Henry Be[illegible]

THE ROYAL INSTITUTION:

ITS FOUNDER

AND

ITS FIRST PROFESSORS

Elibron Classics
www.elibron.com

Elibron Classics series.

ISBN 1-4021-6727-X (paperback)
ISBN 1-4021-0266-6 (hardcover)

This Elibron Classics Replica Edition is an unabridged facsimile of the edition published in 1871 by Longmans, Green, and Co., London.

THE

ROYAL INSTITUTION.

LONDON: PRINTED BY
SPOTTISWOODE AND CO., NEW-STREET SQUARE
AND PARLIAMENT STREET

THE
ROYAL INSTITUTION:

ITS FOUNDER

and

ITS FIRST PROFESSORS.

BY

DR. BENCE JONES,

HONORARY SECRETARY.

LONDON:
LONGMANS, GREEN, AND CO.
1871.

PREFACE.

I begin the history of the Royal Institution, and its professors to the time of Faraday, with the life of its founder, Count Rumford, because his career and character determined its original form. I have written short accounts of the earliest professors because the spirit that has shown itself in them has up to this time been the life of the Institution. Dr. Garnett and Dr. Thomas Young had comparatively little influence there, because the founder took the most active part in the establishment of his Institution; but when Count Rumford and Sir Joseph Banks had left and Mr. Bernard and Sir John Hippesley were the leading managers, Professor Davy gradually became the main supporter of the place, and to him chiefly it owes the form which it now retains.

During the last half-century the name of Faraday has been so blended with that of the Royal Institution that few people know what Davy made it; and fewer still have heard what Rumford at first intended it to be.

The following account will show that the Institution

owes its origin entirely to Rumford, and would certainly have failed but for Davy. Moreover, it will be seen that before Faraday came there, it had been the home of Dr. Garnett and of Dr. Thomas Young; Dr. Dalton had lodged and lectured for weeks there; Sydney Smith, Coleridge, Sir James Smith, Dibden, Dr. Crotch, Campbell, Landseer, Opie, and Flaxman had also lectured there; Sir Joseph Banks and Mr. Cavendish had been managers, and Dr. Wollaston and Dr. Jenner had been members.

I have searched everywhere to find new or forgotten facts about the Institution.

For the sketch of the founder I owe much to the Rev. Dr. G. E. Ellis, of Boston, who has lately written the Life of Rumford for the American Academy of Arts and Sciences. I have found many despatches and letters relating to Rumford in the manuscripts of the American War now in the library of the Royal Institution, and in the unpublished correspondence of Sir Joseph Banks, in the archives of the Foreign Office, and in the State Paper Office.

Not the least strange fact in the history of this original man is that during his life he received no thanks for all that he did for the Royal Institution. Moreover at the present time he is scarcely known as the finder of Davy and the founder of that place where very many of the greatest scientific discoveries of this century have been made.

For the account of the origin and progress of the Institution I have searched the minutes of the meetings of the managers, the proprietors, and the members. I am much indebted to Earl Spencer, who has lent me from the Althorp library a printed copy of the first prospectus of the Royal Institution. This was written by Count Rumford. I have found many forgotten things in the manuscript letters to and from Sir Joseph Banks, to which I have had access by permission of the Knatchbull family; also in a manuscript life of Mr. Webster, the architect of the Royal Institution theatre; and in some letters which belonged to Mr. Savage, the clerk and first printer at the Institution, and for which I am indebted to his daughters.

For the sketch of the lives of Dr. Garnett and of Dr. Young I have been able to find very little original matter.

For the life of Sir Humphry Davy I have met with some new facts in his laboratory note-books. These books give most of his daily work at the time when he was making his great discoveries regarding chemical electricity, the alkalies, and chlorine. I have also had the use of the notes by Faraday of four of the last lectures given by Davy at the Institution. This is the manuscript volume sent to Davy by Faraday when he asked to be employed at the Institution. It consists of 386 small quarto pages. Davy at this time was thirty-three, and Faraday was twenty-one. The one was full of energy to profit by the excellence he could follow, or to shun the evil he could foresee; the other had long reached the climax of his success by his youthful popularity as a lecturer and his early renown as a discoverer; and was about to make a rich and an unsuitable marriage; and before long was to suffer from the restlessness of the failing health that ended in fatal disease.

Whenever a true comparison between these two nobles of the Institution can be made, it will probably be seen that the genius of Davy has been hid by the perfection of Faraday.

Incomparably superior as Faraday was in unselfishness, exactness, and perseverance, and in many other respects also, yet certainly in originality and in eloquence he was inferior to Davy, and in love of research he was by no means his superior.

Davy, from his earliest energy to his latest feebleness, loved research; and, notwithstanding his marriage, his temper, and his early death, he first gained for the Royal Institution that great reputation for original discovery which has been and is the foundation of its success.

H. B. J.

Royal Institution, Albemarle Street,
October 27, 1871.

CONTENTS.

THE

ROYAL INSTITUTION.

CHAPTER I.

LIFE OF RUMFORD BEFORE THE FOUNDATION OF THE INSTITUTION.

1753 to 1799.

At Charlestown, Massachusetts, in the year 1630, James Thompson was among Winthrop's company. He settled about ten miles inland, and the place was called Woburn. In 1752 Benjamin Thompson was there with his father, Captain Ebenezer Thompson, and he married Ruth Simonds, of that place. Their child, the future Count Rumford, was born in his grandfather's farm-house, on March 26, 1753. The house is still to be seen near the meeting-house in North Woburn. When the child was a year old his father died, and when he was three years old his mother married again. 'To the close of her life Rumford wrote to her full of affection, and by the munificent provision which he made for her he showed his tender, grateful regard for her.'

A small inheritance from his grandfather helped to support and to educate the boy. By the law of Massachusetts everyone had a good grammar-school education, and the village school teacher at Woburn was then a graduate of Harvard College and taught a little Latin. From his earliest years the boy was fickle and careless. He neglected regular work, but liked arithmetic. He was full of energy and quick to make what he wanted. When eleven he went to a better school in the neighbouring town of Medford. When thirteen Benjamin Thompson appeared unlikely to make a farmer. He was therefore apprenticed to an importer of British goods and a dealer in everything at Salem, on October 14, 1766. 'Instead of watching for customers over the counter, he busied himself with tools and instruments under it.' When he could he played his fiddle, and played it well. When only fourteen his master allowed him to make small ventures in shipping goods that were paid for by a relative. He was clever at drawing and cutting names, and he thought he had 'invented a machine for making motion perpetual.' When the repeal of the Stamp Act occurred, he blew himself up with fireworks, and was in great danger of death. His master signed the non-importation agreement. Thus his apprentice became useless. When sixteen he returned to his mother. To an elder school-fellow, L. Baldwin, at this time he wrote questions on light, heat, and the wind.

In 1769, when seventeen, he was apprentice and clerk to a drygoods dealer at Boston. There he went to an evening-school to learn French, paying only for the hours he attended.

A note-book made by him about this time still exists. It abounds in caricatures. Has receipts for different fireworks. One of these ends with, 'Love is a noble passion of the mind.' Contains the sum he paid for learning French and for pew-rent, and the sums gained by cutting and carting firewood for relatives. Instructions for the back sword exercise, with a sketch of two combatants; and later there is an account of 'what expense I have been at towards getting an electrical machine,' and 'an account of what work I have done towards getting an electrical machine.'

In the winter of 1770 he was ill for five weeks with fever. Then for eighteen months off and on he boarded with Dr. John Hay, of Woburn, and whilst with him he learned something of anatomy, chemistry, materia medica, surgery, and physic. During the summer, 1771, he went to Cambridge, to attend Mr. Winthrop's lectures on Experimental Philosophy. In the winter of 1771–2 for some weeks he was teaching in a school at Wilmington, and in the spring he taught at Bradford. In the summer he left Dr. Hay for good, because he was asked by Colonel Walker to become the fixed master of a school at Concord, New Hampshire. This place had been called Rumford when it belonged to Essex County, Massachusetts. The name was changed when the disputes as to the county to which it belonged were ended.

The Rev. T. Walker was the first minister of Concord. He was a native of Woburn and connected with the

Thompson family. He was the chief man in Concord. His son was a colonel and a lawyer, and his daughter, when about thirty, was married to Colonel Rolfe, who was sixty. She was left a rich widow in two years, and in the middle of the following year Thompson came as schoolmaster to Concord. He was not yet quite twenty. His friend Baldwin describes him 'as of fine, manly make and figure, nearly six feet high, with handsome features, bright blue eyes and dark auburn hair. His manners were polished and his ways fascinating, and he could make himself agreeable. He had well used his opportunities of culture, so that his knowledge was beyond that of most of those around him, and he was able to give satisfaction as a teacher.'

In the country parsonage and at Colonel Walker's house he frequently met Mrs. Rolfe, and he told his friend Professor Pictet that she married him rather than he her. This was about the end of 1772, when he was nearly twenty. He had to teach no more in school. His marriage made him one of the chief men in Concord.

After his marriage he went with his wife to Portsmouth, where she knew Governor Wentworth. 'He saw in young Thompson not only the representative of a family already known in the public and social life of his province, but also a man of much promise, one likely to work vigorously in whatever he took up.' The Governor soon gave Thompson a commission as major in the second provincial regiment of New Hampshire. The young officer at once became an object of jealousy and ill-will to all the lieutenants and captains of his regiment. The favour of the Governor made all his brother officers his enemies.

The following letter to the Rev. Mr. Williams, at Bradford, afterwards Professor at the college there, shows the influence of Thompson with the Governor, and also some of his scientific thoughts and aims:

Concord, Monday, January 17, 1773.

Dear Sir,—Last Friday I had the honour to wait upon his Excellency, Governour Wentworth, at Portsmouth, where I was very politely and agreeably entertained for the space of an hour and a half. I had not been in his company long before I proceeded upon business, viz. to ask his Excellency whether ever the White Mountains had been surveyed. He answering me in the negative, I proceeded to acquaint him that there was a number of persons who had thought of making an expedition that way next summer, and asked him whether it would be agreeable to his Excellency. He said it would be extremely agreeable, seemed excessively pleased with the plan, promised to do all that lay in his power to forward it,—said that he had a number of Mathematical instruments (such as two or three telescopes, Barometer, Thermometer, Compass, &c.) at Wentworth House, (at Wolfeborough, only about thirty miles from the mountains), all which, together with his library, should be at our service. That he should be extremely glad to wait on us, and to *crown all* he promised, if there were no public business which rendered his presence at Portsmouth *absolutely necessary*, that he would take his tent equipage and go with us to the mountain and tarry with us, and assist us till our survey, which he said he supposed would take about twelve or fourteen days! ! !—! !—! ! ! ! !

During 1773 he was chiefly farming. Whilst on a visit with his wife to Boston he was introduced to

Governor Gage and to several of the British officers. Among those who worked for him on his farm were four deserters from the grenadiers at Boston. He persuaded them to return to their regiment. He wrote to General Gage to beg pardon for them. He asked that his petition might be kept secret. He wished not to excite more enmity among his neighbours. But the use of his influence with the Governor got known. The bitterest feeling was working in the country. Civil war was about to begin. Major Thompson was suspected by the people because he was in favour with the royal Governors. The committees of correspondence and of safety listened to the reports of any of the 'sons of liberty.' Major Thompson was called before a committee of the people in Concord for being 'unfriendly to the cause of liberty.' He denied the charge, and was acquitted. About this time (August 1774) he asks his friend, Mr. Loammi Baldwin, merchant in Woburn, 'to favour him with an easy question, arithmetical or algebraical, and he will give as good an account of it as possible.' In October his only child, Sarah, was born. In November the mob gathered round his house, but by friendly warning he was able to escape to his mother's at Woburn, fifty miles away. Here he sought to busy himself by reading, and he made some experiments on gunpowder; but ill-will soon followed him, and he was driven for shelter to a friend at Charleston. Thence he wrote to his father-in-law at Concord:

December 24, 1774.

REVEREND SIR,—The time and circumstances of my leaving the town of Concord have, no doubt, given you great uneasiness, for which I am extremely sorry. Nothing short of the most threatening danger could have induced me to leave my friends and family; but when I learned from persons of undoubted veracity, and those whose friendship I could not suspect, that my situation was reduced to this dreadful extremity, I thought it absolutely necessary to abscond for a while, and seek a friendly asylum in some distant part.

Fear of miscarriage prevents my giving a more particular account of this affair; but this you may rely and depend upon, that I never did, nor (let my treatment be what it will) ever will do, any action that may have the most distant tendency to injure the true interest of this my native country.

I most humbly beg your kind care of my distressed family; and I hope you will take an opportunity to alleviate their trouble by assuring them that I am in a place of safety, and hope shortly to have the pleasure of seeing them. I also most humbly beseech your prayers for me, that under all my difficulties and troubles I may behave in such a manner as to approve myself a true servant of God and a sincere friend of my country.

To have tarried at Concord and have stood another trial at the bar of the populace would doubtless have been attended with unhappy consequences, as my innocence would have stood me in no stead against the prejudices of an enraged, infatuated multitude,—and much less against the determined villany of my inveterate enemies, who strive to raise their popularity on the ruins of my character. My friends would have been deemed unfriendly to the cause of Liberty, and my defence would have been treated with contempt and disdain. It would have been vain for me to have pretended to curb the fury or calm the rage of this popular whirlwind; but I must have been cast, and condemned to suffer punishments equal to the blackness of my supposed transgressions.

The plan against me was deeply laid, and the people of Concord were not the only ones that were engaged in it. But others to the distance of twenty miles were extremely officious on this occasion. My persecution was determined on, and my flight unavoidable. And had I not taken the opportunity to leave the town the moment I did, another morning had effectually cut off my retreat.

In May his wife and her infant joined him at his mother's home at Woburn. When there, skirmishes took place between the people and troops at Concord, Massachusetts, and Lexington, and in this last fight Major Thompson is said to have taken part with the people; but he was soon the object of ill-feeling, and, although he was saved from immediate arrest by his friend Major Baldwin, a short time afterwards he was arrested, and then he appealed from the Committee of Correspondence of Woburn to the Committee of Safety of the Provincial Congress. When he was acquitted at Woburn and set free, he withdrew his petition from the Committee of Safety. Soon after he was with Major Baldwin at Charlestown, and probably he took part in the battle of Bunker's Hill. He certainly helped to pack up the library at Cambridge, and was only prevented by the officers of the New Hampshire Militia from obtaining a commission from General Washington. When epaulets were ordered for the non-commissioned officers, he had samples made and sent them with the price to his friend, then Colonel Baldwin, offering to take an order for any number that might be wanted.

In August he again writes a long reply to his father-in-law, in answer to letters urging him to express his sorrow that he had done wrong and to ask forgiveness of the people:

Woburn, August 14, 1775.

As to my being instrumental in the return of some Deserters, by procuring them a pardon, I freely acknowledge that I was. But you will give me leave to say that what I did was done from principles the most unexceptionable—the most disinterested—a sincere desire to serve my *King* and *Country*, from motives of *Pity* to those unfortunate Wretches who had deserted the service to which they had *voluntarily* and so *solemnly* tyed themselves, and to which they were desirous of returning. If the designed ends were not answered by what I did, I am sincerely and heartily sorry. But if it is a Crime to act from principles like these, I glory in being a Criminal.

Many other crimes which you do not mention have been laid to my charge, for which I have had to answer both *publicly* and *privately*. My enemies are indefatigable in their endeavours to distress me, and I find to my sorrow that they are but too successful. I have been driven from the Camp by the clamours of the New Hampshire people, and am again threaten'd in this place. But I hope soon to be out of the reach of my Cruel Persecutors, for I am determined to seek for *that Peace* and *Protection* in foreign Lands and among strangers which is deny'd me in my native country. I cannot any longer bear the insults that are daily offered me. I cannot bear to be looked upon and treated as the *Achan* of Society. I have done nothing that can deserve this *cruel usage*. I have done nothing with any design to injure my countrymen, and cannot any longer bear to be treated in this barbarous manner by them.

And notwithstanding I have the tenderest regard for my Wife and family, and really believe I have an equal return of love and affection from them; though I feel the keenest distress at the thoughts of what Mrs. Thompson and my Parents and friends will suffer on my account, and though I foresee and realise the distress, poverty, and wretchedness that must unavoidably attend my Pilgrimage in unknown lands, destitute of fortune, friends, and acquaintance, yet all these Evils appear to me more tolerable than the treatment which I meet with from the hands of my ungrateful countrymen.[1]

I am too well acquainted with your Paternal affection for your Children to doubt of your kind care over them. But you will excuse me if I trouble you with my *most earnest* desires and entreaties for your *peculiar* care of my family, whose distressed circumstances call for every indulgence and alleviation you can afford them.

I must also beg a continuance of your Prayers for me, that my present afflictions may have a suitable impression on my mind, and that in due time I may be extricated out of all my troubles. That this may be the case, that the happy time may soon come when I may return to my family in peace and safety, and *when every individual in America may sit down under his own vine, and under his own Fig-tree, and have none to make him afraid,* is the constant and devout wish of

Your dutiful and affectionate son,

BENJAMIN THOMPSON.

Rev. Tim. Walker.

[1] The following unpublished letter from General Howe to General Washington, written from Philadelphia in 1776, shows what the tyranny of the committees and people was:

'You are not ignorant that numbers even of the most respectable gentlemen in America have been torn from their families, confined in gaols, and their property confiscated; that many of those in this city, whose religious tenets secured them from suspicion of entertaining designs of hostility, have been ignominiously imprisoned, and without

Dr. Ellis, in his admirable biography, says:

Major Thompson remained in and about Woburn two months after writing his last letter to Mr. Walker, in which he so deliberately avowed his intentions. He settled his affairs with his neighbours, collecting dues and paying debts, well assured that his wife and child would lack none of the means of a comfortable support. Having thus made all his preparations, he started from Woburn, October 13, 1775, in a country vehicle, accompanied by his step-brother, Josiah Pierce, who drove him near to the bounds of the province, on the shore of Narragansett Bay, whence young Pierce returned. Thompson was taken on board the 'Scarborough,' British frigate, to Newport and from thence to Boston.

In the Alienation Act of the Senate of New Hampshire in 1778 he was named among the proscribed; and in 1781, the confiscation papers of his property call him 'of Woburn, physician, now an absentee.'

Whilst Mr. Thompson was at Boston the American rebellion became a revolution. General Gage was succeeded by General Howe, and to him Lord Dartmouth

even the colour of a judicial proceeding, banished from their tenderest connections into the remotest part of another province. Nor can it be unknown to you that many have suffered death from tortures inflicted by the unrelenting populace under the eye of usurped yet passive authority; that some have been dragged to trial for their loyalty and, in cruel mockery of law, condemned and executed; that others are now perishing in loathsome dungeons, and that penal edicts are daily issuing against all who hesitate to disavow, by a solemn oath, the allegiance they owe and wish to pay to their sovereign.'

General Howe shows the exasperation of the Royalists also. He says: 'Members of committees, collectors of arbitrary fines, &c., oppressors of the peaceable inhabitants, have been seized by the exasperated inhabitants of different parts of the country and delivered into my hands.'

wrote in September 1775: 'No room was left for any other consideration but that of proceeding against the twelve associated Colonies in all respects with the utmost vigour as the open and avowed enemies of the State,' and he spoke of the great risk and little advantage that are to be expected from the continuance of the army at Boston during the winter, and on the advantages of recovering possession of New York. He tells the general that 'the Empress of Russia, in the fullness of her affection for the British nation, and of gratitude for the benefits she had received under her late difficulties, had made the most explicit declaration and given the most ample assurance of any number of infantry that might be wanted.' When, 'in consequence of this generous and magnanimous offer,' a requisition was made to her for 20,000 men for Canada, objections arose, and 'much embarrassment and disappointment were the only results.'

The Cape Fear expedition failed from ignorance of the depth of the river.

When Lord George Germain became one of his Majesty's principal Secretaries of State, November 10, a commission was issued under the great seal 'for the restoration of public tranquillity among his Majesty's deluded subjects in the affected colonies.' A proclamation said: 'Apprised of the fatal consequence of the conduct they had adopted, and seeing the determined spirit of the nation to maintain its constitutional rights, they will avail themselves of the means which the justice and benevolence of the supreme legislature have held out to them of being restored to the King's grace and peace.' This failed utterly, from ignorance of the depth of opposition in the colonies. Boston was evacuated in March 1776, and Mr. Thompson was sent to England with the news. He was probably thought perfectly qualified to answer every question relative to his Majesty's service. Cuvier says, 'La bonne mine du jeune officier, la netteté et l'étendue des renseignements qu'il donna, prévinrent en sa faveur le secrétaire d'État au département de l'Amérique.' His news caused no great distress, and his information must have reassured the minister, for even in June Lord G. Germain and the Prime Minister wrote to General Howe on the good prospect of an end being put to the rebellion in one campaign. It was the good news from Canada that helped to deceive them.

Mr. Thompson was taken into Lord George Germain's office, and he was appointed Secretary of the Province of Georgia.

In the autumn of 1777 Thompson was at Bath for his health, drinking the waters. Whilst there he made some experiments on the cohesive strength of different substances. These led to no great results, but he communicated them to Sir Joseph Banks, the new President of the Royal Society.

Sir W. Howe was at this time asking for large reinforcements. He thus wrote to Lord G. Germain from Philadelphia:

'From the little attention, my Lord, given to my recommendations since the commencement of my command, I am led to hope that I may be relieved from this very painful service wherein I have not the good fortune to enjoy the necessary confidence and support of my superiors, but which I conclude will be extended to Sir Henry Clinton, my presumptive successor.'

In 1778 Mr. Thompson was with Lord G. Germain at his house, Stoneland Lodge, Sussex. Whilst there Thompson made experiments on testing gunpowder, and on a new method of determining the velocity of projectiles. The results were sent to the Royal Society, in 1781, and were published at great length in the 'Philosophical Transactions.' One good observation is now of great interest. 'Being much struck with the accidental discovery of the great degree of heat that pieces acquire when they are fired with powder without any bullet, and being desirous of finding out whether it is a circumstance that obtains universally, I was very attentive to the heat of the barrel after each of the succeeding experiments, and I constantly found the heat sensibly greater when the piece was fired with powder only than when the same charge was made to impel one or more bullets.'

In order to pursue these experiments he went in 1779, on board of the 'Victory,' of 110 guns, commanded by his friend Sir Charles Hardy. He passed the whole of the campaign on board of the fleet, and the result of the observations that he then made furnished the materials for a chapter which he contributed to Stalkart's 'Treatise on Naval Architecture.' He added to it a code of signals for the navy, which was not published. In his paper on gunpowder, read in 1797 to the Royal Society, he says:

During a cruise which I made, as a volunteer, in the 'Victory,' with the British fleet, under the command of my late worthy friend Sir Charles Hardy, in the year 1779, I had many opportunities of attending to the firing of heavy cannon; for though we were not fortunate enough to come to a general action with the enemy, as is well known, yet, as the men were frequently exercised at the great guns and in firing at marks, and as some of my friends in the fleet, then captains (since made admirals), as the Honourable Keith Stewart, who commanded the 'Berwick,' of 74 guns,—Sir Charles Douglas, who commanded the 'Duke,' of 98 guns,—and Admiral Macbride, who was then captain of the 'Bienfaisant,' of 64 guns, were kind enough, at my request, to make a number of experiments, and particularly by firing a greater number of bullets at once from their heavy guns than ever had been done before, and observing the distances at which they fell in the sea,—I had opportunities of making several very interesting observations, which gave me much new light relative to the action of fired gunpowder.

In 1778 Mr. Thompson was elected a Fellow of the Royal Society.

Great must have been the trouble in his office this year. In October 1778, Sir H. Clinton wrote to Lord G. Germain from New York that he was about to send, as he was ordered, ten thousand men to the West Indies and St. Augustine. 'After a wound in my humble opinion so fatal to the hopes of any future vigour in this army, I trust, my Lord, you cannot wish to keep me in the mortifying command of it.' 'You cannot, I am confident, my Lord, desire that I should remain a mournful witness of the debility of an army at whose head, had I been unshackled by instructions, I might have indulged expectations of rendering serious service to my country.'

Lord G. Germain thought that much good would be done by encouraging the provincial forces, and by promising to the provincial officers half-pay and permanent rank in America.

On January 23, 1779, he wrote to Sir H. Clinton: 'It is likewise his Majesty's pleasure that you publish and make known to his provincial corps, as also to all others his loyal subjects in America, his gracious intention to support and protect them by making the rank of the officers permanent in America, and allowing them half-pay upon the reduction of their regiments, in the same manner as the officers of British reduced regiments are paid.'

This order for promotion immediately excited the discontent of the officers in the army. In their memorial to Sir H. Clinton they ask him 'to prevent our being superseded by officers of yesterday who have served under us.'

In 1780 proposals were made to Lord G. Germain to revive the Association of Loyalists in America, 'so that Government, at a very moderate expense, might be served by a considerable number of men, and Captain Murray offered on behalf of Brigadier Ruggles, who had been Brigadier-General of Provincial Forces in America during the last war, Deputy Surveyor-General of the Woods, and late his Majesty's council in the province of Massachusetts Bay in New England, to raise and to command a regiment of light dragoons, to be called the King's American Dragoons.'

Lord G. Germain wrote to Sir H. Clinton, June 7, 1780, from Whitehall:

The services of Brigadier Ruggles in the last war, and the influence he still retains in those provinces of North America, where his character, his honour, and his name are respected, made me long desirous of seeing that gentleman engaged in the King's service. The enclosed plan of raising a regiment of dragoons was communicated to me by Captain Murray, by authority of Brigadier Ruggles. It appeared to me so fair and so disinterested, that I laid it before his Majesty, and it so far met with his royal approbation that he permitted me to transmit the plan to you. And if the public service requires any provincial cavalry to be raised, his Majesty would be pleased to see Mr. Ruggles placed at the head of such a corps, where he may have an opportunity of again acting with that zeal and spirit which formerly did him so much honour.

In September 1780 Mr. Thompson was made Under-Secretary of State for the Northern Department by Lord George Germain.

In May 1781 the Inspector-General of Provincial Forces wrote to the Under-Secretary, Thompson, to say that the distress for the want of cavalry appointments was beyond conception. 'Had all the appointments,' he says, 'for Brigadier-General Ruggles come out, it would have afforded us a small temporary supply; but only twenty-five helmets have yet appeared.'

Lord G. Germain then moved the Treasury to send fresh and large supplies, and said he had directed Mr. Thompson, the Deputy Inspector-General of Provincial Forces, to procure patterns and estimates and to give information. Lord North, Lord Palmerston, and Sir R.

Sutton referred the question of quality and quantity to the Adjutant-General, who reported that 'it would be doing injustice to Mr. Thompson not to declare that, as far as my judgment goes, he will not only gain great credit for himself, but at the same time essentially serve the public by his disinterested and very attentive execution of the trust that has been reposed in him on this occasion.' Their lordships directed Mr. Thompson forthwith to provide the several articles mentioned, and allowed him one and a half per cent. commission. The sum he received at this time was one hundred and twenty pounds.

Among the exiles in London was Judge Curwen, of Salem, Massachusetts. He kept a journal, and in it he gives a picture of Thompson, May 23, 1781:

On returning home I found a letter from Arthur Savage, informing me of Mr. Thompson's compliments and wish to see me at eleven o'clock to-morrow at his lodgings.

May 24.—Went early, in order to be at Mr. Benjamin Thompson's in time, and being a little before, heard he was not returned from Lord George Germain's, where he always breakfasts, dines, and sups, so great a favourite is he. To kill half an hour, I loitered to the park through the palace, and on second return found him at his lodgings. He received me in a friendly manner, taking me by the hand, talked with great freedom, and promised to remember and serve me in the way I proposed to him [probably the securing the continuance of his allowance unreduced]. Promises are easily made, and genteel delusive encouragement, the staple article of trade, belonging to the courtier's profession, I put no hopes on the fair appearances of outward behaviour, though it is uncandid to suppose all mean to deceive. Some wish to do a service who have it not in their power; all wish to be thought of importance and significancy, and this often leads to deceit. This young man, when a shop-lad to my next neighbour, ever appeared active, good-natured, and sensible; by a strange concurrence of events, he is now Under-Secretary to the American Secretary of State, Lord George Germain, a secretary to Georgia, inspector of all the clothing sent to America, and Lieutenant-Colonel Commandant of Horse Dragoons at New York. His income arising from these sources is, I have been told, near seven thousand a year—a sum infinitely beyond his most sanguine expectations. He is, besides, a member of the Royal Society. It is said he is of an ingenious turn, an inventive imagination, and, by being on a cruise in Channel service with Sir Charles Hardy, has formed a more regular and better-digested system for signals than that heretofore used. He seems to be of a happy, even temper in general deportment, and reported of an excellent heart; peculiarly respectful to Americans that fall in his way.

This statement of the income of Thompson was certainly enormously exaggerated. That about this time he was appointed to the King's American Dragoons the following autograph letter, now in the library of the Royal Institution, shows:

FROM LORD GEORGE GERMAIN TO SIR H. CLINTON.

Stoneland Lodge, September 30, 1781.

SIR,—I beg leave to introduce Mr. Thompson to you, and at the same time to thank you for the favour and protection which you have shewn him in giving him the command of a regiment of light dragoons, which, I trust, will be raised in a manner to entitle the officers of it to your approbation. Lieutenant-Colonel Thompson shows at least a spirit and zeal for the service, in quitting for a time an agreeable and profitable civil situation, in the hopes of being useful to his country, and by his military conduct, shewing himself not unworthy of the protection which you have granted to him. If you do him the honour to converse with him, you will find him well informed, and, as far as theory goes, a good officer in whatever you may think fit to employ him. I can answer for his honour and his ability, and I am persuaded he will ever feel himself attached by gratitude to you for the very kind and obliging manner in which you have protected him and the regiment under his command.

I am, Sir, with great regard, your Excellency's faithful, humble servant,

GEORGE GERMAIN.

On October 4, 1781, Colonel Thompson appointed Mr. Fisher, a clerk in his office, as his attorney, to receive his pay (thirteen shillings daily) and to attend to his clothing commission. He soon after left England in the 'Rotterdam,' a fifty-gun ship, for New York, but contrary winds compelled him to disembark at Charlestown (South Carolina).

In his paper on Gunpowder he shows that he was busy during his passage:

His Majesty having been graciously pleased to permit me to take out with me from England four pieces of light artillery, constructed under the direction of the late Lieutenant-General Desaguliers, with a large proportion of ammunition, I made a great number of interesting experiments with these guns, and also with the ship's guns on board the ships of war in which I made my passage to and from America.

He arrived towards the end of December. Lord

Cornwallis had surrendered, and Charlestown, in Carolina, was in great danger for want of reinforcements and food.

Early in 1782 Lord G. Germain wrote to General Leslie, who commanded at Charlestown: 'I agree with you that mounted troops are the fittest for service in the southern provinces, but I cannot encourage you to expect that any will be sent from home; I am glad, however, you will have Colonel Thompson's assistance in forming what you have. His offer to serve in your army until the season for action to the northward arrives corresponds with that public spirit and zeal for the King's service which prompted him to quit his civil situation and engage in the military line.'

General Leslie wrote to Sir H. Clinton, January 29: 'The army is now well clothed and recovered from the sickness and fatigue it underwent during the last summer.

'The several detached corps of cavalry have been incorporated into distinct ones under the command of Lieutenant-Colonel Thompson. From the unwearied attention and diligent efforts of that officer they are become respectable, and I have everything to expect from this improvement.'

On February 20 Lieutenant-Colonel Thompson wrote to the Honourable Lieutenant-General Leslie that he has not been so fortunate as to meet with the enemy he had come in search of; but the following despatch was sent by him on February 25, 1782:

Duxcent's Plantation, Monday, February 25, 1782.

SIR,—I did not expect, after the affair of yesterday, the enemy would so soon have put it in my power to congratulate you upon another defeat of their troops by those which you have done me the honour to put under my command. We had the good fortune this morning to fall in with a chosen corps, under the command of General Marion in person, which we attacked and totally routed, killing a considerable number of them, taking sixteen prisoners, and driving General Marion and the greatest part of his army into the Santee, where it is probable a great many of them perished.

After resting and refreshing our horses at the plantation where we halted last night, at nine o'clock this morning the cavalry marched back to the Santee, to the ground where we fell in with the enemy yesterday. The infantry marched at the same time for this place, and we promised to join them in the afternoon.

We had advanced about nine miles from the place we left in the morning, when, coming in through a gate-way to the cleared grounds of a plantation, we discovered the enemy about three hundred yards distant, directly in front of us, drawn up in the area between the negroe huts belonging to the plantation.

As soon as the troops were formed I ordered a charge to be sounded, and the line moved forwards. The enemy also sounded a charge, but, instead of coming out to meet us, they were discovered going off by their right in the greatest hurry and confusion, and attempting to gain a swamp that was upon the banks of the river on that side. We immediately charged after them at full speed, and had the good fortune to come up in time to cut off a great part of their rear. Those that gained the swamp were pursued, and many of them were killed in attempting to get into the river, and others were shot and drowned in attempting to swim to the opposite shore. We took near forty horses, many of which are capital chargers.

After the action we collected at our leisure all the cattle from the rebel plantations in that quarter, and have sent them down the road with a proper escort. We shall follow as soon as the troops are refreshed.

In this last affair with the enemy, as well as during the whole time I have had the honour to command this detachment, the troops, both officers and men, have behaved in such a manner as to merit my warmest acknowledgment.

I have the honour to be, with perfect respect, Sir, your most obedient and most humble servant,

R. THOMPSON.

In the general orders on March 1 the General expressed to the army the opinion he entertained of the merit of Colonel Thompson's conduct upon this occasion, and of the spirited behaviour of the troops, and to Sir H. Clinton he wrote, March 12, 1782:

I had the honour to inform your Excellency that Lieutenant-Colonel Thompson having offered his service during his stay here, I had appointed him to the command of the cavalry. He has put them in exceeding good order and gained their confidence and affection. I am very happy to inform your Excellency of his success in a late excursion upon the Santee. [An account of the action is then given in the despatch.] I enclose to your Excellency Colonel Thompson's report to me of this very handsome piece of service, and I assure your Excellency that I have much regret to part with this enterprising young officer, who appears to have an uncommon share of merit and zeal for the service; and could he and his corps be spared to act in this part, where cavalry are so much wanted, I am confident it would tend much to the benefit of his Majesty's service.

Despatches of this date show that in council also Thompson was as efficient as in the field.

General Leslie wrote to Sir H. Clinton:

I beg to know your Excellency's opinion with regard to our putting arms into the hands of the negroes. I have desired Colonel Thompson to speak with your Excellency upon the subject, and to make known to you the particulars of our situation in that respect.

On April 11 Colonel Thompson arrived at New York. Four days afterwards Sir H. Clinton wrote to General Leslie: 'Those parts of your letters to which you have referred for a more full explanation to Lieutenant-Colonel Thompson, I shall answer after consulting with him upon the subject;' and he also says: 'With respect to the disagreeable predicament which you mention Lieutenant-Colonel Balfour and other officers of rank in the Southern army stand in on account of Mr. Green's threats for Colonel Hayne's execution, I shall consult Lieutenant-Colonel Thompson, and let you know my sentiments by the earliest opportunity.'

At this time Sir H. Clinton was about to give up the command he had so often petitioned to resign. He had 'lamented that his happiness was sacrificed to prevent the partial inconvenience which might have arisen from a change,' and later he wrote: 'His Majesty's assent to my petition will crown the many favours of which my heart will ever retain the most grateful remembrance.'

On February 6 General Robinson was appointed to succeed Sir H. Clinton, and soon after Sir Guy Carleton took the command.

Colonel Thompson's chief business was to complete his regiment, which was encamped about three miles from Flushing, in Long Island. There, on August 1, colours were presented to the regiment by Prince William, then a boy of eighteen in the Royal Navy, accompanied by Admiral Digby. On the 6th, on behalf of himself and the officers of the King's American Dragoons, Colonel Thompson petitoned Sir Guy Carleton to order them to enjoy the advantages stipulated on the completion of the regiment; and at the end of August Sir Guy Carleton notifies in the general orders that Colonel Thompson and his officers are entitled to permanent rank in America.

In September Colonel Thompson's name is to be found first on a list of six agents, selected to act for them by those Royalists who were willing to emigrate with their families from Long Island to Nova Scotia.

Two months later it appears, from a bill, that he was building chimneys in the barracks at Huntingdon, Long Island, where his regiment was stationed, when the treaty of peace between America and England was made in Paris without the consent and even without the knowledge of France.

In December every preparation was made for a sudden attack of the French upon New York, and orders were issued by General Robinson in case that event took place. Alarm posts for each of the different corps and the details of the duties of each corps were arranged. 'If an attack was made on Huntingdon, the troops were immediately to assemble and march to the support of Colonel Thompson.'

Early in the spring active measures were proposed against the French in the West Indies. Peace with France stopped these plans, and on April 11, 1783, Colonel Thompson obtained leave of absence, in order that he might return to London to urge the claims of the provincial officers to rank and to half-pay.

Some original documents in the appendix to this chapter will show the energy, the ability, and the perseverance of Colonel Thompson when he arrived in London.

On August 17 Sir Guy Carleton issued an order that all the men who wished to be discharged in America, should hold themselves in readiness to embark for Nova Scotia; and in October the King's American Dragoons were disbanded on the lands appropriated to them, many miles up the river St. John, on the north side of the Bay of Fundy.

On October 25, 1783, Colonel Thompson's half-pay began, and it continued for the remainder of his life. He had at this time began a new career. He determined to go abroad, intending to take part in a war which was then expected between Austria and the Turks.

Gibbon wrote from Dover, September 17, 1783, to Lord Sheffield:

Last night the wind was so high that the vessel could not stir from the harbour; this day it is brisk and fair. We are flattered with the hope of making Calais Harbour by the same tide in three hours and a half, but any delay will leave the disagreeable option of a tottering boat or a tossing night. What a cursed thing to live in an island!

this step is more awkward than the whole journey. The triumvirate of this memorable embarkation will consist of the grand Gibbon, Henry Laurens, Esq., President of Congress, and Mr. Secretary, Colonel, Admiral, Philosopher Thompson, attended by three horses, who are not the most agreeable fellow-passengers. If we survive, I will finish and seal my letter at Calais. Our salvation shall be ascribed to the prayers of my lady and aunt, for I do believe they both pray.

Boulogne.

Instead of Calais the wind has driven us to Boulogne, where we landed in the evening, without much noise and difficulty. . . . Laurens has read the pamphlet, and thinks it has done much mischief. A good sign! [1]

Professor Pictet, of Geneva, has published in the 'Bibliothèque universelle' the notes he made of a conversation with Count Rumford regarding his life at this time. He says:

A purely accidental circumstance had a decisive influence over his destiny. He arrived at Strasburg, where the Prince Maximilian of Deux Ponts, now [1801] Elector of Bavaria, then Field-Marshal in the service of France, was in garrison. This prince, commanding on parade, sees among the spectators an officer in a foreign uniform, mounted on a fine English horse, whom he addresses. Thompson informs him that he comes from serving in the American war. The Prince, in pointing out to him many officers who surround him, says, 'These gentlemen were in the same war, but against you; they belonged to the Royal Regiment of Deux Ponts, that acted in America under the orders of Count Rochambeau.'

[1] The pamphlet here referred to was Lord Sheffield's 'Observations on the Commerce of the American States.'

They engaged in conversation, which became very animated. Colonel Thompson being invited to dine with the Prince, met at the table a number of French officers whom he had encountered on the field in America. They talked at length of the events of this war. The Colonel produced his portfolio, which contained exact plans of the principal engagements, the forts, the sieges, and an excellent collection of maps. One and another recognised the place or the interesting incident which was recalled to him. They conversed a long while, and separated promising to meet again. The Prince was passionately devoted to his profession and intensely eager for information. He invited the Colonel for the next day. They resumed with the same zest the conversation of yesterday. When at last the traveller took leave, the Prince engaged him to pass through Munich, and gave him a friendly letter to the Elector of Bavaria, his uncle.

The season was advanced, and he was in haste to reach Vienna. He had promised to stop at Munich two or three days at most; but he passed there five days, and then did not leave but with regret a city where the tokens of the regard of the sovereign and the attentions of different classes of society were extended to him with that frank cordiality which so eminetly distinguishes the Bavarian nation. He received equally at Vienna the most flattering welcome, and was presented at Court and mingled in the first society. There he passed a part of the winter, and, learning that the war against the Turks was not to be carried on, he yielded to the attractive memories of Munich, and, passing through Venice, where he stopped some weeks, and by the Tyrol, he returned to Brompton by the end of the winter of 1783–84.

In February he was knighted by George the Third, and he received permission to enter into the service of the Duke of Bavaria.

From Munich, July 6, Thompson wrote to Sir Joseph Banks, to tell him that his Electoral Highness had been asked to become a Fellow of the Royal Society. He said:

I should have done myself the honour to have written to you upon this subject some time ago, but I waited for a favourable opportunity to speak to his Electoral Highness about it.

It was only a few days since I came into waiting as aide-de-camp to his Most Serene Highness. I shall continue about his person till September, when I purpose making a tour for a couple of months in the mountains of Tyrol, upon the confines of Bavaria, and the dominions of the Bishop of Saltzburg, a country extremely interesting in several points of view.

. . . .

He gave his direction as 'M. le Chevalier Thompson, colonel et aide-de-camp général au service de S.A.S. l'Élect. Palatin, Duc de Bavière.'

He ended, 'I am, dear Sir, with sincere regard and respect, your most obedient and most humble servant.'

He again wrote to Sir Joseph Banks on July 24. He began by asking if he could have one of the two hundred medals for Cook's voyages given to Fellows of the Royal Society, and he ended with a postscript:

I beg you would make my best compliments to Mr. Blagden when you see him, and tell him I hope he will not entirely forget an old correspondent who remembers him with great affection.

Cuvier, in his *éloge* of Count Rumford, says of the Electors of Bavaria:

Les souverains agrandis à l'époque des guerres de

religion, par suite de leur zèle pour le catholicisme, avaient longtemps porté les marques de ce zèle bien au-delà de ce que réclame un catholicisme éclairé : ils encourageaient la dévotion et ne faisaient rien pour l'industrie; on comptait dans leurs états plus de couvents que de fabriques. L'armée y était à peu près nulle ; l'ignorance et l'inertie dominaient dans toutes les classes de la société.

The first work in Bavaria of Sir Benjamin Thompson was to rearrange the military service and introduce a new system of order, discipline, and economy among the troops. In the execution of this commission he says : 'I was ever mindful of that great and important truth that no political arrangement can be really good except in so far as it contributes to the general good of society. I have endeavoured to unite the interest of the soldier with the interest of civil society, and to render the military force, even in the times of peace, subservient to the public good.' To make soldiers citizens, and citizens soldiers, the soldier was better paid, better clothed, better housed, better taught, better occupied, better amused, and, above all, allowed to earn money and to spend it as he pleased. Fixed garrisons were formed, and the army was used as a means of introducing useful improvements into the country. Thus military gardens were formed to introduce the culture of the potato. Workhouses for manufacturing clothing for the army were founded, first at Mannheim for the troops of the Palatinate and Duchies of Juliers and Bergen, and a few months afterwards at Munich for the fifteen Bavarian regiments. The greatest order and economy were used in the military manufactory and magazine, and after six years Sir B. Thompson wrote that the net profit on the various trades and manufactures in the Munich Workhouse up to that time was 100,000 florins; and he could refer to its growing reputation, its extensive connexions, which reached even to foreign countries, to the punctuality with which all its engagements were fulfilled, to its unimpeached credit, and to its growing wealth. The amount of orders executed in the sixth year of its establishment did not fall much short of half a million of florins.

Among the various measures that occurred to Sir B. Thompson by which the military of the country might be made subservient to the public good in time of peace, 'none,' he says, 'appeared to me of so much importance as that of employing the army in clearing the country of beggars, thieves, and other vagabonds, and in watching over the public tranquillity.'

The beggars swarmed everywhere. They were dissolute, sturdy, shameless, importunate robbers.

A system of mounted police was formed throughout the country by four regiments of cavalry. Means were taken, first, to furnish suitable employment for those who were able to work; and, secondly, to provide the necessary assistance for those who, from age, sickness, or other bodily infirmities, were unable by their industry to provide for themselves.

'To make vicious and abandoned people happy, it has generally been supposed necessary *first* to make them virtuous. But why not reverse this order? Why not make them first happy and then virtuous?'

A large building, once a manufactory, was taken in

one of the suburbs of Munich; arrangements were made for a kitchen, an eating-room, a bakehouse, workshops for carpenters, smiths, turners, tool-makers, spinners of cotton wool and worsted, for weavers of all kinds, a dyers' shop, a fulling mill, a washhouse.

Everything was done that could be desired to make the inmates really comfortable by good food, raiment, and cleanliness. The rooms were scrupulously clean, well warmed, and well lighted; the people were well fed, well taught, and well paid for their work. 'They had the kindest usage from every person, from the highest to the lowest. No ill usage, no harsh language, was permitted; and at the end of five years not a blow had been given to anyone, not even to a child by its instructor,' and Sir B. Thompson could say: 'The pleasure I have had in the success of this experiment is much easier to be conceived than described; would to God that my success might encourage others to follow my example! If it were generally known how little trouble and how little expense are required to do much good (the heartfelt satisfaction which arises from relieving the wants and promoting the happiness of our fellow-creatures is so great), I am persuaded acts of the most essential charity would be much more frequent, and the mass of misery among mankind would consequently be much lessened.'

New Year's Day having been long specially set apart for giving alms early that morning in 1790, three regiments of infantry, with their officers, were stationed in the streets, and Sir B. Thompson assembled the magistrates and asked their assistance to take up all the beggars and to provide for the poor. Accompanied by the chief magistrate, he went into the street, and the first beggar who asked for alms he arrested with his own hands, and orders were given to all the other officers, who also were accompanied with magistrates, to do the same. In less than an hour no beggar was to be found in the streets. They were taken to the Town Hall, inscribed in printed lists, and then told to go to the newly-erected Military Workhouse. An address was opened to the public, asking for perfectly voluntary subscriptions to put an end to begging; monthly sums were given, and daily supplies of bread, meat, and soup were collected.[1]

Several good spinners of hemp were engaged at the House of Industry, and this was the first occupation of the poor. Knitting, sewing, and carding wool were early occupations, but the object to be desired was woollen work for the clothing of the army. If the poor did well, they were rewarded; if they came late, their food was lessened. They slept at their own homes, and when ill they received relief at home. Everything was done to encourage industry and emulation. 'To incite activity and inspire with a true spirit of persevering industry, it was necessary to fire the poor with emulation—to awaken in them a dormant passion whose influence they had never felt; the love of honest fame; an ardent desire to excel, the love of glory, or by what other pompous name this passion, the most

[1] So great was the economy practised that the daily expense for firewood in the kitchen, where dinner was provided for 1,000 people, was only twelve Kreutzers, or fourpence halfpenny. Sometimes 1,500 were fed in one day.

noble and most beneficent that warms the human heart, can be distinguished.'[1]

To excite emulation praise, distinctions, rewards are necessary; and these were all employed.

The House of Industry for the Poor and the Military Workhouse were quite separate in their management, though they were so dependent on each other that neither of them could subsist alone; one building served for both.

Twice yearly small sums were given to the poor to assist them in paying for lodgings, and ultimately a large house was bought and fitted up as an hospital for those who were infirm and unable to take care of themselves.

Means were adopted for giving relief to those who never were beggars, but who, from poverty and inability to provide the necessaries of life, were involved in distresses and difficulties which they bore in silence.

Persons of distinguished birth even sent to the House of Industry at Munich for flax, or wool, or linen, which they manufactured into goods, and received the usual amount of wages; and some who had been accustomed

[1] The great mistake which has been committed in most of the attempts to introduce a spirit of industry where habits of idleness have prevailed, has been the too frequent use of coercive measures. Force will not do. It is address which must be used on those occasions. The children in the House of Industry at Munich who, being placed on elevated seats round the hall where other children worked, were made to be idle spectators of that amusing scene, cried most bitterly when their request to descend from their seats and mix in that busy crowd was refused; but they would most probably have cried still more had they been taken abruptly from their play and forced to work. Men are but children of a larger growth, and those who undertake to direct them ought ever to bear in mind that important truth.

to sumptuous fare took the soup furnished gratis from the public kitchen to the poor.

The warming, lighting, clothing, feeding, occupying the poor, seemed the sole object of all Sir B. Thompson thought and of all he did. His success must be told in his own words.

My hopes of engaging others to follow my example are chiefly founded upon my success in the enterprise. Then why should I not mention even the marks of affectionate regard and respect which I received from the poor people for whose happiness I interested myself? And will it be reckoned vanity if I mention the concern which the poor of Munich expressed in so affecting a manner when I was dangerously ill? That they went publicly in a body in procession to the cathedral church, where they had divine service performed, and put up public prayers for my delivery. That four years afterwards, on hearing that I was again dangerously ill at Naples, they of their own accord set apart an hour each evening after they had finished their work in the Military Workhouse to pray for me.

Let the reader, if he can, picture my situation. Sick in bed, worn out by intense application, and dying, as everybody thought, a martyr in the cause to which I had devoted myself, let him imagine, I say, my feelings upon hearing the confused noise of the prayers of a multitude of people, who were passing by in the streets, upon being told that it was the poor of Munich, many hundreds in number, who were going in procession to the church to put up public prayers for me; public prayers for me! for a private person, a stranger, a Protestant! I believe it is the first instance of the kind that ever happened; and I dare venture to affirm that no proof could well be stronger than this that the measures adopted for making these poor people happy were really successful; and let it be remembered *that this fact is what I am most anxious to make appear* IN THE CLEAREST AND MOST SATISFACTORY MANNER.

Cuvier says: 'Il convient lui-même que cet acte spontané de reconnaissance religieuse en faveur d'un homme d'une autre communion lui parut la plus touchante des récompenses; mais il ne se dissimulait pas qu'il en avait obtenu une autre qui sera plus durable. En effet, c'est en travaillant pour les pauvres qu'il a fait ses plus belles découvertes . . .

'Chacun sait que dans ses plus belles espérances on eut pour objet la nature de la chaleur et de la lumière, ainsi que les lois de leur propagation; et c'était là effectivement ce qu'il importait le plus de bien connaître pour nourrir, vêtir, chauffer et éclairer avec économie un grand rassemblement d'hommes.'

Other measures for the benefit of the country were carried out at the same time.

A Military Academy was formed, principally with a view to bring forward extraordinary talents and employ them in the civil or military public service. Anyone was admissible. The children of the meanest mechanics and day-labourers, provided they had *very extraordinary natural genius*, a healthy constitution, and a good character, were educated. It was an establishment designed for the encouragement of genius, and for calling forth into public utility talents which would otherwise remain buried and lost in obscurity.

Measures were adopted for improving the breed of horses and horned cattle in Bavaria and the Palatinate. An attempt was made to put an end to usury in Munich and to improve the highways and public roads, by employing the soldiery in repairing them and preserving order and public tranquillity on them.

A new English Garden was formed, beginning upon the ramparts of the town. It was nearly six English miles in circumference. Within the Garden was a fine and very valuable farm, with thirty of the finest cows procured from Switzerland, Flanders, the Tyrol, and other places. There was a public coffee-house in the middle of the Garden for refreshment and public resort.

The scientific work which Sir B. Thompson did whilst in the service of the Elector of Bavaria between 1783 and 1794, shows his energy and originality, his accuracy and his depth.

When at Mannheim in July 1785 he made experiments in the presence of Professor Hemmer, of the Electoral Academy of Sciences of Mannheim, on the propagation of heat through various substances; on the increased difficulty of conduction of heat through the torricellian vacuum; on the effect of humidity in increasing the conducting power of the air; and on the effect of air of different degrees of density. The Duke ordered the meteorological instrument maker to the academy at Mannheim to come to Munich, and to spare neither labour nor expense in providing the complete apparatus necessary for the experiments.

These experiments, on the relative conducting powers of mercury, water, air, and a torricellian vacuum, were read to the Royal Society, March 9, 1786.

He then proceeded to make experiments on the relative warmth of various substances used in making artificial clothing; relative quantities of the same substance; different qualities of substance chemically, as charcoal, ashes, dust. All his experiments indicated that the air which occupies the interstices of substances used in forming coverings for confining heat acts a very important part in that operation. Air is a perfect non-conductor of heat. These experiments were chiefly made in 1787. They were not read before the Royal Society until January 19, 1792.

Early in the winter of 1787, as soon as the cold was sufficiently intense, he began to repeat the experiments of Dr. Fordyce ('Transactions of the Royal Society,' vol. lxxv.) on the weight said to be acquired by water in the act of freezing; and, being possessed of a most excellent balance belonging to the Duke of Bavaria, he soon came to the conclusion that all attempts to discover any effect of heat upon the apparent weights of bodies would be fruitless.

He had previously, in April 1785, convinced himself of the errors that arose from currents of air and from the drying of the cords by which the scales were hung.

These experiments were made into a paper entitled 'An Inquiry concerning the Weight Ascribed to Heat.' This was read before the Royal Society, May 2, 1799.

In May and June 1786 he made experiments on the production of air from water exposed to light. These were read before the Royal Society, Febuary 15, 1787.

When engaged in his experiments on the conducting powers of various bodies with respect to heat, and particularly of such substances as are used for clothing, he made experiments on the relation between their conducting power and their power of absorbing moisture, but found none. Flannel and fur, contrary to his expectation, absorbed much more moisture from the air than silk and cotton. On this he forms an idea of the good of wearing flannel. This, the weakest of his papers, was read to the Royal Society, March 22, 1787.

In the spring of 1791 a large building was erected in the neighbourhood of Munich, on the ground destined for the exercise of the artillery, where a most complete apparatus was put up for measuring the velocities of cannon bullets by the recoil of the gun, and also by the pendulum at the same time, and with this apparatus a great number of interesting experiments were made.

He observed that the force of the charge was always sensibly increased when the gun was discharged by firing a pistol (constructed for that use) into the vent, instead of using a priming and a common match for firing off the gun.

These experiments were continued in 1792, and in 1793 they were shown to Dr. Blagden, who was in Munich during the absence of Sir B. Thompson in Italy for his health.

The principal objects in view were to determine the expansive force of the elastic vapour generated in the combustion of gunpowder in its various states of condensation, and to ascertain the ratio of its elasticity to its density, and to measure the utmost force of this fluid in its most dense state.

In order to find the most economical method of lighting his Workhouse at Munich, he devised a new way of measuring the relative quantities of lights by their shadows. His arbitrary standard was a London made Argand lamp. He first experimented on the resistance of air to light, then on the loss of light in its passage through different kinds of glass, and in its reflection from a plate glass mirror, then on the relative quantities of oil burnt by different lamps and relative quantities of light emitted by different substances, and lastly on the transparency of flame.

He made these experiments into a paper on the 'Relative Intensities of the Light Emitted by Luminous Bodies,' and it was read before the Royal Society, February 6, 1794; and on February 20 another paper was read, being an 'Account of some Experiments on Coloured Shadows,' and he came to the conclusion that our eyes are not always to be believed, even with respect to the presence or absence of colours.

For his national and scientific work he received various honours between 1783 and 1794.

In 1785 he was elected member of the Bavarian Academy of Sciences, which had been established in 1758, and he was made chamberlain to the Elector.

In 1786 the King of Poland, at the request of the Elector of Bavaria, conferred on him the Order of St. Stanislaus. This was done because the statutes of Bavaria did not allow a foreigner to receive any national honours.

In 1787, when in Prussia, he was made a member of the Berlin Academy of Sciences.

In 1788 the Elector made him Major-General of Cavalry and Privy Councillor of State, and he was placed at the head of the war department.

On May 29, 1789, he was elected a foreign honorary member of the American Academy of Arts and Sciences, and he was made Lieutenant-General of the Bavarian Armies and received the command of a regiment of artillery.

In 1791, in the interval between the death of the Emperor Joseph and the coronation of Leopold II., the Elector of Bavaria was one of the Vicars of the Empire, and he made Sir Benjamin Thompson a Count of the Holy Roman Empire, and gave him the Order of the White Eagle.

Early in the following year the wife of Count Rumford, who had been a great invalid, and who had lived with her son by her first husband and with her daughter, the child of Rumford, died at the age of 52. Her own property had given her every comfort that her ill health required.

At the end of this year Count Rumford was in correspondence with his early friend Colonel Baldwin, through whom probably for some time previously he had sent money to his mother. He wrote to Colonel Baldwin from Munich, January 18, 1793:

You could hardly conceive the heartfelt satisfaction it would give me to pay a visit to my native country. Should I be kindly received? Are the remains of party spirit and political persecutions done away? Would it be necessary to ask leave of the State?

It is possible you may see me at Woburn before you are

aware of it. I wish exceedingly to be personally acquainted with my daughter. I wish to know her real character, and how I must go to work to lay a solid foundation for her future happiness. I wish once more to have the satisfaction of seeing my most kind and affectionate mother. I wish to prove to her how dear she is to me, and how grateful I am for all her goodness to me. My dear, beloved parent! What would I give to see her, were it but for one hour! I should be much obliged to you for any accounts you may from time to time send me of her situation, and of others, my friends, in your neighbourhood. Desiring to be remembered to all those of my old acquaintance who interest themselves in my welfare, I am, my dear Sir, with unfeigned regard and much esteem, yours most affectionately.

Count Rumford, in the spring of 1793, left Munich for Italy on account of his health. He was absent sixteen months. At Verona the directors of the two great hospitals La Pieta and La Misericordia, containing 350 and 500 poor, accepted his offer to rebuild the kitchens. Seven-eighths of the fire-wood were saved, and he made arrangements to supply the poor with clothing from the Munich House of Industry at a saving of twenty per cent.

On May 11, 1793, Sir C. Blagden, who was travelling with Lord Palmerston, wrote to Sir Joseph Banks from Rome:

Count Rumford is come into Italy. I have just received a very friendly letter from him, in which he desires me to appoint a meeting. It will probably be at Milan.

Three months later he wrote from Augsburg:

Thompson, now Count Rumford, met me by appointment at Pavia. Volta showed us his experiments on animal electricity, and said he had sent off his paper for the Royal Society about three weeks before, probably not time enough for it to be read before the vacation. I thought his experiments proved that there is no particular animal electricity, and that the animals serve only the purpose of very delicate electrometers; but they leave other circumstances unexplained.

On his return to London Sir C. Blagden wrote on November 21 to Sir Joseph Banks:

From Italy I brought two papers by Count Rumford, one on 'Coloured Shadows,' the other on a 'Method of Measuring the Comparative Intensities of the Light Emitted by Luminous Bodies.' In the former he shows neatly enough that the colours ascribed to these shadows depend entirely on comparing them with light of another colour. The method referred to in the second paper is that of the intensity of the shadows produced by the different luminous bodies. These two papers will furnish matter for nearly three meetings of the Royal Society.

Count Rumford had another serious illness in Naples in the early part of 1794. He returned to Munich in August.

He left Munich for London in 1795. He had spent the year after his return from Italy in comparative quiet. He was unfit for public business and he chiefly occupied himself by writing out the results that he had obtained. He thus made a series of essays.

In order to publish these in England and to meet his daughter, who was about to come to him from America, and to recover further his health, he obtained leave of absence from the Elector of Bavaria.

In his paper on Gunpowder in 1781 he said he would make experiments on the strength of various bodies. In 1797, when he had another paper in the 'Philosophical Transactions' on this subject, he added this note:

Since writing the above I have met with a misfortune which has put it out of my power to fulfil this promise. On my return to England from Germany, in October 1795, after an absence of eleven years, I was stopped in my post-chaise in St. Paul's Churchyard, in London, at six o'clock in the evening, and robbed of a trunk which was behind my carriage, containing all my private papers and my original notes and observations on philosophical subjects. By this cruel robbery I have been deprived of the fruits of the labours of my whole life, and have lost all that I held most valuable. This most severe blow has left an impression on my mind which I feel that nothing will ever be able entirely to remove. It is the more painful to me, as it has clouded my mind with suspicions that never can be cleared up.

These essays were published at different times separately between 1796 and 1802. The two first volumes were reprinted in 1800.

His first essay gave an account of an establishment for the poor in Munich; the second was on establishments for the poor in general. It contains the germ of the Royal Institution.

This was a 'proposal for forming in London by private subscription an establishment for feeding the poor and giving them useful employment, and also for furnishing food at a cheap rate to others who may stand in need of such assistance, connected with an institution for introducing and bringing forward into general use new inventions and improvements, particularly such as relate to the management of heat and the saving of fuel, and to various other mechanical contrivances by which domestic comfort and economy may be promoted, submitted to the public by A.B.' Dated January 1, 1796. Count Rumford begins by saying that *no person* shall *find means* to make a job of the proposed establishment. That the general arrangement of the establishment and all its details shall be left to the author of these proposals, who will be responsible for their success. He engages, however, in the prosecution of this business to adhere faithfully to the plan here proposed, and never to depart from it on any pretence whatever.

He proposed first to establish a public kitchen with every useful invention and improvement by which fuel may be saved.

As soon as the measures for feeding the poor and giving them employment are carried into execution the secondary object will be attended to—the formation of a grand repository of all kinds of useful mechanical inventions, particularly such as relate to furnishing houses and are calculated to promote domestic comfort and economy.

He concluded thus: 'The author of these proposals will think himself most amply repaid for any trouble he may have taken in the execution of this scheme by the heartfelt satisfaction he will enjoy in the reflection of having been instrumental in doing essential service to mankind.'

In the summer of 1796 a conversation took place between the Bishop of Durham, Mr. Wilberforce, Mr. Bernard, and the Honourable Edward James Eliot, and in consequence of this a society was formed for encouraging industry and promoting the welfare of the poor.

The object of this Society was everything that concerned the happiness of the poor, everything by which their comforts could be increased; to correct the abuses of workhouses; to assist the poor in placing out their children; to add to and meliorate their means of subsistence by public kitchens, by the union of liberal and benevolent minds, by circulating information and by personal assistance and influence.

The Bishop of Durham and Mr. Thomas Bernard were the chief contributors to the funds. Mr. Bernard was the third son of Sir Francis Bernard, Governor of New Jersey and Massachusetts Bay. He was a graduate of Harvard College, New England. He was the original promoter of the School for the Indigent Blind, of an Institution for the Protection and Instruction of Climbing Boys, of a Society for the Relief of Poor Neighbours in Distress, of the Cancer Institution, of the London Fever Hospital. He was also the founder of the British Institution for Promoting the Fine Arts in the United Kingdom, and the originator of the Alfred Club.

The first meeting of the new Society was held on December 21, 1796, when the King declared himself the patron of it. On February 24, 1797, the Society resolved that, 'in consideration of the extraordinary services of Count Rumford for the benefit of the poor, and as a testimony of the respect and esteem with which this Society regards his services in the promotion of the general objects of the institution, he be elected and declared a member of the Society and one of the general committee for life.'

In consequence Count Rumford wrote to Thomas Bernard, Esq., from Germany:

Munich, April 28, 1797.

I feel myself very highly honoured by the distinguished mark of esteem and regard which the Society for Bettering the Condition of the Poor has conferred on me, and I beg leave through you to return the Society my respectful and grateful acknowledgments.

This flattering proof of the approbation of those most respectable persons who compose the Society will tend very powerfully to encourage me to persevere in those endeavours to promote the important objects they have in view, by which I first obtained their notice and esteem.

I am very sanguine in my expectations of the good which will be done by this Society; they will, however, be able to do much more by examples—by *models* that can be seen and felt—than by anything that can be said or written.

The following year he wrote:

Munich, May 13, 1798.

The rapid progress you are making in your most interesting and laudable undertakings affords me a high degree of satisfaction. It proves that I was not mistaken when I concluded that, notwithstanding the alarming progress of luxury and corruption of taste and of morals in England, there is still good sense and energy to be found, even in the highest classes of society, where the influx of wealth has operated most powerfully. Go on, my dear sir, and be assured that when you shall have put *doing good* in fashion, you will have done all that human wisdom can do to retard and prolong the decline of a great and powerful nation that has arrived at, or passed, the zenith of human glory.

And again:

Munich, June 8, 1798.

I have received your letter from Brighton of the 12th ult. You can hardly imagine the high degree of pleasure and satisfaction which I feel at your success in your most laudable undertakings. Go on, my dear sir, and be assured that you will contribute more essentially to the revival of taste and morals, of energy, industry, benevolence, and *prosperity* in your favoured country than all the speculators and reformers in the three kingdoms.

When society is arrived at a certain degree of torpid indifference and enervation of mind and body, which are the unavoidable effects of wealth, luxury, and inordinate indulgence, mankind must either be *allured* or *shamed* into action. Precepts and admonitions have no effect on them.

As they are too indolent to take the trouble either to investigate or to choose, they must be led to acts of useful benevolence as they are led in everything else—by *fashion*; when you shall have rendered it perfectly ridiculous for a man of fashion and fortune *to have the appearance* of being insensible to the most noble and most delightful of human enjoyments—that which results from doing good—you will have done more for the relief of the poor than all that the Poor Laws can ever effect. Deeply impressed with the necessity of rendering it *fashionable* to care for the poor and indigent, and contribute to their relief and comfort, in order to diffuse in England that spirit of active benevolence you are kindling, I am apt to insist, perhaps with too much prolixity, on that important point.

I am anxious to hear of the execution of your plan with regard to Bridewell. A well arranged House of Industry is much wanted in London. It is indeed absolutely necessary to the success of your undertaking, for there must be something *to see* and *to touch*, if I may use the expression, otherwise people in general will have but very faint, imperfect, and transitory ideas of those important and highly interesting objects with which you must make them acquainted in order to their becoming zealous converts to our new philosophy, and useful members of our community. Pray read once more the 'Proposals,' published in my second essay. I really think that a public establishment like that there described might easily be formed in London, and that it would produce infinite good. I will come to London to assist you in its execution whenever you will in good earnest undertake it.

The third essay was on 'Food and Feeding the Poor; Rumford Soup and Soup-Kitchens.' The fourth on 'Chimney Fire-Places.' The fifth on 'Several Public Institutions Founded in Bavaria; on Nurseries for Genius; for Horses and for Cattle.'

During 1797 and 1798 Rumford published in England a second volume containing four essays.

These were on the 'Management of Fire and the Economy of Fuel;' on the 'Propagation of Heat in Fluids,' extending to liquids, the doctrine which he had before advanced respecting elastic fluids; on the 'Propagation of Heat in various Substances;' and an 'Experimental Inquiry concerning the Source of Heat Excited by Friction.'

An account of this last essay must be given here, because from it Count Rumford derives his chief scientific reputation.

Whilst directing the military affairs of the Duke of Bavaria he had to organise the field artillery, and he found no cannon foundry in Bavaria. The arsenal at Munich was filled with cannon, but by far the greater part of them were perfectly useless, being too heavy to be moved. There was a very good foundry at Mannheim, the capital of the Elector's dominions on the Rhine, but the distance between Munich and Mannheim is so great that it would have cost more to have sent the Bavarian guns to Mannheim to be re-founded and to have brought them back than was required to defray the expense of establishing a new manufactory for the construction of artillery in Bavaria.

A foundry was accordingly established at Munich, and neither pains nor expense were spared to make it as perfect as possible. A most excellent machine was erected for boring cannon, with workshops adjoining to it for the construction of gun-carriages and ammunition waggons.

Whilst engaged in superintending the boring of the cannon he was struck by the heat produced in a brass gun and with the still more intense heat of the metallic chips separated by the borer.

He says: 'The more I meditated on these phenomena the more they appeared to me to be curious and interesting. A thorough investigation of them seemed even to bid fair to give a further insight into the hidden nature of heat, and to enable us to form some reasonable conjectures respecting the existence or non-existence of an igneous fluid.

'Whence comes the heat actually produced?

'Does it come from the metallic chips? If so, their capacity for heat must be changed; but by repeated experiments I found that no change of capacity was caused by the boring. Determination of the actual heat produced and of the amount of chips showed that there was no relation between them. That the heat did not come from the gun itself was shown by the absence of every sign of exhaustion in the metal, notwithstanding the large quantities of heat given off.

'Did the heat come from the air? Exclusion of the air did not in the smallest degree diminish the heat.

'It would be difficult,' he says, 'to describe the surprise and astonishment expressed in the countenances of the bystanders on seeing a large quantity of cold water heated and actually made to boil without any fire.

'Though there was, in fact, nothing that could justly be considered as surprising in this event, yet I acknowledge fairly that it afforded me a degree of childish pleasure which, were I ambitious of the reputation of a grave philosopher, I ought most certainly rather to hide than to discover.'

The amount of heat given out in a continual stream by his borer he estimated at that of nine wax candles each of three-quarters of an inch in diameter. This was produced by the work of two horses. 'But,' he adds, 'no circumstances can be imagined in which this method of procuring heat would not be disadvantageous; for more heat may be obtained by using the fodder necessary for the support of a horse as fuel.'

He concludes thus:

'Anything which any insulated body or system of bodies can continue to furnish without limitation cannot possibly be a material substance, and it appears to me to be extremely difficult, if not quite impossible, to form any distinct idea of anything capable of being excited and communicated in these experiments except it be MOTION.

'I am far from pretending to know how that

particular kind of motion which has been supposed to constitute heat is excited, continued, and propagated. Nobody surely in his sober senses has ever pretended to understand the mechanism of gravitation, and yet what sublime discovery was our immortal Newton enabled to make merely by the investigation of the laws of its action!'

The account of these experiments was read to the Royal Society, January 25, 1798.

Some interesting facts regarding this paper are to be found in the correspondence of Sir C. Blagden with Sir J. Banks.

DEAR SIR JOSEPH,—Count Rumford's paper on Friction, together with your letter, were safely delivered to me by Lord Palmerston. The paper is by no means incorrect in itself, nor has the copyist made any remarkable blunders, and it is valuable from the large scale on which the experiments were tried, and the quantity of heat produced in consequence. As the result of the experiments was such as the Count himself foresaw, and as every other philosopher would have expected, they do not furnish any *new* argument in favour of the opinion he has adopted that heat is motion, though perhaps they add force to the old ones. There is, however, an experiment of some consequence if it can be depended upon; namely, *that* which seemed to show that the shavings cut by the borer out of the cannon had the same capacity for heat as the metal on which the borer had not acted; but I do not feel much confidence in experiments of this nature. You will recollect that one opinion pretty much adopted on this subject is that the heat produced in boring a cannon depends on the compression of the metal of the cannon by the borer, in consequence of which it gives out heat; on the principle that the same body has a less capacity for heat when it is in a denser than when it is in a rarer state. I wish the Count had ascertained whether the metal shavings he tried had really a greater specific gravity than that of the chips of metal he had sawed off.

Whilst in England Rumford at this time strove to advance scientific knowledge not only by the publication of his own discoveries, but also by his benefactions for the promotion of discovery by others, and by the further practical application of some of the results which he had obtained.

On July 12, 1796, he wrote to the Honourable John Adams, President of the American Academy of Arts and Sciences at Boston, to offer 5,000 dollars in the 3 per cent. stocks, 'to the end that the interest may be spent every second year on a silver and gold medal as a premium to the author of the most important discovery or useful improvement on heat or on light; the preference always being given to such discoveries as shall, in the opinion of the Academy, tend most to promote the good of mankind.'

In 1829 the fund accumulated to 20,000 dollars, and in 1870 to 37,000 dollars. The Academy applied to the Legislature to use the money for the purchase of books and apparatus, and to pay for experiments, lectures, and treatises, and this was decided in 1831. During the first fifty years only one award of the medals was made. This was to Dr. Hare, of Philadelphia, 1839. They have been since given to Mr. Ericsson, Professor Treadwell, Mr. Alvan Clark, and Mr. Corliss.

On the same day in 1796 Count Rumford wrote to

Sir Joseph Banks, the President of the Royal Society, offering 1,000*l.* stock on the same conditions to the Royal Society of London.

Sir Joseph Banks was requested by the council to return their sincere thanks to Count Rumford, and at the same time to inquire 'how far improvements or discoveries in optics and chemistry might come under the Count's views.'

Count Rumford wrote to Sir Joseph Banks, from Munich, April 20, 1797:

I think the premium should be limited to new discoveries tending to improve the theories of fire, of heat, of light, and of colours, and to new inventions and contrivances by which the generation and preservation and management of heat and of light may be facilitated. In as far, therefore, as chemical discoveries or improvements in optics answer any of these conditions they may, I think, fairly be considered as being within the limits assigned to the operation of the premium. The objects which I had more particularly in view to encourage, are such practical improvements in the generation and management of heat and light as tend directly and powerfully to increase the enjoyments and comforts of life, especially in the lower and more numerous classes of society.

The first award of the Rumford medal was made, in November 1802, to Count Rumford himself for his own discoveries on heat and light. In 1870 the award was made for the twenty-sixth time. Eleven foreigners have received the honour, and thus added to the reputation of the prize. The greatest English discoverer on the subject of light is not on the list, but when sending the medal to M. Fresnel (who was on his death-bed) in 1827, Young, as foreign secretary of the Royal Society, wrote to him: 'I also should claim some right to participate in the compliment which is tacitly paid to myself in common with you by this adjudication, but, considering that more than a quarter of a century is passed since my principal experiments were made, I can only feel it a sort of anticipation of *posthumous* fame, which I have never particularly coveted.'

In order further to apply some of his scientific researches to practice in the spring of 1796, on the invitation of his friend Mr. Secretary Pelham, Rumford went to Dublin.

In the house of the Dublin Society he fitted up a laundry and a model kitchen for private families, and also a cottage fire-place, and a model lime-kiln in the courtyard of the house of the Society; also in the hall in which the meetings of the Royal Irish Academy are held he fitted up two chimney fire-places. He contrived a fire-place for heating one of the principal churches in Dublin, and he promised to give a plan for heating the superb new building destined for the meeting of the Irish House of Commons. In the Linen Hall at Dublin he fitted up an oblong square boiler as a model for bleachers.

He was made a member of the Royal Irish Academy and of the Society for the Encouragement of Arts, and he received after he left the country the public thanks of the Grand Jury of the County of Dublin, and of the Lord Mayor of the city, as well as of the Lord Lieutenant as the head of the Government.

Upon his return to London he superintended some

improvements at the Foundling Hospital for his friend Mr. Bernard, who was treasurer there. Roasters and boilers were put up, but he was obliged to return to Munich before the kitchens were entirely finished.

His daughter left America to join her father in England in January 1796. By her Colonel Baldwin wrote from Woburn, January 26, 1796:

In answer to your inquiry, I can say that it is my opinion that you can freely return to America, either with or without official leave from the State, as you may choose; and that you would realise a hearty welcome from all your old friends and citizens in general. I can say, for one, that there is not a person on earth that I should rejoice so much to see.

Rumford answered:

London, March 26, 1796.

I return you many thanks for your friendly letter, which I received by my daughter, and I beg you would accept my warmest acknowledgments for all the kindness you have shown to my daughter for the many years she has been known to you.

Her gratitude to you is without bounds, and she says nothing on earth will ever make her forget your goodness to her. I do not despair of being able, at some future period, to express to you in person, by word of mouth, the sense I entertain of your kindness to my dear child. You will not expect that I should attempt to describe the pleasure I felt at seeing my dear girl after an absence of twenty years!

Some years afterwards the daughter gave a vivid picture of her father at this time.

Count Rumford, my father, having passed several preceding years at Munich, in Bavaria, had come to England to have published some of his essays. He took the opportunity to send for me, my mother being dead, and I requiring protection. Many were the scenes he had passed through after leaving me as an infant, and erroneous were the ideas I had formed of him, particularly of his appearance; we having had only a small profile of him in shade, giving ever an imperfect idea of the person. Indeed, so different from what I had thought were his looks, that I could hardly fancy him the person I sought after, and would willingly have run from him, and ended in a violent fit of crying, which he did not consider as a compliment, asking me afterwards what I meant by it. The playfulness of his character (at times) secured love to my father. Witness his laughter, quite from the heart, nothing made up about it. The expression of his mouth, ornamented with the most finished pearls, was sweetness itself. But to see him accidentally, he did not strike one as handsome, or very agreeable, though not exactly to the contrary. At the time I met him, having been ill, he was very thin and pale—again a reason of my disappointment. My opinion of him was naturally romantic, perhaps, as young people's often are. I had heard him spoken of as an officer. I had attached to this an idea of the warrior, with the martial look, possibly the sword, if not the gun, by his side. His profile being in black, made me suppose him dark in complexion, possibly sunburnt; in short, in stature, size, and looks the perfect warrior. Yet my mother often spoke of him as carroty, his hair being red; but later not so, a very pretty colour. My father pretended I looked better than he expected to find me. It is true he had had a most unfavourable likeness of me in a small miniature.

Though it was a trying scene to meet, yet it was nothing to finding out each other's disposition in the end, and my father began with being much alarmed about me. He himself resided in a large hotel in Pall Mall, but could not have me with him, putting me to board not far off, at a Mrs.

Lackington's. He had brought his valet, Aichner, with him, and for me a maid, by the name of Anymeetle, both Germans. I was to be presented to Lord and Lady Palmerston, Sir Charles Blagden, Sir William Pepperell and family (Americans), and other of his friends.

My father was often at the Royal Society, and intimate with its president, Sir Joseph Banks. I would be invited to the dinners Sir Joseph gave to the select ones of his royal learned Society. Through the kindness and civility of Lady and Miss Banks, his wife and sister, I several times found myself one of their party. Lady Banks was so kind, and, most likely out of civility to my father, she would allow me to be with her for days together, taking me about with her, letting me see things—in short, trying to amuse me. I recollect she took me to a Lord Mayor's ball, where I saw the princes and royal family for the first time. As may be supposed, the select dinners of the Royal Society were highly interesting, and where, I think, ladies were seldom or never admitted. I was allowed to accompany Lady and Miss Banks as a mere nobody; but this did not prevent my making observations which never have been and never will be forgotten. The idea of very learned people suggests that of pedantry. At these dinners there was nothing of the kind, differing only from other refined societies when remarks were made to convey perhaps new ideas, discoveries, or highly entertaining instruction, sometimes there being no such talk at all.

The daughter wrote to Mrs. Baldwin in America, June 13, 1796:

We should have been gone long before this time to Germany if some business had not called my father to Ireland.

I enjoy very good health, and am very happy. I should think it strange if I were not to be. I am indulged in everything I wish, and I am under the protection of a parent that I have not only reason to love, but to be proud of.

. . . . . .

The state of Europe at this time caused Rumford to return to Munich. At the close of the campaign of 1794 between France and the German Empire, when Prussia made peace with France, Bavaria desired to be neutral. It was not until the spring of 1796 that the Republicans under Moreau, who had crossed the Rhine at Strasburg, threatened Munich. Rumford was recalled. The Elector took refuge in Saxony eight days after Rumford arrived. He had appointed Rumford head of a council of regency and commander of the Bavarian troops. The Austrians, defeated by the French near Augsburg in August, retreated on Munich. They found Count Rumford determined to oppose them. On the arrival of the French troops he refused to admit them also, and by his firmness and wisdom the neutrality of Munich was preserved. The inhabitants of the town fully recognised that they owed the preservation of their city to Count Rumford alone.

The defeat of Jourdan on the Lower Rhine obliged Moreau to retreat. The Bavarian territory was evacuated, and the Elector returned to Munich. He made Rumford head of the General Police of Bavaria, and about 200*l*. of the pension which had been granted to him was settled on his daughter for her life. She was also received at Court as a Countess of the Empire.

In December 1797 Rumford wrote to his friend Baldwin from Munich:

My daughter never ceases her solicitations to engage me to pay a visit to my friends in America, and her wishes are so powerfully seconded by my own feelings and longing desires to breathe once more my native air, that I have come to the resolution to make the journey as soon as the restoration of peace and the arrangement of my concerns in this country will permit it. If the public affairs of Europe and of America take the turn I expect, and if no unforeseen event should happen to prevent my carrying my schemes into execution, I think you will see us in America in fifteen or sixteen months from this time.

Meanwhile his daughter amused herself at Munich. The Elector was old and had married a young wife, so that there was gaiety at Court during this winter, and the attentions of one of the aides-de-camp of her father made rides, and dinners, and balls pleasant to the Count's daughter; but she says 'all her fine castles were demolished by one blow from her father, and Count Taxis was ordered to join his regiment in the country.' Ill health followed, and change of air and scene was advised. 'My father appeared to try how agreeable he could make himself, as if wishing to wear off by it some of the disagreeable impressions of his late conduct in drawing so many tears from my poor eyes. . . . When quiet and happy himself he was, like others, agreeable; but when perplexed with cares and business, or much occupied, there was no living with him.'

In the autumn of 1798, partly on account of his health, he determined to return to England with his daughter. The Elector of Bavaria, to show his esteem for Rumford, appointed him Minister Plenipotentiary and Envoy Extraordinary to the Court of St. James.

On September 14, 1798, Lord Grenville sent a despatch to the Hon. Arthur Paget at Munich, saying, 'It is, I apprehend, a thing if not wholly unprecedented, at least extremely unusual, to appoint a subject of the country to reside at the Court of his natural sovereign in the character of minister from a foreign prince. I am to direct you in the last resort to state in distinct terms that his Majesty will by no means consent to receive Count Rumford in the character which has been assigned to him. You will observe that the circumstance of Count Rumford having heretofore filled a confidential situation (that of Under-Secretary of State in the American Department) under his Majesty's Government, makes the appointment in his person peculiarly improper and objectionable.'

On Count Rumford's arrival on September 19 he wrote to Lord Grenville to say that, notwithstanding the information and the intimation which had been communicated to him by Mr. Canning, Under-Secretary of State for Foreign Affairs, he considered it his duty formally to notify that, having been appointed Envoy Extraordinary and Minister Plenipotentiary, he had come to England in consequence of that appointment, and was charged with a letter to the King, which he ought to endeavour to obtain permission to deliver with his own hands. He therefore asked an audience or personal interview with the minister, to state the objects of his mission, and to receive such information as would enable him to give a clear, authentic, and satisfactory account to the sovereign who had entrusted him with the management of his affairs.

The day but one after, Lord Grenville shortly answers that 'he conceives it will be more agreeable to Count Rumford that the substance of the representation with which Mr. Paget was charged should be transmitted by Count Rumford to the Elector rather than through any other channel.'

The same day a despatch to this effect was written to the Hon. Arthur Paget at Munich.

No other notice was taken of Count Rumford's appointment. He did not return to Munich, and the following year his master, the Elector Charles Theodore, died.

The thoughts of Rumford, when rejected as minister of Bavaria, were directed to his native land. He thus wrote to his friend Baldwin in America:

London, September 28, 1798.

I arrived in this city last week from Germany, and I expect to be able to remain here several months. I have, indeed, some hopes of being able to pay you a visit in America in the spring. But these hopes, though apparently well founded, may easily be disappointed, for there are several events, none of which are very improbable, that would render it impossible for me to be absent from Europe next year. It is, however, my fixed intention to pay a visit to my friends in America as soon as ever it shall be in my power, which most probably will be in the course of a year or two. I have even a scheme of forming for myself a little quiet retreat in that country, to which I can retire at some future period and spend the evening of my life. Perhaps you may be so good as to assist me in carrying this plan into execution. As I am not wealthy, and prefer comfort to splendour, I shall not want anything magnificent. From forty to one hundred acres of good land, with wood and water belonging to it, if possible in a retired situation, from one to four miles from Cambridge, with or without a neat, comfortable house upon it, would satisfy all my wishes.

Among his friends in England was the Honourable Rufus King, the American minister.

Mr. King wrote to Colonel Pickering, the Secretary of State in America:

London, December 8, 1798.

Count Rumford, late Sir Benjamin Thompson, whose name and history are probably known to you, and whose talents and services have procured the most beneficial establishments and reforms in Bavaria, was lately named by the Elector to be his minister at this Court. On his arrival he has been informed that, being a British subject, it was contrary to usage to receive him, and that therefore he could not be acknowledged. The intrigues and opposition against which he had for some years made head in Bavaria probably made him desire the mission to England. The refusal he has here met with has decided him to return and settle himself in America. He proposes to establish himself at or near Cambridge, to live there in the character of a German count, to renounce all political expectations, and devote himself to literary pursuits. His connexions in this country are strictly literary, and his knowledge, particularly in the military department, may be of great use to us. The Count is well acquainted with and has had much experience in the establishment of cannon foundries; that which he established in Bavaria is spoken of in very high terms, as well as certain improvements that he has introduced in the mounting of flying artillery.

He possesses an extensive military library, and assures me that he wishes nothing more than to be useful to our country. I make this communication by his desire, and my wish is that he may be well received, as I am persuaded that his principles are good, and his talents and information uncommonly extensive. It is possible that attempts may be made to misrepresent his political opinions; from the inquiry that I have made on this head, I am convinced that his political sentiments are correct.

Be good enough to communicate this letter to the President.

Count Rumford soon after wrote to Mr. King:

I send you herewith a small pamphlet,[1] which will explain to you the causes which have rendered it impossible for me to go to America this spring, as I had intended. I have not, however, given over all ideas of visiting that country at some future period; very far from it, I really hope and expect to be able to go there next spring, and will most certainly do so, if it should be possible, provided you should continue to advise it, and to encourage me with the hope of a kind reception.

The model of a field-piece[2] on a new, and I believe on an improved construction, which I have destined as a present to the United States, I shall pack up and send to you, in order to its being shipped for America as soon as I shall get it from his Royal Highness the Duke of York, who has desired to have a copy of it.

You will recollect that in a conversation we had at your house on the great importance to the United States of the speedy establishment of a military school or academy, I

[1] This was the prospectus of the Royal Institution.

[2] This was a model one quarter of the full size of the new Bavarian six-pounder with its ammunition waggon. The Elector permitted him to present it to the United States.

took the liberty to say that to assist in the establishment of so useful an institution I should be happy to be permitted to make a present to the academy of my collection of military books, plans, drawings, and models. I now repeat this offer, and with a request to you that you would make it known to the Executive Government of the United States, and that you would let me know as soon as may be convenient whether this offer will be accepted.

Another letter written the following day to his friend Colonel Baldwin also gives the reason why Rumford stayed in England.

March 14, 1799.

I will not attempt to describe the painful disappointment I feel at being obliged to give up all hopes of seeing you and the rest of my dear friends in America this year. A small pamphlet which you will receive with this letter will acquaint you with the reasons which have induced me to postpone my intended voyage; and you will, I am confident, agree with me in opinion that I have done right in sacrificing the pleasure that voyage would have afforded me to the more important objects to which my attention has been called. I beg you would be so kind as to give my dear mother the earliest notice of this change in my plans, and that you would at the same time endeavour to give her just ideas of the very great importance of the undertaking in which I have been called upon to give my assistance, and show her how impossible it was for me to refuse that assistance, especially as it was asked in a manner so honourable to myself. And as the success of the undertaking will be productive of so much good, and will place me in so distinguished a situation in the eyes of the world and of posterity, you will, I am persuaded, find little difficulty in persuading her that I have done perfectly right, and in reconciling her to the disappointment she will naturally feel at not seeing me arrive in America at the time appointed.

The undertaking was the Royal Institution, and the pamphlet was the 'Proposals' for its foundation.

On September 8 Mr. King again wrote to Count Rumford:

London, September 8, 1799.

I have more than once expressed to you a wish that you might find leisure, as well as inclination, to revisit your native country, where I have been persuaded you would meet with a friendly and cordial reception, and by your presence and advice might be of great advantage to our public institutions, the establishment of which, upon approved principles, is an object of the highest consequence. I am happy that I have it in my power to assure you that I have not been mistaken in these sentiments, and it affords me peculiar satisfaction to execute the order that I have lately received from my Government to invite you in its name to return and reside among us, and to propose to you to enter into the American service.[1]

Count Rumford answered:

Brompton, September 12, 1799.

I am deeply sensible of the honour that has been conferred upon me by the Government of the United States, by the kind invitation they have sent me to come and reside in my native country, and also by the other distinguished and most flattering proofs of their confidence and esteem with which that invitation has been accompanied.

[1] The President wrote to Secretary McHenry: 'I should not scruple to give him any of the appointments you mention, and leave it with you to make such proposals to him through Mr. King within the limits you have drawn in your letter as you should think fit.'

Nothing could have afforded me so much satisfaction as to have had it in my power to have given to my liberal and generous countrymen such proof of my sentiments as would in the most public and ostensible manner have evinced, not only my gratitude for the kind attentions I have received from them, but also the ardent desire I feel to assist in promoting the prosperity of my native country.

His affection for his mother, his daughter, and his friend is seen in the following letter to Colonel Baldwin, which he wrote the day before his daughter sailed for America:

Brompton, near London, August 24, 1799.

I cannot permit my daughter to return to America without charging her with a few lines for my *oldest* friend and schoolfellow, the companion of my earliest youth. In straining my recollection as much as possible, in order to look back into that dark cloud that covers the early period of my life, I can remember no person distinctly, longer than yourself, except it be my mother. I must therefore consider you as one of my oldest acquaintances, and I have never ceased to regard you and to love you as one of my best friends. A few months ago I flattered myself with the hope of soon seeing you, but events happened to frustrate those hopes. But though my voyage to America is postponed, it is by no means abandoned. On the contrary, I really think it very likely that I shall pay you a visit next spring.

My daughter will tell you what I am doing in this country, and will acquaint you with my plans and wishes respecting her establishment in America. If you can further the execution of my schemes, I have no doubt but you will do it. There is nothing I have so much at heart as to make my dear mother perfectly comfortable and happy during the remainder of her life.

And a year later he wrote to Colonel Baldwin:

Royal Institution, June 9, 1800.

I must begin my letter with a subject which is ever uppermost in my mind. My daughter and my dear mother will probably be in your neighbourhood when this letter reaches you. I most earnestly recommend them both to your kind attentions. I have one wish, and one only, respecting them, which is, that they may be as happy as possible. As I am at so great a distance from them, I am but ill qualified to judge of their wants and their wishes. Pray assist them in every way in which your friendly assistance can be of use to them, or make them comfortable and contented.

Perhaps my daughter may marry (which she has my leave to do whenever she pleases, and with whom she pleases).[1] This may greatly alter her relative situation with me and with my mother. She may perhaps wish at some future period to make me another visit in Europe, and even in this scheme I shall not oppose her inclinations, if her heart should be set on the gratification of them. I do not mean to be an indulgent father in theory only.

Tell me how I must act to make two persons who are very dear to me as happy as possible.

[1] Notwithstanding this his daughter said her father objected to her marrying Sir C. Blagden.

CHAPTER II.

LIFE OF RUMFORD AFTER THE FOUNDATION OF THE INSTITUTION.

1799 to 1814.

THE history of the life of Count Rumford in 1799, 1800, 1801 to May 1802 is chiefly the history of the Royal Institution. The foundation of it forms an episode which must be separated from the rest of his career. But some of the letters and events of these years which are more closely related to his future life will be recorded here.

Before he began the Institution he had almost determined to go to America, and before the building was finished he wrote to his daughter regarding the time 'when I shall be at liberty,' and soon after he spoke of going to Munich, but before his plans for the Institution were carried out he went to Paris, where new attractions put an end to all he intended to do in America and in England, and he never revisited his native or his adopted country.

On June 9, 1800, Sir C. Blagden wrote to Rumford's daughter in America :

It will give me great pleasure to see you again either here or in America. Do not depend upon the Count's going to visit you there. It is indeed possible that the fancy may suddenly strike him, and then he will set off in an instant, almost without giving notice. But his favourite child, the Institution, cannot yet walk alone, and, if he quits it at the time he talks of, will be a helpless cripple, even if it should continue to exist at all. I still see with regret his time and powers wasted on an object so inferior, in my opinion, to those which presented themselves to him in America. But he views the thing in a different light, and I suspect will be led on to stay here one year after another, till you are worn out with expecting him, and the opportunity of distinguishing himself in a rising country will be past.

Count Rumford thus wrote to his daughter :

Royal Institution, London, March 2, 1801.

MY DEAR CHILD,—I am still established at the Institution. I have been exceedingly busy, but desire to be thankful that all is now nearly completed, when I shall be at liberty. We have found a nice able man for this place as lecturer—Humphry Davy. Lectures are given, frequented by crowds of the first people. Lady Palmerston and her two daughters, Frances and Elizabeth, are pretty constant attendants.

They would not receive me as minister here, but seem disposed now to make it up to me by the respect they show the Institution—originally and chiefly my work. Bernard says they are crazy about it. It was certainly gratifying to me to see the honourable list of lords, dukes, &c., as fifty-guinea subscribers. It is a very extensive establishment, and will cost a great deal of money ; but I hope it will be an equal advantage to the world, as the expense and labour of forming it have been great. To strive for good things I view as a laudable ambition, as I hope you do, my dear Sally. But I hope, above all, to hear of your being well and happy, not doubting the rest.

I hope to be undisturbed by visitors this morning, or

workmen, from my being thought to be at Harrogate, and to be allowed quietly to fill this sheet. You can form no idea of the bustle in which I live since I have taken up my residence in this place. In short, the Royal Institution is not only the fashion but the rage. I am very busy indeed in striving to turn the disposition of the moment to a good account for the permanent benefit of society.

I have the unspeakable satisfaction to find that my labours have not been in vain. In this moment of scarcity and general alarm the measures I have recommended in my writings for relieving the distresses of the poor are very generally adopted, and public kitchens have been erected in all the great towns in England and Scotland. Upwards of sixty thousand persons are fed daily from the different public kitchens in London.

The plan has lately been adopted in France, and a very large public kitchen for feeding the poor was opened in Paris three weeks since. A gentleman present tells me that the founders of the institution did me the honour to put my name at the head of the tickets given to the poor authorising them to receive soup at the public kitchens. At Geneva they have done still more to show me respect. They have marked their tickets with a stamp on which my portrait and my name are engraved.

I am not vain, my dear Sally, but it is utterly impossible not to feel deeply affected at these distinguished marks of honour conferred on me by nations at war with Great Britain, and in countries where I have never been, or know little of the inhabitants. But my greatest delight arises from the silent contemplation of having succeeded in schemes and labours for the benefit of mankind.

Sir C. Blagden wrote to Rumford's daughter, September 10, 1801:

Your father is indeed going to Munich, and talks of setting out in a fortnight. I had at one time almost settled to go with him, but he then proposed to stay there all this winter and next summer. Two or three weeks ago he changed his plan, and determined to make this only a preparatory visit, and to return hither within three months. For my own part I sincerely wish that he had found it expedient to make a voyage to America instead of this journey on the Continent. I would then certainly have accompanied him across the Atlantic, notwithstanding the unsettled state of affairs here. He every day talks more and more coolly about going to America, and though I really think that he means to make *you* a visit there some time or other, yet it does not seem as if he promised himself much satisfaction besides.

As to his health, it is nearly the same as usual, except that he is rather thinner, having lived long upon a very spare diet. The constant agitation of his mind, and the irritable constitution with which it is connected, will necessarily prevent him from enjoying a regular state of good health.

Again, in September, writing to his daughter, Rumford says that the new Elector has invited him to return with assurances of his warm friendship, and 'that though many salaries and pensions have been suspended through the war, his shall be paid.' He says he is going to Munich, 'but that if the Elector will excuse him he does not intend to stay long, the Royal Institution still requiring his oversight.'

He reached Munich by way of Mannheim, and thence wrote to his daughter:

Munich, October 2, 1801.

MY DEAR SALLY,—I arrived here late last evening, and early this morning went to pay my respects to the Elector, who received me with all imaginable kindness. He appears to have plenty of business for me in an academy he is about building, but, as things are not yet in readiness to begin, I am excused from remaining; instead of which I return to England, to put an end to the work begun there—that of the Royal Institution. I owe so much to the Elector, it is my duty to do all in my power to give him satisfaction. Besides, he says I shall be president of the academy when done.

In another letter he speaks of the kindness he met with in Bavaria.

He left Munich on October 13, and again wrote to his daughter on his arrival in Paris on the 25th. His daughter says this was her father's first visit to Paris. The reception he met with was 'simply enchantment.' His inventions were in common use; his name was familiar to everyone. He made a multitude of acquaintances; parties were made for him every day; and he particularly liked one lady. Two letters written to Sir Joseph Banks from Paris in 1801 are of great interest.

Hôtel de Caraman, Paris, November 11.

MY DEAR SIR JOSEPH,—I arrived here from Munich about a fortnight ago, and I purpose staying here three weeks longer. My reception has been very flattering, and I find many interesting objects of curiosity that engage my attention. I have already made the personal acquaintance of most of the men of eminence in science, and I have attended several of the meetings of the National Institute. At the last meeting of the mathematical and physical class the First Consul came in, and, fortunately for the complete gratification of my curiosity, he happened to come and seat himself very near me. One person only (Lagrange) was between us. He stayed about an hour—till the meeting was over. Volta read a memoir on Galvanism and explained his theory of the action of the voltaic pile or battery. His opinion is that all the appearances that are called galvanic are owing to the action of an electric fluid, and he says that the simple tact of two metals—silver and zinc, for instance—is sufficient to set the electric fluid in motion; and if the metals are insulated, one of them will become electrified positively and the other negatively. This assertion was proved by an experiment which was made before the assembly, and this fact is the foundation on which his explanation of the phenomena of the galvanic pile is established. After Volta had finished his memoir the First Consul demanded leave from the President to speak, which, being granted, he proposed to the meeting to reward M. Volta with a gold medal, and to appoint a committee to confer with M. Volta on the subject of his experiments and investigations respecting galvanism, and to make such new experiments as may bid fair to lead to further discoveries. He delivered his sentiments with great perspicuity and displayed a degree of eloquence which surprised me. He is certainly a very extraordinary man and is possessed of uncommon abilities. The expression of his countenance is strong, and it is easy to perceive by his looks that he can pronounce the magic words 'je le veux' with due energy. I was presented to him by the Bavarian minister at his last public audience, and was received by him with marked attention. He gave me to understand that he knew me by reputation very well, and intimated that the French nation had adopted several of the improvements I had recommended. A few minutes after I came home from the audience I received a note from him, inviting me to come and dine with him that day. The foreign ministers dined with him, but no other stranger except myself was invited; consequently my being invited was considered as a marked distinction. It was the next day that I saw him again at the National Institute.

I have had opportunities of making the acquaintance of several of the most distinguished characters now in power in this country. I am very intimate with Chaptal, the

Minister of the Interior, and frequently see Talleyrand, the Minister for Foreign Affairs. I have dined with both of them, and visit them often. Laplace and Bertholet are very civil and attentive to me, and have each of them given me a dinner, where I met most of the men of science of the first distinction in Paris. Fourcroy has also given me a dinner. In short, I am treated with the utmost civility, and I spend my time very agreeably and very usefully. I hope to see you in London about the 6th or 8th of December.

Ever yours most faithfully,

RUMFORD.

He again wrote:

November 22, 1801.

MY DEAR SIR JOSEPH,—I do wrong perhaps, but I cannot help telling you that your name is at the head of the list of those ten persons whom the Class of Mathematics and Physics have resolved to present to the National Institute at their next general meeting, in order to their being elected foreign members of the Institute. You were proposed to the class by the Section of Botany. Your name is followed by those of Maskelyne, Cavendish, Herschel, Priestly, Pallas, Volta, and three others. I was present when the ballot of the class was taken, and had the satisfaction to see that all the votes agreed in placing your name at the head of the list. I was politely told that my name would have been near that of my friend, had it not been that the second class of the Institute had claimed me as belonging to them and had placed me on their list. The three first names on that list are, I am told, Mr. Jefferson, President of the United States, Count Rumford, and Major Rennell; the others I did not learn.

I was proposed to the class by the Section of Political Economy. The classes propose to the Institute, and the Institute elects at a general meeting. The number of foreign members is limited to twenty-four. As the election will not take place for some weeks to come, I beg you would make the most prudent use of the information I have given you. I shall not mention the subject to anybody but yourself.

I hope to see you in London in about three weeks from this time.

My health is much improved, and is still improving every day. My stay in Paris has afforded me much amusement, but I begin to be impatient to see my friends in England. I hope everything is going on well at the Royal Institution.

I am, my dear Sir Joseph, with unalterable esteem and attachment, yours most faithfully,

RUMFORD.

In another letter to his daughter, written January 15, 1802, he says that he returned to Brompton on December 20, and that he was three months on the Continent and seven weeks of the time in Paris. He spoke of his intention to enjoy again the delights of the French capital on his way, in the course of the summer, to Munich and to get excused from any longer residence at Munich. The Elector continued friendly to him, and had lately written to him a very gracious letter, in which he expresses his pleasure at the cordiality extended towards Rumford in France, and advises him to cultivate an acquaintance with a certain lady there, who, among other attractions, was said to have great wealth. When he made this second visit to Paris, the Count accepted an invitation which he had received to stay with the Bavarian ambassador.

Before he left England again, May 9, 1802, he published the third volume of his essays.

His tenth essay was on 'Kitchen Fire-Places and Utensils;' his eleventh on 'Chimney Fire-Places.'

His twelfth on the 'Salubrity of Warm Rooms in Cold Weather;' his thirteenth on the 'Salubrity of Bathing and the Construction of Warm Baths.' His fourteenth consisted of 'Supplementary Observations on the Management of Fires;' his fifteenth was on the 'Use of Steam for Transporting Heat.'

In May 1802 he also published a volume of his philosophical papers, with a dedication to his Most Serene Highness Maximilian Joseph, Elector Palatine of Bavaria. In this he says he must ever feel himself greatly indebted to his Most Serene Electoral Highness

for the kind assurances you gave me of your esteem, protection, and friendship on your succeeding to your present Bavarian dominions on the death of your late uncle, my kind friend and benefactor; but I am bound to you still more, if it be possible, by the flattering invitation you have lately given me to come to you and reside at your Court and assist in the local work of carrying into execution the vast plans you have formed for promoting the prosperity of your subjects.

From Brompton, May 6, 1802, he writes to his daughter: 'In three days I shall set out for Dover, on my way to Paris, where I expect to stay four or five weeks, and then to proceed to Munich.' He sent by way of Holland two carriages and much baggage.

On May 20 Sir C. Blagden wrote from Paris to Sir Joseph Banks: 'Count Rumford arrived here last Friday (the 14th) in remarkably good health. Travelling agrees with him, and he seems very happy. We purpose to set out for Bavaria before the middle of next month.'

Writing to his daughter, June 25, Rumford says: 'I did not propose to stay here long, but the Elector has written commissioning me to transact some business for him of a political nature in which he is much interested.'

On June 8 Sir C. Blagden writes to Sir Joseph Banks: 'I was preparing everything to set off for Germany, and had even applied to Mr. Merry for a passport, when Count Rumford told me he had received permission from the Elector to stay a few weeks longer at Paris. This considerably deranges my plans.'

On July 19 Rumford wrote to Sir Joseph Banks:

Rue de Clichy, 356, July 19, 1802.

MY DEAR SIR JOSEPH,—The print[1] you sent me has afforded me much amusement, and, even more than that, it has given me real satisfaction. It is just that 'those who take up the sword should perish by the sword.' I never had a doubt who was the author of another print which certainly was not designed to give me pleasure. Although it has long been said, and I believe with truth, that those who render themselves conspicuous by their superior genius, their talents, and, above all, by their usefulness to society, must necessarily be exposed to the shafts of envy and to the hatred of all bad men, yet, much as I am desirous of deserving the approbation of mankind, so far from feeling any secret satisfaction at seeing myself distinguished by those miscreants, who may justly be considered as the vermin of society, I lament that I am not permitted to finish

[1] Probably the caricature by Gilray of the Royal Institution and Sir John Hippesley, published on May 23. Count Rumford was caricatured on June 12, 1800.

my days in peace and quietness. But the established order of things cannot be changed, and I must endeavour to support with patience and dignity all those evils which cannot be avoided.

I continue to pass my time here in Paris very agreeably. The society in which I live most is very pleasant, and I am surrounded by a great variety of interesting objects of curiosity. I have very often the satisfaction of hearing your name mentioned, and always in terms of the highest possible respect. No individual was ever in more complete possession of the enlightened world than yourself. It is indeed true that no man ever deserved it more.

An extraordinary meeting of the first class of the Institute was held on Saturday last for the purpose of deciding a dispute which had arisen among the Ingénieurs des Ponts et Chaussées relative to an intended canal from Cambray to St. Quentin, to form a communication by water between the Belgique and the interior of France. Two plans had been proposed, one by a M. Laurent and the other by M. Vicque.

Laurent proposed to form the junction by one straight subterranean canal about six French leagues in length; Vicque proposed to avail himself of a valley, in order to diminish the length of the subterranean passage to about three leagues. The latter was almost unanimously approved by the Institute, though the total length of the canal of Vicque is more than a third greater than that of Laurent, and though it has two subterranean passages instead of one. The First Consul was present at the discussion of this question by the Institute, and took a very active part in the debate. He displayed very uncommon abilities. He is indeed a very extraordinary man. He hears with patience and with the utmost attention every argument opposed to his own opinions, and he states the question in dispute in so clear a light, and divests it so completely from every consideration that is not essential, that every difficulty seems to be removed and the decision rendered quite plain and obvious.

I was at the public audience of the 14th of July, and dined with the First Consul, and also stayed and spent the evening at the Tuileries. We sat down to table about 240 persons, and about 60 or 80 of the company stayed and spent the evening. There were a few card tables—not more than four or five. The First Consul did not play, but walked about and talked to the company. He went out two or three times upon an elevated terrace, or rather large open platform, on the level of the apartment we were in to see the illuminations of the gardens. As often as he appeared, the crowd below saluted him by clapping hands.

He went to the opera the next evening, and, instead of occupying his private box, which is grillé, he went and took his place in the front of Madame Bonaparte's box, where he was exposed to the view of the whole house. The applause he received was quite enthusiastic and lasted near a quarter of an hour. 'Vive Bonaparte!' was heard from every part of the theatre, and the actors were obliged to stop for some time. These applauses were again repeated when he went away. He came to the meeting of the Institute on Saturday without any guards, and accompanied only by his brother-in-law, General Murat. I followed him down the stairs when he went away. I found his carriage waiting for him, surrounded by about ten or twelve grenadiers, who kept the crowd at a small distance from the carriage and formed a line from the foot of the staircase. He was received by the populace with shouts of applause, and he drove away without guards and with a single footman behind his carriage, which was a coach.

Thursday Morning, July 31.

This letter will be forwarded by M. d'Ifeffel, the Elector's chargé d'affaires at London, who will leave Paris this evening. My stay at Paris is very uncertain; I fancy, however, that I shall set out for Munich in the course of three or four weeks. The Elector writes me the kindest and most flattering letters, and I have the satisfaction to think that my stay here has been of some use to him. I avoid most carefully every appearance of interfering in public business, but I now and then find opportunities of putting in a word privately where it is not lost. I fancy the Elector will be well treated in the general arrangement which is about to take place.

I thank you for the information you have given me relative to the Royal Institution. It is impossible for me not to feel very deeply interested in its fate. I hope it will prosper; I know it will if you can support and protect it. It would grieve me to see it fall to the ground. My health is much improved since I have been in France. I am, indeed, now quite well. I continue to spend my time here very agreeably. If there should be anything I could do for you here, I hope and trust that you will have no scruples in favouring me with your commands.

I am, and shall ever be, my dear Sir Joseph, with unalterable attachment, yours most faithfully,

RUMFORD.

On August 10, Tuesday, Sir C. Blagden writes: 'I am on the point of setting out with Count Rumford for Munich. We go first to Mannheim, and I expect to be there next Sunday; afterwards, perhaps, through that tract of country bordering on Switzerland which will be ceded to the Elector as a compensation, so as to reach Munich about the latter end of this month.'

On August 30, from Munich, Sir C. Blagden wrote to Sir Joseph Banks:

I wrote to you from Paris on the day of our departure, and left the letter to be sent by post next day. Our journey hither was made during the hottest time of this summer; we had the thermometer in the carriage one day at 93°, and several days within a degree or two of it; but this great heat did not injure our health or materially impair our spirits or appetite.

It is really pleasant to see with what respect and affection Count Rumford is treated here by all ranks of people. I do not mean to say that he is without enemies, for surely he has many, but all, as far as I can learn, from envy, jealousy, or competition of interests. The great mass of the people consider him as a public benefactor, and would rejoice to see the government of the country thrown into his hands. This, however, as far as I can judge from what he says, as well as from his actions, is by no means his own wish, and, indeed, I think he can do as much good, leading at the same time a vastly pleasant life, if he remains simply as the Elector's friend. In our way we called at a convent in Bavaria, and it was surprising to see how much attachment the monks show to him, though they must consider him as a heretic. In spite of religious differences he has found the means to persuade them of his general good intentions. The Elector and every person in his family behave to the Count with great respect, and are extremely gracious to me, evidently for the purpose of showing regard to his introduction.

On September 1, Rumford wrote to his daughter that he found his English Garden grown more beautiful than ever, the Elector sparing no expense upon it. But his House for the Poor had not been well attended to, though there were few or no beggars to be met with in the streets. The Count says that he was received by the public with the most flattering marks of esteem and respect. The Emperor of Russia sent him an invitation to visit St. Petersburg, but the Count could not make up his mind to the undertaking. He writes:

My health requires that I should keep more quiet. It is

all I ask here. I have and ask no augmentation of appointments. Many cannot understand why I am not more anxious for places and money. People even pretend I am going to be Minister of State; but for a certainty I am not, neither do I desire to be. I want only quiet.

In her summary of a letter from her father, dated from Mannheim, November 30, 1802, his daughter says that 'he alludes to his love concern: says he has got into full employment at Munich, but would rather be in Paris; and the *certain lady* would rather have him there.'

At Christmas he was still at Mannheim, and thence he wrote to the clerk at the Institution: 'As I have no correspondent but you who can inform me how you are going on at the Royal Institution, you will oblige me very much by writing to me now and then, and letting me know what you are doing, and how the Institution stands in the public opinion. You will easily believe that I must be very anxious to hear of its welfare and prosperity.' He said that he hoped to be back in April or May. In January he sent his compliments to Dr. Young and to Mr. Davy.

Writing to his daughter again from Munich, January 22, 1803, Rumford says he is unsettled there, and therefore that he cannot conveniently have her with him, but that at a future time, not far distant, he will attempt it. He spoke of the style in which he was living, having his servants, the Aichners, with him, with his carriages. While he was at Munich he was joined by Madame Lavoisier.

Sir C. Blagden wrote to Sir Joseph Banks:

Paris, October 15, 1802.

As a good occasion of making the journey to Paris presented itself, I left Munich about a week sooner than I originally intended, and have now been some days in this capital.

Count Rumford was in very good health, and proposed to spend the winter at Munich; he was going into a magnificent house, or rather palace, lent him by one of the nobility, an old friend, in which he meant to give concerts as he used to do. The Elector continued to treat him with the most marked distinction, but he did not seem to be engaging in any public business. Indeed, the country was rather in a state of alarm, on account of the menacing appearances of the Emperor, who evidently wants part of Bavaria as a further compensation to the Grand Duke. The Count's opinion when I quitted him was that he should be in Paris next spring, and thence return to England.

Two months later Sir C. Blagden said: 'The Count finds the climate of Mannheim much milder and more suitable to his constitution than that of Munich, which is really sharp and trying.' And afterwards he wrote regarding the French Institute:

Count Rumford has been removed from the third class to the first, a change which I believe he very much desired. In consequence there is now only one vacancy to be filled up in the first class, and I think that Volta will be the man chosen at the next election.

Unless we are all sent away by the war, I shall probably stay near a fortnight longer than the 5th of April.

The Count expects to be in England some time in the summer. He is very busy making experiments on heat, and says his new-invented instruments have already put him in possession of several new and interesting facts.

Sir C. Blagden wrote to Rumford's daughter from London, August 8, 1803:

When my letter of last June was written I thought your father pretty much fixed at Munich, and therefore ventured to suggest to you that it might contribute to your happiness if you were to be established at that Court. But I learn since that the Elector has set him more at his liberty, and that in consequence he intends to return to England this autumn. Political difficulties may possibly stand in the way of this journey, but he hopes to avoid them. I am still as much at a loss as I was in June to answer your question whether your father be going to marry. He is now, as I told you in that letter, making the tour of Switzerland with a very amiable French lady. But I have no reason to think that they have any idea of matrimonial connexion. When the Count comes to England she is to return to Paris; at least so he writes me word.

He wrote to Sir Joseph Banks:

Count Rumford has sent me a letter from Mannheim, dated the 13th of September. He had applied for leave to pass through France to England, but was refused. I suppose the French Government thought that he too would act the spy.[1]

He professes himself still uncertain whether he should not attempt the journey by the north of Germany, but I am myself pretty well satisfied that he will not. In the meantime he desires me to assure you that he will certainly contrive to send the paper on Heat before Christmas. The King and Queen of Sweden were then at Mannheim. He had been presented to and had dined with them.

Later he wrote:

Soho Square, September 29.

My last letter from Count Rumford was of July 31, but I have learned otherwise that he was at Geneva about the

[1] Blagden himself had just been accused of being a spy.

20th of August, setting out for a tour to the icy mountains of Savoy. He has permission, therefore, to travel in that part of the French territory. Whether he will be allowed to return to England through France, or whether he will come at all, I do not yet know.

Whilst in Switzerland Rumford wrote 'Some Observations on the Glaciers of Chamouni, and on the Propagation of Heat in Liquids.' This paper was sent to the Royal Society, of which he was then vice-president, December 15. It was published in the 'Philosophical Transactions' for 1804.

On December 5, 1803, Sir C. Blagden again wrote to Rumford's daughter:

All I can tell you about your father is this: He continued travelling with the French lady till about the middle of September, when she left him at Mannheim and returned to Paris. Your father had applied to the French Government for leave to come to England through France, but was refused. In consequence he remained at Mannheim till the middle of October, when, having by some means, I do not know how, induced the French Government to change their resolution, and allow him to travel in France, he set out for Paris; and I know that he was in that city on the 1st of November. In the last letter I received from him, which was written the day before he set out from Mannheim, he said that he had great hopes of being in England before the end of this year. Since that time I have heard nothing from him. He continues very intimate with the lady, but whether it will end in a marriage I cannot say. My own opinion is rather inclined to the negative, yet I have no good foundation for it.

Since this was written I have received a letter from your father, dated at Paris, November 11. By this it is evident that he expects to marry the French lady, though nothing is yet finally determined.

On March 12, 1804, he again writes from Liverpool:

The last account I received of your father was dated the 19th of January. He was then at Paris, very assiduous in his attentions to the French lady, with whom, indeed, he spent most of his time. But I believe she had not then determined to marry him, and I am still inclined to think she never will. In the meantime he is entirely losing his interest in the country. His residence at Paris this winter, whilst we were threatened with an invasion, is considered by everyone as very improper conduct, and his numerous enemies do not fail to make the most of it. He has quarrelled with Mr. Bernard and others of his old friends at the Royal Institution, and they do all they can to render him unpopular. Probably he has written to you more than once by American ships since his residence at Paris. To me he wrote on the 12th of November, about a fortnight after his arrival there. But I expect no other letter from him, as it would certainly be imprudent in him to keep up a correspondence with this country during his residence in France.

On January 22, 1804, Rumford wrote to his daughter:

I shall withhold this information from you no longer. I really do think of marrying, though I am not yet absolutely determined on matrimony. I made the acquaintance of this very amiable woman in Paris, who, I believe, would have no objection in having me for a husband, and who in all respects would be a proper match for me. She is a widow, without children, never having had any, is about my own age, enjoys good health, is very pleasant in society, has a handsome fortune at her own disposal, enjoys a most respectable reputation, keeps a good house, which is frequented by all the first philosophers and men of eminence in the science and literature of the age, or rather of Paris, and, what is more than all the rest, is goodness itself. . . . She is very clever (according to the English signification of the word); in short, she is another Lady Palmerston. She has been very handsome in her day, and even now, at forty-six or forty-eight, is not bad-looking; of a middling size, but rather *en bon point* than thin. She has a great deal of vivacity and writes incomparably well.

He soon after writes again of the lady: 'She is fond of travelling, and wishes to make the tour of Italy with me. She appears to be most sincerely attached to me, and I esteem and love her very much.'

On February 7, 1804, the Count writes again from Paris. He and Madame Lavoisier were then making preparations for their marriage. She deposited in his name one hundred and twenty thousand *livres* in the five per cent. French funds, which was to go to the survivor of the three—herself, himself, or his daughter. An income of six thousand a year out of her own property was secured to Madame Lavoisier. Her house in Paris, as well as the Count's at Brompton, was to revert to the survivor of the two.

On July 2 he said:

MY DEAR SALLY,—This letter, which will be entirely devoted to very serious and important business, will, no doubt, obtain your serious attention.

In order to be able to complete in a *legal manner* some domestic arrangements of great importance to me and to you, I have lately found, to my no small surprise, that certificates of my birth and of the death of my former wife are indispensably necessary. You can, no doubt, very easily procure them—the one from the town clerk of Woburn, the other from the town clerk of Concord. And I request that you would do it without loss of time, and send them to me under cover, or rather in a letter addressed to me and sent to the care of my bankers in London. As an accident may possibly happen to that letter, I beg you would at the same time send another set of these certificates directly to Paris, addressed to me, rue de Clichy, No. 356.

On July 3 he wrote to Mr. Savage, the clerk of the Royal Institution:

With regard to the outstanding bills which you mention, as I intend and expect to come to England soon, they may as well stand on till my arrival. Some of the charges require examination. It gives me great pleasure to hear that my house is kept in good order. I hope to inhabit it next winter.

On August 10 the Count left Paris for Munich.

On May 1, 1805, he wrote to the clerk of the Royal Institution:

Munich, May 1.

I have written to Mr. Herries respecting the letting or selling of my house. I hear that the Royal Institution is become a great favourite with the public. I am sorry, however, to find that the Journals of the Institution have not been continued. I desire you would make my compliments to Mr. Davy, and tell him that I am still employed in my researches on heat and light. I should be glad to know what he is doing, for I am sure he cannot be idle. It is now more uncertain than ever when I shall have it in my power to visit England.

To his daughter he wrote, June 18, from Munich:

I left Paris the 9th of June, and arrived here the 16th. My stay here is uncertain, for many things are yet wanting that are indispensably necessary for the success of such an establishment as the Academy of Arts and Sciences.[1] I

[1] It was not until May 1, 1807, that King Maximilian Joseph, 'having extended the bounds of his kingdom, gave a new constitution to the Bavarian Academy, proportioned to the existing state of science and to his new empire.' The first public meeting was held on July 27.

continue to pursue my philosophical researches, and that will ever be the most pleasing occupation I can have.

On September 17 he was again in Paris.

He wrote to his daughter:

Rue d'Anjou, No. 39, Paris, October 25, 1805.

You will have intelligence by the papers of the events that have lately taken place in Germany. Foreseeing the storm, I left Munich the day before the Elector left it. I have brought Aichner and his whole family, not being willing to leave them behind. I succeeded in so winding up my affairs in Bavaria as in the future to be able to live where I please. I shall, of course, go from time to time to pay my respects to the Elector, for he has ever treated me with too much respect for me to be negligent on that account towards him.

I have informed you before of the arrangements Madame Lavoisier and I had made in case of our marriage, which, in fact, took place yesterday.

I have the best-founded hopes of passing my days in peace and quiet in this paradise of a place, made what it is by me—my money, skill, and directions. In short, it is all but a paradise, removed from the noise and bustle of the street, facing full to the south, in the midst of a beautiful garden of more than two acres, well planted with trees and shrubbery. The entrance from the street is through an iron gate, by a beautiful winding avenue, well planted, and the porter's lodge is by the side of this gate; a great bell to be rung in case of ceremonious visits.'

The daughter's comment on this letter is: 'It seems there had been an acquaintance between these parties of four years before marriage. It might be thought a long space of time enough for perfect acquaintance. But, ah Providence! thy ways are past finding out.'

Dr. Ellis, the biographer of Rumford, says:

An interval, though a very brief one, of cheerfulness and satisfaction was enjoyed by the Count after his marriage. There were but two letters to his daughter recognising this state of content and pleasant anticipation. He informed her that he left Munich under the pleasantest relations with the Bavarian sovereign and his friends at that Court. He had received a letter from Maximilian, congratulating him on his marriage and approving of his settling himself in France, and at the same time adding four thousand florins a year to his pay.

One letter was dated from Paris, December 20, 1805, two months after his marriage:

I gave up my lodgings on quitting Munich, and managed so as to settle all concerns of business. I flatter myself I am settled down here for life, far removed from wars and all arduous duties, as a recompense for past services, with plenty to live upon and at liberty to pursue my own natural propensities, such as have occupied me through life—a life, as I try to fancy, that may come under the denomination of a benefit to mankind.

Next spring we are going to travel into Italy and the south of France, to be gone two years, so you must patiently stay where you are for the present.

You will wish to know what sort of a place we live in. The house is rather an old-fashioned concern, but in a plot of over two acres of land, in the very centre and finest part of Paris, near the Champs Elysées and the Tuileries and principal boulevards. I have already made great alterations in our place, and shall do a vast deal more. When these are done I think Madame de Rumford will find it in a very different condition from that in which it was, that being very pitiful with all her riches.

Our style of living is really magnificent. Madame is exceedingly fond of company, and makes a splendid figure in it herself. But she seldom goes out, keeping open doors; that is to say, to all the great and worthy, such as the philosophers, members of the Institute, ladies of celebrity, &c.

On Mondays we have eight or ten of the most noted of our associates to dinner. Thursdays are devoted to evening company, of ladies and gentlemen, without regard to numbers. Tea and fruits are given, the guests continuing till twelve or after. Often superb concerts are given, with the finest vocal and instrumental performers.

At this time Sir C. Blagden wrote to Sir Joseph Banks:

I have received a letter, dated November 22, from a lady in Paris, which contains no kind of news except the following article about Count Rumford and his lady: 'Madame Lavoisier s'appelle à présent Madame de Rumford. J'ai vu Madame de Rumford [the writer of the letter has been returned to Paris only two days]. Ils ne donnent ni l'un ni l'autre aucun détail sur leur mariage ni sur l'époque; un jour ils l'ont dit à leurs amis, et il n'y a pas eu plus de formalité que cela. Ils sont sur un pied fort amical, mais ils étaient ainsi depuis longtemps. La maison de Mdme. de Rumford est charmante. Elle l'embellit tous les jours et avec beaucoup de goût.'

On January 15, 1806, Rumford wrote to his daughter:

The newspapers will acquaint you with the other particulars of this peace, which will occasion a great change in the political state of Germany, as, in fact, of all Europe. I hope that I shall not, and I do not think that I shall, lose by any of these changes. At all events the Elector, or rather the new King, has just written me a very kind letter, giving me hopes, rather than suggesting fears of anything of a disagreeable nature. But dependencies like mine can never be otherwise than uncertain, as I feel it, notwithstanding my marriage. I may make a change, after all, but never certainly to the disadvantage of anyone. Between you and myself, as a family secret, I am not at all sure that two certain persons were not wholly mistaken, in their marriage, as to each other's characters. Time will show. But two months barely expired, I forebode difficulties. Already I am obliged to send my good Germans home—a great discomfort to me and wrong to them.

On March 8, 1806, Sir C. Blagden, who had quarrelled with his friend because he thought that Count Rumford had not defended him from the imputation of acting as a spy in Paris in 1803, wrote to Rumford's daughter regarding the marriage :

They are now living together in Paris, and, as far as I can learn, very happily. I know nothing of it from your father himself, which is not surprising, as I some time since intimated to him my wish that our correspondence should cease. We are not, to the best of my knowledge, on terms of enmity, but it is not likely that any kind of confidence or friendship should subsist between us again.

In 1806 and 1807 Count Rumford sought for relief by the pursuit of science. He published in the Memoirs of the mathematical class of the Institute a continuation and extension of his investigations on light and heat. These were in the sixth, seventh, and eighth volumes, and made nine papers. 1. 'A Description of a New Thermoscope or Differential Thermometer.' 2. 'Researches on Heat, Showing the Effect of Difference of Surface on Radiation.' 3. 'Further Experiments on the Effect of Blackening the Surface.' 4. 'Researches Continued on the Different Properties of Bodies with Respect to Radiation and to Conducting

Powers.' 5. 'Further Researches on the Passage of Heat through Solids.' 6. 'Experiments on the Heat of the Solar Rays.' 7. 'Remarks on the Temperature of Water at the Maximum Density.' He made it 41° F. or 5° C. This paper was published in the 'Philosophical Transactions.' 8. On the 'Dispersion of the Light of Lamps by Screens of Ground Glass, Silk, and so forth, with a Description of a New Lamp.' He had an illuminator constructed and presented to the Institute. This paper was published in England as his sixteenth essay on the 'Management of Light in Illuminations.' 9. On the 'Cooling of Liquids in Vases of Porcelain, Gilt or not Gilt.'

In October 1806 he gave this sad account to his daughter:

MY DEAR CHILD,—This being the first year's anniversary of my marriage, from what I wrote two months after it, you will be curious to know how things stand at present. I am sorry to say that experience only serves to confirm me in the belief that in character and natural propensities Madame de Rumford and myself are totally unlike, and never ought to have thought of marrying. We are, besides, both too independent, both in our sentiments and habits of life, to live peaceably together—she having been mistress all her days of her actions, and I, with no less liberty, leading for the most part the life of a bachelor. Very likely she is as much disaffected towards me as I am towards her. Little it matters with me, but I call her a female dragon—simply by that gentle name! We have got to the pitch of my insisting on one thing and she on another.

It is possible that, had the war ceased raging, and had we gone into Italy, where she is dying to go, and with me too, she having heard me speak much of the delights of that country, she having been very happy, too, in travelling with me in Switzerland, it might have suspended difficulties, but never have effected a cure. That is out of the question. Indeed, I have not the least idea of continuing here, and, if possible, still less the wish, and am only planning in my mind what steps I shall take next—to be hoped more to my advantage. Communication with England is prohibited, and it makes me sad.

He wrote more pitiably a year later:

Rue d'Anjou, Paris, October 24, 1807.

I can do no more, my dear Sally, than simply give you the latest news upon this the anniversary of my marriage, for I am still here, and so far from things getting better they become worse every day. We are more violent and more open, and more public, as may really be said, in our quarrels. If she does not mind publicity, for a certainty I shall not. As I write the uncouth word *quarrels*, I will give you an idea of one of them.

In the first place be it known that this estate is a joint concern. I have as good a right to it as Madame, she having paid rather more in the beginning, but I an immensity of money in repairs and alterations, &c. &c., besides a great deal of my own time and care spent while we have been here.

I am almost afraid to tell you the story, my good child, lest in future you should not be good; lest what I am about relating should set you a bad example, make you passionate, and so on. But I had been made very angry. A large party had been invited I neither liked nor approved of, and invited for the sole purpose of vexing me. Our house being in the centre of the garden, walled around, with iron gates, I put on my hat, walked down to the porter's lodge and gave him orders, on his peril, not to let anyone in. Besides, I took away the keys. Madame went down, and when the company arrived she talked with them, she on one side, they on the other, of the high brick wall. After that she goes and pours boiling water on some of my beautiful flowers.

And the wretched climax came the next year:

Rue d'Anjou, St. Honoré, No. 39, Paris, April 12, 1808.

After what you know, my dear Sally, of my domestic troubles you will naturally be anxious to know the present state of things. There are no alterations for the better. On the contrary, much worse. I have suffered more than you can imagine for the last four weeks; but my rights are incontestable, and I am determined to maintain them. I have the misfortune to be married to one of the most imperious, tyrannical, unfeeling women that ever existed, and whose perseverance in pursuing an object is equal to her profound cunning and wickedness in framing it.

It is impossible to continue in this way, and we shall separate. I only wish it was well over. It is probable I shall take a house at Auteuil, a very pleasant place, with the Seine on one side and the Bois de Boulogne on the other, about a league from Paris. I have seen a very handsome house there which I can have—rather dear, but that matters little can I but find quiet. It would be truly unfortunate, after the King of Bavaria's late bounties joined to former ones, if I could not live more independently than with this unfeeling, cunning, tyrannical woman.

Little do we know people at first sight! Do you preserve my letters? You will perceive that I have given very different accounts of this woman, for *lady* I cannot call her.

Now, my dear Sally, as soon as I get settled, enjoying again independence, I shall wish you to join me.

In the meantime believe me your affectionate Father.

The Count bought the lease of his villa at Auteuil in April 1808.

For the last two or three months of his most miserable

married life he was seriously ill. The nature of his illness is seen by the remedies that benefited him. He told his daughter that the King of Bavaria, having knowledge of his domestic discomforts, had recently written him a letter that had done him much good. 'He speaks most kindly to me, and encourages me to bear my misfortunes like a man of firmness who has nothing to reproach himself with.'

The separation took place amicably on June 30, 1809. He soon after wrote to his daughter:

I find myself relieved from an almost insupportable burden. I cannot repeat too much how happy I am, gaining every day in health, which, from vexations, had become seriously deranged. I am persuaded it is all for the best. After the scenes which I have recently passed through I realise, as never before, the sweets of quiet, liberty, and independence. My household consists of the most faithful, honest people, attached to me, without dissension, bribery, or malice. And, above all, that eternal contradiction. Oh! happy, thrice happy, am I to be my own man again!

Later he wrote:

Madame de Rumford is well. I see her sometimes, though very seldom. After what is past a reconciliation is impossible. She now repents of her conduct, but it is too late. The less I see her the better. I now enjoy peace and tranquillity, and my health improves every day.

Again:

Auteuil, October 24, 1809.

DEAR SALLY,—The 'Mentor' arrived some weeks since, when I was expecting you. Without doubt the reason you did not come was owing to your not finding proper protection, and in these terrible times of war you cannot be too particular. This unfortunate war chains me to the spot, for I am so situated between three governments that I am obliged almost to turn into a cypher. It is to England I want to go, but dare not risk it. And it is there I should much prefer receiving you than here.

By the date of this letter you will perceive it to be the anniversary of my wedding-day with Madame Lavoisier to-day four years. I own I make choice of this day to write to you, in reality to testify joy, but joy that I am away from her, as has been the case for the last six months. It would be difficult to describe what I suffered there for the last year. I often wished for you, but am now exceedingly glad you did not come, as it would have made you unhappy and perhaps have done me no good. I was made quite ill at last, but now, thank Heaven, I am recovering my health and spirits fast. I am like one risen from the dead. Adieu, my dear child. You will hear from me soon again, and I hope to see you soon. I have some pretty rooms prepared for you. I had one of the Aichners to come and wait upon you, but she did not exactly please me, and I sent her back again. My old servants, her father and mother, are nicely established, owing to mine and the Elector's kindness, at Munich, and are very happy.

Auteuil, November 12, 1809.

MY DEAR DAUGHTER,—Here is another month past, and you do not come. I know all the difficulties of travelling either by sea or by land, so do not blame you; am only sorry. Sorry on several accounts—on one account that I want to see you. For do you recollect, my dear, that it is many years since we saw each other? We will not say how many, lest the time should seem longer. And little did I think, when you quitted me at Brompton, it would have been for such a length of time, nor would it have been but for this unfortunate marriage. Never were there two more distinct beings than this woman (for I cannot call her a lady) before and after marriage. But undoubtedly she was pushed on by those looking forward to her fortune, fearing some of it would light on me. She is the most avaricious woman I ever saw, and the most cunning—things which I could not possibly know before marriage.

I suffered more for the last fourteen months—indeed, the whole three years and a half that I lived with her—than I had an idea I could have gone through. Luckily I have money enough of my own, but war and these terrible times prevent me from receiving money from Bavaria, or my half-pay from England. Yet I am obliged to keep up a certain consequence, besides being disgusted with everything. I am afraid you will have to quit the world if you stay with me.

Auteuil, January 10, 1810.

Here month after month arrives, but you do not come. I am very impatient to see you, but I am more anxious lest something should happen to you on the way, for discord reigns everywhere.

Later he said:

I am absolutely obliged to set out for Munich, so if you come in the time you must make yourself comfortable. If I find you here on my return, it will give me much pleasure.

The King has been in Paris, and invited me so kindly I thought it my duty to go; but he assures me I shall not be detained there on any business of importance.

On his arrival in Munich he wrote:

My reception here has been most kind and flattering. The whole town is in expectation of seeing me again fixed here and employed in the public affairs of the country.

But I know positively, and it is my greatest consolation, that I shall be permitted to return quietly to my retreat at Auteuil.

Adieu, my dear Sally. I shall write to you again, I think, before leaving Munich; but you had better not write me, lest I should be already set out on my return.

My health is perfectly good, and I am very happy. All my late sufferings are forgotten. I feel as if just relieved from an insupportable weight. God be thanked for my delivery! All your friends here have desired to be remembered to you. Adieu, my dear Sally; make yourself as comfortable and happy as you can, and be assured that I have at length quite recovered my reason, and that I am now persuaded that all that has happened to me has been most fortunate for me. I am now a free man.

Munich, October 24, 1810.

You will perceive that this is the anniversary of my marriage. I am happy to call it to mind, that I may compare my present situation with the three and a half horrible years I was living with that tyrannical, avaricious, unfeeling woman. You can have no idea, my dear Sally, what I had to suffer during the last fourteen months—indeed, during the whole three years and a half I lived in that house—but the closing six months was a purgatory sufficiently painful to do away the sins of a thousand years.

The Prince Royal was married on the 12th, and we have had continued *fêtes* and rejoicings. The English Garden is in high beauty; no expense is spared upon it. I am allowed to dine with the King pretty much as often as I wish, but to-morrow I take leave of him, of Munich, and the rest of my friends; so you will soon, my dear Sally, see me at Auteuil.

In December 1811 his daughter arrived at Auteuil, and found him in excellent health. She writes:

I had not been many days at Auteuil before we had a visit from his separated lady, for they seemed to be on good terms—at least on visiting terms. The lady was gracious to me, and I was charmed with her, nor did I ever after find reason to be otherwise, for she was truly an admirable character. Their disagreements must have arisen from their independence of character and means; being used always to having their own ways. Their pursuits in some particulars were different. He was fond of his experiments, and she of company.

A picture of Madame de Rumford was thus drawn by M. Guizot in 1841, five years after her death:

Soit affection pour son mari, soit disposition naturelle, Madame Lavoisier s'associa à ses travaux comme un compagnon ou un disciple. Ceux-là même qui ne l'ont connue que bien loin de la jeunesse ont pu démêler que sous une apparence un peu froide et rude, et presque uniquement préoccupée de sa vie de société, c'était une personne capable d'être fortement saisie par un sentiment, par une idée, et de s'y adonner avec passion. Elle vivait dans le laboratoire de M. Lavoisier, l'aidait dans ses expériences, écrivait ses observations sous sa dictée, traduisait, définait pour lui. Elle apprit à graver, pour qu'il fût sûr d'un ouvrier exact jusqu'au scrupule, et les planches du 'Traité de Chimie' furent bien réellement l'œuvre de ses mains. Elle publia, parce qu'il le désirait, la traduction d'un ouvrage du chimiste anglais Kirwan sur 'la Force des Acides et la Proportion des Substances qui composent les Sels neutres,' et elle avait acquis, de la science qu'ils cultivaient ensemble, une intelligence si complète que lorsqu'en 1805, onze ans après la mort de Lavoisier, elle voulut réunir et publier ses mémoires scientifiques, elle put se charger seule de ce travail et l'accomplit en effet, en y joignant une préface parfaitement simple, où ne se laisse entrevoir aucune ombre de prétention.

Un intérieur aussi animé par affection réciproque et des

occupations favorites, une grande fortune, beaucoup de considération, une bonne maison à l'Arsenal, recherchée par les hommes les plus distingués, tous les plaisirs de l'esprit, de la richesse, de la jeunesse, c'était là, à coup sûr, une existence brillante et douce. Cette existence fut frappée, foudroyée par la Révolution, comme toutes celles qui l'entouraient. En 1794 Mdme. Lavoisier vit monter le même jour sur l'échafaud son père et son mari, et elle n'échappa elle-même, après un emprisonnement assez court, qu'en plongeant avec la patience la plus persévérante dans la plus complète et silencieuse obscurité.

Quand les proscriptions cessèrent, quand l'ordre et la justice revinrent apaiser et ranimer en même temps la société, Mdme. Lavoisier reprit sa place dans le monde, entourée de toute une génération de savants illustres, les amis, les disciples, les successeurs de Lavoisier, Lagrange, Laplace, Berthollet, Cuvier, Prony, Humboldt, Arago, charmés en honorant sa veuve de trouver dans sa maison, en retour de l'éclat qu'ils y répandaient, les agréments d'une hospitalité élégante. M. de Rumford arriva parmi eux. Il était alors au service du roi de Bavière et jouissait dans le public d'une grande popularité scientifique; son esprit était élevé, sa conversation pleine d'intérêt, ses manières empreintes de bonté. Il plut à Mdme. Lavoisier; il s'accordait avec ses habitudes, ses goûts, on pourrait presque dire avec ses souvenirs. Elle espéra recommencer en quelque sorte son bonheur. Elle l'épousa le 22 October, 1805, heureuse d'offrir à un homme distingué une grande fortune et la plus agréable existence.

Leurs caractères ne se convinrent point. A la jeunesse seule il est facile d'oublier au sein d'un tendre bonheur la perte de l'indépendence. Des questions délicates furent élevées, des susceptibilités s'éveillèrent. Mdme. de Rumford en se remariant avait formellement stipulé dans son contrat qu'elle se ferait appeler Madame Lavoisier de Rumford. M. de Rumford, qui y avait consenti, finit par le trouver mauvais. Elle persista. 'J'ai regardé comme un devoir, comme une religion,' écrivait-elle en 1808, 'de ne point quitter le nom de Lavoisier. . . . Comptant sur la parole de M. de Rumford je n'en aurais pas fait un article de mes engagements civils avec lui, si je n'avais voulu laisser un acte public de mon respect pour M. Lavoisier et une preuve de la générosité de M. de Rumford. C'est un devoir pour moi de tenir à une détermination qui a toujours été une des conditions de notre union ; et j'ai dans le fond de mon âme l'intime conviction que M. de Rumford ne me désapprouvera pas et qu'après avoir pris le temps d'y réfléchir . . . il me permettra de continuer à remplir un devoir que je regarde comme sacré.'

Ce fut encore là une espérance trompée. Après des agitations domestiques, que M. de Rumford avec plus de tact eût rendues moins bruyantes, la séparation devint nécessaire, et elle eut lieu à l'aimable le 30 juin, 1809.

Depuis cette époque et pendant vingt-sept ans aucun événement, on pourrait dire aucun incident, ne dérangea plus Mdme. de Rumford dans sa noble et agréable façon de vivre. Elle n'appartint plus qu'à ses amis et à la société, tantôt étendue, tantôt resserrée, qu'elle recevait avec un mélange assez singulier de rudesse et de politesse, toujours de très-bonne compagnie et d'une grande intelligence du monde même dans ses brusqueries de langage et ses fantaisies d'autorité.

In February 1812 Count Rumford gave his mother 10,000 dollars in 3½ per cent. stock as a free gift, and he wrote to her:

I desire that you will accept of it as a token of my dutiful affection for you, and of my gratitude for the kind care you took of me in the early part of my life. I have the greatest satisfaction in being able to show my gratitude for all your goodness to me, and to contribute to your ease and comfort. I request that you will consider this donation as being perfectly free and unconditional, and that you would enjoy and dispose of what is now your property just as you shall think best and most conducive to your happiness and to your satisfaction, without any regard to any former arrangements you have made at my request.

My health continues to be good, and I yet feel none of those infirmities of age which sometimes render the evening of life painful. I have the satisfaction to think that I have done my duty through life, and that is a great consolation to me as I approach the end of my course. I shall never cease to be, my dear mother, your dutiful and affectionate child,

Benjamin.

On January 23 he had a paper read before the Royal Society which he published as his seventeenth essay. It was an 'Inquiry Concerning the Source of the Light which is Manifested in the Combustion of Inflammable Bodies.'

His object was to prove by decisive experiments that the light which accompanies the complete combustion of any given quantity of pure inflammable matter is variable, and therefore light cannot be one of the chemical products of combustion.

If light were a substance, as has been supposed, it seems highly probable that means would long since have been found to discover where and how it exists; but if it be nothing more than a blow given to the eye by the repercussion of an ethereal fluid which touches that organ and at the same time every other body in the universe, it is evident that all attempts to discover it in a state of combination must be vain.

Nobody, I imagine, ever thought of searching for sound in a fulminating powder. Is it more reasonable to search there for the light that accompanies the combustion of substances?

The greatest light may be obtained by preserving the heat of the flame. Thus several flat flames placed together, in order that they may mutually cover and defend each other against the powerful cooling influence of surrounding bodies, form a lamp that has answered far beyond my most sanguine expectation.

I lose no time in giving an account of the principles on which it is constructed, in hopes that others may be induced to assist in improving it.

So far from being jealous of their success I shall rejoice in it, and shall ever be most ready to contribute to it by all the means in my power.

On February 24 he had a paper read before the French Institute on the 'Heat Manifested in the Combustion of Inflammable Substances.'

On August 1 he published his last essay, the eighteenth, of the 'Excellent Qualities of Coffee and the Art of Making it in the Highest Perfection.

In 1813 the founder of the Royal Institution once more met Davy, then the great discoverer who by his eloquence and genius had saved the Rumford Institution from an early death.

In the 'Life of Davy,' by Dr. Paris, it is said, probably on the authority of Mr. Underwood, 'On November 10 they (Underwood and Davy) dined at Auteuil with Count Rumford, at this time a prisoner in France, who showed his laboratory to Davy. This was exactly eight months before the poor, broken-hearted Count sank into the grave, the victim of domestic torment and of the persecutions of the French savans, instigated by his wife, the widow of the celebrated Lavoisier.'

The following account of Count Rumford's life at Auteuil was probably also written by his friend Mr.

Underwood. It was published in the 'Gentleman's Magazine' in 1814:

After the death of his worthy friend, the illustrious Lagrange, he saw only his next-door neighbour, the Senator Leconteux Caneleux; Mr. Underwood, a member of the Royal Institution, who assisted him in his experiments; and an old friend, Mr. Parker, a learned American, who possesses a splendid mansion in Paris and a very fine landed estate and agricultural establishment in its environs. He ceased to attend the sittings of the National Institute; but for the perpetual secretary, Cuvier, a man as morally estimable as his talents are superior to his French fellow-members, he always preserved the highest admiration and esteem.

One object of his later occupations was a work—not yet finished, though it has been constantly going on for more than twenty years—on the 'Nature and Effects of Order,' which, had he been spared to finish it, would probably have been one of the most valuable presents ever made to domestic society. No man in all his habits had more the spirit of order; everything was classed; no object was ever allowed to remain an instant out of its place the moment he had done with it, and he was never behind his time in an appointment a single instant.

He was also latterly employed on a series of experiments on the propagation of heat in solids. He had by him several unpublished works, particularly one of considerable interest on Meteorolites, in which he demonstrated that they came from regions beyond the atmosphere of the earth. He has left several memoirs in French (of which he had a few copies printed for the use of his friends) on the quantity of heat obtained by the combustion of various substances and the relative quantity of light from others, with a description of different improvements in the construction of lamps, which he had the satisfaction of seeing very generally adopted in Paris. His admirable paper on the

'Advantages of Broad Wheels to Carriages' is well known. He put this in practice in his own chariot; but, though there could be no doubt of their advantages, they were not used by others, the Count's being the only carriage in Paris that had them. Nor did anyone follow (which is not to be wondered at) his whimsical winter dress, which was entirely white, even his hat. This he adopted agreeably to the law of nature, that more heated rays are thrown from a dark body than from a light one. I do not know whether his very simple, and I may add perfect, calorimeter is known in England. The apparatus with which he was making a series of experiments on the relative conducting powers of different solid bodies for heat, and which death prevented his completing, is of the greatest beauty. It consists of a cylindrical vessel of cork (which is a perfect non-conductor of heat), in the centre of the bottom of which the small solid cylinder of the substance to be experimented upon is fitted into an aperture of exactly the same diameter as the cylindrical vessel, which is then filled with water, and heat from the flame of a spirit-lamp is applied to the lower extremity of the substance; the time the heat takes to pass through and raise the temperature of the water indicates the relative conducting powers of the different substances through which it is made to pass. He has repeatedly declared to me it was his decided opinion that heat and light were the result of vibrations in bodies, and were not bodies themselves. He had lately brought to the greatest perfection a lamp for burning spirits of wine, and by which all explosion was rendered impossible. This in France is of the greatest convenience, where, from the low price of alcohol, it is nearly as economical as any other fuel for heating water.

The Count met with considerable plague in his pursuits from the malignant disposition and jealousies of his fellow-members of the National Institute, in consequence of having differed in opinion on capillary attraction from their despotic leader, Laplace. He often used to exclaim that no one who had not lived a considerable time in France could imagine how contemptible a nation they are, and how void of honour and even honesty. Whenever he ordered any instrument at a mathematical instrument maker's a similar one was instantly made for some one of the Great Nation, though of the intended use they were at the moment ignorant; but the hope of supplanting a foreigner and of arrogating to themselves a discovery (a common practice with them) incited them to adopt this dishonourable practice. This forced him to send for a workman from Germany, whom he constantly employed, and who lived in his house. I was one day with the Count at a sitting of the first class of the Institute, when we heard one of the leading members declare that they would set their faces against any discovery which did not originate among themselves.

The Count displayed extraordinary spirited conduct and firmness in refusing the French the passage of the city of Munich. He used often to dwell with much pleasure on having been the means of bringing forward two celebrated characters, the Bavarian general Wieden and Sir Humphry Davy—the former originally a lawyer, or a land steward, and possessing great military dispositions; Count Rumford, then Minister of War to the Elector of Bavaria, gave him a commission: and the latter was recommended to him when he had the direction of the Royal Institution by Mr. Underwood, and was made Lecturer on Chemistry.

The climate of France agreeing with him far better than that of Bavaria, he received permission of the King of Bavaria to reside there; and his half-pay as lieutenant-general in his service and pension of retreat as minister of his late father [uncle] were regularly paid him, amounting to about twelve hundred pounds sterling *per annum*. It was this which prevented his return to England, as Bonaparte would not, in that case, have allowed his vassal, the King of Bavaria, to have paid the Count.

When Bavaria joined in the coalition for the emancipation of Europe it was agitated in Bonaparte's council to send the Count away. However, as it was proved that he scarcely ever stirred out of his house, he was allowed to remain.

The German, French, Spanish, and Italian languages were as familiar to the Count as the English, both in speaking and writing. His only recreations were playing at billiards against himself, for want of one to play with, and walking in his garden, of which he was very fond, though ignorant of botany and even of the common names of the commonest plants. He was very fond of chess, at which he played well, but rarely enjoyed this pleasure, as he said that after a few minutes' play his feet became like ice and his head like fire. He drew with great skill the designs of his own inventions, but of painting and sculpture he had no knowledge and little feeling; nor had he any taste for poetry. He had, however, great taste for landscape-gardening.

His habits of life were latterly most abstemious, so much so that he had not sufficient vital strength to resist a nervous fever, which carried him off on the 21st of August, after three days' illness, when he was on the eve of returning to England, to which as long as he lived he retained the most devoted attachment.

In the 'Moniteur Universel' of August 25, 1814, the death and burial of Count Rumford are mentioned. An address was pronounced over his grave by the Baron Benjamin Delessert, his friend and banker in Paris, on the 24th.

The news of Count Rumford's illness and burial reached the French Academy at the same time, so that the members were unable to attend his funeral. On January 9, 1815, Baron Cuvier read his éloge to the Academy. In it he said:

Nous l'y avons vu, en effet, pendant dix ans honoré des Français et des étrangers, estimé des amis des sciences, partageant leurs travaux, aidant de ses avis jusqu'aux moindres artisans, gratifiant noblement le public de tout ce qu'il inventait chaque jour d'utile. Rien n'y aurait manqué à la douceur de son existence si l'aménité de son commerce avait égalé son ardeur pour l'utilité publique.

Mais il faut l'avouer, il perçait dans sa conversation et dans toute sa manière d'être un sentiment qui devait paraître fort extraordinaire dans un homme si constamment bien traité par les autres, et qui leur avait fait lui-même tant de bien: c'est que c'était sans les aimer et sans les estimer qu'il avait rendu tous ces services à ses semblables. Apparemment que les passions viles qu'il avait observées dans les misérables commis à ses soins ou ces autres passions non moins viles que sa fortune avait excitées parmi ses rivaux l'avaient ulcéré contre la nature humaine. Aussi ne pensait-il point que l'on doit confier au commun des hommes le soin de leur bien-être; ce besoin qui leur semble si naturel d'examiner comment ils sont régis n'était à ses yeux qu'un produit factice des fausses lumières. Il avait sur l'esclavage à peu près les idées d'un planteur, et il regardait le gouvernement de la Chine comme le plus voisin de la perfection, parce qu'en livrant le peuple au pouvoir absolu des seuls hommes instruits, et en élevant chacun de ceux-ci dans la hiérarchie selon le degré de son instruction, il fait en quelque sorte de tant de millions de bras les organes passifs de la volonté de quelques bonnes têtes—doctrine que nous exposons sans prétendre la justifier en rien et que nous savons de reste être peu propre à faire fortune chez nos nations européennes. M. de Rumford a éprouvé lui-même à plus d'une reprise qu'il n'est pas si aisé dans l'occident qu'en Chine d'engager les autres à n'être que des bras; et cependant personne ne s'était autant préparé que lui à bien se servir de bras qu'on lui aurait soumis. Un empire tel qu'il le concevait ne lui aurait pas été plus difficile à conduire que ses casernes et ses maisons de pauvres; il se confiait surtout pour cela à la puissance de l'ordre. Il appelait l'ordre l'auxiliaire nécessaire du génie, le seul instrument possible d'un véritable bien et presque une divinité subordonnée régulatrice de ce bas monde. Il se proposait d'en faire l'objet d'un ouvrage qu'il regardait comme devant être plus important que tous ceux qu'il a écrits; mais on n'en a trouvé dans ses papiers que quelques matérieux informes. Lui-même de sa personne était sur tous les points et sous tous les rapports imaginables le modèle de l'ordre; ses besoins, ses plaisirs, ses travaux, étaient calculés comme ses expériences. Il ne buvait que de l'eau: il ne mangeait que de la viande grillée ou rôtie, parce que la viande bouillie donne sous le même volume un peu moins d'aliment. Il ne se permettait enfin rien de superflu, pas même un pas ni une parole, et c'était dans le plus strict qu'il prenait le mot *superflu.*

C'était sans doute un moyen de consacrer plus sûrememt toutes ses forces au bien, mais ce n'en était pas un d'être agréable dans la société de ses pareils; le monde veut un peu plus d'abandon, et il est tellement fait qu'une certaine hauteur de perfection lui paraît souvent un défaut quand on ne met pas autant d'efforts à la dissimuler qu'on en a mis à l'acquérir.

Quels que fussent au reste les sentiments de M. de Rumford pour les hommes, ils ne diminuaient en rien son respect pour la divinité. Il n'a négligé dans ses ouvrages aucune occasion d'exprimer sa religieuse admiration pour la Providence et d'y offrir à l'admiration des autres les précautions innombrables et variées par lesquelles elle a pourvu à la conservation de ses créatures; peut-être même son système politique venait-il de ce qu'il croyait que les princes doivent faire comme elle et prendre soin de nous sans nous en rendre compte.

Cuvier finished his éloge with this epitaph: 'L'homme qui par l'heureux choix des sujets de ses travaux a su lui donner à la fois pour appui l'estime des savans et la reconnaissance des malheureux.'

Dr. Young, who, whilst Professor at the Royal Institution, knew Rumford well, said of him in the 'Encyclopedia Britannica:'

Count Rumford certainly possessed considerable facility of conversation, and there was a very laudable spirit of originality in his views and mode of reasoning, although he had never leisure to acquire profound learning in any department of study. In person he was above the middle size, with a dignified and pleasing expression of countenance and a mildness in his manner and tone of voice. He was ambitious of fame and distinction, and had too great a propensity to dictate without sufficiently regarding the opinions of those who were of equal authority with himself. His mode of life was abstemious, and his health was even supposed to have suffered from too great abstinence, though his regimen was much more the result of medical opinion regarding his health than of his own peculiar taste for temperance.

By his will, of which Lafayette was a witness, he made a bequest to his daughter, and another to Harvard College

for the purpose of founding, under the direction and government of the corporation, overseers, and governors of that university, a new institution and professorship, in order to teach by regular courses of academical and public lectures, accompanied with proper experiments, the utility of the physical and mathematical sciences for the improvement of the useful arts, and for the extension of the industry, prosperity, happiness, and well-being of society.

He left all his military books and papers to the Government of the United States, and the snuff-box given to him by the Emperor of Austria to Baron Delessert, and his gold enamelled watch to his friend Mr. Parker. He thus showed his regard for Davy:

I give to Sir Humphry Davy, Knight, Professor of Chemistry in the Royal Institution of Great Britain, my plain gold watch, as a token of my esteem.

Madame de Rumford gave up her interest in the lease of the Count's house at Brompton to his daughter, who went to London in May 1815 and lived there for twenty years, during which period she returned to Paris for three years. In 1835 she went to America, and then she returned to Paris until 1844, when she revisited America. In the room in which she was born she died, when seventy-eight years of age, December 21, 1852. She left her property chiefly to form the Rolfe and Rumford Asylum for the Poor and Needy at Concord.

The memory of Count Rumford is preserved in Munich by a stone monument in the English Garden, erected by public subscription in 1795, and by a bronze statue placed in 1867 by the present King in the finest street in the city.

In Paris a street once bore his name, and his gravestone in the cemetery at Auteuil is the only material mark of his residence in France.

In America the Rumford medals which he founded, and the institutions he originated, form his enduring monuments.

In England the highest scientific reward which the Royal Society can bestow, and the place where the greatest scientific discoveries of this century have been made, should both in gratitude be inseparably united with the name of Rumford.

CHAPTER III.

EARLY HISTORY OF THE ROYAL INSTITUTION, 1799-1800; WITH THE LIFE OF PROFESSOR GARNETT.

THE history of the Proposals for founding the Royal Institution is thus given by Count Rumford in 1799:

Having long been in a habit of considering all useful improvements as being purely *mechanical*, or as depending on the perfection of machinery and address in the management of it, and of considering *profit* (which depends much on the perfection of machinery) as the only incitement to *industry*, I was naturally led to meditate on the means that might be employed with advantage to diffuse the knowledge and facilitate the general introduction of such improvements; and the plan which is now submitted to the public was the result of these investigations.

In the beginning of the year 1796 I gave a faint sketch of this plan in my second essay; but, being under a necessity of returning soon to Germany, I had not leisure to pursue it farther at that time, and I was obliged to content myself with having merely thrown out a loose idea, as it were by accident, which I thought might possibly attract attention.

After my return to Munich, I opened myself more fully on the subject in my correspondence with my friends in this country, and particularly in my letters to Thomas Bernard, Esq., who, as is well known, is one of the founders and most active members of the Society for Bettering the Condition and Increasing the Comforts of the Poor.

This gentleman I found, on my return to England in September 1798, not only agreeing with me in opinion in regard to the utility and importance of the plan I had proposed, but very solicitous that some attempts should be made to carry it into immediate execution in this capital.

After several consultations, that were held at Mr. Bernard's apartments in the Foundling Hospital and at the house of the Lord Bishop of Durham, at which several gentlemen assisted who are well known as zealous promoters of useful improvement, it was agreed that Mr. Bernard should report to the Committee of the Society for Bettering the Condition of the Poor the general result of these consultations, and the unanimous desire of the gentlemen who assisted at them, that means might be devised for making an attempt to carry the scheme proposed into execution.

The gentlemen of the Committee agreed with me entirely in the opinion I had taken the liberty to express, that the Institution which it was proposed to form would be too conspicuous, and too interesting and important, to be made *an appendix* to any other existing establishment, and, consequently, that it must stand alone, and on its own proper basis; but as these gentlemen had no direct communication with any persons, except with the members of their own Society, they appointed a Committee, consisting of eight persons, from their own body, to confer with me on the subject of the plan.[1]

I had the honour to meet this Committee on this business on the 31st of January, at the house of Richard Sulivan, Esq., where a plan I had previously drawn up for forming the Institution in question was read and examined, and its principles unanimously approved; but, as some of the

[1] The gentlemen chosen were the Earl of Winchelsea, Mr. Wilberforce, the Rev. Dr. Glasse, Mr. Sullivan, Mr. Richard Sulivan, Mr. Colquhoun, Mr. Parry, and Mr. Bernard.

gentlemen present were of opinion that the plan entered too much into detail to be submitted to the public in the beginning of the business, I undertook to revise it, and to endeavour to accommodate it to the wishes of the Committee.

Having made such alterations in it as I thought might satisfy the Committee, I sent a corrected copy of it to them, accompanied by the following letter:

'GENTLEMEN,—Inclosed I have the honour to send you a corrected copy of the Proposals I took the liberty of laying before you on Thursday last, for forming in this capital, by private subscription, a public Institution for diffusing the knowledge and facilitating the general and speedy introduction of new and useful mechanical inventions and improvements; and also for teaching, by regular courses of philosophical lectures and experiments, the application of the new discoveries in science to the improvement of arts and manufactures, and in facilitating the means of procuring the comforts and conveniences of life.

'The tendency of the proposed Institution to excite a spirit of inquiry and of improvement amongst all ranks of society, and to afford the most effectual assistance to those who are engaged in the various pursuits of useful industry, did not escape your observation; and it is, I am persuaded, from a conviction of the utility of the plan, or its tendency to increase the comforts and enjoyments of individuals, and at the same time to promote the public prosperity, that you have been induced to take it into your serious consideration. I shall be much flattered if it should meet with your approbation and with your support.

'Though I am perfectly ready to take any share in the business of carrying the scheme into execution, in case it should be adopted, that can be required, yet there is one preliminary request which I am desirous may be granted me, and that is, that the Government may be previously made acquainted with the scheme before any steps are taken towards carrying it into execution; and also that his Majesty's Ministers may be informed that it is in the contemplation of the founders of the Institution to accept of my services in the arrangement and management of it.

'The peculiar situation in which I stand in this country, as a subject of his Majesty, and being at the same time, by his Majesty's special commission, granted under his royal sign manual, engaged in the service of a foreign prince, this circumstance renders it improper for me to engage myself in this important business, notwithstanding that it might perhaps be considered merely as a private concern, without the knowledge and the approbation of the Government.

'I am quite certain that my engaging in this, or in any other business in which there is any prospect of my being of any public use in this country, will meet with the most cordial approbation of his Most Serene Highness the Elector Palatine, in whose service I am; for I know his sentiments on that subject; and although I do not imagine that his Majesty or his Majesty's Ministers would disapprove of my giving my assistance in carrying this scheme into execution, yet I feel it to be necessary that their approbation should be asked and obtained; and, if I might be allowed to express my sentiments on another matter, which, no doubt, has already occurred to everyone of the gentlemen to whom I now address myself, I should say that, in my opinion, it would not only be proper, but even necessary, to inform Government of the nature of the scheme that is proposed and of every circumstance relative to it, and at the same time to ask their countenance and support in carrying it into execution; for although it may be allowable in this free country for individuals to unite in forming and executing extensive plans for diffusing useful knowledge and promoting the public good, yet it appears to me that no such establishment should ever be formed in any country without the knowledge and approbation of the Executive Government.

'Trusting that you will be so good as to excuse the liberty I take in making this observation, and that you will consider my doing it as being intended rather to justify myself, by explaining my principles than from any idea of its being necessary on any other account, I have the honour to be, with much respect, Gentlemen, your most obedient and most humble Servant,

(Signed) 'RUMFORD.

'Brompton Row, February 7, 1799.

(Addressed)

'To the Gentlemen named by the Committee of the Society for Bettering the Condition of the Poor to confer with Count Rumford on his scheme for forming a new Establishment in London for Diffusing the Knowledge of Useful Mechanical Improvements, &c.'

The Committee above mentioned having, in the meantime, made their report to the Society for Bettering the Condition and Increasing the Comforts of the Poor, that Society came to the following resolution:

'At a meeting of the Society for Bettering the Condition and Increasing the Comforts of the Poor, on Friday, the 1st of February, 1799,

'*Present*:

The BISHOP OF DURHAM, in the chair,
PATRICK COLQUHOUN, Esq.,
THOMAS BERNARD, Esq.,
WILLIAM MANNING, Esq.,
JOHN SULLIVAN, Esq.,
The REV. DR. GLASSE,
JOHN J. ANGERSTEIN, Esq.,
WILLIAM WILBERFORCE, Esq.,
RICHARD JOSEPH SULIVAN, Esq.,
MATTHEW MARTIN, Esq., Secretary,

the Committee appointed to confer with Count Rumford reported that they had had a conference with the Count, and that they were satisfied that the Institution proposed by him would be extremely beneficial and interesting to the community; that, in order to provide the pecuniary funds of the Society at its commencement, it was proposed that subscribers of fifty guineas each should be the perpetual proprietors of the Institution, and be entitled each to perpetual transferable tickets for the lectures and for admission to the apartments of the Institution; and that as soon as thirty such subscribers offered it was proposed to call a meeting of those thirty subscribers, in order to lay the plan before them and elect managers for the Institution.

'Resolved,—That the said report be approved of, and that it be referred to the gentlemen of the Select Committee to communicate the outlines of the plan to the members of the Committee of the Society, and to such other persons as they shall think fit, desiring that those who wish to have their names inserted among the original subscribers to the Institution would communicate their wish to the Special Committee.

'Extracted from the Minutes.

'M. Martin, Secretary.'

In consequence of this resolution a paper was printed by the gentlemen of the Select Committee containing the outlines of the plan, and sent round privately among their friends and others whom they thought likely to countenance the scheme, accompanied by a printed copy of the foregoing resolution, with a request that those who were willing to allow their names to be put down among the original subscribers and proprietors of the Institution would be so good as to communicate their intentions by a letter addressed to Thomas Bernard, Esq., at the Foundling Hospital.

The Proposals that were circulated in this manner met with so much approbation that fifty-eight of the most respectable names were sent in before measures could be taken for holding a meeting, and these successful beginnings encouraged those who were principally concerned in forming and bringing forward the plan to make some alterations in it, and particularly in respect to the time and manner of choosing the first set of managers, and in regard to an application for a charter for the Institution, which it has been determined to make, in order to place the establishment on a more solid and more respectable foundation, and to give full security to the subscribers against all future claims upon them.

IN THIS STAGE OF THE BUSINESS, and especially as a meeting of the subscribers is to be held in a few days for the purpose of determining what other steps shall be taken for carrying the proposed plan into execution, I have thought it to be my duty to lay all these particulars before the subscribers, and at the same time to state to them at length the general outline of the plan I have taken the liberty to propose, and in the execution of which, if it should be adopted, I am ready to take any part that the subscribers may wish me to take.

RUMFORD.

Brompton Row, March 4, 1799.

THE PROPOSALS FOR FORMING BY SUBSCRIPTION, IN THE METROPOLIS OF THE BRITISH EMPIRE, A PUBLIC INSTITUTION FOR DIFFUSING THE KNOWLEDGE AND FACILIATING THE GENERAL INTRODUCTION OF USEFUL MECHANICAL INVENTIONS AND IMPROVEMENTS, AND FOR TEACHING BY COURSES OF PHILOSOPHICAL LECTURES AND EXPERIMENTS THE APPLICATION OF SCIENCE TO THE COMMON PURPOSES OF LIFE WERE THESE:

THE two great objects of the Institution being the speedy and general diffusion of the knowledge of all new and useful improvements, in whatever quarter of the world they may originate; and teaching the application of scientific discoveries to the improvement of arts and manufactures in this country, and to the increase of domestic comfort and convenience, these objects will be constantly had in view, not only in the arrangement and execution of the plan, but also in the future management of the Institution.

As much care will be taken to confine the establishment within its proper limits as to place it on a solid foundation, and to render it an ornament to the capital and an honour to the British nation.

In the execution of the plan it is proposed to proceed in the following manner:

A place having been fixed on by the managers for forming the Institution,

Spacious and airy rooms will be prepared for the reception and public exhibition of all such new and mechanical inventions and improvements as shall be thought worthy of the public notice, and more especially of all such contrivances as shall tend to increase the conveniences and comforts of life, to promote domestic economy, to improve taste, or to promote useful industry.

The most perfect models of the full size will be provided and exhibited in different parts of this public repository of all such new mechanical inventions and improvements as are applicable to the common purposes of life. Under this head will be included :

Cottage Fire-places and Kitchen Utensils for Cottages.
A complete Kitchen for a Farm-house, with all the necessary Utensils.
A complete Kitchen, with Kitchen Utensils, for the family of a gentleman of fortune.
A complete Laundry for a gentleman's family, or for a public hospital, including Boilers, Washing-room, Ironing-room, Drying-room, &c.
Several of the most approved German, Swedish, and Russian Stoves, for heating rooms and passages.

In order that those who visit this establishment may be enabled to acquire more just ideas of these various mechanical contrivances, and of the circumstances on which their *peculiar merit* principally depends, the machinery exhibited will, as far as it shall be possible, *be shown in action*, or in *actual use*, and with regard to many of the articles it is evident that this can be done without any difficulty and with very little additional expense.

Open Chimney Fire-places on the most approved principles will be fitted up as models in the different rooms, and fires will be kept constantly burning in them during the cold season.
Ornamental as well as Economical Grates, for Open Chimney Fire-places, will also be exhibited ; as also,
Ornamental Stoves, in the form of elegant Chimney-pieces, for halls, drawing-rooms, eating-rooms, &c.

It is likewise proposed to exhibit *working models*, on a reduced scale, of that most curious and most useful machine the Steam Engine.
Of Brewer's Boilers, with improved Fire-places.
Of Distiller's Coppers, with improved Fire-places and improved Condensers.

Of large Boilers for the kitchens of hospitals, and of Ships' Coppers, with improved Fire-places.

Further it is proposed to exhibit in the repository of the Institution—

Models of Ventilators for supplying rooms and ships with fresh air.

Models of Hot-houses, with such improvements as can be made in their construction.

Models of Lime-kilns on various constructions.

Models of Boilers, Steam-boilers, &c., for preparing food for cattle that are stall-fed.

Models of Cottages on various constructions.

Spinning-wheels and Looms, on various constructions, for the use of the poor, and adapted to their circumstances, together with such other machinery as may be useful in giving them employment at home.

Models of all such new-invented Machines and Implements as bid fair to be of use in Husbandry.

Models of Bridges on various constructions, together with *models of all such other machines and useful instruments as the managers of the Institution shall deem worthy of the public notice* and proper to be publicly exhibited in the repository of the Institution.

It is proposed that each article exhibited should be accompanied with a detailed account or description of it, properly illustrated by correct drawings. The name of the maker and the place of his abode will also be mentioned in this account, together with the price at which he is willing to furnish the article to buyers.

In order to carry into effect the second object of the Institution—namely, TEACHING THE APPLICATION OF SCIENCE to the USEFUL PURPOSES OF LIFE—

A lecture room will be fitted up for philosophical lectures and experiments, and a complete LABORATORY and PHILOSOPHICAL APPARATUS, with the necessary instruments, will be provided for making *chemical* and other *philo. sophical experiments.*

In fitting up this lecture room (which will never be used for any other purpose than for giving lectures in natural Philosophy and Philosophical Chemistry) convenient places will be provided and reserved for the subscribers, and care will be taken to warm and light the room properly, and provide for a sufficient supply of fresh air, so as to render it comfortable and salubrious.

In engaging lecturers for the Institution care will be taken by the managers to invite none but men of the first eminence in science to officiate in that most important and most distinguished situation; and no subjects will ever be permitted to be discussed at these lectures but such as are strictly scientifical, and immediately connected with that particular branch of science publicly announced as the subject of the lecture. The managers to be responsible for the strict observance of this regulation.

In case there should be places to spare in the lecture room, persons not subscribers will, on the recommendation of a subscriber, and on paying a certain small sum to be determined by the managers, be permitted to attend the public lectures or any one or more of them.

Among the various branches of science that will occasionally be made the subjects of these public lectures may be reckoned the following, *viz.*: These lectures will treat—

Of Heat, and its application to the various purposes of life.

Of the Combustion of Inflammable Bodies, and the relative quantities of Heat producible by the different substances used as fuel.

Of the Management of Fire and the Economy of Fuel.

Of the Principles of the Warmth of Clothing.

Of the Effects of Heat and of Cold, and of hot and of cold winds, on the human body in sickness and in health.

Of the Effects of breathing vitiated and confined air.

Of the Means that may be used to render Dwelling-houses comfortable and salubrious.

Of the Methods of procuring and preserving Ice in Summer, and of the best principles for constructing Ice-houses.

Of the Means of preserving Food in different seasons and in different climates.

Of the Means of cooling Liquors in hot weather, without the assistance of ice.

Of Vegetation, and of the specific nature of those effects that are produced by Manures, and of the Art of composing Manures and adapting them to the different kinds of soil.

Of the nature of those changes that are produced on substances used as food in the various processes of cookery.

Of the nature of those changes which take place in the Digestion of Food.

Of the Chemical Principles of the process of Tanning Leather, and of the objects that must particularly be had in view in attempts to improve that most useful art.

Of the Chemical Principles of the art of making Soap, of the art of Bleaching, of the art of Dyeing, and in general of *all the Mechanical Arts*, as they apply to the various branches of manufacture.

Of the Funds of the Institution.

It is proposed to raise the money necessary for defraying the expense of forming this Institution, and also for the future expense of keeping it up, in the following manner:

1st. By the sums subscribed by the original founders and sole *proprietors* of the Institution, at *fifty guineas each person*, to be but once paid.

2dly. By the sums contributed by those who shall subscribe *for life*, at *ten guineas* each person, to be but once paid.

3dly. By the sums contributed by the *annual subscribers* at two guineas *per annum* for each person.

4thly. By the particular donations and legacies that may be expected to be made for the purpose of extending and improving so interesting and so useful an Institution; and,

Lastly. By the sums that shall be received at the door from strangers who shall visit the repository of the Institution, or who shall obtain leave to frequent the philosophical lectures.

PRIVILEGES OF THE ORIGINAL SUBSCRIBERS OR PROPRIETORS OF THE INSTITUTION.

1*mo*. These subscribers, who will *never be called upon for any further contributions* after the sum subscribed (fifty guineas) shall have been once paid, will be effectually secured against all future legal claims and demands upon them on account of any debts the managers of the Institution may contract, as a charter for the Institution will be applied for and obtained, for the express purpose of providing for that security, before any other step shall be taken for carrying this plan into execution, and before any part of the money subscribed will be demanded.

2*do*. Proprietors will not be deemed liable to serve, either as managers or as visitors, against their consent; and none will be considered as candidates for either of those offices, or will be entered on the lists as candidates, or be proposed as such, except it be those who shall have previously signified their willingness to serve in one of those offices in case of their being elected.

3*tio*. For the still greater security of the proprietors, as well as to found the Institution on a more solid basis, one-half of the sums subscribed by the original subscribers and proprietors of the Institution will be permanently vested in the public funds, or in the purchase of freehold property, and the annual produce thereof employed in defraying the expense of keeping up the Institution.

4*to*. Each original subscriber and proprietor of the Institution to be an hereditary governor of the Institution —to have a perpetual *transferable* share in all the property belonging to it—to have a voice in the election of the managers of the Institution, as also in the election of the Committee of Visitors—to have, moreover, two *transferable* tickets of perpetual admission into the establishment, and into every part of it, and two *transferable* tickets of admission to all the public philosophical lectures and experiments.

5*to*. Although the shares of proprietors and all the privileges annexed to them are hereditary, and are also *transferable* by sale or by donation, yet those to whom such shares are conveyed by sale or by donation must, in order to their being rendered capable of holding them, have obtained the approbation and consent of the majority of the managers for the time being. Those who shall become possessed of these shares by inheritance will not stand in need of the consent of the managers to be qualified to hold them, and to enjoy the rights and privileges annexed to them.

6*to*. Proprietors' tickets will admit any persons who shall be the bearers of them.

7*mo*. Proprietors will have the privilege of recommending persons for admittance to the philosophical lectures and experiments, and the persons so recommended will be admitted in all cases where there shall be room for their accommodation, provided that the persons so admitted conform to the rules and regulations which will be established by the managers for the preservation of order and decorum within the walls of the Institution.

8*vo*. No more than *forty per cent.* of the sum subscribed by each proprietor will be wanted immediately, and the remainder may be furnished in three equal payments at the expiration of the three next succeeding half-years; but it will be in the option of proprietors to pay the whole sum of fifty guineas at once if they should prefer doing it.

PRIVILEGES OF THE SUBSCRIBERS FOR LIFE.

Each subscriber of this class will receive *one* ticket for life, but not transferable, of free admission into the Institution, and into every part of it, together with *one* other ticket for life, but not transferable, of free admission to all public philosophical lectures and experiments.

PRIVILEGES OF ANNUAL SUBSCRIBERS.

Each annual subscriber will receive *one* ticket for one year, but not transferable, of admission into the Institution, and into every part of it; as also *one* ticket for one year, but not transferable, of admission to all the public philosophical lectures and experiments. Subscribers of this class will, moreover, have a right of becoming subscribers for life, on paying at any time within the year for which they subscribe an additional sum of eight guineas.

PRIVILEGES THAT ARE COMMON TO SUBSCRIBERS OF ALL DENOMINATIONS.

1*mo*. Subscribers for life and annual subscribers, as well as the proprietors of the Institution, will be entitled to have copies or drawings (made at their own expense, however) of any of the models in the repository, and this even when such copies are designed for the use of their friends, as well as when they are wanted for their own private use; and for their better and more speedy accommodation workshops will be prepared, and workmen provided under the direction of the managers, for executing such work properly and at reasonable prices. And, to prevent mistakes, all copies or drawings that shall be made of the machines, models, and plans lodged in the repository of the Institution will be examined by persons appointed for that purpose, and marked with a seal or stamp of the Institution.

2*do*. Tradesmen and artificers employed in executing any work after any of the models lodged in the repository will, on the recommendation of a proprietor or of a subscriber for life, or for one year, be allowed free access to such model as often as shall be necessary; and any workman or artificer so recommended who shall be willing to furnish to buyers any article exhibited in the repository that is in his line of business, will be allowed to place a specimen of such article of his manufacture in the repository, with his name and place of abode attached to it, together with the price at which he can furnish it, such specimen having been examined and approved by the managers.

Of the Government and Management of the Institution.

1*mo*. All the affairs of the Institution will be directed and governed by *nine* managers, chosen by and from among the proprietors of the Institution.

2*do*. For the greater convenience of the proprietors, and to spare them the trouble of a general meeting, all the elections of managers, after the first, will be made by ballot, by means of sealed lists of names sent in by the proprietors individually to the Institution, which lists will be opened, and the result of the election ascertained and published, by the united committees of the managers and of the visitors for the time being.

3*tio*. The first set of managers will be chosen by the

first fifty or more original subscribers, at a general meeting of them to be held for that purpose; and of this first set of managers three will be chosen to serve *three years*, three to serve *two years*, and three to serve *one year*, reckoned from the 25th day of March, 1799.

4to. All managers, as well those of the first set as others, will be capable of being *re-elected* without limitation.

5to. The elections of managers to be made annually on the 25th day of the month of March,[1] and fourteen days previous to each election the managers for the time being will send to each proprietor individually a printed list containing the names of all such of the proprietors as shall have offered or consented to be candidates for the places among the managers that are to be filled up. On this printed list, which each proprietor will receive, he will indicate the persons to whom he gives his suffrage by making a mark with a pen and ink in the form of a small cross just before the names of those persons; and, this being done, he will seal up the list without signing it and send it to the Institution, directed 'To the United Committee of the Managers and of the Visitors.' In order that these lists may be recognised on their being returned to the Institution, they will all be marked with the stamp of the Institution previous to their being issued or sent to the proprietors. And, for still further security, each proprietor will be requested to send in his or her sealed list of names under an additional cover, signed with his or her own name, which additional cover will be taken off, and all the sealed lists mixed together in an urn, previous to any of them being opened—an arrangement that will effectually prevent the vote of any individual subscriber being known.

[1] If any other season should be thought more convenient for these elections, it will of course be chosen instead of that here proposed.

6to. The managers are to serve in that office without any pay or emolument or pecuniary advantage whatever; and by their acceptance of their office they shall be deemed solemnly to pledge themselves to the proprietors of the Institution and to the public for the faithful discharge of their duty as managers, and also for their strict adherence to the fundamental principles of the government of the Institution as established at its formation.

7mo. The managers are to take care that the property of the Institution, as far as it shall be practicable, be insured against accidents by fire.

8vo. The managers will cause exact and detailed accounts to be kept of all the property belonging to the Institution, as also of all receipts and expenditures. They will also keep regular minutes of all their proceedings, and will take care to preserve the most exact order and the strictest economy in the management of all the affairs and concerns of the Institution.

9mo. The managers are never, on any pretext, or in any manner whatever, to dispose of any money or property of any kind belonging to the Institution in *premiums*, as the design or object of the Institution is NOT TO GIVE REWARDS to the authors of ingenious inventions, but to *diffuse the knowledge of such improvements as bid fair to be of general use*, and to facilitate the general introduction of them; and to excite and assist the ingenious and the enterprising by *the diffusion of science*, and by awakening a spirit of inquiry.

10mo. The ordinary meetings of the managers for the despatch of the current business of the Institution will be held weekly—namely, on every   , at the hour of   , —and extraordinary meetings will be held as often as shall be found necessary.

11mo. Any three or more of the managers being present at any ordinary or at an extraordinary meeting, the others having been duly summoned, to be a quorum.

12*mo*. The managers will be authorised to make all such standing orders and regulations as they shall deem necessary to the preservation of order and decorum in the Institution, as also such regulations respecting the manner of transacting the business of the Institution as they shall think proper and convenient, or that may be necessary in order to regulate the responsibility of the managers for their acts and deeds; all such standing orders and regulations must, however, in order to their being valid, be approved by six at least of the managers, and they must all be published and made known to all the proprietors.

OF THE COMMITTEE OF VISITORS.

1*mo*. The Committee of Visitors will be composed of *nine* persons, the first set to be elected three months after the opening of the Institution.

2*do*. Three persons of the nine of which this Committee will consist will be chosen for *three years*, three of them to serve *two years*, and three of them to serve *one year*, reckoned from the 25th of March, 1799.

3*tio*. Any three or more of the members of this Committee being present at any meeting of the Committee, the others having been duly summoned, to make a quorum.

4*to*. It will be the business of this Committee formally to inspect and examine the Institution, and every part and detail of it, once every year—namely, on the 25th day of the month of March—and to give a printed account or report to the proprietors, and to the subscribers of all denominations, of its state and condition, and of the degree and manner in which it is found to answer the important ends for which it was designed. This Committee will also once every year—namely, on the 25th of the month of March—examine and audit the accounts of the receipts and expenditures of the Institution kept by the managers or by their orders; and the report of the Committee of Visitors on this audit will always make the first article in their public annual reports.

5to. A person actually serving as a visitor will not be eligible as a manager, nor can his name be put on the list of candidates for that office till one whole year shall have elapsed after he shall have ceased to belong to the Committee of Visitors. Those, however, who serve as visitors will be capable of being *re-elected* on that Committee without limitation.

MISCELLANEOUS ARTICLES.

1mo. The managers will take care to procure, and to exhibit in the repository as early as possible, models of all such new and useful mechanical inventions and improvements as shall, from time to time, be made in this or in any other country.

2do. All presents to the Institution, and all new purchases and acquisitions of every kind, will be and remain the joint property of the proprietors of the Institution and of their heirs and assigns, and all the surplus of the income of the Institution, over and above what shall be found necessary for maintaining it and keeping it up, will be employed by the managers in making additions to the local accommodation of the Institution, or in augmenting the collection of models, or in making additions to the philosophical apparatus, accordingly as the managers of the Institution for the time being shall deem most useful.

3tio. In order that the proprietors of the Institution and the subscribers may have the earliest notice of all new discoveries and useful improvements that shall be made, from time to time, not only in this country, but also in all the different parts of the world, the managers will employ the proper means for obtaining, as early as possible, from every part of the British Empire, and from all foreign countries, authentic accounts of all such new and interesting discoveries in the various branches of science, and in arts and manufactures, and also of all such new and useful mechanical improvements as shall be made; and a room will be set apart in the Institution where all such information will be lodged, and where it will be kept for the sole and exclusive use and inspection of the proprietors and subscribers, and where no stranger will ever be admitted.

At a general meeting of the proprietors, held at the house of the Right Honourable Sir Joseph Banks, Bart., K.B., in Soho Square, on the 7th day of March, 1799, the Right Hon. Sir Joseph Banks in the chair, the following list of the proprietors and original subscribers of fifty guineas each was read:

Sir Robert Ainslie, Bart.
J. J. Angerstein, Esq.
Right Hon. Sir Joseph Banks, K.B.
Thomas Bernard, Esq.
Scrope Bernard, Esq., M.P.
The Earl of Besborough.
Rowland Burdon, Esq., M.P.
James Burton, Esq.
Timothy Brent, Esq.
Henry Cavendish, Esq.
Rich. Clarke, Esq., Chamb. of London.
Sir John Colpoys, K.B.
John Craufurd, Esq.
The Duke of Devonshire, K.G.
Andrew Douglas, Esq.
The Lord Bishop of Durham.
The Earl of Egremont.
George Ellis, Esq., M.P.
Joseph Grote, Esq.
Sir Robert Bateson Harvey, Bart.
Sir John Cox Hippesley, Bart.
Henry Hoare, Esq.
John Spalding, Esq., M.P.
The Earl Spencer, K.G.
Sir George Staunton, Bart.
John Sullivan, Esq.
Richard Joseph Sulivan, Esq.
Lord Teignmouth.
John Thomson, Esq.
Lord Hobart.
Lord Holland.
Henry Hope, Esq.
Thomas Hope, Esq.
Lord Keith, K.B.
William Lushington, Esq., M.P.
Sir John Macpherson, Bart., M.P.
William Manning, Esq., M.P.
The Earl of Mansfield.
The Earl of Morton, K.T.
Lord Ossulston.
Thomas Palmer, Esq.
The Lord Viscount Palmerston, M.P.
Edward Parry, Esq.
Right Hon. Thomas Pelham, M.P.
John Penn, Esq.
William Morton Pitt, Esq., M.P.
Sir James Pulteney, Bart., M.P.
Sir John Buchanan Riddell, Bart.
Count Rumford.
Sir John Sinclair, Bart., M.P.
Lord Somerville.
Samuel Thornton, Esq., M.P.
Henry Thornton, Esq., M.P.
George Vansittart, Esq., M.P.
William Wilberforce, Esq., M.P.
The Earl of Winchelsea.
Hon. James Stuart Wortley, M.P.
Sir William Young, Bart., M.P.

The following Resolutions were agreed to unanimously:

I.—That before any measures are taken for carrying the plan into execution, a petition be presented to his Majesty, praying that he would be graciously pleased to grant a charter to the Institution.

II.—That an outline of the plan be laid before the Right Honourable Mr. Pitt and his Grace the Duke of Portland.

III.—That for these purposes it is expedient to elect the Committee of Managers.

IV.—That the following proprietors (*who have agreed to serve in case they shall be elected*) be now elected as the *first managers* of the Institution:

For three years.
The Earl Spencer.
Count Rumford.
Richard Clark, Esq.

For two years.
The Earl of Egremont.
Rt. Hon. Sir Joseph Banks.
Rich. Joseph Sulivan, Esq.

For one year.
The Earl of Morton.
The Rt. Hon. Thomas Pelham.
Thomas Bernard, Esq.

V.—That the said managers be desired to solicit a charter for the Institution, upon principles conformable to the Proposals which have been printed and distributed, and (as soon as the charter is obtained) to publish the plan for the benefit of the public, in such manner as they shall deem most expedient; and also to take preparatory measures for opening the Institution.

That these resolutions be inserted in the public papers.

Jos. Banks, Chairman.

Sir Joseph Banks having quitted the chair,

Resolved,—That the thanks of the meeting be given to him for his conduct in the chair.

After this meeting of the proprietors a meeting of the managers was held, and the following resolutions taken:

At the first meeting of the Managers of the Institution, held at the house of the Right Honourable Sir Joseph Banks, in Soho Square, Saturday, March 9, 1799,

On a motion made by Count Rumford—

I.—Resolved, That Sir Joseph Banks be requested to take the chair, and that he do continue to preside at all future meetings of the managers, until a charter shall have been obtained from his Majesty for the Institution.

II.—Resolved, That all acts and deeds of the managers, in carrying on the business of the Institution, be transacted and done in the name of the managers of the Institution.

III.—Resolved, That at each meeting of the managers one of the managers present be elected by a majority of those present to act as secretary to the managers at that meeting.

IV.—Resolved, That the minutes of the proceedings of each meeting of the managers for the despatch of the business of the Institution, as well as all orders, resolutions, and other acts and deeds of the managers, be signed by the person who acts as president, and also by the person who acts as secretary at the meeting at which such business is transacted.

V.—Resolved, That the persons present at this meeting do now proceed to make choice of one of their number to act as secretary at the present meeting.

VI.—Resolved, That Thomas Bernard, Esq., is duly elected to act as secretary at the present meeting.

VII.—Resolved, That the Proposals for forming the Institution, as published by Count Rumford, be approved and adopted by the managers, subject, however, to such partial modifications as shall be by them found to be necessary or useful.

VIII.—Resolved, That the Earl of Morton, the Earl Spencer, Sir Joseph Banks, and Mr. Pelham, or any one or more of them, be requested to lay the Proposals for forming the Institution before his Majesty and the Royal Family, and before his Majesty's Ministers and the Great Officers of State.

IX.—Resolved, That the Proposals for forming the Institution be laid before the Members of both Houses of Parliament, and also before the members of his Majesty's Most Honourable Privy Council and the twelve Judges.

Messrs. Cadell and Davies, booksellers in the Strand, having generously offered to make a donation to the Institution of 500 copies of the original Proposals for forming the Institution, published by Count Rumford :—

X.—Resolved, That the thanks of the managers be given to Messrs. Cadell and Davies for this donation; that it be accepted; and that these 500 copies of the Proposals be distributed among such persons as the managers may think most likely to give their assistance in forming the Institution.

At the next meeting of managers, on March 23, Count Rumford was elected secretary.

It was decided that ladies should be admitted as proprietors and subscribers, and entitled to all privileges, 'excepting only that ladies will not be called upon to take any part in the management with the officers of the Institution.'

And on the 30th, Mr. Bernard being secretary, the draft of the charter was read.

On April 30 Dr. Glasse was elected honorary secretary, and Mr. Bernard treasurer. Mr. Mellish's house in Albemarle Street was ordered to be bought. Count Rumford was asked to see the Rev. Mr. Farish regarding lectures on experimental philosophy. Mr. Swan was chosen as clerk assistant to the treasurer and secretary. Mr. Webster, a young architect twenty-six years old, was engaged as Clerk of the Works. He had been educated at Aberdeen, and had studied at the Royal Academy and with an eminent architect. At this time he had also a small school for about a dozen mechanics.

In May it was decided that the treasurer and secretary should be entitled to assist at all the deliberations of the managers, and a committee of expenditure was appointed.

On Wednesday, June 5, the managers first met in Albemarle Street.

In the second volume of the 'Reports of the Society for Bettering the Condition of the Poor,' Mr. Bernard gives an account of the Institution 'so far as it may be expected to affect the poor.' He thus gives a view of the Institution as it was intended to be, June 1, 1799: 'Besides having a general view to the benefit of arts and manufactures and to the advancement of taste and science in this country, the Institution should specifically direct itself to the improvement of the *means of industry and of domestic comfort among the poor.* In bettering the condition of the poor there is very little prospect of these difficulties being removed until a *centre of action* can be fixed, to which persons may apply for examples, for models, and for engravings accompanied by printed instructions, without being any longer compelled implicitly to rely on the talents, the docility, and the conscientious moderation of the different tradesmen who may be employed to make and sell them.

'A convenient house was proposed for the purpose of lectures and experiments, and for a public exhibition of all such new and useful inventions and improvements as are applicable to the common purposes of life, and especially those which tend to increase the conveniences and comforts of mankind, and to promote domestic economy and useful industry. In the priority of introduction it was proposed that regard should be had to the degree of public utility, and particularly as they might benefit the general mass of the people.

'Of the subjects of the lectures there are few which appear peculiarly to apply to the poor. Such as those on heat, on the principles of the warmth of clothing, and on the effects of the different temperatures of the air on the human body.

'The models and inventions in which the poor are most immediately concerned will be those which may promote economy in food and fuel, and tend to correct and purify the air in cottages and workhouses, and which may supply means and instruments of industry on a cheap and simple construction.

'Thus the models to be exhibited will consist of improved fire-places and kitchens, and of flues and louvres for supplying rooms either with tepid or fresh air.

'There will be small models of inventions at a very cheap price, with engravings and explanatory descriptions useful to those who are unable to employ the persons recommended by the Institution or to examine them in actual and constant use at the Institution.'

Mr. Bernard's report ends thus: 'Though the charter is not yet obtained, and the Institution may be considered only in its infancy, the subscriptions already exceed 8,000*l*.

'It is not very easy to calculate what may be eventually the progress of the Institution, and what its influence on the condition of the poor. If it is followed up with an equal zeal and attention on the part of the conductors, and it receives the support it merits from the public, its effects must be extremely beneficial and important. For, without adverting to the general advantage of a new species of employment and amusement being afforded to the higher classes of life; and science and useful occupation being brought into some degree of fashion; it must be apparent to everyone that, without some such means, the poor can never receive all that benefit and assistance which the efforts and co-operation of many are now directed to procure for them; and that the improvement of the domestic comfort and means of industry in the cottage, the promotion of health, the economy and well-being of the inhabitants of poor-houses, hospitals, manufactories, and other public establishments will never be effectually obtained without such an establishment as the Institution.'

It is difficult to believe that the Royal Institution of the present day was ever intended to resemble the picture given of it in this report.

In June the Earl of Winchester became the first president, and the King became the patron, and he allowed the Institution to be called Royal. At the last meeting in the month Count Rumford was authorised to carry into effect his proposition for a repository of models, and to employ such artisans as he might think necessary, paying according to his discretion for their services. He was instructed to procure such instruments and utensils as relate more immediately to the management of fire; and he was empowered to draw 500*l*. to fit up the house for their reception.

On July 6 he submitted to the managers a form of advertisement to be inserted in the public papers, in order to carry out the exhibition of models.

In September Count Rumford was requested to engage Dr. Garnett as lecturer and scientific secretary and Editor of the Journals, with lodgings in the house and 300*l*. emolument, with a prospect of a gradual increase to 500*l*., provided the funds of the Institution in future authorised this additional expenditure. A committee was formed to prepare a lecture room on the first floor for the next winter.

Mr. Webster was appointed clerk to the treasurer and secretary, as well as Clerk of the Works, and a long report from him was read to the managers by Count

Rumford on the formation of an industrial school for mechanics at the Institution.

A letter written by Mr. Webster to Dr. Garnett in August 1800, and another in 1801 to a friend, give an explanation of this proposal.

Probably August 1800.

The original object of the Institution was certainly to disseminate knowledge in the most effectual way possible; and for this purpose, while the higher ranks of society were amused and instructed by lecturers on science and its too much neglected applications to the purposes of common life, it was conceived necessary to do somewhat in order to enlighten the minds of that class which had not enjoyed the advantages of a liberal education, and yet whose improvement was necessarily connected with the progress of the useful arts.

This was always considered as an object of so much importance by Count Rumford, who has certainly had the greatest share in establishing the Institution, that he repeatedly declared to me when I first knew him that it was his intention to do everything in his power to establish a school for science under the auspices of the Institution and particularly calculated for working mechanics, a class of men whose deficiency in knowledge proves one of the greatest drawbacks to the progress of art. It was through the prospect of being employed in this way, which would have been as agreeable to my habits of thinking as useful to my interest, that I was induced to give up the school which I then kept and the other business in which I was engaged, and to accept of a situation and salary in the Institution by no means equivalent to what I should have considered myself as entitled to under other circumstances.

Later Mr. Webster wrote to a friend:

You have heard, no doubt, that I was employed as draftsman to the Royal Institution at its first formation, and was besides engaged by Count Rumford to take the management of a school for mechanics which he then proposed to establish. In order to overcome the scruples of some of the managers of the Institution on this subject, as well as to give a specimen of my abilities for conducting such an establishment, I addressed a paper to Count Rumford in August 1799, in which I gave him my opinion of the kind of school which would prove most useful to the public, and also entered into a detail of the plan which I proposed to follow. This paper, which the Count read at the meeting of the managers, was highly approved of, and I had then every reason to expect that something would be done which would be creditable to the Institution and useful to myself. I was induced in consequence to give up the school which I then had, and which promised to answer pretty well. But, after remaining some time in suspense, I found some reason to be apprehensive that those who are at the head of an Institution which professes to be a grand and national establishment were not altogether possessed of that liberality of sentiment and knowledge of the subject necessary for carrying into effect plans which can only be accomplished by those whose industry has made them acquainted with the arts and sciences taught. In short, I saw but little prospect of its being done in the way I wished, and I had no desire to engage in it otherwise. I am not certain that the plan has been entirely abandoned, but I think it is not likely to take place.

In 1837 Webster gave the following account of the intention to form an industrial school at the Institution:

Whilst employed as an architect, having occasion to direct various workmen, I had observed their frequent inability to do what was required from them through their deficient education, and that it was no easy matter to find those who could understand either drawings or directions; one had also frequently to contend with a species of perverseness and conceit often the result of ignorance. In attempting our improvements in fire-places, &c., I felt this the more as this kind of work demanded a superior class of artificers. Knowing from previous experience what it was possible to effect in their improvement, I conceived the idea of giving to mechanics for this purpose a species of scientific education suited to their condition, and I believe I was the first person in this country who took active steps for effecting so desirable an object. I was not unacquainted with the political feelings of that time, but I did not think a little learning was a dangerous thing *if judiciously bestowed*, although without due caution it might be capable of doing more harm than good. My idea was to make *good mechanics*, not to force them like hot-bed plants out of the sphere in which they are so useful.

I proposed, then, to found a school for mechanics in the house of the Royal Institution, in which they should be taught such principles of science as would be useful in their several occupations, which I considered would in a great degree promote the 'application of science to the common purposes of life.' In the house of the Institution itself the men would be under the eye of the higher classes, and anything wrong would easily be put a stop to. With this view I wrote a long letter to Count Rumford, detailing my views and plans. He was delighted with them, and he read my letter to the board of managers; the idea was favourably received, and my letter was inserted upon the Minutes of the Institution, where of course it may be seen (Managers' Minutes, Sept. 14, 1799). Some difficulties were, however, suggested. It was thought that Sir Joseph Banks, then president, would object, and I was requested to take the minute book to him and do what I could to win him over. I accordingly saw Sir Joseph, and, by explaining to him how much the arts would gain by intelligent operatives, I overcame a few political scruples which he had. At last all objections were silenced, and everyone seemed to rejoice in the prospect that opened of adding to the Royal Institution a decided proof of liberal feeling. The general idea and intention with respect to this school were published in the Journals of the Institution;[1] and the news reached every corner of the kingdom that the managers of the Royal Institution of Great Britain, among whom were persons of the highest rank, instead of being adverse to the diffusion of knowledge, had actually formed a school for the instruction of mechanical classes.

It is saying little to assert that the Institution acquired some popularity by this measure. It gained much not only here but all over Europe; and in June 1801 Professor Pictet, of Geneva, the well-known and learned editor of the 'Bibliothèque Universelle,' in his published account of a tour which he made through England at this time, speaks of it as one of the most important branches of the Institution. It is unnecessary to enter into a detailed account of my plan, which was, in fact, intended as an experiment. It was generally to educate a number of mechanics sent by the proprietors of the Institution. At first all were to learn the same elementary principles, but afterwards they were to branch off according to their several trades. My first intention was to instruct bricklayers, joiners, tinmen, and ironplate workers, as those were the trades most connected with our improvements at this time. In a large room on the ground floor we built up for practising the men chimneys and fire-places of all kinds in a slight manner, pulled them down, and built up others. We fitted up improved fire-places within, models of old-fashioned

[1] No notice of workshops exists in the first number of the Journal, dated April 1800. In the second number, containing the report to the managers on May 25, 1801, it is said that eighteen or twenty young men are to be boarded and lodged in the house (p. 27, Journal).

cottage chimneys, also boilers of various kinds, and showed how smoky chimneys might be cured, &c.; models of various culinary vessels were made from ideas of Count Rumford, and were put in the model room for the inspection of the public. Of the workmen to be instructed some were sent by Lord Winchelsea, by Sir Thomas Barnard, Lady Palmerston, &c., and when they were thought to be sufficiently instructed they returned to the part of the country from which they had come, and practised what they had learned and taught others. Thus by degrees a laudable zeal was created amongst various classes of society, even the highest, for acquiring useful knowledge and diffusing it by their several exertions. Never was there a period when this was felt in a stronger degree, and the establishment of the Royal Institution ought to be considered as the commencement of a new era in the history of science in this country. I should not here forget to mention the then existing Society for Bettering the Condition of the Poor, composed of men of the highest rank, such as the Bishop of Durham, &c.; and to this Society, which met in the house of the Royal Institution (December 23, 1799), I was made assistant secretary for the purpose of letting me the better into their views.

It is impossible to state the whole of the good that has proceeded from these liberal endeavours to improve society, and the country owes more than is generally known to the benevolent spirit thus excited.

After September 14 Count Rumford was absent until February 3. During this time six meetings only of the managers were held, one in October, when Sir John Hippesley brought at great length the question of the arms of the Institution before the managers. Another meeting was on December 23, when the Society for Bettering the Condition of the Poor were granted a room for the committee meetings.

The prospectus and charter were ordered to be printed in octavo, and Dr. Garnett laid before the managers the plan of his lectures for the following year.

Thus, then, in 1799 the Rumford Institution began in the house of Sir Joseph Banks, the President of the Royal Society, and in the first year of its life it became the Royal Institution in Albemarle Street. It had its origin in the work which Count Rumford did for the poor in Munich, and its primary objects were models, workshops, and useful knowledge to benefit the poor; lectures, researches, and scientific experiments to amuse and interest the rich and to advance science were comparatively the secondary intentions of its founder.

In 1800 a new and very long prospectus was written by Count Rumford. It was printed with the charter, bye-laws, and names of the proprietors and subscribers, and published on January 23. It again said, 'the two chief purposes of the Institution were the speedy and general diffusion of the knowledge of all new and useful improvements, in whatever quarter of the world they may originate; the application of scientific discoveries to the improvement of arts and manufactures in this country, and to the increase of domestic comfort and convenience.' There is a remarkable addition in May of two paragraphs to the edition in quarto of this publication. They read as if some one had pointed out the absence of all mention of attraction for the rich. These words were added: 'But, in estimating the probable usefulness of this Institution, we must not forget the public advantages that will be derived from the general diffusion of a spirit of experimental investigation and improvement among the higher ranks of society. When the rich shall take pleasure in contemplating and encouraging such mechanical improvements as are really useful, good taste, with its inseparable companion good morals, will revive; rational economy will become fashionable; industry and ingenuity will be honoured and rewarded; and the pursuits of all the various classes of society will then tend to promote the public prosperity.'

On the 13th of January Sir J. Hippesley read to the managers a letter proposed to be sent to every proprietor and subscriber. It stated that the charter had been approved, and would be sealed the next seal day; that temporary accommodation for lectures was completed; and that Mr. Professor Garnett would lecture early in February; that the subscribers' rooms, containing the periodical scientific publications, foreign and domestic, would be opened at the same time. All subscribers were requested to pay their subscriptions immediately to Professor Garnett, or to Mr. Webster, the clerk of the Institution, or to one of the six bankers of the Institution.

At the end of the month Mr. Webster was ordered to prepare plans for a new lecture room. When an old man he thus spoke of his work: 'After nearly forty years the theatre of the Royal Institution is pronounced to be *the most perfect room of the kind in the kingdom* for possessing the properties of allowing the lecturer to be well heard and seen by the audience, and for affording them easy entrance and exit, &c. I have never "puffed" myself respecting it, as is very common in similar cases, and hence, probably, my name is scarcely known as connected with it. But I may *now* say, "that it has been stated by Faraday, in his late examination before a committee of the House of Commons, to be 'almost perfect as a lecture room,' and that 'although architects are continually measuring and drawing it to copy from, and many other rooms have been built in imitation of it in which he has tried his voice, yet none of them proved equal to that in question.'"

'*After my designs were quite finished, and after it was resolved by the Institution that they should be carried into execution by me*, Mr. Saunders, then architect of the British Museum, offered his assistance should any difficulties arise. I willingly accepted his offer, as his name would be some sanction and security in a case where I knew I had enemies as well as friends, and I took care to show him everything I did in the construction of the building; but the whole of the working drawings, even the details of the mouldings, &c., were made by my own hand. The estimate and contract were made by me and not by Saunders, and every person employed was under my *immediate direction*. My designs were not in the smallest degree altered by him.

'Soon after my designs were made they were taken away by one of the managers (whose name I shall not mention at present) and put into the hands of Mr. Spiller, an architect, in order that he might make another set of designs, thereby giving him the advantage of my ideas. This was accordingly done. His lecture room was upon the second story and mine was upon the first. His was covered by a lofty dome highly enriched; my ceiling was flat. His estimate was 10,000*l.*; mine was 5,000*l.* His would take two years to execute; mine was to be finished in six months. I shall pass over the unpleasant circumstances to which this affair gave rise, my resigning my situation in the Institution, being requested by the managers to retain it, &c., and shall only say both the sets of designs were submitted to the members of the Institution at their annual meeting, and *mine were* adopted, and it was resolved that they should be executed under my superintendence. Mr. Spiller claimed and got, I believe, 150*l.* I received nothing as an architect, because I was an officer of the Institution at a very small salary, and Count Rumford had in the beginning caused a strange regulation to be made and *printed* "that no one should ever be *rewarded* by the Institution for any services which he might perform."'

In another note he says:

'In designing the lecture room of an institution so peculiar (unique indeed at that time) my object was to adapt it for different ranks in society, for any attempt to destroy all distinctions must be absurd. I constructed a gallery intended for those who either wished to be less observed, or who, for obvious reasons, would not like to sit down by their employers. It was also to receive such ingenious mechanics as had gained a title to be there. To this gallery *a separate stone staircase led from the street.* The whole of this *was built.*' [1]

On January 15 Count Rumford wrote to Sir Joseph Banks from Broadlands:

I certainly am in much better health than I was when I came here, which I attribute as much to my having left off taking medicines as to the salubrious air of the country. I think that I shall stay here about a fortnight longer, and shall then return to Brompton, and shall be at the disposal of the managers of the Institution for the remainder of the winter. I am very glad indeed that you like Webster. I am much deceived if he does not turn out to be a very useful acquisition. I hope Dr. Garnett will do well, but I must own that I am not as prepossessed in his favour as I am in favour of Webster.

If more active and more useful men could be found to serve as managers in lieu of two or three of ours who seldom or never attend, I think it would be advisable to accept their resignation. *One* has *privately* offered me to resign whenever I may wish it, and I should think it would not be difficult to persuade two others to follow the example. But we will talk this matter over when we meet.

I have been very busy here for the last fortnight putting up a public kitchen in the town of Romsey. It is now nearly finished, and begins to attract public curiosity. As it contains a complete well-arranged kitchen for a private family as well as cottage fire-places, German stoves, nests of small ovens, large soup boilers, &c., it almost deserves the name of a public repository, and I have no doubt but it will be useful as such. If Webster were here for a few days, he might take drawings of the whole for the use of the Royal Institution.

[1] This gallery staircase has left its mark in the Institution, and is drawn in the old plans of the house. There was originally no door into the theatre under the gallery.

A week after he wrote: 'I am expecting the arrival of Webster every moment. I am glad you have sent him here, for the drawings he will make of the works that have been executed in the Romsey public kitchen will save me much trouble (for I must have made them), and his seeing the kitchen here will enable him to be of great use to me in directing the works in Albemarle Street.'

On February 3 Count Rumford was again present. Doubtless the following passage in the Managers' Minutes refers to him: 'The unfortunate illness and long confinement of one of the managers, whose zeal had been so conspicuous in the formation and success of the Institution, was another obstacle to the commencement of many interesting arrangements, which he necessarily considered as essential to superintend in person.'

The same day Sir John Hippesley made a long report to the managers to be laid before the proprietors of the Institution on the 10th.

He alluded to a proposal for private boxes in the new theatre, and spoke of accommodating nearly 1,000 persons, and said that the floor under the theatre was for a repository, and that the sunk floor of the new building was designed for a complete laboratory, 'which unfortunately this great metropolis of the British Empire has hitherto failed to produce, but which is an essential appendix to the Royal Institution.'

It was proposed to raise 5,000*l.* by transferable debentures, and the sum subscribed during the meeting was 5,200*l.*

At the next meeting a building committee, consisting

of Earl Morton, Count Rumford, and Sir J. Hippesley, was appointed. The following week this was made to include all the managers.

In this month Count Rumford went to live in the house, and the managers resolved 'that as long as he did so he should be required to superintend all the works going on in the house, and to see that the servants in the house and the different workmen employed discharge their various duties with diligence and due decorum, and that the proprietors, subscribers, and others who visit the Institution are received with civility and treated with proper respect and attention.'

Sir Joseph Banks drew up the bye-laws, and Count Rumford was afterwards asked, agreeably to a provision in the draft bye-laws, to prepare internal regulations for conducting the business of the Institution. An under-librarian and clerk to the managers was also appointed.

The meeting of managers on March 31 was the starting point of the Journal of the Institution. The publication was left to the superintendence of Rumford.

A printing press was ordered to be bought as soon as possible, and a scientific committee of council was formed. This was to be a standing committee 'to examine the syllabuses of the professor of natural philosophy and chemistry, to the end that no false scientific doctrine might be taught at the Institution, and to superintend all the new philosophical experiments that might be made in the house of the Institution, and, when made, to cause to be drawn up an account of the same for the managers and for the Royal Society of London.'

This committee consisted of Cavendish, Maskelyne, Blagden, Rennell, Planta, Gray, Vince, Farish, and Hatchett.

The managers also decided that fourteen committees should be appointed for the purpose of specific investigation and improvement. Persons in no way connected with the Institution might be appointed. The chairman and deputy chairman were to be nominated by the managers. The meetings were to be held in the house, and the results were to be published in the Journals. The subjects were, 1, making bread; 2, soup; 3, cottages; 4, stoves; 5, kitchen fire-places and utensils; 6, household furniture; 7, food for cattle; 8, cooking in ships and distilling fresh water at sea; 9, lime-kilns; 10, fire-balls and combustible cakes; 11, mortar and cements; 12, composition houses; 13, useful machines of all descriptions; 14, iron founding and working and refining iron and steel.

Dr. R. J. Thornton offering to lecture on botany as connected with agriculture, it was resolved that the cultivation of natural history and agriculture was not included in the original plan of the Royal Institution, and that it was not expedient to accept the offer.

On April 5 the first number of the 'Journal of the Royal Institution of Great Britain' was published. It contains, 1. The proceedings of the managers of March 31 and the report to the proprietors made on February 10. 2. An advertisement respecting the publication of the Journal, 'that threepence would be the price of a number of eight pages, and sixpence if sixteen pages; that no stated period could then be fixed, but it is expected a number would appear as often at least as once every fortnight.' 3. A short account of the works now carrying on at the house of the Institution. Mention is made of the theatre, and under it a spacious airy semicircular repository for receiving various useful machines which will be exhibited as models for imitation. Immediately under the repository will be constructed a lofty and capacious laboratory for chemical experiments. The fire-places, the kitchen, the boilers, the ovens, the complete roaster, steamers, and other articles of kitchen furniture on new principles were either prepared or preparing for exhibition. An account is given of the number of the proprietors, 248; life subscribers, 259; annual subscribers, 297; ladies, annual, 97; and a notice of the philosophical lectures for the following week.

The second number of the Journal did not appear for nearly fourteen months.

In May Mr. Savage was engaged as printer; and 'a good cook for the improvement of culinary advancement, one object, and not the least important, for the Royal Institution.' A resolution was passed that as Count Rumford had, at the request of the managers, undertaken to superintend the house, no new works should be undertaken in it, nor any alterations made in it, nor any furniture ordered for it, or brought into it, or placed or displaced in it unless it be with his knowledge, and by his orders; and he was requested, whilst he continued to lodge in the house, to superintend all the servants, to preserve order and decorum, and to control the expenses of housekeeping. It is most probable that this resolution was intended to control Dr. Garnett. A printing-press was bought. Sir John Hippesley was elected treasurer.

Count Rumford wrote to Sir Joseph Banks:

Royal Institution, May 29, 1800.

I am very sorry to find, on making inquiry of Doctor Garnett, that your information was accurate respecting his having ascribed the late discoveries of our friend Volta to the French. Had I been apprised of his intention to mention this discovery at his lectures, I should certainly have taken care that he should have mentioned it in a proper manner; but I knew nothing of the matter until it was too late to prevent the mistake. I have, however, insisted on its being rectified as far as it is possible in some future lecture, and I am promised that it will be done. I know not from whom the Doctor procured his information respecting his discovery, but I learnt by accident late last evening that he borrowed the apparatus with which he exhibited the experiments at the lecture from Mr. Howard. I dined out and did not come home till his lecture was nearly over.

The next day Rumford wrote again:

Royal Institution, May 30, 1800.

Doctor Garnett is perfectly ready to make the following public declaration this evening at his lecture at the Institution, or he will say anything else on the subject in question which you may think will be more proper for him to say to atone for his mistake and to make amends to Professor Volta:

'Having by mistake on Wednesday, in the course of my public lecture, ascribed to the French philosophers a new and interesting discovery relative to galvanism, which, on inquiry, I find belongs to Professor Volta, of Milan, I feel it to be my duty to state this fact in a public manner, in order that Professor Volta may not be deprived in any degree of the honour of a discovery which so justly belongs to him and to him alone. The first news of this discovery, which arrived in this country in the beginning of last month, was communicated in a letter from Professor Volta to the President of the Royal Society, and it was in consequence of the information contained in that letter that Dr. Carlisle, Mr. Nicholson, Mr. Howard, and others have been enabled to construct the necessary apparatus, and to repeat the ingenious Professor's very interesting experiments.'

Any alterations you may wish in the above shall be made, if you will point them out.

In June Count Rumford reported that, in consequence of the request of the managers, he had transmitted through the envoy of the United States of North America to each of the philosophical societies, academies, universities, &c., in that country a copy of the prospectus, charter, ordinances, bye-laws, and regulations of the Royal Institution of Great Britain.

Copies were sent to different public institutions abroad.

Dr. Garnett finished his lectures on June 10. He then wrote to the managers to say that he proposed to go into the country, but would at all times be ready to obey the summons of the managers if his attendance should be wanted before the commencement of the lectures.

On June 12, 1800, Count Rumford wrote to Sir Joseph Banks:

Royal Institution, Thursday Morning, 6 o'clock.

I hope you can make it convenient to come and give me a lift this morning at our meeting, for I want you very much. Our treasurer[1] has not qualified, and he does not seem to be in any hurry to do so. I mentioned to him at our last meeting the embarrassments we were under for the want of a treasurer to furnish money to the new Committee of Expenditure; but he proposed, as an *expedient*, that I should draw on Ransom and Co., who he said would not refuse my draft. I see no reason why business should be done in this irregular way, when it may and ought to be done in the manner specially and clearly pointed out in our bye-laws. Our lectures are over for this season, and Garnett is going into the country to stay there till January next. I see no good reason why we should keep up our present numerous and expensive establishment of servants, especially as a great part of the house is coming down, and we shall soon have no place in the house to lodge them.

All we can possibly want till January next are—

Our clerk of the works . . .	Webster
Our clerk	Savage
Our messenger, who may act as porter and messenger	
And one housemaid . . .	Blanchett

This arrangement will enable us to discharge—

Dr. Garnett's assistant . . .	Sadler
The porter	Wharton
The housekeeper	Mrs. Wharton
And one housemaid	

If this scheme should meet with your approbation, I beg that *you* would move the necessary resolutions to-day, and there will be more than one difficulty removed. As soon as this disagreeable business shall be completed, and everything in the house belonging to the Institution

[1] Sir J. Hippesley, elected May 19.

delivered over to the care of those persons who are to take and have the charge of them, my mind will be at rest, and I can go to Harrogate and give these waters a fair trial, which, as things are now circumstanced, would be impossible.

The expensive establishment was at once ordered to be reduced, and the assistant to the Professor was discharged.

The agreement for building the new premises was this month sealed and signed, the treasurer qualified, and the weekly meetings of managers ceased to be held.

As soon as the basement of the new building was finished, it must have been apparent that it was much too dark and low for a laboratory, and this part of the intended plan was given up.

Many years afterwards Mr. Webster said of the present laboratory: 'I may perhaps just mention that the chemical laboratory in which so many valuable discoveries have been made was not only designed and built by me, but owes to me its very existence, for, though I inserted it in my plans, the managers did not at first consider it necessary.'

In August Mr. Webster thus wrote to Count Rumford, who was then at Harrogate:

I have deferred writing to you so long in expectation of being able to send you drawings of the proposed mode of building the laboratory. Mr. Hatchett has been several times at the Institution and has given his opinion respecting it, from which the drawings have been made out. There was a meeting of managers on Monday last, at which

Mr. Saunders laid before them the drawings and an estimate of several works which he proposed to do, and which were not included in the original contract. These are the engine and reservoir on the staircase, the removal of the water-closet from the place where it now stands to the roof of the laboratory; taking down the present stack of chimneys from the great kitchen, together with the breast-work in the kitchen which contains the range, roasters, and oven, which he considers necessary in order to fit up a strong closet in the managers' room; together with a small addition to the fitting up of the laboratory itself, which it is proposed to do in a more complete and more expensive way than was provided for by the contract. All these additions, Mr. Saunders informs me, the managers approved of, and he is accordingly preparing the necessary agreements with Mr. Hancock for executing them.

Everything in the new building goes on briskly and well. We have got as high as the lecture-room floor, and I expect in a month we shall be ready for the roof. No deviation whatever has been made from the plans, and all the works hitherto done have been executed to the satisfaction of Mr. Saunders.

I wished to send you the drawings of the laboratory, but they not being quite ready, I shall take the next opportunity.

In September he wrote again:

The timbers of the roof are on, and we are beginning to board it for slating. The brickwork of the laboratory is also nearly completed.

Hitherto I have found employment for Mr. Wincks, the model-maker; when I had nothing else for him to do he has been at work upon the model of the pile engine, which will now be finished in a day or two; and, as I have not any further occasion for him to assist me, I shall be happy if you will write whether there is anything he might be employed upon until you come to town.

In another letter he says:

The buildings are advancing rapidly, and I hope the lecture room at least will be ready by the 1st of January. The laboratory will, I think, be found very convenient, being airy and well lighted.

During his stay at Harrogate Rumford made careful experiments on himself with regard to the warm bath. These are given in his thirteenth essay, on the 'Salubrity of Warm Bathing.' He found that a daily bath at ninety-six degrees or ninety-seven for half-an-hour two hours before dinner for five weeks increased the appetite, the digestion, the spirits, the strength, and the insensibility to cold.

On leaving Harrogate he went to Scotland.

A visit of ceremony was paid him by the magistrates of Edinburgh; he was consulted respecting the abolition of mendicity, and the measures which he recommended were speedily executed with complete success.

He was made an honorary member of the Royal Society and of the Royal College of Physicians of Edinburgh, and he received a gold snuff-box as a compliment for his assistance in reforming the culinary establishment of Heriot's Hospital, and was elected a member of the Society of Scotland for Bettering the Condition of the Poor. His letters of thanks for these last honours are preserved.

To the Lord Provost of Edinburgh he wrote:

I shall always remember with pleasure, and with the most sincere gratitude, the kind and flattering attentions

I received in Edinburgh during my stay there. The public honours that were conferred on me by the corporation of the city and by the University were highly gratifying to me; but nothing affected me so deeply as the deference which was paid to my opinions and advice on subjects of public utility by men in the highest stations and of the most respectable character and abilities, and the liberality, zeal, and perseverance with which the measures I took the liberty to recommend were adopted and pursued.

May the important undertaking in which the inhabitants of Edinburgh are now engaged—the prevention of that most disgusting and disgraceful of public evils, mendicity—and the formation of a permanent establishment for the *instruction* and *employment* of the poor be completely successful, and may it serve as a model for imitation to every city and every town in Great Britain and Ireland.

To the Rev. George Baird, Principal of the University of Edinburgh, he wrote from the Royal Institution, March 21, 1801, thanking him for the honour which the Society in Scotland for Bettering the Condition and Improving the Comfort of the Poor had conferred on him by electing him a member.

During the autumn Webster wrote to Dr. Garnett to ask if he would help him to become his assistant. He wished this place in order to make himself a better teacher of operatives, and to have employment when the additional buildings were finished. Dr. Garnett, in his reply, says 'an operator's time ought to be dedicated to natural philosophy.' 'Nevertheless,' he said, 'the School of Mechanics might perhaps be carried on by the operator.' In Webster's answer to

Dr. Garnett the position of the School of Design at the end of September 1800 is seen.

When I mentioned that teaching mechanics might probably form a part of my employment I did not speak from any certain knowledge on the subject, but merely because such a thing had once been in agitation. I have now very little reason for supposing that such a plan will be at all put in practice, but if ever it should, no doubt the managers will take care that it shall not prove any inconvenience to you. I could not myself engage in it upon any other conditions. Setting that aside, therefore, as extremely uncertain if not improbable . . . .

At the end of the year hot-water pipes were ordered for warming the theatre.

The chief events in the history of the Institution during the year 1800 may be thus summed up: The new theatre was built; large committees for scientific investigation were formed; and the first number of the Journal was published. No advance was made in the formation of a repository for models; or in the foundation of a school of design. The lectures of Dr. Garnett were successful, but he was refused permission to practise his profession as a physician and to bring his children to live at the Institution. Count Rumford himself ordered and superintended *everything* in the house. Early the next year there was a visible rupture between him and Dr. Garnett regarding the prospectus of the lectures for the season, and in June 1801 Dr. Garnett resigned.

The causes of this will be best seen by a short sketch of his life.

Dr. Thomas Garnett was born in 1766 in Westmoreland. He was apprenticed to a medical man in the country and graduated as a physician in Edinburgh in 1788. Dr. Brown at that time was teaching his new theory of medicine, and Dr. Garnett became a strong Brunonian. In an inaugural essay on Health, which was published ultimately, he showed with great clearness how the doctrine of accumulated and exhausted excitability could be applied to explain the movements in the body in health and disease.

He left Edinburgh to study medicine in London, and in 1790 he went to Bradford to practise his profession; there he gave some private lessons in natural philosophy and chemistry.

In 1791, when twenty-five, he thought he should succeed better by practising at Knaresborough in the winter and at Harrogate in the summer. He analysed the waters at Harrogate, and in 1794 he built a house there and determined to practise only at Harrogate. An engagement to be married made him form a new plan for success. He persuaded his intended wife reluctantly to agree to emigrate to America after their marriage, which took place in the following year. Then he sold his house in Harrogate and purchased apparatus for lectures on natural philosophy and chemistry. On their way to America they went to Liverpool. There, whilst waiting for a ship, he was persuaded to give a course of lectures. This was successful, and he was invited to give the same course on chemistry and experimental philosophy at Manchester. He was still more successful, and invitations came to him from Warrington, Lancaster, Birmingham, and Dublin. He did not give up his intention of emigrating until he was offered the professorship in Anderson's Institution at Glasgow. His wife had borne him a daughter, and she earnestly urged him to settle in Glasgow.

In November 1796, when thirty, he published the 'Outlines of a Course of Lectures on Natural and Experimental Philosophy.' His subjects were the properties of matter, astronomy, electricity, magnetism, pneumatics, hydrostatics and hydraulics, optics and mechanics.

When the session at Glasgow was over he went to Liverpool to repeat his course of lectures. In the autumn he returned to Glasgow and made known his intention of practising as a physician there. Fortune continued to favour him; his reputation increased and he soon had the best prospect of the leading practice in Glasgow.

In 1797, when thirty-one, he published his 'Outlines of a Course of Lectures on Chemistry.' His twenty-seventh lecture was on Agriculture; his twenty-eighth on Bleaching; his twenty-ninth on Dyeing and on Calico Printing; and his last on the Analysis of Mineral Waters.

On Christmas Day, 1798, his wife died in childbirth, and on New Year's Day he wrote this feeling letter:

Oh! my dear cousin, little did I expect that I should begin the new year with telling you that I am now deprived of all earthly comforts; yes, the dear companion of my studies, the friend of my heart, the partner of my bosom, is now a piece of cold clay. The senseless earth is closed on that form which was so lately animated by every virtue, and whose only wish was to make me happy.

Is there anything which can now afford me any consolation? Yes, she is not lost, but gone before; but still it is hard to have all our schemes of happiness wrecked when our bark was within sight of port. When we were promising ourselves more than common felicity it struck upon a rock; my only treasure went to the bottom, and I am cast ashore friendless and deprived of every comfort. My poor dead love had been as well as usual during the two or three last months, and even on the dreadful evening (Christmas Eve) she spoke with pleasure of the approaching event. My spirits were elevated to so uncommon a pitch by the birth of a lovely daughter, that they were by no means prepared for the succeeding scene; and they have been so overwhelmed that I sometimes hope it may be a dream out of which I wish to awake. The little infant is well, and I have called it Catherine, a name which must ever be dear to me, and which I wish to be able to apply to some object whom I love; for, though it caused the death of my hopes, it is dear to me as being the last precious relic of her whom everybody, who knew her, esteemed, and I loved. I must now bid adieu to every comfort and live only for the sweet babes. Oh! 'tis hard, very hard!

THOMAS GARNETT.

In the summer of 1799 Count Rumford wrote to Dr. Garnett, to whom he was then an entire stranger, for information regarding the nature and economy of Anderson's Institution and the plan of the lectures given there. This led finally to the proposal that Dr. Garnett should become the first lecturer at Rumford's new Institution in London.

On October 15 Dr. Garnett informed a special

meeting of the managers of Anderson's Institution of his wish to resign his situation in order to go to London. When Dr. Garnett arrived, December 23, the managers of the Royal Institution resolved that he should be styled Professor of Natural Philosophy and Chemistry to the Royal Institution. He sent to the board a letter from which a view of the earliest lectures at the Institution can be obtained.

PROFESSOR GARNETT TO THE MANAGERS.

December 23, 1799.

To the Managers of the Royal Institution. — Count Rumford requested me to arrange and put on paper my ideas concerning the plan and economy of the Royal Institution for the perusal of the managers. On looking over the prospectus, however, I find the plan so well digested that I cannot make any improvement or even advantageous alteration. I shall therefore confine myself in the following observations to what I conceive to belong more particularly to my department—I mean the arrangement of the lectures—and shall propose a plan which, from experience, I think most likely to be useful; but I propose it with the utmost deference to the opinions of the managers, and shall be ready to make any alterations which they may think proper to point out.

Our object ought undoubtedly to be both amusement and instruction. We shall have two classes of auditors, the one consisting of those who will come chiefly for amusement or because it may be fashionable. These it is our business to amuse, while at the same time I hope we shall be able to interest them in the subjects, and communicate considerable knowledge without any trouble to themselves.

For these I would propose a popular course of experimental philosophy, in which all abstract reasoning shall be avoided, the most entertaining and interesting experiments introduced, and the whole calculated to afford pleasure and instruction to those who have not had an opportunity of examining these subjects and to refresh the memory of those who have.

On the supposition that the lectures of the Institution should open the first week in February, if we appropriate one evening a week to it, we can comprise this course in eighteen or twenty lectures, each lecture to continue only an hour, that the attention may not be fatigued.

A course of lectures on chemistry; popular and amusing, at the same time sufficiently scientific, might be given twice a week. This course would contain the elements of chemistry and the application of this science to the arts and manufactures, and would be illustrated by interesting and pleasing experiments.

For the sake of the second class of auditors, which would not at first be the most numerous, but which would continually increase in number, even though the auditors of the other course should diminish—I mean those attached to scientific pursuits—I would propose a full and scientific course of experimental philosophy on the plan generally adopted in universities. In this course particular attention should be paid to mechanics, hydrostatics, hydraulics, and pneumatics, which are the most useful branches of mechanical philosophy. The mathematical demonstration of the propositions would first be given, next the experimental proof, and lastly the application of each to the mechanical and chemical arts.

In this way those who could follow the mathematical demonstration would see the coincidence between theory and experiment, and those who could not would be satisfied with the experimental proof.

As an instance we may take one proposition.

The momentum or force of a moving body is proportioned to the quantity of matter multiplied by its velocity;

this will first be demonstrated mathematically, then experimentally, and afterwards applied to the explanation of mechanical powers in machinery, projectiles, &c., illustrated by familiar examples and calculations.

If we suppose that five mornings in the week should be devoted to this course, we shall be enabled to go through one hundred lectures before the conclusion of the session.

It is scarcely necessary to observe that in this course opportunity will be taken to show working models of machinery and chemical processes in their proper places.

This would be the most useful course, and, as was before observed, the numbers who attend it would gradually increase. At least this was the case at Glasgow. A morning hour would probably be best for this course.

My apparatus is elegant and good. It was made for me by the late Mr. Adams. What the Institution will chiefly want will be of the supplementary kind, and will not, I apprehend, cost more than 150*l.* or 200*l.*, supposing we purchase the most complete and elegant instruments, which I would strongly advise. My own apparatus shall be at the service of the Institution while I continue among you, which I hope will be while I live, and it is my intention eventually to bequeath it to the Institution. As it will be necessary to come to an arrangement as speedily as possible, Mr. Webster and myself, after having carefully surveyed the house, are of opinion that the apparatus should be placed in cases with glass doors, and that the best situation for it would be round the large room[1] on the same floor with the lecture room, and what could not conveniently be placed there, either on account of their bulk or inelegant appearance, might be put in the small room[2] adjoining to it. This would render this room very interesting to strangers, and, even considering it as a lounging room, it would be much better to have an elegant apparatus to look at than bare walls. It would likewise be much the most convenient as

[1] Now the anteroom. [2] Now the lecturers' room.

an apparatus and model room with respect to its vicinity to the lecture room—a circumstance of no small importance.

With respect to a lounging room, in which persons might meet before the lecture, or to which they could retire during the lecture, I assume with submission that such a place should not *on any account* be allowed. Wherever I have had accidentally such a convenient room in the vicinity of a locture room I have been obliged to lock it up; otherwise the disturbance to the company by persons coming in and going out is intolerable. The lectures will always begin at a certain hour to a minute. If any find themselves a few minutes too soon, they will find an elegant lecture room, well warmed. This will prevent their coming into the room in a body and disturbing the audience and the lecturer after the lecture is begun.

That matters might be put in a proper train it would, I think, be best to agree immediately upon the arrangement of the house, and to give Mr. Webster and myself, with one or more of the managers, the power of seeing the arrangement executed.

I am, with much respect, your most obedient Servant,

Thos. Garnett.

On January 6, 1800, the managers resolved that the morning lectures of Dr. Garnett should be given on Tuesday and Thursday at two, and the evening lectures at eight, on Monday, Wednesday, and Friday.

The first lecture was on Tuesday, March 4. The two rooms which now make the upper library formed the theatre. It had been fitted up to accommodate the greatest possible number of auditors, 'with a greater deference to their curiosity than to their convenience.'

In the first number of the Journal of the Institution the account of Dr. Garnett's lectures for the week beginning April 7 shows the arrangements that then existed.

MORNING LECTURES.—On Tuesday, the 8th, the lecture will be on Charged Electrics and the Theory of the Leyden Phial, with experiments. On Thursday, Respiration and Animal Heat will be continued, with the Effects of Oxygen in the Blood. On Saturday, on Hydrogen Gas and the Composition of Water, Sulphurated and Phosphorated Hydrogen; and a specimen of the philosophical fireworks with the inflammable air will be exhibited.

EVENING LECTURES.—On Monday evening, the 7th, the subject will be Spontaneous Evaporation, Ignition, and Inflammation, with some Remarks on Light. On Wednesday evening, the Different Powers of Bodies as Conductors of Heat; and some Experiments with the Passage Thermometer. The method of confining heat and applying it to useful purposes with economy.

Friday being Good Friday, no lecture will be given on that day.

Those who come to the lectures in carriages are requested to give orders to their coachmen to set down and take up with their horses' heads towards Grafton Street.

A contemporary account says:

During the winter the lecture room was crowded with persons of the first distinction and fashion, as well as by those who had individually contributed much to the promotion of science, and although the northern accent, which he still retained in a slight degree, rendered his voice somewhat inharmonious to a London audience, his modest and unaffected manner of delivering his opinions, his familiar and at the same time elegant language rendered him the object of almost universal kindness and approbation.

Dr. Garnett left Glasgow with the expectation that he should have accommodation for his family in the house of the Institution, and the first disappointment he met with was the opposition to his wishes in this respect. When he gave up his position in Glasgow he fully intended to enter into practice as a physician in London, but from this also he was restrained in great measure by the managers of the Institution.

His biographer says:

The exertions of the winter in some degree injured his health, and the uncertainty he saw in his prospects tended greatly to depress his spirits. He determined, however, to keep his place at the Institution.

In the summer he rejoined his children in Westmoreland, but his anxiety of mind was not diminished or consequently his health improved by the relaxation from active employment. He walked over the same ground and viewed the same prospects that he had formerly enjoyed in the company of his wife. He had not resolution to check the impressions as they arose, and thus, instead of being solaced by the beauties which surrounded him, he gave the reins to his melancholy fancy, which, unchecked by any other remembrance, dwelt only on the affection and virtues of her whose loss he had ever to deplore, the want of whose society he imagined to be the chief source of his misery.

Dr. Garnett showed his own position when he answered the application of Webster for his recommendation as chemical operator.

Kirkby-Lonsdale, September 27, 1800.

DEAR SIR,—I have received your letter, and, in answer to it, must observe that such is my opinion of both your industry and abilities that it would give me pleasure to serve you, and I should with the greatest willingness recommend you to any situation for which I knew you qualified. That you could in time qualify yourself for the situation of operator there is not the smallest doubt, but still it must have been evident to you that if *you* had acted in that capacity last year, imperfect as the lectures were, they must have been much more so; for though I had an operator capable of preparing any experiments that could be made, still it was with the greatest difficulty that I could get through it. How, then, could I have done had my time been taken up with instructing an operator? And, having the greatest number of chemical things to prepare, I could not have got through it with any credit to myself or satisfaction to the managers. You are better acquainted with the duty of an operator than you were before the commencement of the lectures, and can therefore form some judgment concerning the knowledge requisite and the labour which it requires. It is unnecessary to say that an operator must give up his whole time to it; and, as we are to have a good laboratory, it seems to me necessary that he should be a good practical chemist, which he cannot be without working some years in a laboratory. Sadler could do anything in that way, and, were he a little more steady, would be invaluable in the Institution. You say nothing what has become of him. I was in hopes he might have been employed again next year. Indeed, the managers ought, in my opinion, to endeavour to have an operating chemist who would be permanent.

That you could in time do everything required I am very far from doubting, and, should it be the wish of the managers, I shall be far from opposing it; on the contrary, were you qualified, there is not one person whom I should so much wish to have it. But, before you come to a determination, you must well consider whether you would relish the many dirty jobs to which it will subject you as well as the labour; and, if it be still your wish and determination, it would certainly be proper to attend an autumnal course of lectures. If it be your intention to remain in the Institution and to continue as operator, which probably might be carried on along with the School of Mechanics (though of this I am not certain, as an operator's time ought to be dedicated to natural philosophy), I would do all in my power to instruct you properly; but to have the weight upon myself without the prospect of being relieved from it another year is what I dare scarce look at.

In deciding put everything out of the question but the good of the Institution, for unless you can promote that you cannot promote your own by its means. You will, I hope, excuse my having spoken thus freely on the subject which so much concerns us both; consider it well and favour me with your sentiments again. I suppose that I shall be in town in about a month, but I should wish to hear from you before. There are probably some of my objections which you can remove.

I am, dear Sir, yours sincerely,

THOS. GARNETT.

Towards the latter end of the autumn Dr. Garnett returned to the Institution. The differences between him and the managers soon appeared. He prepared the outlines of a course of lectures on Natural and Experimental Philosophy, to be delivered in 1801, and he printed this preface: 'This pamphlet contains the outlines of the popular course on Natural and Experimental Philosophy, delivered at the Royal Institution every Tuesday at two o'clock during the present session.—Royal Institution, February 2, 1801.'

At the same time he printed another pamphlet—'Outlines of a Course of Lectures on Chemistry delivered at the Royal Institution,' and to it he put this preface: 'This work contains the outlines of the course of chemistry delivered at the Royal Institution by the Professor of Natural Philosophy and Chemistry, every Thursday and Saturday at two o'clock during the present season.—Royal Institution, February 2, 1801.'

In the table of contents he gave thirty lectures, and it was almost exactly a reprint of the table of contents of the lectures on chemistry published by him in 1797.

There can be no doubt that Dr. Garnett printed these pamphlets, the one of twelve and the other of two hundred and sixteen pages, without consulting the managers; for at their meeting on February 2, 1801, they resolved that the annual courses of philosophical and chemical lectures at the Royal Institution should commence 'as soon as the new theatre can be got ready for them, and that Count Rumford be authorised to take all such steps on the part of the managers as shall be necessary in that business;' and they also resolved that Sir Joseph Banks, Henry Cavendish, and Count Rumford be a committee to superintend the drawing up and publication of a suitable syllabus or account of the philosophical and chemical lectures given at the Royal Institution. They further resolved that no syllabus of lectures or other account of what is doing or done, or to be done, at the Royal Institution, be published by any person or persons without the permission of the aforesaid committee, or the express leave of the managers formally signified in writing. This last resolution shows that Count Rumford had then probably determined that Dr. Garnett should give up his professorship at the Royal Institution.

On February 16 the managers resolved that their resolutions of February 2 should be communicated to

Dr. Garnett, and on this day they determined to engage Mr. Humphry Davy as Assistant Lecturer on Chemistry. Still the managers did not decide on the removal of Professor Garnett, for the following letter shows that Count Rumford at this time had some conversation with him as to the terms upon which he would give up his rooms in the house. On February 22 Dr. Garnett wrote to Count Rumford:

SIR,—I have considered the matter you did me the honour to desire I would deliberate upon, and I place much confidence that when you and the other managers of the Royal Institution reflect upon the necessary expenditure for rent, coals, and candles, domestics and other out-goings, the sum of 100*l.* per annum will not be considered as an improper allowance for giving up the apartments and advantages assigned me in the house of the Institution by the honourable managers.

You will allow me to add that I have also considered the possibility of my residing out of the house occasioning any inconvenience to the interests of the Institution, and that if upon the maturest consideration I was not confident no such inconvenience could arise, there is no personal compensation that could tempt me to quit my residence in the house of the Institution.

It is with great deference I take the advantage at the same time to submit to your and the other managers' consideration whether the funds of the Institution are in your and their judgment in a condition to authorise any of that gradual increase of my salary of 300*l.* which the resolution of September 14, 1799, gave me well-founded reason to hope for, and which I now most cheerfully and with perfect confidence beg to leave to the candour and liberality of yourself and the managers.

I have the honour to be, with the greatest respect, Sir, your very obedient Servant,

THOS. GARNETT.

On February 23 it was resolved that the consideration of Dr. Garnett's letter be postponed till the annual accounts of the Institution for the present year be made up and the state of its finances ascertained.

The lectures began in February. His biographer says: 'The transactions of the winter almost completely undermined his constitution. He became sallow, listless, melancholy. A gloomy day or the smallest disappointment gave him inconceivable distress.

'The effect produced upon his lecturing was remarkable. Debility of body as well as uneasiness of mind incapacitated him. His spirited and, at the same time modest, method of delivery was changed into one languid and hesitating. He would have resigned in the middle of his course, and on one occasion at least Count Rumford, at a few hours' notice, found a substitute to lecture for him.' This was on the evening of March 2, when with the shortest possible notice Count Rumford got Dr. Crichton to give the lecture on account of the illness of Dr. Garnett.

He again wrote to the managers on May 11, and on the 25th a special meeting of the managers was held, and it was resolved that 'the managers, taking into consideration the two applications of Dr. Garnett, are unanimously of opinion that they cannot agree to make any alteration in his present salary and situation.'

On June 1 Davy was appointed Lecturer on Chemistry.

On June 15 it was resolved by the managers unanimously that Dr. Garnett's resignation should be accepted, that his salary up to the end of the year should be paid to him by the Committee of Expenditure, and that his letter of resignation should be preserved. Unfortunately this letter does not exist now.

'Dr. Garnett had long determined to apply himself to medical practice, and at the same time to give private lectures, to secure that income of which he seemed fated to be disappointed.'

In the summer of 1801 he removed to Great Marlborough Street, and brought his family to London, and he sought for practice as a physician. He built a lecture room; he made arrangements for editing the 'Annals of Philosophy, Natural History, Chemistry, Literature, Agriculture, and Fine Arts' for the year 1800, intending to continue it yearly; and he prepared himself to give not less than eight courses of lectures during the winter. At his own house he gave two courses on Chemistry, one on Mineralogy, one on Botany, two on Experimental Philosophy, and a private course on this subject also; he gave a course on Botany at Brompton, and in a room at Tom's Coffee House, in the City, a course of popular lectures on Zoonomia, or the Laws of Animal Life in Health and Disease. This was for the convenience of medical students and others in that part of the town.

A return of ill health prevented him from completing some of these courses, but he used every means to increase his private practice. In May 1802 he was elected physician to the Marylebone Dispensary, which he thought would bring the success which he seemed never able to obtain. Very weak in body and not exempt from anxiety of mind, he began the hard work of his Dispensary. He caught typhus fever from one of the patients in June, and died on the 28th of that month.

He left his children penniless.

On August 2 Dr. Garnett's executor, Mr. Parker, asked permission to have the popular lectures on the Laws of Animal Life, the Zoonomia, printed at the press of the Royal Institution, and that the printer to the Institution, Mr. W. Savage, might receive subscriptions for the publication of the work. The managers resolved to subscribe for the Institution 50*l.*, and in 1804, when the work was published in quarto, they allowed it to be dedicated to them, a privilege which they refused on many occasions afterwards. The dedication was in these words :

> To the Right Honourable and Honourable the Managers of the Royal Institution of Great Britain these Lectures, composed by a man who, in his lifetime, was honoured by their selection as their first lecturer, and whose infant family have since experienced their benevolence and protection, are, with permission, dedicated by the trustees of the subscription in favour of these orphans.

The amount of the subscription was nearly two thousand guineas.

CHAPTER IV.

THE PROGRESS OF THE INSTITUTION TO THE RESIGNATION OF PROFESSOR YOUNG.

1801 to 1803.

WITH THE LIFE OF DR. THOMAS YOUNG.

1773 to 1829.

IN 1801 Count Rumford continued to carry out his plans at the Institution. In February he engaged Mr. Humphry Davy as Assistant Lecturer on Chemistry, Director of the Chemical Laboratory, and Assistant Editor of the Journals. On March 11 Davy arrived at the Institution and took possession of his situation, and in April he began to lecture.

In this month the managers decided to build five new bed-rooms, forming the south attics, equalising the height of the house.

Sir John Hippesley declined to continue the treasurership. He drew up the following abstract of accounts from the commencement to April 30 of this year: Receipts, 19,257*l.* 8*s.*; Expenditure, 12,601*l.* 2*s.* 1*d.*; Consols, costing 4,471*l.* 5*s.*; Balance at Banker's, 2,185*l.* 0*s.* 11*d.*; Debts due, 4,400*l.*: making a disposable sum of between 10,000*l.* and 11,000*l.* 'Now, as all bills are paid, there are sufficient grounds to hope that the managers will be able not only to finish all the new works, but also to furnish the different apartments and workshops, and complete the arrangement of the establishment in all its details, without incurring any permanent debt, or calling upon the subscribers for any part of the 7,000*l.* which was generously offered for defraying the expense of the new buildings.' Lord Kinnaird was elected treasurer.

In May Count Rumford reported that, 'as a Master of the Workshops will soon be wanted, he had taken considerable pains to find out some person qualified for that office, and he had found a sober, steady, single, mathematical instrument maker, to whom he proposed to give 80*l.* a year and a room in the house.'

Sir Joseph Banks recommended Mr. Böekman, a German chemist, to be engaged in the laboratory at 50*l.* a year and a room in the house.

On May 25 Count Rumford laid before the managers his report on the progress, present state, and probable future prosperity and utility of the Institution. This was ordered to be printed in the Journals of the Institution, and this report, with a paper by Count Rumford—'Observations Relative to the Means of Increasing the Quantities of Heat Obtained in the Combustion of Fuel'—forms the second number of the Journals edited by Rumford alone.

In this paper a picture is seen of the Institution as Rumford wished it to be. Except when prevented by illness and care for his health, he had worked night and day with all his energy to make his prospectus of February 1799 a realised fact. After twenty-eight months the idea was carried out. Rumford's Institution was formed. He gives a long account of all he had done and of all he intended to do. Hence this report is a record of his mind as well as a record of the Institution.

He dismisses the professors, and lectures, and lecture rooms with four lines. He dwells at more length on the spacious and complete chemical laboratory, furnished for carrying on upon a large scale all the various processes of practical chemistry and chemical analysis and for making new and interesting experiments. He speaks of a director of the laboratory, a chemical operator, and an assistant in the laboratory (a very ingenious German chemist), who will devote his whole time to the business of it. Nearly a page is given to the workshops of the Institution, 'where models of new and useful inventions will be constructed and sold at reasonable prices to professors and subscribers.' 'These are quite finished, and are now furnished with the most complete set of tools that can be procured.'

He speaks of the Master of the Workshops, who will take care of the philosophical apparatus and direct the workmen, and says he will likewise superintend and instruct all such ingenious and well-behaved young men as may, at the recommendation of the professors, be admitted into the workshops of the Institution to receive instruction and to complete their education in any one or more of the mechanic arts. The following workmen, he says, are already engaged for the workshops of the Institution, viz.—

A mathematical instrument maker, a model maker, a

cabinet maker, a carpenter, a worker in brass and copper, a tin-plate worker, and an iron-plate worker. To these will soon be added bricklayers and stonemasons, who will be instructed and enabled to instruct others in setting new-invented grates, roasters, ovens, boilers, &c.

A complete kitchen for a small family has been put up for examination in the housekeeper's room. The principal kitchen will be begun in a few weeks. It will contain roasters, ovens, boilers, steamers on the newest and most improved construction, and will be kept in daily use. In order that the proprietors and inventors may be enabled to judge from actual experiment of the merit of any new-method of cooking, or any new dish that may be proposed, a dining room has been built, and will soon be ready for use, at the house of the Institution, in which the managers will occasionally order *experimental dinners*, to which the proprietors and subscribers will be invited, in as far as the accommodations will admit. The expense of such dinners to be defrayed by those who partake of them.

A conversation room has been set apart, so that silence may be kept in the reading rooms. There will be maps, pens, and ink in the conversation room, and as soon as some necessary previous arrangements (which are now actually making) shall be finished, those who frequent this room will be furnished at the most reasonable prices from the housekeeper's room below with soups of various kinds, tea, coffee, chocolate, and other refreshments.

Two letter-boxes have been established in the great hall.

A complete printing office exists. The Journals will appear at regular intervals, probably once a week. The reports of the various committees for specific scientific investigations (which will soon be appointed by the managers) will no doubt furnish much interesting matter for the Journals of the Institution.

Twenty-five foreign periodical scientific publications, and twenty-four domestic periodical scientific and literary publications are regularly taken in. Twenty-four new foreign publications on scientific subjects have been purchased for the library, and many valuable books have been presented. Nine daily newspapers are taken in.

He goes on to say:

One of the most interesting details of the Institution still remains to be mentioned. It is the repository. The measures necessary for forming it have not been neglected, but from its nature it cannot be finished, nor indeed can it be begun, till the establishment is quite complete in all its other essential parts. Models of mechanical inventions and contrivances, in order to their being really useful, must be so made as to serve for imitation; consequently they must be constructed with the greatest care, and they cannot be made in the workshops of the Royal Institution till those shops are fitted up and furnished with the best tools and the best workmen. These workshops will soon be completed and properly manned. In the meantime a spacious and elegant room, 44 feet long and 32 feet wide, with the ceiling supported by two rows of columns, has been built for the repository, and will be finished in a month and ready to receive machines for public inspection. [This was the room beneath the theatre.] It may be useful to observe here that it never was the intention of the managers, nor of any of them, to expose to public view models of machines of all kinds indiscriminately. Considerable alarms have, it is said, been occasioned among some of our principal manufacturers from an idea that the construction of their machines and the valuable secrets of their trade, on which the excellence of their manufactures depend, are in danger of being disclosed by means of the public lectures and exhibitions of the Royal Institution, but the event will show that these apprehensions are without foundation.

The measure lately adopted by the managers for completing the attic story will be finished before the end of November.

As soon as this addition to the buildings shall be completed, and not before, there will be room in the house for the accommodation of a certain number of young men, from eighteen to twenty in number, of different mechanical professions, who, at the recommendation of proprietors, will be taken into the house to be instructed; who will be boarded and lodged in the house and be employed in the workshops, and for whose improvement in drawing, practical geometry, and mathematics an evening school, under the direction of the Clerk of the Works (Mr. Webster), who was formerly a teacher in such a school, will be established in the house in a room adjoining the workshops. As most of the young men who will be admitted to this seminary will probably come from distant parts of the country, and will return home after a residence of three or four months at the Institution, carrying with them a perfect knowledge of such new and useful inventions applicable to the common purposes of life as may be deserving of being generally known and adopted, it is easy to foresee that this arrangement will be of great and extensive public utility. It is, perhaps, that part of the establishment precisely which will be the most interesting, and which will contribute the most powerfully to the attainment of the principal object of the Institution—*the diffusing the knowledge and facilitating the general introduction of useful mechanical inventions and improvements.*

The proprietors, he says, were 325; life subscribers, 268; and annual subscribers, 527.

He concludes thus:

We may safely look forward with confidence to a period not far distant when the Royal Institution of Great Britain, complete in all its details, and in full activity, will become so interesting that every person of liberality and discernment who takes pleasure in contemplating the process of human improvement, will be desirous of belonging to it and willing to assist in promoting its permanent prosperity.

In June Davy was made Lecturer, instead of Assistant Lecturer, in Chemistry, and in a few days Dr. Garnett resigned. A permanent committee, consisting of Charles Hatchett, chairman, Lord Dundas, Mr. Howard, Mr. Chenevix, Mr. Pepys, Dr. G. Pearson, Mr. Nicholson, and Mr. Carlisle, was appointed for the purposes of chemical investigation and analysis; to make such experiments in the laboratory of the Institution as they think useful; Messrs. Hatchett, Howard, and Nicholson were requested to draw up a few short rules for the ordinary meetings and manner of conducting the business of the committee; and once a month or once a fortnight the committee was to be allowed to dine together at the house of the Institution.

The managers resolved that on November 2 Mr. Davy should begin a course of lectures on Tanning; that he should have leave of absence in July, August, and September, to learn the practical part of the business; and that respectable persons of the trade, if recommended by proprietors of the Institution, should be admitted gratis.

In order to obtain more support Count Rumford drew up in his own name a letter to be sent as a circular with a printed fly-leaf. The heading of it ran thus:

Being desirous of becoming a member of the Royal Institution of Great Britain, I request that Count Rumford would propose me to the managers of the said Institution as a candidate for election in the class pointed out in the column below, in which my name is subscribed.

1st class proprietors, who up to May 1802 pay seventy guineas; 2nd class life subscribers, who pay twenty guineas; 3rd class annual subscribers, three guineas.

The letter states that, as the Institution will certainly become more interesting and more useful in proportion as it is made more complete and more extensive in all its numerous details, it is very desirable that as great a number as possible of respectable individuals should be induced to unite in its support and interest themselves in its prosperity; and then, after mentioning that its plan has been much praised abroad, it says:

And if some persons in this country, influenced by misrepresentation or by groundless apprehensions or other motives, have been withheld from giving to the undertaking their countenance and support, the character, reputation, and distinguished rank of many of those who have been most active in promoting it, and who certainly may be supposed to be best acquainted with its nature and tendency, and above all the ostensible patronage of our most gracious Sovereign, who has given so many proofs of his solicitude to encourage useful improvements and to discourage dangerous and doubtful innovations, ought to be sufficient to relieve the doubts of all, and to recommend the Royal Institution of Great Britain to the support of all those who take pleasure in contributing to the diffusion of useful knowledge and the encouragement of industry and ingenuity.

The postscript says:

Any one or more gentlemen of your acquaintance whom you shall recommend will be proposed to the managers, and will no doubt be elected.

Soon after the third number of the Journal was edited by Rumford alone. It contained a paper on the 'Use of Steam as a Vehicle for Conveying Heat, from one Place to another,' by Count Rumford, and 'An Account of a New Eudyometer,' by Mr. Davy.

In July Count Rumford returned to his own house, but he was requested to continue his general superintendence of the works in the same manner as if he had continued to reside in the house. Dr. Young, at the recommendation of Sir Joseph Banks, was made Professor of Natural Philosophy, Editor of the Journals, and Superintendent of the House, with 300*l*. a year and rooms. In the autumn Dr. Young alone edited the fourth number of the Journal, which consisted only of the outlines of a view of galvanism, which Davy had made his first course of lectures.

In August the Committee of Chemistry agreed to the following rules: To meet by summons the third Wednesday of every month at 7 P.M. That all decisions should be by ballot. The decisions respecting experiments to be undertaken should be made by a majority, consisting of three or more members. That the orders to the proper officers of the Institution concerning experiments should be strictly attended to, and be immediately carried into effect. That by unanimous ballot the Committee should elect new members. That every question should be put in writing, proposed, and seconded. That apparatus or materials, if immediately required, should be obtained without reference to the Committee of Managers. That the clerk should attend and take notes of all the proceedings of the Committee.

The managers immediately agreed that no person should be added to any committee without previous consultation with the committee on the qualification of the candidate proposed for election.

In the autumn Count Rumford went to Paris and Germany, and made the acquaintance of Madame Lavoisier. He returned by Paris. The clerk, Mr. W. Savage, wrote to him, probably in December:

In obedience to your commands, I annex an account of the present state of the works at the Royal Institution.

He then gives the state of the laboratory, the workshops for iron and copper, the joiners' workshops, the kitchen, the library, the hall, and passage to the conversation room.

He then says:

The repository is in the same state you left it; indeed, it has been, and is at present, a workshop for the plumbers and glaziers.

The printing office. We are busy printing Dr. Young's syllabus and beginning Mr. Davy's. Dr. Young's is expected to make 10 or 12 sheets. Of Mr. Davy's there is none printed off. It is meant to be 6 sheets. We print 1,000 on common paper and 100 on large paper of Dr. Young's, and 500 on common paper and 50 large of Mr. Davy's. We have printed one sheet for a number of the Journals which contains part of Mr. Davy's paper on Galvanism, but it appears very uncertain when we shall publish it. [This was No. 4.]

The apparatus for warming the lecture room is fitted up. They have tried it, but have not yet been able to raise the temperature more than 5 degrees. It is considerably hotter under the seats, and they have bored a great number of holes through the front of them to admit the hot air into the room.

Mr. Davy's rooms are fitted up; he does not mean to give

separate courses of lectures on tanning, and on staining and printing cotton, but purposes to incorporate them in his general course. The attic floor is far from being finished; they have not yet begun to plaster it, but it is all lathed. There are three additional annual subscribers, one of them through your letter (the circular). The Committee of Chemistry have resolved to recommend to the managers to provide apparatus to the amount of 314*l*. 11*s*. for the laboratory, and to stop the passage through and attach the servants' hall to the laboratory.[1]

He ends his letter thus:

I anxiously wish for your return, as I can perceive that the Institution begins to feel the want of you. I have the honour to be, with the greatest respect, Sir, your most humble Servant,
W. S.

The energy of supervision and the power of organisation of Count Rumford enabled him in 1801 to work out most of his plan; but to keep it in action far more money was wanted than he had obtained, and to perfect it he must have continued much longer to act the part of a dictator. Before 1801 was ended a new and powerful interest began to draw him away from his Institution and from England.

In three years he had made more or less perfect working models of an industrial school for mechanics; of a society for diffusing useful knowledge by publications and lectures; of a mechanical exhibition of things useful to the poor and to the rich; of an association for the promotion of scientific investigation by means of different committees of workers; and of a convenient modern club, with a school of cookery

[1] This was part of the front area.

attached to it. He had included all these objects in one design, and had placed them under one roof.

He was not yet fifty years old, and after the events through which his energy had carried him he saw no difficulty, and thought it would be easy to make his most complicated Institution prove to the world how scientific knowledge might be useful to the lower as well as to the higher classes. He expected to gain the support of the whole nation. He wished that his Institution should be approved by all the world.

The difficulties and dangers that arose as he worked out his plan became only stimulants to his energy, and if engagements at Munich and attractions at Paris had not interfered, he would not have allowed his original Institution to fail from any want of support or from any opposition to his designs.

Already he had made enemies and met with difficulties, and early in 1802 political necessity and private interest led him abroad, and made him agree to changes which affected the foundations of his Institution, and caused it to approach in some respects nearer to its present form. Thus the year 1802 saw the first great change in the management of the Royal Institution.

In the sixth number of the Journal of the Institution the lectures of Young, and in the seventh number the lectures of Davy, which began on January 21, are mentioned by Young thus:

As the object of the Journals is to present to their readers discussions tending either to practical utility or to the lustrations of the principles of science, so particulars of any mode of demonstration either new or not commonly known that may occur in the lectures will be noticed.

Not that anything like an abstract is intended, for this may be found in the compendiums already published; but it may be the more proper to notice some experiments as it has not been possible to introduce an enumeration of experiments into those compendiums.

In a meeting of the Committee of Chemistry of the Institution on the 20th of January it was resolved that—

The Committee of Chemistry, having taken into consideration the present state of knowledge respecting the history of metallic alloys, and being of opinion that this branch of chemistry (so eminently important to science and so useful to various arts) has not been hitherto investigated with due accuracy, resolve that a series of experiments shall be made in the laboratory of the Royal Institution, in order to ascertain with all possible precision the physical and chemical properties of these metallic compounds.

This is probably the germ of Faraday's investigation of the alloys of steel.

Count Rumford moved that all the stock 7,000*l.* in the funds belonging to the Institution should be sold out to pay for the new buildings and other debts.

Early in February it was resolved that each proprietor should have an extra transferable ticket, 'to facilitate the admission of such artists and mechanics as may derive advantage from the public lectures delivered at the Institution, which will give admittance to the gallery only of the great lecture room and to no other part of the house.

'Resolved,—That this new arrangement, which is intended as an experiment, do continue as long as the managers shall deem it expedient.'

On April 12 Count Rumford passed a resolution to increase the payments of life subscribers to forty guineas and of annual subscribers to four guineas, and to elect a new class of subscribers to the lectures only, the payment being two guineas. A requisition had been drawn up and signed to call a general meeting of the proprietors to enlarge the body of managers and visitors to fifteen, and to stop the election of more proprietors. Count Rumford did not sign this requisition. The managers who signed it were Winchelsea, Morton, Pelham, Banks, Sullivan, and Hatchett.

That the management of the Institution at this time was by no means harmonious is seen by a letter of Mr. Webster to his mother, and by his recollections, written some time afterwards, of the failure of the school for mechanics, of which he was to have been master.

January 8, 1802.

I wish I could give you a more favourable account of my situation at the Institution. I believe I told you it did not by any means answer my expectations; the men who conduct it at present cannot always be its managers, and its very system may and probably will be very much altered at some future period. . . . Except some change takes place in the domestic arrangements of the Institution, I do not think that I shall sleep there again; I am sorry to say that whatever good qualities the managers possess—and they are by no means deficient in them—they have shown very little attention to the comforts of those employed in it.

In his recollections he says:

But this project for improving mechanics, well intended as it was, which promised to be so useful, and which had already gained for the Institution 'golden opinions,' was doomed to be crushed by the timidity (for I shall forbear to speak more harshly) of a few. I was asked rudely (by an individual whom I shall not now name) what I meant by instructing the *lower classes* in science. I was told likewise that it was resolved upon that the plan must be *dropped* as *quietly as possible*. It was thought to have a dangerous political tendency, and I was told that if I persisted I would become a *marked man*! It was in vain to argue—the time was unfavourable—and I found the necessity of yielding. No notice was ever given publicly that the idea of instructing the mechanic was abandoned, and I have no doubt but that in many parts of the kingdom the Institution got the credit of great liberality long after the mechanics' school had become extinct.

I have no wish to detail now a thousand circumstances curious enough in a historical point of view connected with my residence in the house of the Royal Institution; suffice it to say that, notwithstanding I became much known and had many friends, yet my chief views being evidently thwarted, and there being no prospect of my situation becoming valuable in a pecuniary way, I thought it was high time to think of my own interest, and I determined on becoming a landscape painter, a profession which then offered considerable prospects in a very agreeable and independent occupation. Count Rumford left England about the same time, certainly neither rewarded nor thanked in proportion to the good he had done.

The management of the Institution now fell into other hands, and, from what appeared to me very erroneous reasoning, my mechanics' stone staircase was pulled down at a considerable expense. All the culinary and other contrivances which the Count and I had taken so much trouble to fit up in the kitchen as an exhibition—and many of them were really good things—were put away. The workmen employed in the house to make models were discharged, there being no one to direct them. The lecture room had been warmed by steam and satisfactorily. When the boiler was worn out (as things will in time) the whole steam apparatus was taken away by the ironmonger then employed, and something of his own was put up, which for years was an annoyance to Mr. Faraday, who did not even know that steam had ever been employed till I informed him. In short, it might seem as if the then managers had resolved that the Institution should *not* be for the application of science to the common purposes of life.

On April 26 Mr. Webster was allowed leave of absence for the benefit of his health until December 1, and he was given 50*l.* on account of his salary. This was his retirement from the Institution. In 1826 he was appointed house secretary of the Geological Society, and Curator of the Museum. He died in 1844, Professor of Geology in the (then) London University.

At the meeting of managers and visitors on the same day Count Rumford made a report on the present state of the Institution. This was the last meeting of the managers that he ever attended.

He said: 'I shall briefly state what has been accomplished since my last report on May 25, 1801, and what still remains to be done to complete this great and interesting establishment in all its details.'

He spoke of the new lecture room as holding nine hundred persons; 'a whisper may be distinctly heard from one extremity to the other, and no echo is ever perceived in it on any occasion.'

This theatre is warmed in cold weather by steam, which, coming in covered and concealed tubes from the lower part of the house, circulates in a large semicircular copper tube eight inches in diameter and above sixty feet long, which is concealed under the rising seats of the pit.

The repository already contains a considerable number of specimens of new and useful mechanical contrivances. The chemical laboratory, in which there is provision made for placing and using no less than sixteen furnaces of different kinds at the same time, is quite finished.

All the workshops of the Institution are now quite finished, and they have been furnished with the most complete sets of tools that could be procured, and several excellent workmen are now employed in them; and a great variety of useful articles designed as models of imitation have already been manufactured in the house, and are ready to be delivered to any of the proprietors or subscribers to the Institution who may be disposed to purchase them.

The great kitchen at the house of the Institution has been furnished, and now contains a variety of new and useful utensils and implements of cookery, many of which are in daily use, and others (which are not) are so exposed to view as to be easily understood and their merit appreciated.

He then gives an account of each room. The present lower library was divided into two rooms, the first for foreign newspapers, the other for books. Over these rooms was the second lecture room, which at some future period was to become the library.

It will be useful for occasional lectures, and for exhibiting new experiments, and for the meetings of the committees.

The conversation room has been furnished, and everything has been prepared for its being used as a coffee room. It is now set apart for the daily papers.

The proprietors since June had increased 16, the life subscribers 16, and annual subscribers 122. All the new works to be done and every demand would amount to 3,900*l.* The balance at the banks and the debts to the Institution came to 8,100*l*. The Institution has been completed without any debt, and the annual income is quite sufficient to defray all the expenses of keeping it up.

He ended thus:

The Royal Institution of Great Britain may therefore be considered as finished and freely established. That it may long continue to flourish is no doubt the ardent wish of those who are connected with it, and also of all those who are acquainted with the principles on which it is founded, and who know how powerfully it must contribute to the general diffusion of an active spirit of inquiry and useful improvement among all the ranks of society.

Such was Count Rumford's favourable statement when he was about to take leave for a time, and, as it proved, for ever, of the Institution he had founded.

The contrast between this report and that which he made to the managers only one week afterwards shows that he was very suddenly made aware of the changes which his absence would occasion in the Institution.

This, his last report, was dated May 3, and it was taken into consideration by the managers the day after he left for Bavaria. He begins by saying that at the desire of the managers he has made some inquiries and taken some preparatory steps for making several new arrangements in the internal regulation of the house of the Institution.

First, of the Journals, to relieve the managers from the care and anxiety which is ever inseparably connected with the direction of business of account, of multifarious detail, and where inspection and control are difficult and sometimes impossible. It was proposed to put the publication of the Journals into the hands of Dr. Young, Mr. Davy, and

Mr. Savage, on conditions which made them take the printing-office without the power of disposing of it.

Second, of the workshops of the Royal Institution. These are proposed to be put into the hands of some respectable tradesman, to be managed by him under certain regulations at his own expense and for his own benefit. Mr. Feetham, a respectable ironmonger of Oxford Street, offered to take charge of the workshops of workers in metal,[1] which is immediately under the managers' room, and carry on at his own expense and risk the same kinds of work with the same workmen.

Charles Royce, who, in the absence of Mr. Webster, acts as an assistant of the professor and chemical lecturer, is ready to engage to carry on the business of the model-makers' workshops at the house of the Institution on his own account, and at his own private expense and risk, promising to furnish at fair prices to all proprietors and subscribers such models as they may order. He will likewise continue to assist Dr. Young and Mr. Davy at their public lectures.

If these arrangements are carried out, the office of Steward of the House and Master of the Workshops, held by Mr. M'Cullock, might be suppressed. Mr. Royce will only require a boy to clean the laboratory.

Of the coffee room and dining room. It has been proposed to give the management of these to some individual who shall agree to furnish the proprietors and subscribers with refreshments at his own account and risk.

He ended his dictatorship with these abdicating words:

All the different subjects mentioned in this report remain for future discussion among the managers.

Many proofs exist that Count Rumford took little counsel from others in founding the Royal Institution.

[1] Now the chemical laboratory, 1871.

In the works of Peter Pindar (Dr. Walcot) (vol. v. p. 458) there is an epistle to Count Rumford containing these lines and this note:

'But what an insolence in me to prate,
Pretend to him to open Wisdom's gate,
Who spurns advice, like weeds, where'er it springs,
Disdaining counsel,[1] though it comes from kings.'

[1] 'Here I must beg leave to differ from the Count. Although a man may, like the Count, possess *extraordinary intellect*, and though a man may be the *best judge* of *himself*, nevertheless it is *indecorous* to treat the opinions of *others* with contempt. The Count's constant assertion is, 'I never was yet in the wrong; I know everything.' Granting this to be true, the declaration nevertheless is *arrogant* and supercilious.'

In the 'Monthly Magazine, or British Register' for May 1815, in a memoir of Count Rumford, speaking of his connexion with the Royal Institution, and of the quarrels which arose among the managers, this passage occurs:

We feel it proper to state that the Count assumed the character of absolute controller, as well as the projector, of this establishment, and conducted himself with a degree of *hauteur* which disgusted its patrons, and almost broke the heart of our amiable friend and its first professor, Dr. Garnett.

And in Dr. Thomas Thompson's 'Annals of Philosophy' for April 1815 a biographical account of Count Rumford is given, and the following inaccurate statement is made:

I pass over his quarrel with the managers of the Royal Institution, about the nature of which I am not fully informed, though I suppose it was an attempt on the part of the Count to retain in his own hands the entire management of that Institution. Be that as it may, the result of the dispute induced him to leave London, to which he never again returned.

Differences with the managers had nothing to do with Count Rumford's departure from London. The immediate cause is seen in his letter to his daughter from Munich on October 2, 1801. He had promised the new Elector to return as soon as the Royal Institution was in order. Dr. Young states that the superiority of the climate of France was partly, if not entirely, the cause of his leaving England. Probably the influence of Madame Lavoisier had its full effect.

Count Rumford left England for Munich on May 9. It is quite certain that when he left he intended to return to his Institution and his house, to his housekeeper and his servants in Brompton Row. It is equally certain that he no longer was on terms of intimacy with Mr. Bernard, who was still a visitor of the Institution, and that he kept up no correspondence during his absence with the other managers regarding his Institution except with Sir Joseph Banks. Before he had left England one month those objects which he had considered likely to bear the best fruits at the Institution were marked for destruction, and they gradually withered away.

The state of the funds was the cause of the immediate change. The bills due were 3,900*l.*, the balance at the bankers' was 3,180*l.* The arrears came to 4,960*l.* 10*s.*, but these were chiefly bad debts.

In 1799 the income was 6,379*l.*; in 1800, 11,047*l.*; in 1801, 3,474*l.*; whilst in 1802 it was only 2,999*l.* Moreover the expenditure was increasing.

Meeting after meeting was held in May 1802 to make arrangements for reducing the expenditure in the workshops and printing-office.' In June the resolution of Count Rumford to increase the rates of subscription to be paid by life and annual subscribers was unanimously rescinded.

In July Dr. Young, when applying for leave of absence, had to ask for the balance of his salary, and Mr. Davy at the same time requests that he may be allowed a part of his salary.

In the autumn the managers seem from the Minutes to have held only two meetings between July 5 and December 6.

But on December 20 Mr. Bernard, visitor, Lord Kinnaird, treasurer, and Mr. Auriol, secretary, were requested by the managers to take into consideration the state of the Institution, and to report their opinion upon such measures and regulations as may appear to them eligible to be adopted for reducing the expenses and increasing the benefit of the Institution.

An accident, as it may be called, this year led the thoughts of Davy to agricultural chemistry, and ultimately gave him a reputation in the country resembling that which Liebig afterwards obtained.

During the summer it was resolved that the Board of Agriculture should be allowed the use of the lecture room for a course of lectures on the Application of Chemistry to Agriculture, provided the subscribers and the proprietors of the Institution were allowed admission; and 'if the professors of the Institution can be of any service in assisting or forwarding the wishes of the Board of Agriculture in giving these lectures, the managers have no objection to their being employed.'

The following year Davy gave in consequence his first course on Agriculture.

In 1803 the existence of the Royal Institution was in peril. This is apparent from a letter written by Sir John Hippesley, in 1820, to the President of the Board of Agriculture suggesting an amalgamation of the two societies. He said: 'I recollect with pain that when I was of the Committee of Managers in the year 1803 (scarcely three years after the date of the charter) our capital was exhausted and the corporation was 3,000*l.* in debt, insomuch that a proposal was then made at the board to shut up the house of the Institution and to bring all the effects to a sale for a discharge of its debts. Fortunately a better determination prevailed. A liberal subscription among the members immediately took place. The debt was paid off and near 3,000*l.* was invested for a time in the public funds. I say for a time, as unfortunately the Institution since that period has not been exempted from the pressure of the general difficulties of the times, and has had to struggle with their severity while its efforts nevertheless have not relaxed in fulfilling the great objects of its establishment. To your Lordship I need not insist upon the extent of these efforts nor the credit due to the general management as well as to the eminent talents and exertions of the able professors and lecturers who have so justly maintained the high scientific celebrity of the Institution in every part of Europe.'

On January 17 Lord Kinnaird, Mr. Bernard, and Mr. Auriol made their first report.

They proposed to continue the existing scientific establishment alone; to reduce the workmen, the printers, and the domestics; and to appoint a sub-committee to watch the expenditure.

Two thousand pounds were wanted for immediate payment of bills, and the managers, visitors, treasurer, and secretary subscribed 100*l.* each, to be repaid to them without interest.

The committee asked for more time in February to prepare the accounts of the Institution.

Early in March an accountant was called in 'to arrange the accounts from the first.'

The result of this investigation is best seen in a report which was drawn up by Mr. Bernard, and which was presented by the visitors to the proprietors, May 2, 1803.

Mr. Bernard reviewed all the expenditure from the first, beginning with the purchase of the house (and the two adjoining houses held under it) for 4,850*l.* For the charter, 583*l.* For arms, 101*l.* For lecture room, repository, laboratory, and workshop, 5,227*l.*, which was 1,800*l.* less than was expected, and 'it has been completed, as the visitors conceive, in a manner and with a degree of attention and economy very creditable to those who undertook the care and direction of it.'[1] . . . 1,181*l.* was paid for fitting up and furnishing the workshops and for experiments incidental to the use of them. 'It is to be observed that a part of this expense ought regularly to be charged to the apparatus. Some loss, however, will probably be incurred upon this article of expenditure, as that part of the arrangement seems to be in a great measure given up. The

[1] This and a line below are the only traces of praise of Count Rumford that are to be found in the records of the Institution.

loss, however, it is hoped, will be inconsiderable, as by a plan recently brought forward by a very scientific member of the Committee of Managers (Mr. Hatchett), it is proposed to form for the use of proprietors, and for the benefit of the Institution, in these and the adjoining rooms, the establishment of a very extensive and useful laboratory, upon a scale of magnitude and with a degree of advantage that are not likely to be equalled in any part of his Majesty's dominions.'

After reviewing the domestic expenditure and the expenditure of the invested principal Mr. Bernard said:

Upon the whole the visitors have the pleasure of stating to the annual meeting that, in the examination of the expenditure incurred in a concern of so great magnitude, under some peculiar circumstances and difficulties and during a period of near four years, they have found the whole of the accounts correctly stated, verified, and balanced except as to a small deficit of 47*l.* 14*s.* 10½*d.* entered as such by mistake, the vouchers for which having been actually produced; and they conceive that there is nothing that merits censure and much that deserves approbation.

With regard to the present state and progress of the Institution he said:

In the supply of useful models, one of its original and most important objects, very little advance is yet made. The lectures and public experiments connected with them will be considerably augmented in the coming season. The new plan for the laboratory promises to increase the scope and utility of it, and at the same time very much to diminish, if not eventually provide for, the expense of that part of the Institution. The library and proposed collection of books of reference will form a library establishment honourable to the British nation, favourable to science, advantageous to the pursuits of scientific men, and very conducive to the increase of the funds and of the utility, prosperity, and permanency of the Institution.

He thus ended his report:

> The fabric of the Royal Institution is now completed by the efforts of individuals. . . . The attempt has been as arduous as the object has been great and important—not less than that of giving fashion to science and of forming a centre of philosophical and literary attraction, for supplying instruction to the young, and rational amusement to mature life, with essential advantages to the public and increase of resources to the country by new discoveries and improvements in the arts and manufactures.

Early in January the managers resolved that Dr. Young and Mr. Davy should give one hundred lectures in the ensuing season, to begin on October 26.

On January 21 Dr. Young proposed to the managers a preface to the second volume of the Journal of the Institution. It was referred to the Select Committee, who advised that at the present period, when, on account of the situation of the finances and expenses of the Institution, a considerable alteration is become necessary in their arrangements, any publication of the kind proposed by Dr. Young had better be deferred for the present. This preface, written by Dr. Young, never was published, and, as it gives a good view of the Institution as it was left by Rumford, it is of interest as a record of the past.

Plan and Regulations of the Royal Institution of Great Britain, Albemarle Street, written by Dr. Thomas Young.

THE professed object of the Royal Institution is the diffusion of useful knowledge, derived from science, and applicable to the purposes of life.

The means proposed for attaining this end are, first, an annual delivery of lectures on the various branches of natural philosophy and chemistry, familiar enough to be intelligible to moderate capacities, and extensive enough to comprehend the most important applications of theory to practice; secondly, the furnishing of a spacious repository with models of such machines, instruments, and utensils as, after sufficient experimental examination, can with confidence be recommended for introduction into common use; thirdly, the establishment of a chemical laboratory, with proper apparatus and materials to be employed in such investigations as are of the greatest practical utility; fourthly, the provision of reading rooms, supplied as well with periodical publications as with works of acknowledged merit, particularly relative to the sciences and the arts; and, lastly, the extension of the benefits derived from the Institution, by publishing from time to time, in its Journals, such improvements as may either have been made by its means, or may have been otherwise suggested by individuals in foreign countries or in our own.

These objects are indeed of too great magnitude to be completely obtained at once; but a considerable progress has already been made in the pursuit of them, and a continuance of the public support alone is required for rendering the Royal Institution as well a natural ornament as a private accommodation.

The lectures are already established on an unprecedented scale, in the order of the systematic compendiums which have been published; and weekly notice is given to the subscribers of the subjects of each lecture. The laboratory has been provided with an ample apparatus; and a number of original experiments have already been made in it, which are immediately connected with the useful arts. The reading rooms are furnished with all new works of importance, both foreign and domestic, which relate to the arts and sciences, as well as with newspapers and all other periodical publications; and they are open daily, from nine in the morning till midnight. A volume of the Journals is completed, and may serve as a specimen of what is to be expected from them when their editors shall be more at leisure to prepare materials for them. But a more complete collection of models and of apparatus can only be obtained by degrees, and in proportion as the funds of the Institution are enabled to support the expense.

The affairs of the Institution are directed by a president and nine managers, elected out of the proprietors at large. Their meetings are usually the first Monday in every month, or oftener.

The professors engage to deliver, annually, not less than fifty lectures each, on natural philosophy and the mechanical arts; and on chemistry, and the chemical arts respectively; to direct and superintend, with the approbation of the managers, the construction of apparatus necessary for their lectures, and of other models and experimental machines proper to be placed in the repository; to collect such information as is requisite for these purposes; and to provide jointly sufficient matter for the publication of the Journals. The Superintendent of the House is charged with the regulation of its internal economy; and the Director of the Laboratory is empowered to make such experiments in it as he may judge likely to promote the views of the Institution.

The clerk is required to attend in the house in general from nine to five, and on the evenings when lectures are delivered from seven to nine; but in particular to be never absent between twelve and four; to be ready every day at one o'clock, to show the various parts of the house to all persons who are entitled to admission; to inspect and arrange the library, to receive payment of subscriptions, to deliver tickets, and to keep all the accounts, under the direction of the managers and of the Superintendent of the House.

The mathematical instrument maker, and other workmen in the immediate service of the Institution, are employed in the construction and repair of apparatus for the lectures and for the repository. The Superintendent of the Workshops assists also in the experiments exhibited by the professors in their lectures, and has the charge of the preparation of all necessary apparatus.

Besides these officers, and the domestic servants of the house, six workmen are at present constantly employed in various departments of the Institution.

Such persons as are desirous of becoming proprietors of the Royal Institution, or subscribers for life, or for any number of years, must be nominated by one of the managers, at a meeting prior to that in which they are elected; but in cases of emergency they may receive temporary tickets of admission as soon as they are nominated, paying their subscriptions, to be returned in case of non-election.

A proprietor pays at present 80 guineas. He receives two transferable tickets of admission to the lectures and to the house in general; but such tickets do not admit the bearer to the reading rooms, unless they have been personally transferred to him, with the consent of the managers, for a time not less than a year.

Subscribers for life pay 20 guineas, and annual subscribers 3 guineas a year. Their tickets admit the possessors to all parts of the house, but they are not transferable.

Ladies who are desirous of subscribing must be recommended by one of the ladies holding books for the purpose. For personal admission to the lectures each lady pays a guinea for the season, but her ticket is not transferable, except among daughters of the same family subscribing with their mother. Ladies subscribing three guineas are entitled to introduce to each lecture any one lady of their acquaintance.

All subscriptions must be paid, either to the clerk or to one of the bankers of the Institution, upon or before the receipt of a ticket of admission; and no annual subscriber can be admitted after the expiration of a former year before the payment of his subscription for the succeeding one.

The lectures are delivered daily at two o'clock, excepting Tuesdays and Fridays, when they are at eight in the evening.

The Journals are usually published every month or oftener, in numbers of two sheets or more; they are sold at the price of a shilling each at the house of the Institution and by the principal booksellers, and they are regularly sent to the houses of all those who wish to be considered as subscribers to them.

Ladies empowered to recommend subscribers:

Duchess of Devonshire, .	Piccadilly.
Countess of Sutherland, .	Arlington Street.
Countess Spencer, . .	St. James's Place.
Countess of Bessborough, .	Cavendish Square.
Viscountess Palmerston, .	Hanover Square.
Hon. Mrs. Barrington, .	Cavendish Square.
Lady Campbell, . . .	Wimpole Street.
Mrs. Sullivan, . . .	Grafton Street.
Mrs. Bernard, . . .	At the Foundling.
Mrs. Crewe, . . .	Lower Grosvenor Street.

Bankers of the Royal Institution:

Messrs. Down, Thornton, Free, and Cornwall, Bartholomew Lane.

Messrs. Herries, Farquhar, and Co., St. James's Street.

Messrs. Hoare, Fleet Street.
Messrs. Ladbrook and Co., Bank Buildings.
Messrs. Pybus, Call, Grant and Hale, Bond Street.
Messrs. Ransom, Morland, and Co., Pall Mall.

The second volume of the Journals never was published. Three sheets only were printed, chiefly containing papers by Young and a few extracts by Davy, and then the Journals of the Institution ceased, and were not revived until 1830, when they were edited for a year and a half by Professor Brande.

On April 21 Dr. Young wrote to the managers a letter, which is lost. On the 26th the managers answered that 'they cannot consent to grant him the increase of salary which he desires for the next year, and with respect to the other situations (Librarian and Keeper of the Library of Reference) which he mentions, as they are appointments which do not at present exist, the managers cannot now say anything regarding them.' This resolution was not communicated to Dr. Young until June 6, and he then gave notice of his wish to resign his appointment. He was asked whether it would be agreeable to him to deliver twenty lectures in the next season, and what would be his subject and his terms. At the next meeting it was resolved that the balance of two years' complete salary should be paid to Dr. Young, and that his engagement with the Institution should terminate from that time, and that, in consideration of his services, he should be proposed to the next meeting to be admitted gratuitously to the privileges of subscribers for life.

In 1804 Dr. Young, in his reply to the articles of Lord Brougham in the 'Edinburgh Review,' gave the following account of his engagement and of its termination:

The reviewer has thought proper to unite, in several instances, with his invectives against me some ridicule of the objects of the Royal Institution of Great Britain—an Institution in which its managers have studied to concentrate all that is useful in science or elegant in literature. This connexion appears to him to add so much weight to his arguments that he has chosen, without further provocation, to insinuate its existence more than a year after it has been dissolved. I accepted the appointment of Professor of Natural Philosophy in the Royal Institution as an occupation which would fill up agreeably and advantageously such leisure hours as a young practitioner of physic must expect to be left free from professional cares. I was led to hope that I should be able to impress an audience, formed of the most respectable inhabitants of the metropolis, with such a partiality as the moderately well-informed are inclined to entertain for those who appear to know even a little more than themselves of matters of science. While I held the situation I wished to make my lectures as intelligible as the nature of the subjects permitted; but I must confess that it was not my ambition to render them a substitute for those of any superficial experimenter that was in the habit of delivering courses of natural philosophy for the amusement of boarding schools. Whatever may have been the imperfections of my lectures, it cannot be asserted, except perhaps in the 'Edinburgh Review,' that they were fit for audiences of ladies of fashion only. After fulfilling for two years the duties of the professorship, I found them so incompatible with the pursuits of a practical physician that, in compliance with the advice of my friends, I gave notice of my wish to resign the office.[1]

[1] *Edinburgh Review*, Nos. II. and IX., 1803, 1804.

In March the Select Committee made their second report.

It recommended the supply and completion of the library, and the formation of an *additional* collection of books for the reference of scientific men, as one of the measures most likely to give permanency and stability to the Royal Institution.

On March 21 Mr. Bernard laid before a meeting of the managers and visitors a plan for these libraries which he had prepared. By April 4 he had obtained subscriptions to the amount of 2,828*l*., and at a meeting of the subscribers they appointed a select committee to consider and report upon the arrangements proper to be made. On April 14 another general meeting of subscribers to the library and collection of reference decided on an address to the proprietors and subscribers to the Royal Institution. Further resolutions were adopted on April 20 and on April 29, the subscriptions having reached 3,798*l*. Regulations were drawn up, and ultimately bye-laws regarding the library and collection of books of reference were made on May 2. The total subscriptions to February 6, 1806, came to 5,395*l*. 10*s*.

This library and collection was an institution within an institution. It had its chief patron, chairman, deputy chairman, treasurer, secretary, and other patrons, its general committee and sub-committees, its accounts, its bankers. Its great object, in addition to the immediate completion of the library, was 'the formation of an extended collection of books of reference, comprehending not only the best publications in practical science, but a library of general and authentic history, political economy, finances, topography, and other departments of knowledge that may be useful to individuals of the United Kingdom, and also to scientific persons of other nations.'

This was formed in the room which is now the upper library. Before the theatre was built it had been the lecture room.

In June Mr. Harris, who had been employed at Mr. Egerton's, the bookseller in Whitehall, was engaged to correct and arrange the library, and to buy the London Library, in Hatton Garden, if he thought it was desirable to do so. It was found to be in a very bad state and was declined.

On July 27, 1803, at the meeting of the general committee of the patrons of the library and collection of reference of the Royal Institution, a letter was read from Mr. Dibden to Mr. Bernard, applying for the situation of principal librarian of the Royal Institution.

> Being a married man with a young family, and having a particular partiality to the study of bibliography, such a situation would be an eligible one and agreeable to my general habits and pursuits.

He enclosed a testimonial from Dr. Jenner.

It was resolved that Mr. Dibden be informed 'that it is not intended to proceed to the choice of a librarian until after Christmas next.'

At the end of April Mr. Hatchett laid before the managers a report on the chemical department of the Institution. He said:

Chemistry was always a primary object of the Institution. A laboratory was therefore erected at an early period, and was furnished with such apparatus as was immediately requisite; but, as the Institution was then in a nascent state, great attention was paid to economy in the chemical department, and although much was in reality wanted to render the laboratory complete, yet nothing more was expended on this part than was absolutely necessary to the immediate demands of the lectures delivered in the Institution. On this account the laboratory has remained in a state inferior to that which might justly be expected in such a liberal and splendid establishment; but, as some extension may now be expected in a department so instructive, so interesting, and so eminently useful, the following intended regulations are submitted to the consideration of the Committee of Managers: 1st. That the workshop lately occupied by Mr. Feetham shall in future be annexed to the laboratory. 2nd. The forge to be adapted to chemical purposes. 3rd. An air-furnace and reverberatory furnace to be built. 4th. Presses and shelves to be added to contain vessels and chemical preparations.

This laboratory will be equal, or indeed superior, to any in this country, and probably to any on the Continent. Such a laboratory, therefore, will accord with the respectability and liberal views of this Institution, which, on the other hand, may henceforward regard this part of its establishment not only as very conducive to its honour, but as likely to produce real and substantial advantages. But to procure these some further regulations appear necessary: 1. Crude materials to prepare pure products should be bought. 2. The Professor shall be assisted by a person well versed in practical chemistry, who shall be expressly engaged to attend the laboratory and assist in the chemical lectures. 3. Operations in the laboratory should be taught. The Institution will derive therefrom honour and profit, and, as far as chemistry is concerned, that one of its chief purposes will be accomplished—the diffusion of knowledge and the application of science to the improvement of arts and manufactures.

On May 2 it was resolved 'that a Committee of Science should be appointed from among the managers to regulate the lectures and public experiments; to direct the publication of the Journals; and to report as to any experiments, or additions to apparatus, or models.' It was to meet weekly and be appointed monthly. Spencer, Banks, Cavendish, Hatchett, Symonds, formed the first committee.

On May 16 the managers resolved 'that the Committee of Science should carry out improvements in the laboratory, that the workshops should be thrown into the laboratory and fitted up as a lecture room for 120 persons.' For nearly sixty years this laboratory theatre remained unchanged.

Other traces of the activity of this Committee of Science are to be found. On May 27 Sir Joseph Banks, in the name of the Committee of Science of the Royal Institution, wrote to the Board of Agriculture:

The Committee do not expect in agricultural analysis the same degree of precise accuracy as is necessary in that intended to illustrate philosophical experiments; it will be enough for them if the component parts of substances and their respective proportions to each other are marked with sufficient precision to demonstrate the probable effects on vegetables.

The Committee are aware that at present the science of agricultural chemistry is in its infancy, and that till it has been more matured each analysis will take up a considerable portion of time; they trust, however, that it will not be long before Mr. Davy himself, or some one named by him and acting under his superintendence, will undertake the business of analysing soils and manures for individuals at a moderate fixed price for each substance that shall be brought to them.

The Royal Institution wish to have Mr. Davy's lectures repeated at their house, and have desired me to ask whether the Board of Agriculture have any objection to a measure which appears to them likely to extend still further.

. . . .

Having been requested to suggest what I think a proper recompense to Mr. Davy on account of his six lectures delivered at the Board, and also a plan for securing his services in future to the Board of Agriculture, I beg leave to propose that sixty guineas be given by the Board to Mr. Davy as a remuneration for his six lectures, being at the rate of ten guineas for each lecture, and that the office of Professor of Chemical Agriculture to the Board, with a salary of 100*l.* a year, be offered to his acceptance; the duty of his professorship to consist of reading lectures in the spring at such time as shall be fixed by the Board, on the application of chemistry to the improvement of the art of agriculture, and in making an analysis of such substances as shall be put into his hands by the Committee, in case he is of opinion that the result of such analysis is likely to throw light on the theory and practice of that most useful art.

This Committee of Science also, as early as July 18, proposed that in the ensuing session Mr. Dalton should be engaged to lecture.

The form which the Institution was at this time about to take is well seen in the joint report of the committees of science and accounts on the plan of the lectures and experiments and other proposed arrangements for the ensuing year. This was made on November 28, 1803; the reporters were Sir Joseph Banks, Henry Cavendish, Sir J. Hippesley, Mr. Bernard, Mr. Sullivan.

They said:

With regard to the lectures on Natural Philosophy, it is presumed that the subjects may be advantageously arranged in the three distinct courses. The first should be a complete course of experimental philosophy; the second should relate to practical mechanics; and the third should be on optics and astronomy.

Abstruseness should in all cases be avoided, the processes of the arts should be particularly described, and the operations should be on such a scale as to instruct by their applications and to interest and amuse by the distinctness and brilliancy of their appearance.

The lectures on Chemistry, it is supposed, may be included in two courses. The first would relate to the chemistry of natural history and the chemical economy of nature, and the second to theoretical and practical chemistry. From the progression of this branch of knowledge it will be easy to develope in both these courses many new objects, and it is supposed that they may at once be rendered useful and made to excite attention and gratify curiosity.

It would be very advantageous to institute a particular and distinct series of public experimental operations, showing such new facts in elementary and natural philosophy as are connected with splendid and curious phenomena or highly useful applications.

During the season it was proposed that there should be one hundred lectures and twenty public experiments—about four lectures weekly.

For affording more practical and minute information concerning the objects of science, first, in relation to mechanical sciences and arts, the models of useful inventions should be increased and made more available; second, in relation to chemistry, the examination of the private experimental processes performed in the laboratory might be given as private instruction, for which those who thought proper to attend should make some annual contribution for defraying the extra expense, as it would be impossible to admit all the proprietors and subscribers.

With the reduction of expenses and the strict economy that has taken place in the establishment, it is submitted to the managers that it will not be necessary to increase at present the annual subscription.

The Committee concludes the report with observations on the progress which has been recently made and is now making in the Institution. After mentioning the lectures and the apparatus for the lectures, it is said the laboratory for experimental processes has been enlarged by the addition of the former workroom, and has been improved by many new arrangements, and provision has been made in it for preparing the different reagents and tests employed in philosophical chemistry and for carrying on various new and interesting researches.

The foundation of a mineralogical collection has been laid by the exertions of Mr. Professor Davy. For the purpose of extending it one proprietor has offered 100*l.*, and others promised to give minerals. A collection of fossils was also made.

The reading library is now completed. The room for the collection of reference, fitted up for 10,000 volumes, some part of which are already purchased. It was proposed to open it to the proprietors and subscribers early in the ensuing season. The funds subscribed amounted to 4,368*l.* 15*s.* As this would not be sufficient to purchase the whole of the desired collection, it was hoped that other proprietors and subscribers 'would enjoy the pleasure of adding their contributions.'

On November 24 Mr. Dalton wrote to Mr. Savage, the clerk:

RESPECTED FRIEND,—As it will not be convenient to me to be in town before the 17th or 18th of next month, I should be glad to know previously whether my accommodation as to board and lodging would be in the Institution; if not, whether you know of any place in the vicinity where the same would probably be procured. It will be necessary for me to spend a considerable portion of time to make myself acquainted with the structure and use of some of the apparatus, and therefore I am the more solicitous on the above heads. Pray, what is the usual duration of a lecture—one or two hours? An immediate reply to these inquiries will much oblige,

Yours respectfully,

J. DALTON.

Apartments were ordered by the managers to be prepared in the house for Mr. Dalton before December 17.

On Monday, December 22, at two, he gave the introduction to a course of four lectures on Mechanics and Physics. In this lecture he dwelt on the objects of natural philosophy, division of the science, utility of the study, plan of the lectures. The second lecture was on Monday, 26, at eight P.M., on the Properties of Matter; extension, impenetrability, divisibility, inertia, various species of attraction and repulsion, *motion*, *forces*, composition of forces, *collision*, *pendulums*. The third lecture was on Wednesday, 28, at two. *Projectiles*; resistance of the air, *mechanic powers*, strength of timber. The fourth on Thursday, at two. Pneumatics; nature of electric fluids, the atmosphere, air-pump, spring and weight of the air proved by experiments, barometer. The last lecture was given on Saturday, 31, at eight. This was followed by other courses, making altogether twenty lectures.

After his return to Manchester Dalton wrotè to his brother, February 1, 1804:

DEAR BROTHER,—I have the satisfaction to inform thee that I returned safe from my London journey last seventh day, having been absent six weeks. It has on many accounts been an interesting *vocation* to me, though a very laborious one. I went in a great measure unprepared, not knowing the nature and manner of the lectures at the Institution nor the apparatus. My first was on Thursday, December 22, which was introductory, being entirely written, giving an account of what was intended to be done; and on natural philosophy in general. All lectures were to be one hour each, or as nearly as might be. The number attending were from one to three hundred of both sexes, usually more than half men. I was agreeably disappointed to find so *learned* and *attentive* an audience, though many of them of rank. It required great labour on my part to get acquainted with the apparatus and to draw up the order of experiments and repeat them in the intervals between the lectures, though I had one pretty expert to assist me. We had the good fortune, however, never to fail in any experiment, though I was once so ill prepared as to beg the indulgence of the audience as to part of the lecture, which they most handsomely and immediately granted me by a general plaudit. The scientific part of the audience was wonderfully taken with some of my original notions relative to heat, the gases &c., some of which had not before been published. Had my hearers been generally of the description I had apprehended, the most interesting lectures I had to give would have been the least relished; but, as it happened, the expectation formed had drawn several gentlemen of first-rate talents together, and my eighteenth, on Heat and the Laws of Expansion, &c., was received with the greatest applause; with very few experiments. The one that followed was on *Mixed Elastic Fluids*, in which I had an opportunity of developing my ideas, that have already been published on the subject, more fully. The doctrine has, as I apprehended it would, excited the attention of philosophers throughout Europe. Two journals in the German language came into the Royal Institution whilst I was there from Saxony, both of which were about half filled with translations from the papers I have written on this subject and comments upon them.

Dr. Ainslie was occasionally one of my audience, and his sons constantly. He came up at the concluding lecture, expressed his high satisfaction, and he believed it was the same sentiment with all or most of the audience.

I saw my successor, William Allen, fairly launched. He gave his first lecture on Tuesday, preceding my conclusion. I was an *auditor* in this case—the first time—and had an opportunity of surveying the audience. Amongst others of distinction the Bishop of Durham was present. In lecturing on optics I got six ribbands—blue, pink, lilac, red, green, and brown—which matched very well, and told the various audience so. I do not know whether they generally believed me to be serious, but one gentlemen came up immediately after and told me he perfectly agreed with me. He had not remarked the difference by candle light.

Throughout the year 1803 scarcely a trace of Count Rumford's name can be found in the records of the Institution. On January 24, when writing from Munich to the clerk, Mr. Savage, about his house in Brompton Row, he only begs his compliments to Dr. Young and to Mr. Davy, and on November 11, the clerk having asked him about an account relating to the Institution, he wrote from Paris:

I assure you that I have not the smallest recollection of having received from Mr. Hunter, the solicitor of the Institution, the account you mention in your letter of the 7th ult.; and had I in fact received it, I should most undoubtedly have laid it before the managers of the Institution. I can imagine no reason which could have induced me to keep it back; and, as all the affairs of the Institution in my hands were kept with the utmost care and regularity, as you can testify, it is not likely that I should have mislaid and forgotten it. This is all I can say on the subject, and I hope and trust that this declaration will be satisfactory to the managers of the Royal Institution and to Mr. Hunter.

I expect to be in England in the course of the winter.

Gradually the 'usefulness of science to the poorer classes and to the common purposes of life' ceased to be the prime object of the Institution. The school for mechanics, the workshops, and the models, the kitchens and the Journals, died away; and the laboratory, the lectures, and the library became the life of the new Institution, and its object became 'the diffusion of knowledge and the application of science to the improvement of arts and manufactures.'

The most memorable scientific incident in the history of the Rumford Institution was its relationship with Dr. Thomas Young. His lectures on physics must even now be held to rank as the greatest work in the literature of the Institution. As Professor and Superintendent of the House he had no great success; and he had no great influence on its fortunes; but by his genius he anticipated the progress of science, and his reputation has risen until it now ranks with that of Davy and Faraday.

A short sketch of his life will bring this period of the history of the Institution to a close.

Thomas Young was born in Somersetshire on June 13, 1773. Both his parents were Quakers, and to their tenets he was accustomed to attribute his resolution to effect any object on which he was engaged. This determination he brought to bear on all he did, and by this he educated himself almost from infancy 'with little comparative assistance or direction from others.'

His earliest years were passed with a grandfather, a merchant at Minehead, who had some classical taste. He encouraged his precocious grandchild and often repeated to him that—

> A little learning is a dangerous thing;
> Drink deep or taste not the Pierian spring.

From 1780 to 1787 (7 to 14) he was chiefly at school. He gives an account of his acquirements in an autobiography written in Latin at this time—writing, arithmetic, Latin, Greek, mathematics, natural philosophy, introduction to the Newtonian philosophy, turning, telescope making, bookbinding, colour making, drawing, Hebrew, botany, fluctions, Priestly on Air, Italian, Chaldee, Syriac, Samaritan. He was a prodigy at fourteen.

His father had a neighbour, a man of great ingenuity, by profession a land-surveyor, in whose office during the holidays the boy was given the use of mathematical and philosophical instruments and the perusal of three volumes of a dictionary of arts and science. He got some practical knowledge of land-surveying. This led him to botany; and to examine his plants he made a microscope. This required a knowledge of optics, and thence he went to mathematics and fluctions.

From 1787 to 1792 (14 to 19) his studies and his position were equally extraordinary. He became classical tutor to a boy a year and a half his junior. Mr. Barclay, of Youngsbury, took him as companion to his grandson, Hudson Gurney, who had a tutor. Young taught the tutor Greek, and taught his companion Latin and Greek, whilst he taught himself Latin, French, Italian, mathematics, natural philosophy, botany, and entomology.

When 16 (1789) he was threatened with consumption. His uncle, Dr. Brocklesby, the friend of Burke, attended him, and through him Burke and Porson and others became interested in the great classical knowledge of the youth, and encouraged him in his translations of Shakespear into Greek iambics.

It was at this period that his character was most strongly formed:

He was never known to relax in any object which he had once undertaken. During the whole term of these five years he was never seen by anyone on any occasion to be ruffled in temper. Whatever he determined on he did. He had little faith in any peculiar aptitude being implanted by nature for any given pursuits. His favourite maxim was, that whatever one man had done another might do; that the original difference between human intellects was much less than it was generally supposed to be; that strenuous and persevering attention would accomplish almost anything; and at this season, in the confidence of youth and consciousness of his own powers, he considered nothing that had been compassed by others beyond his reach to achieve; nor was there anything which he thought worthy to be attempted which he was not resolved to master.

In 1792 he entered the medical profession, learning anatomy from Hunter in London.

In 1793 he became a pupil at St. Bartholomew's Hospital, and on May 30 he had a paper read to the Royal Society on the 'Structure of the Crystalline Lens,' which he thought to be muscular. Hunter claimed the discovery as his, and was only prevented by death from giving the Croonian lecture at the Royal Society in proof of his right. Sir E. Home, in the Croonian lecture the following year, stated that neither Young nor Hunter was right.

In 1794 (æt. 21) he was elected a Fellow of the Royal Society.

About this time the Duke of Richmond, at Bath, thus wrote to Dr. Brocklesby:

Bath, May 5, 1794.

I need not write much about myself, as your nephew, who dined with us yesterday, will give you a good account of my health. I have, however, still returns of headache, and my legs continue very weak. But I must tell you how much pleased we all are with Mr. Young. I really never saw a young man more pleasing and engaging. He seems to have already acquired much knowledge in most branches and to be studious of obtaining more; it comes out without affectation on all subjects he talks upon. He is very cheerful and easy without assuming anything, and even on the peculiarity of his dress and Quakerism he talked so reasonably that one cannot wish him to alter himself in any one particular. In short, I end as I began, by assuring you that the Duchess and I are quite charmed with him, and shall be happy to renew our acquaintance with him when we return to London.

Later in the autumn the Duke, who was Master-General of the Ordnance, offered to make him his private secretary.

In a letter to his mother Young says:

I have very lately refused the pressing offer of a situation which would have been the most favourable and flattering introduction to political life that a young man in my circumstances could desire. I might have lived at a duke's table, with a salary of 200*l.* a year, as his secretary, and with hopes of a more lucrative appointment in a short time. I should have been in an agreeable family, have had time enough for study, a library, a laboratory, and philosophical apparatus at my service; and I was not ashamed to allege my regard for our society as a principal reason for my not accepting the proposal.

In the winter of 1794–5 he went to Edinburgh to study medicine. He learnt Spanish, German, music in theory and by playing the flute, dancing; and he went as much as he could into society and to the play.

Soon after he left Edinburgh in June he wrote to his friend and fellow-student Dr. Bostock:

I have seen Mrs. Siddons in 'Douglas,' the 'Grecian Daughter,' the 'Mourning Bride,' the 'Provoked Husband,' the 'Fatal Marriage,' 'Macbeth,' and 'Venice Preserved.' She was neither below nor much above my expectation. I can form an idea of something more perfect. My friend Cruikshanks, when I went to take my leave of him, took me aside and, after much preamble, told me he heard I had been at the play, and hoped that I should be able to contradict it. I told him 'I had been several times, and thought it right to go,' &c. &c., as civilly as I could. 'I know you are determined to discourage my dancing and singing, and I am determined to pay no regard whatever to what you say. You think I shall never be able to play the flute well, and I am pretty sure that I may if I choose; as to dancing, the die is cast.'

At this time he gave up the dress and all the other peculiarities of the Quakers.

On June 5 he started on a journey through the Highlands 'in se totus teres atque rotundus,' as a friend described him.

I was mounted on a stout, well-made black horse, fourteen hands high, young and spirited, which I had purchased from my friend Cathcart. I had before me my oiled linens, the spencer with a separate camlet cover; under me a pair of saddle-bags, well filled with three or four changes of linen, a waistcoat, and breeches; materials for writing and for drawing; paper, pens, ink, pencils, and colours; packing-paper and twine for minerals; soap, brushes, and a razor; a small edition of Thomson's 'Seasons,' a third flute in a bag; some music, principally Scotch, bound with some blank music-paper; wafers; a box for botanising; a thermometer; two little bottles with spirits for preserving insects; a bag for picking up stones; two maps of Scotland—Ainslie's small one and Sayer's; letters of recommendation. The bags had pockets at the end, one containing a pair of shoes, the other boards with straps and paper for drying plants. I found my bags at first an encumbrance, but became afterwards more reconciled to them. They are to a saddle what pockets are to a coat; and who objects to wearing pockets? But they were wetted the first day and stained their contents. This will make me more careful in future.

Some of his notes at Gordon and Inverary Castles are cabinet pictures.

It was Lady Georgina's birthday (afterwards Duchess of Bedford); the flag was hoisted. Lord Alexander's regiment of little boys was paraded, and employed in racing and dancing on the green, and in the evening a ball was given to the servants; all the family went downstairs and amused themselves with observing the agility of the lads and lasses. Every person employed about the house, except one man, is married, and most of them are descended from those who have served the family before them. The Duchess proposed, in honour of the day, that Sir George Abercrombie and I should dance a reel with the two younger ladies; for they danced nothing but reels. Afterwards the Duke danced with one of the upper servants. Some time after our party joined again in the amusement at the same time with two others; when it was late, and Sir George was tired, we took a girl in his place and resumed the sport. Lady Madeline (Sinclair) sat by, and made the music play till the other sets quitted the field, and left us victorious to reel through the whole room. I have now written as much of dancing in my tour as Johnson has in his, and as much more as a young man may be expected to write of it than an old one.

At Inverary [he writes] after breakfast the party were to ride, and the Doctor gravely submitted to my determination whether I would go at a slow pace with him and the Duke to view the country leisurely on the way, or ride with the ladies and be galloped over. I told him that of all things I liked to be galloped over, and therefore should be of the youthful party. . . .

After dinner the Duke rode again, and the younger men of the party took a walk. I left them about nine, and joined the ladies at tea. I was showing Lady Charlotte some of my sketches; she begged to see my notes, and I showed the greatest part of them. All the family are musical; the ladies sing admirably. Cards and a fine piano occupied the evening. After supper, besides other songs, I heard a most beautiful canzonet by Jackson, beginning 'Love in thy eyes.' It was twelve o'clock when we retired. After breakfast I took my leave, not without regretting that I had so little time to observe the beauties of Inverary. Lady Charlotte is handsomer than Lady Augusta: she sings better, but she has less good sense and less sweetness. An innocent girlishness sometimes gives her the appearance of a little affectation. She is to Lady Augusta what Venus is to Minerva. I suppose she wishes for no more. Both are goddesses.

On October 7 he left London to graduate at Göttingen; he went by Hamburg.

On December 14 he wrote to Dr. Bostock:

You will be pleased, as a lover of the fine arts, to hear that I am taking lessons in drawing. You will not be surprised that I receive in this study, as well as in music and dancing, full approbation from my masters for application and accuracy. At the same time they honestly tell me that ease is wanting, and you will also readily believe that I have the assurance not to be discouraged with this character, while they all assert that I may confidently expect sufficient advancement in due time. . . .

I have not exhibited myself at a public dance. My master, who is a very sensible fellow, advising me against it, as he observed that a person seldom loses the character which he obtains from the first impressions; but we have agreed that I may venture at the next *pique nique*.

On the alternate Sundays we have a dance: either a tea dance or a supper dance; one from four to eight, and the other from five to one. This is called a *pique nique*, and in its constitution resembles a Scotch oyster dance.

Soon after, to his uncle, he says:

Blumenbach has shown me many civilities, but I am most at home at Arnemann's, under whose roof I live, and who has been long in Britain, and brought an English wife home with him. You need not be afraid of my following his example and marrying a German lady. I am not likely to lose my heart here, though there are some tolerably agreeable girls with whom I wish to be more acquainted for the sake of exercise in the language; for conversation with women gives both a fluency of expression and a delicacy of manners which are never to be learned from men.

On April 30 he passed his examination before the Medical Faculty.

I made [says he] no preparatory study, as is usual here, and also at Edinburgh not uncommon, under the name of grinding. The examination lasted between four and five hours. The four examiners were seated round a table, well furnished with cakes, sweetmeats, and wine, which helped to pass the time agreeably. The questions were well calculated to sound the depth of a student's knowledge in practical physics, surgery, anatomy, chemistry, materia medica, and physiology; but the professors were not very severe in exacting accurate answers. Most of them were pleased to express their approbation of my replies. We were all previously obliged to give a summary account of the manner in which our lives had been spent.

He wrote to his uncle towards the close of his residence in Göttingen thus:

I have this morning been upon the back of the Springer. To mount this terrestrial Pegasus is considered here something like *Summos in re equestri honores*, and is seldom attained without long practice. I finish my lessons this week and look back with satisfaction on the health and amusement which have repaid my time and money. It might, perhaps, be more useful to me to take some instruction how to sit in a doctor's chariot; but it is impossible to possess any qualification which one may not want, and capabilities are but light burdens. We have another fashionable exercise, which I think adequately corresponds to the athletic schools of the ancients—vaulting on a wooden horse in various positions—and I am much more known among the students for excelling in this than for writing Greek, of which they have little knowledge and not much more respect.

After being nine months at Göttingen he returned by Brunswick, Gotha, Weimar, Jena, Dresden, and Berlin to England in February 1797. At Brunswick he had a favourable opportunity of exhibiting his personal agility at a court masquerade, where he made his appearance with great success in the character of Harlequin.

From Berlin he wrote, December 12, to his uncle: 'You say my Thesis (for his medical degree, on the conservative forces of the human body) is caviare to the general; but do not you think people have a greater respect for anything out of the common way? It seems a fatality that almost everything I do, or produce, should be termed stiff; in this case it may arise from my having been obliged to treat the subject in a short compass.'

Finding, when he came back from Germany, that the College of Physicians of London required two years' continuous attendance at one university for a licence to practise, and shut out from the Fellowship all who were not graduates at Cambridge or Oxford, he went as fellow-commoner to Emmanuel College, Cambridge; and the account given by one who was afterwards tutor of the college brings the Professor of the Royal Institution most clearly into view.

When the Master [says the writer] introduced Young to his tutors, he jocularly said, 'I have brought you a pupil qualified to read lectures to his tutors.' This, however, as might be concluded, he did not attempt; and the forbearance was mutual: he was never required to attend the common duties of the College.

He had a high character for classical learning before he came to Cambridge; but I believe he did not pursue his classical studies in the latter part of his life—he seldom spoke of them, but I remember his meeting Dr. Parr in the College Combination Room; and when the Doctor had made, as was not unusual with him, some dogmatical observation on a point of scholarship, Young said firmly, 'Bently, sir, was of a different opinion,' immediately quoting his authority and showing his intimate knowledge of the subject. Parr said nothing, but when Dr. Young retired asked who he was, and, though he did not seem to have heard his name before, he said, 'A smart young man that.'

He had a great talent for Greek verse, and on one occasion I remember a young lady had written on the walls of the summer-house in the garden the following lines:—

Where are these hours on airy pinions borne,
That brought to every guiltless wish success,
When pleasure gladdened each succeeding morn,
And every evening closed with dreams of peace?

On the next morning appeared a translation in Greek elegiacs, written under them in Young's beautiful characters.

It may be here mentioned that when his mode of writing Greek was laid before Porson, he said that if he had seen it before he would have adopted it.

The views, objects, character, and arguments of our mathematicians were very different then to what they are now, and Young, who was certainly beforehand with the world, perceived their defects. Certain it is that he looked down upon the science, and would not cultivate the acquaintance of any of our philosophers. Wood's books I have heard him speak of with approbation, but Vince he treated with contempt, and Vince afterwards returned the compliment.

He never obtruded his various learning in conversation, but if appealed to on the most difficult subject he answered in a quick, flippant, derisive way, as if he was speaking of the most easy; and in this mode of talking he differed from all the clever men that I ever saw. His reply never seemed to cost him an effort, and he did not appear to think there was any credit in being able to make it. He did not assert any superiority, or seem to suppose that he possessed it, but spoke as if he took it for granted that we all understood the matter as well as he did. He never spoke in praise of any of the writers of the day, even in his own particular department, and could not be persuaded to discuss their merits. He was never personal; he would speak of knowledge in itself of what was known or what might be known, but never of himself or any other as having deserved anything, or as likely to do so.

His language was correct, his utterance rapid, and his sentences, though without any affectation, never left unfinished; but his words were not those in familiar use, and the arrangement of his ideas seldom the same as those he conversed with. He was, therefore, worse calculated than any man I ever knew for the communication of knowledge.

I remember his taking me with him to the Royal Institution to hear him lecture to a number of silly women and dilettante philosophers. But nothing could show less judgment than the method he adopted; for he presumed, like many other lecturers and preachers, on the knowledge, and not on the ignorance, of his hearers.

In his manners he had something of the stiffness of the Quaker remaining, and, though he never said or did a rude thing, he never made use of any of the forms of politeness. Not that he avoided them through affectation; his behaviour was natural, without timidity, and easy without boldness. He rarely associated with the young men of the College, who called him, with a mixture of derision and respect, 'Phenomenon Young,' but he lived on familiar terms with the Fellows in the Common Room. He had few friends of his own age or pursuits in the University, and not having been introduced to many of those who were distinguished either by their situation or talent, he did not seek their society, nor did they seek him; they did not like to admit the superiority of anyone in *statu pupillari*, and he would not converse with anyone but as an equal.

It is difficult to say how he employed himself; he read little, and though he had access to the College and University libraries he was seldom seen in them. There were no books piled on his floor, no papers scattered on his table, and his room had all the appearance of belonging to an idle man.

I once found him blowing smoke through long tubes, and I afterwards saw a representation of the effect in the 'Transactions of the Royal Society,' to illustrate one of his papers upon sound; but he was not in the habit of making experiments. He walked little and rode less; but, having learnt to ride the great horse abroad, he used to *pace* round Parker's Piece on a hackney: he once made an attempt to follow the hounds, but a severe fall prevented any future exhibition.

He seldom gave an opinion, and never volunteered one. He never laid down the law like other learned doctors, or uttered apophthegms or sayings to be remembered. Indeed, like most mathematicians (though we hear of abstract mathematics), he never seemed to think abstractedly. A philosophical fact, a difficult calculation, an ingenious instrument, or a new invention, would engage his attention; but he never spoke of morals, of metaphysics, or of religion. Of the last I never heard him say a word, nothing in favour of any sect, or in opposition to any doctrine; at the same time, no sceptical doubt, no loose assertion, no idle scoff, ever escaped him.

On July 8, 1799, he sent from Emmanuel College a paper to the Royal Society, entitled 'Outlines of Experiments and Inquiries respecting Sound and Light.' In it he established the great principle of the interference of sounds, and he wrote one section on the analogy of sound and light. In 1800 he referred, in the 'British Magazine,' to a young gentleman of Edinburgh 'who certainly promises, in the course of time, to add considerably to our knowledge of the works of nature, but who had a paper in the "Philosophical Transactions" for 1798, in which what was new was not true, and what was true was not new.' Dr. Robison, in his article on Music in the 'Encyclopædia Britannica,' criticised Young's papers. In Nicholson's 'Philosophical Journal' for 1801 Young answered Robison, and published an extension of the principles of interferences from sound to light. This was the preliminary announcement of his views regarding the undulatory theory of light.

His first paper on the 'Theory of Light and Colours' was read to the Royal Society, November 12, 1801. His second paper on this subject was read July 1, 1802, and his third November 24, 1803. His 'Syllabus of Lectures at the Royal Institution,' dated January 19, 1802, p. 116, gives the first printed account of his views.

He says, 'Speaking of Newton's views, it will be sufficient for our present purpose to enumerate the respective explanations of the principal phenomena of light as they are furnished by the Newtonian system, and by the theory lately submitted to the Royal Society'; and (p. 117) he says, 'The colours of thin and of thick plates, and the fringes produced by inflection, are referred by Newton to the very complicated effects of an undulating medium on the corpuscles of light, but without any attempt to accommodate the explanations to the measures obtained from his own accurate and elegant experiments; those of striated surfaces he has not noticed. But the general law by which all these appearances are governed may be very easily deduced from the interference of two coincident undulations which either co-operate or destroy each other in the same manner as two musical notes produce an alternate intermission and remission in the beating of an imperfect unison.

'The young gentleman of Edinburgh,' afterwards known as Lord Brougham, in the 'Edinburgh Review,' January 1803, criticised the Royal Society papers.

It is difficult [he said] to argue with an author whose mind is filled with a medium of so fickle and vibratory a nature. Were we to take the trouble to refute him, he might tell us, *My opinion is changed*, and *I have abandoned that hypothesis, but here is another for you.* We demand if the world of science which Newton once illuminated is to be as changeable in its modes as the world of taste, which is directed by the nod of a silly woman or a pampered fop? Has the Royal Society degraded its publications into bulletins of new and fashionable theories for the ladies who attend the Royal Institution? *Proh pudor!* Let the

Professor continue to amuse his audience with an endless variety of such harmless trifles, but, in the name of science, let them not find admittance into that venerable repository which contains the works of Newton, and Boyle, and Cavendish, and Maskelyne, and Herschel.

Young's most famous experiment of stopping the rays which passed on one side of a thin card exposed to a sunbeam in a dark chamber Brougham threw aside, with the assertion that the experiment was inaccurately made. Dr. Young replied:

The reviewer has here afforded me an opportunity for a triumph, as gratifying as any triumph can be where an enemy is so contemptible. Conscious of inability to explain the experiment, too ungenerous to confess that inability, and too idle to repeat the experiment, he is compelled to advance the supposition that it was incorrect. 'Let him make the experiment, and then deny the result if he can.'

He took no special means to make his answer known, and only one copy of his reply was sold. The poison sank deep into the public mind, and Dr. Young's researches remained comparatively unnoticed until Arago, in 1815, when reporting upon the optical discoveries of Fresnel, showed that a greater discoverer than Newton had anticipated the researches of the French philosopher.

Dr. Young gives the following account of his discovery of the general law of the interference of light:

It was in May 1801 that I discovered, by reflecting on the beautiful experiments of Newton, a law which appears to me to account for a greater variety of interesting phenomena, than any other optical principle that has yet been made known. I shall endeavour to explain this law by a comparison:—Suppose a number of equal waves of water to move upon the surface of a stagnant lake, with a certain constant velocity, and to enter a narrow channel leading out of the lake; suppose, then, another similar cause to have existed, another equal series of waves will arrive at the same channel with the same velocity, and at the same time with the first. Neither series of waves will destroy the other, but their effects will be combined. If they enter the channel in such a manner that the elevations of one series coincide with those of the other, they must together produce a series of greater joint elevations; but if the elevations of one series are so situated as to correspond to the depressions of the other, they must exactly fill up those depressions, and the surface of the water must remain smooth; at least I can discover no alternative either from theory or from experiment.

Now I maintain that similar effects take place whenever two portions of light are thus mixed, and this I call the general law of the interference of light.

Within three months he became Professor at the Royal Institution.

In 1801, on the 6th of July, Count Rumford reported to the managers that, 'at the recommendation of Sir Joseph Banks, he had had a conversation with Dr. Young respecting his engaging as Professor of Natural Philosophy at the Royal Institution and Editor of the Journals, together with a general superintendency of the house, and it appearing from the report of Count Rumford that Dr. Young is a man of abilities equal to these undertakings, it was resolved that Count Rumford be authorised to engage Dr. Young in the aforesaid capacities at a salary of 300*l.* per annum.'[1]

[1] See Appendix II.

On August 3, at the managers' meeting (Count Rumford in the chair; present, Henry Cavendish, R. J. Sullivan; secretary J. P. Auriol), Count Rumford reported that, agreeably to the authority granted him by the managers, he had engaged Dr. Thomas Young. A copy of his letter to Dr. Young, expressing the conditions of his engagement, was at the same time laid before the committee.

The first number of the Journal had been published by Rumford on April 5, 1800. Dr. Young alone edited the fourth number in the autumn of 1801, the fifth number in December 1801, and, after editing two more numbers alone, he joined with Davy in the editorship till the Journal stopped in 1803.

On January 19 Dr. Young printed, at the press of the Royal Institution, a syllabus of his first course of lectures.

The first part was on Natural Philosophy; the second part on Hydrodynamics; the third part on Physics; and the fourth part on Mathematical Elements.

Each had a Greek or Latin motto prefixed, and the following advertisement to the first part was printed:

In order to adapt the delivery of these lectures as much as possible to the convenience of different persons who may be disposed to attend them, they will be divided into three parts of nearly equal magnitude, and in great measure independent of each other. Two parts will be delivered in succession on Mondays and Wednesdays, at two o'clock, and the third on Friday evenings at eight. And in future winters, each part will be taken in turn for the evening lecture, so that the whole course may be heard at either hour. The fourth part contains all the preliminary knowledge that is necessary for those who may wish to enter mathematically on the various subjects of the lectures; it will save considerable pains in consulting other authors, and the most experienced may often find it convenient for occasional reference. It was the more desirable that something of this kind should be inserted, as mathematical arguments will be avoided as much as possible in the lectures; and for this reason the demonstrations which occur in the syllabus are distinguished from the principal text by a smaller type, and a separate place in the page. In a future edition a fifth part will probably be added, containing a catalogue of the best authors, with references to their works upon each subject. One acknowledgment must, however, be inserted here for the extensive use that has been made of the valuable articles contributed by Professor Robison to the 'Encyclopædia Britannica.'

Royal Institution, Albemarle Street,
January 19, 1802.

The volume forms an octavo of upwards of 250 pages; and it is quite evidence enough that the matter, no less than the manner of the lectures of Dr. Young, were more fitted for Cambridge than for the Royal Institution.

Dr. Paris thus contrasts Davy's manner with that of Young:

To judge fairly of the influence of a popular style we should acquaint ourselves with the effects of an opposite method, and, if an appeal be made to experience, I may very safely abide the issue. Dr. Young, whose profound knowledge of the subjects he taught no one will venture to question, lectured in the same theatre, and to an audience similarly constituted to that which was attracted by Davy, but he found the number of his attendants diminish daily, and for no other reason than that he adopted too severe and didactic a style.

The first afternoon lecture was given by Dr. Young, on Wednesday, January 20, 1802, and the first evening lecture on Friday, January 22.

At the commencement he gave an introductory view of the nature and objects of the Royal Institution and of the particular plan of the lectures. Afterwards he proceeded to the subject of mechanics with the doctrine of motion.

In the introductory lecture, when dwelling on the objects of the Royal Institution and the dissemination of elementary knowledge, he said:

Those who possess the genuine spirit of scientific investigation, and who have tasted the pure satisfaction arising from an advancement in intellectual acquirements, are content to proceed in their researches without inquiring at every step what they gain by their newly-discovered lights, and to what practical purposes they are applicable; they receive a sufficient gratification from the enlargement of their views of the constitution of the universe, and experience in the immediate pursuit of knowledge that pleasure which others wish to obtain more circuitously by its means. And it is one of the principal advantages of a liberal education that it creates a susceptibility of an enjoyment so elegant and so rational.

On the subject of the education of females at the Royal Institution he said:

The many leisure hours which are at the command of females in the superior orders of society may surely be appropriated with greater satisfaction to the improvement of the mind, and to the acquisition of knowledge, than to such amusements as are only designed for facilitating the insipid consumption of superfluous time.

The Royal Institution may in some degree supply the

place of a subordinate university to those whose sex or situation in life has denied them the advantage of an academical education in the national seminaries of learning.

With regard to the special objects of the Institution, the theory of practical mechanics and of manufactures, he said:

> We must be more practical than academies of science and more theoretical than societies for the improvement of arts; while we endeavour at the same time to give stability to our proceedings by an annual recurrence to the elementary knowledge which is subservient to the purposes of both and, as far as we are able, apply to practice the newest lights which may from time to time be thrown on particular branches of mechanical science. It is thus that we may most effectually perform what the idolised sophists of antiquity but verbally professed—to bring down philosophy from the heavens and to make her an inhabitant of the earth.
>
> We may venture to affirm that out of every hundred of fancied improvements in arts or in machines ninety at least, if not ninety-nine, are either old or useless; the object of our researches is to enable ourselves to distinguish and to adopt the hundredth. But, while we prune the luxuriant shoots of youthful invention, we must remember to perform our task with leniency, and to show that we wish only to give additional vigour to the healthful branches, and not to extirpate the parent plant.

He spoke of the repository of models as being a supplementary room for apparatus exhibited and described in the lectures, and 'where a few other articles may perhaps deserve admission.' He mentioned the library and the Journals as free from commercial shackles, but made no mention of the workshops nor of the education of artisans.

When all the advantages which may reasonably be expected from this Institution shall be fully understood and impartially considered, it is to be hoped that few persons of liberal minds will be indifferent to its success or unwilling to contribute to it and to participate in it.

To that regulation which forbids the introduction of any discussions connected with the learned professions I shall always most willingly submit and most punctually attend. It requires the study of a considerable portion of a man's life to qualify him to be of use to mankind in any of them, and nothing can be more pernicious to individuals or to society than the attempting to proceed practically upon an imperfect conception of a few first principles only. In physic the wisest can do but little, and the ignorant can only do worse than nothing; and anxiously as we are disposed to seek whatever relief the learned and experienced may be able to afford us, so cautiously ought we to avoid the mischievous interference of the half-studied empiric. In politics and in religion we need but to look back on the history of kingdoms and republics, in order to be aware of the mischiefs which ensue when fools rush in where angels fear to tread.

With regard to his prospectus and lectures he said:

For the sake of those who are not disposed to undertake the labour of following with mathematical accuracy all the steps of the demonstrations on which the doctrines of the mechanical sciences are founded, I shall endeavour to avoid in the whole of this course of lectures every intricacy which might be perplexing to a beginner, and every argument which is fitter for the closet than for a public theatre. Here I propose to support the same propositions by experimental proofs, not that I consider such proofs as the most conclusive, or as more interesting to a truly philosophic mind, than a deduction from general principles, but because there is a satisfaction in discovering the coincidence of theories with visible effects, and because objects of sense are of advantage in assisting the imagination to comprehend, and the memory to retain, what in a more abstracted form might fail to excite sufficient attention. With regard to the mode of delivering these lectures, I shall in general entreat my audience to pardon the formality of a written discourse in favour of the advantage of a superior degree of order and perspicuity. It would unquestionably be desirable that every syllable advanced should be rendered perfectly easy and comprehensible even to the most uninformed, that the most inattentive might find sufficient variety and entertainment in what is submitted to them to excite their curiosity, and that in all cases the pleasing, and sometimes even the surprising, should be united with the instructive and the important. But, whenever there appears to be a real impossibility of reconciling these various objects, I shall esteem it better to seek for substantial utility than temporary amusement; for if we fail of being useful, for want of being sufficiently popular, we remain at least respectable; but if we are unsuccessful in our attempts to amuse, we immediately appear trifling and contemptible. It shall, however, at all times be my endeavour to avoid each extreme, and I trust that I shall then only be condemned when I am found abstruse from ostentation or uninteresting from supineness. The most difficult thing for a teacher is to recollect how much it cost himself to learn, and to accommodate his instruction to the apprehension of the uninformed. By bearing in mind this observation I hope to be able to render my lectures more and more intelligible and familiar, not by passing over difficulties, but by endeavouring to facilitate the task of overcoming them; and if at any time I appear to have failed in this attempt, I shall think myself honoured by any subsequent inquiries that my audience may be disposed to make.

The division of the whole course of lectures into three

parts was originally suggested by the periodical succession in which the appointed hours recur, but it appears to be more convenient than any other for the regular classification of the subjects. The general doctrines of motion and their application to all purposes, variable at pleasure, supply the materials of the first two parts, of which the one treats of the motions of solid bodies and the other of those of fluids, including the theory of light. The third part relates to the particular history of the phenomena of nature, and of the affections of bodies actually existing in the universe independently of the art of man, comprehending astronomy, geography, and the doctrine of the properties of matter, and of the most general and powerful agents that influence it.

The synthetical order of proceeding from simple and general principles to their more intimate combinations in particular cases, is by far the most compendious for conveying information with regard to sciences that are at all referable to certain fundamental laws. For these laws being once established, each fact, as soon as it is known, assumes its place in the system, and is retained in the memory by its relation to the rest as a connecting link. In the analytical mode, on the contrary, which is absolutely necessary for the first investigation of truth, we are obliged to begin by collecting a number of insulated circumstances, which lead us back by degrees to the knowledge of original principles, but which, until we arrive at these principles, are merely a burden to the memory. For the phenomena of nature resemble the scattered leaves of the Sibylline prophecies; a word only, or a single syllable, is written on each leaf, which, when separately considered, conveys no instruction to the mind, but when, by the labour of patient investigation, every fragment is replaced in its appropriate connexion, the whole begins at once to speak a perspicuous and a harmonious language.

On July 5 he requested leave of the managers to be absent during the months of August and September, taking care in the meantime to provide sufficient matter for the publication of the Journals. He went with the late Duke of Richmond and his brother to France. At Paris he was introduced to the First Consul at the Institute.

This year he was appointed foreign secretary of the Royal Society, and he held this office for the remainder of his life. He refused the appointment of secretary in 1812, because he thought it would interfere with his medical reputation.

In 1803, on January 26, the lectures at the Institution recommenced. Young and Davy each gave weekly two day lectures and one evening lecture. On Tuesday and Friday the lectures were in the evening.

On February 21 Young proposed his preface[1] to the second volume of the Journal of the Institution.

This year, in March, he took his first Cambridge medical degree; he did not receive his degree as Doctor of Medicine until 1808.

On July 4 the engagement of Dr. Young with the Royal Institution terminated.[2]

On October 3 he was elected a subscriber for life for his services to the Institution.

On November 6 he wrote to the managers:

40 Welbeck Street.

I beg to return you my sincere thanks for the privileges of a life subscriber to the Royal Institution, which

[1] See p. 205. [2] See p. 210.

you have conferred upon me. I consider this honour both as a flattering mark of your approbation of the unremitting attention which it was my endeavour to pay to the objects of the Institution while I was employed in its service, and as a substantial advantage in giving me access to a collection of books so valuable as that which is now forming in it. For this privilege I cannot show my gratitude better than by endeavouring to make such use of it as to render the publication of my lectures, which I am preparing, more and more worthy of the Institution in which they were delivered, and fitted to co-operate in its exertions for the advancement and dissemination of mechanical knowledge

After this time Dr. Young took no part in the progress of the Royal Institution. A very short sketch of the remainder of his life, therefore, will be given.

When between thirty-one and forty-one years of age he used his utmost endeavours to succeed in practice in Welbeck Street. In 1804 he married, and he built a house at Worthing, where he practised in the autumn for sixteen years. In 1807 he tried to become physician to the Middlesex Hospital. In this he failed, but he lectured there on Chemistry, Physiology, Nosology, Practice of Medicine, and Materia Medica. Many of the lectures formed afterwards part of his work on 'Medical Literature.'

This year he published his 'Course of Lectures at the Royal Institution' in two quarto volumes. The long delay was occasioned partly from the increase of matter and partly from the difficulty of the engravings. Through the bankruptcy of his publisher, Johnson, he lost the 1,000*l.* he was to receive for his work. The Dean of Ely says of these volumes: 'They form altogether the most comprehensive system of natural philosophy and of what the French call physics that has ever been published in this country; equally remarkable for precision and accuracy in the enunciation of the vast multitude of propositions and facts which they contain, for the boldness with which they enter upon the discussion of the most abstruse and difficult subjects, and for the addition or suggestion of new matter or new views in almost every department of philosophy.'

In the autumn of 1810 he wrote to Sir Joseph Banks an account of 'an agricultural micrometer for measuring the fineness of wool.' See Appendix II.

On January 24, 1811, he was elected one of the physicians of St. George's Hospital. The contest, he says, was almost unparalleled. 'The Cabbells were very naturally confident of triumphant success; parliamentary influence and the natural wish to serve a man who is likely to be Lord Chancellor made Sir S. Romilly's nephew, Dr. Roget, very formidable.' 'Mrs. Young has emerged from death to life by the event of this contest.' Before and after this time he wrote frequently for the 'Quarterly Review,' to which he contributed eighteen articles. Perhaps the most celebrated was on the 'Herculanean Manuscripts,' of which eighteen hundred were discovered. 'It is a consolation to know,' said a friend, 'that Brougham, who took advantage of the growing circulation of the 'Edinburgh Review' to desseminate his vile abuse of you, and Jeffery, who permitted him to do so, should be condemned to hear your praises on all sides, and to feel that the publication in which they are engaged is suffering, and is likely to suffer, by your means.'

In 1814 he was asked to contribute to the new supplement of the 'Encyclopædia Britannica,' but he declined, because 'it was necessary to abstain as much as possible from appearing before the public as an author in any department of science not immediately medical.'

During the next ten years of Dr. Young's life the failure of his efforts to succeed as a physician led him to the highest literary success that could be attained.

In 1814 he began his 'Hieroglyphical Researches,' and throughout the summer and autumn he worked at the Rosetta Stone.

At the end of the year he wrote to Mr. Hudson Gurney, who had got him Champollion's book—'Egypt under the Pharaohs:' 'I have only spent literally five minutes in looking over Champollion, turning by means of the index to the parts where he has quoted the inscription of Rosetta. He follows Akerblad (a Swedish attaché at Paris, a good classical and first-rate Coptic scholar, who had written a letter on this stone to Silvestre de Sacy) blindly, with scarcely any acknowledgment. But he has certainly picked out the sense of a few passages in the inscription by means of Akerblad's investigations, although in four or five Coptic words which he pretends to have found in it he is wrong in all but one, and that is a very short and a very obvious one. My translation is printed; it is anonymous, and must for some time remain so, but everybody whose approbation is worth having will know the author.' In the summer of this year Arago and Gay-Lussac visited him at Worthing. Young then learned what Fresnel was doing on the diffraction of light, and they saw what Young had published in his lectures in 1807.

In 1816 he proposed to the editor of the 'Encyclopædia Britannica' to write for him. He says: 'I would also suggest (in addition to sound) alphabet, annuities, attraction, capillary action, cohesion, colour, dew, Egypt, eye, forms, friction, halo, hieroglyphics, hydraulics, motion, resistance, ship, strength, tides, and waves. Anything of a medical nature which you might think desirable would of course be doubly so to me. Nor should I be difficult with respect to any other subject that might occur to you. L' alti non temo, e l' umili non sdegno.' He contributed sixty-three articles; forty-six were biographical. This year he published his 'Translation of the Hieroglyphics' with a correspondence with De Sacy and Akerblad.

In 1818 he wrote the article 'Egypt' for the Encyclopædia. 'It was pronounced to be the greatest effort of scholarship and ingenuity of which modern literature could boast; yet it was only a popular and superficial sketch of the vast mass of materials which his diligence had collected and his genius had interpreted.'

He was this year appointed superintendent of the 'Nautical Almanac' and secretary of the Board of Longitude, which was established to relieve the Astronomer Royal from all scientific questions regarding the interests of navigation. He immediately set himself to correct all the errors of the Almanac that endangered the safety of ships, but, considering it as intended for nautical and not astronomical use, he resisted the changes which practical astronomers strongly urged on him and on the Government.

In 1822 he wrote to Mr. Gurney from Paris:

In my own pursuits I have found abundance of novelty to interest me, both the scientific and literary departments of the Institute happening at this moment to be particularly engaged with my investigations, and a Frenchman having in each of them been engaged in going over my own ground without being fully acquainted with what I had done, and having had to exclaim, 'Pereant qui ante nos nostra dixerunt.' Fresnel, a young mathematician of the civil engineers, has really been doing some good things in the extension and application of my theory of light, and Champollion, the author of the book you brought over, has been working still harder upon the Egyptian characters. He devotes his whole time to the pursuit, and he has been wonderfully successful in some of the documents which he has obtained.

How far he will acknowledge everything which he has either borrowed or might have borrowed from me, I am not quite confident, but the world will be sure to remark que c'est le premier pas qui coûte, though the proverb is less true in this case than in most others, for here every step is laborious.

The best comparative estimate of the value of the work of Young and Fresnel on light was given by Sir John Herschel, in 1827, at the end of his view of the undulating theory of light in the 'Encyclopædia Metropolitana':

Such is the beautiful theory of Fresnel and Young, for we must not, in our regard for one great name, forget the justice which is due to the other; and to separate them, and to assign to each his share, would be as impracticable as invidious, so intimately are they blended together throughout every part of this system—early, acute, and pregnant suggestion characterising the one, and maturity of thought, fulness of systematic development, and decisive experimental illustration equally distinguishing the other.

During the last five years of Dr. Young's life, when he was between fifty-one and fifty-six years old, he ceased to be a practising physician, and occupied himself with science and literature only.

In 1827, at the anniversary of the Royal Society, after the resignation of the presidency by Sir Humphry Davy, the claims of Dr. Young were too strong to be altogether neglected.

Writing to his sister he says;

I find there has been pretty general conversation about making *me* President of the Royal Society, and I really think if I were foolish enough to wish for the office, I am at this *moment* popular enough to obtain it; but you well know that nothing is further from my wishes.

Davies Gilbert was chosen. 'I told him,' says Young, 'that he had not quite enough of the devil in him, that Sir Joseph Banks should have left his *eyebrows* to go with his cocked hat, if he had left the Society nothing else.'

In the summer of 1828 he visited Paris for the last time on his way to Geneva. He was then one of the eight foreign associates of the Academy. To Mr. Gurney he wrote:

My principal object was Champollion, and with him I have been completely successful as far as I wanted his *assistance*, for, to say the truth, our conferences have not been very gratifying to my *vanity*. He has done so much more and so much better than I had any reason to believe he would or could have done, and, as he feels his own importance more, he feels less occasion to be tenacious of any trifling claims which may justly be denied him, and in this spirit he has borne my criticisms with perfect good humour, though Arago has charged me with some degree of undue severity, and wanted to pass the matter over as not having been published as mine; but to this I could not consent: and, supposing that Champollion might have been unacquainted with the remarks, I thought it a matter of conscience to carry them to him this morning, before I allowed him to continue his profuse liberality in furnishing me with more than I want.

From Geneva Young sent Arago, at his request, a statement of his claims. He gave full justice to Champollion. But when Arago, a few years later, read his éloge of Young, he still said that Young's principle of phonetisation of the hieroglyphics was mixed with error, chiefly by making symbols stand for words and syllables, instead of for letters only. He also denied Young's knowledge of two or more signs for the same letter.

His health up to this time, with the exception before mentioned, had been perfect. During this summer excursion he was most easily fatigued, and appeared to age rapidly.

In a letter written soon after his return he says:

As for myself, I am perfectly content with the life I lead—walking on business of routine every day from eleven to two, the rest of the day sitting over my hieroglyphics, or my mathematics, and conversing in my library with people beyond the Alps or the Mediterranean. I have lost all ambition for a more bustling life, or more active scenes, and I believe I am as happy as a person so old in *soul* is capable of being. In mental faculties I am not yet old, and I amuse myself almost daily with some petty bonnes fortunes among some of the nine sisters. I hear nothing whatever from the Admiralty, and so much the better, except receiving 300*l.* a year instead of four. As for Croker, I never believe a word of his going out, and he may remain in for aught I care, and be Lord Melville's master if he chooses; for the stronger of two heads will generally direct the weaker in the long run. I am deep in the value of life, and I really begin to think that people do live longer than was formerly supposed, though not in the extravagant degree that was asserted.

In 1828, at the Royal Society, when the President, Davies Gilbert, announced Wollaston's donation of 2,000*l.* for the promotion of scientific research and his own gift of 1,000*l.*, Young, as senior officer, returned thanks for the Society. He tells Mr. Gurney, 'I summoned up courage to take the first opportunity of muttering out, "Mr. President, a gentleman on my right says he never heard me make a speech."'

In January 1829 he wrote:

Our new Committee of Longitude is settled, at least for the present, though the radical abuse of the 'Nautical Almanac' is likely to continue; but, fortunately for my security, they have put the Admiralty and the 'Nautical Almanac' together; so they may do their worst. Croker has appointed Sabine and Faraday and me to constitute a scientific committee to advise the Admiralty, which was all that the Board of Longitude would do, and it is better that things should be called by their right names.

Immediately a memorial was sent to the Prime Minister, the Duke of Wellington, against the 'Nautical

Almanac.' A report on this paper was made by Dr. Young in February.

Though his health was at this time rapidly declining, his observations were written with his usual precision and ability, giving way in one instance only to feelings of personal resentment, if a stronger term may not be used, which had been provoked by attacks of unusual violence and bitterness. It is hardly necessary to add that he adhered substantially to the views which he had previously maintained. His death, which took place on May 10, put an end to the contest.

The life of Dr. Young began, continued, and ended strangely. Throughout he was a phenomenon. His course was very different from what might have been expected and quite opposed to that which would have been most suited to him.

He was the great physicist of his time, and yet 'at no period of his life was he fond of repeating experiments or even of originating new ones. He considered that, however necessary to the advancement of science, they demanded a great sacrifice of time; and that, when a fact was once established, that time was better employed in considering the purposes to which it might be applied or the principles which it might tend to elucidate.' He was kind by nature and a Quaker by education, and yet he was always at war for his discoveries. He never was free from a scientific or literary controversy. As a professor at the Royal Institution, as a hospital physician at St. George's, and still more as a practitioner of medicine in London and Worthing, his powers were entirely misdirected.

With a culture like that of Newton what noble fruit might not Young have brought forth! The work he did for science was undervalued during his life; nevertheless he was content; and nothing shows that he foresaw or wished for that great reputation which has gradually gathered round his name. Two years before his death, writing to his sister-in-law regarding the praise which Herschel had given him in his 'Treatise on Light,' he said:

> I think he has divided the prize very fairly, and I dare say poor Fresnel, if he had lived, would have preferred his share of the honour as much as I do mine. It was *before I knew you* that mine was earned, and acute suggestion was then—and indeed always—more in the line of my ambition than experimental illustration. But surely one that is conscious that such things may be said with some truth (or who imagines it) has no further temptation to be President of the Royal Society even if he could.

His character was drawn by Sir Humphry Davy thus: 'A man of universal erudition and almost universal accomplishments. Had he limited himself to any one department of knowledge he must have been first in that department. But as a mathematician, a scholar, and hieroglyphist he was eminent; and he knew so much that it is difficult to say what he did not know. He was a most amiable and good-tempered man; too fond, perhaps, of the society of persons of rank for a true philosopher.'

Mr. Davies Gilbert, the President of the Royal Society, in his speech from the chair on the death of Young, said:

He came into the world with a confidence in his own talents, growing out of an expectation of excellence entertained in common by all his friends, which expectation was more than realised in the progress of his future life. The multiplied objects which he pursued were carried to such an extent, that each might have been supposed to have exclusively occupied the full powers of his mind; knowledge in the abstract, the most enlarged generalisations, and the most minute and intricate details were equally effected by him; but he had most pleasure in that which appeared to be most difficult of investigation. The example is only to be followed by those of equal perseverance.

CHAPTER V.

THE PROGRESS OF THE INSTITUTION TO THE TIME OF FARADAY.

1804 to 1814.

IN 1804 the change in the original management and objects of the Royal Institution was completed. The place which Rumford, with the help of Sir Joseph Banks, had held was taken by Mr. Bernard, who was supported by Sir John Hippesley. He knew nothing of science but much of the world, and his aim for the Institution can be given in his own words. 'The object has been great and important, not less than that of giving fashion to science.'

In the spring the report of the visitors reflected the picture of Mr. Bernard's management, but the shadow of future greatness was there. Mention was made of the intention to carry on original inquiries upon new objects of science.

The visitors said:

There is every reason to suppose that a general interest in favour of the establishment has been created among the inhabitants of the metropolis.

The laboratory has been enlarged by the old workshop; some of the space has been filled up with seats as a theatre for those who attend the experiments of research; an arched opening is being made in the wall in front of the table of the laboratory. This part of the establishment is now found to answer very completely the end of enabling the Professor of Chemistry and his assistants to prepare materials for the chemical lectures, and to carry on original inquiries upon new objects of science. A collection of minerals has been formed of more than 3,000 specimens, principally from presents. Great progress has been made in the library in the old lecture room; the library of the late Thomas Astle, Esq., has been purchased for 1,000 guineas. It contains a variety of scarce and valuable books in ancient British history, topography, and antiquities. It will soon be opened. The model room has been re-arranged, and the number of models slightly increased, but the adequate supply of useful models still continues a desideratum in our establishment, and seems to call for every exertion, as forming so interesting a part of the original prospectus of the Institution. The printing press has been removed; its utility has not been found adequate to its expense. At the same time it has occupied a space in the upper story which may hereafter be employed to greater advantage.

The number and variety of the public lectures have been advantageous.

The great improvements made during the year offer every reasonable prospect of increased advantage and extended utility.

In January Mr. Bernard was full of energy for the lectures. To the managers he said he had reason to flatter himself that Mr. Fletcher, of Cecil Street, would lecture on Natural Philosophy (but Mr. Fletcher could not find room for his course, as Mr. Allen was engaged on the same subject). Mr. Crowe would lecture on History; Dr. Stanger on Physiology, and give another course on Medicine; Dr. James Smith on Botany; John Opie on Painting; Astley Cooper on Comparative Anatomy (but he did not give the lectures). All these courses were not to cost 150*l.*, if in two or three instances the privileges of a life subscriber were granted. Davy was asked to report on the means of escape in case of fire; on lighting the theatre; and whether a plan could be formed for the regular publication of the Journal.

In February the printing office was discontinued and the Journals were given up. Mr. Savage bought the printing press and type and removed them in May, and became printer to the Royal Institution on his own account.

In April all Sir Guy Carleton's manuscripts on the American War, including a copy of the treaty of peace between England and America, signed by Benjamin Franklin, were given to the library. The bye-laws regarding the library of reference were made less strict. In May Mr. Bernard announced his arrangements for the autumn and spring lectures.

Davy agreed to give three courses; the Rev. Sydney Smith two courses of ten lectures each on Moral Philosophy, one from November 10 to January 30 and the other from February 20 to May 20, for 50*l.* and the compliment of a life admission to him and Mrs. Smith. Mr. Fletcher was to give twenty-four lectures on Natural Philosophy; Mr. Landseer, three lectures on Engraving at eight o'clock on Monday evenings; Dr. Crotch, six lectures on Wednesday and Friday evenings.

Two letters written at this time by Sir Joseph Banks to Count Rumford at Paris give some insight into the divisions among the managers, the causes of disagreement, and the different motives that had been working in the Institution almost from its commencement. It is clear that Count Rumford and Sir Joseph Banks especially desired the promotion of scientific knowledge among the poor and the rich, and that Mr. Bernard and Sir John Hippesley believed that the success of the Institution depended upon fashionable popularity. For the first three years the advancement of scientific knowledge was the chief object of the Institution; in the fourth and fifth years this object gave way to that of fashionable popularity, which was sought for until the original investigations of Davy again made science, in the noble function of new discovery, the life of the Royal Institution.

SIR JOSEPH BANKS TO COUNT RUMFORD.

April 1804.

I am very glad to find by your letter that you are well and happy where you now are. In truth, you seem so much so that your friends here begin to suppose you will take root in the soil where you now grow. I cannot, however, disguise that your not appearing in England last year, as I had reason to expect you would have done, has been a material disappointment to me and a great detriment to the Royal Institution.

It is now entirely in the hands of the profane. I have declared my dissatisfaction at the mode in which it is carried on and my resolution not to attend in future. Had my health and spirits not failed me, I could have kept matters in their proper level, but, sick, alone, and unsupported, I have given up what cannot now easily be recovered.

The Royal Society, however, goes on extremely well; our members are industrious, especially Mr. Hatchett, whose chemical discoveries do him every day more and more credit. We shall not now, I trust, go astray, as I think we have not one attending member who is at all addicted to politics.

All our subordinate societies also seem to prosper, and labour diligently in their respective departments; we have newly formed one for the improvement of horticulture, which promises to become very numerous. I send you a book on the subject of heat, &c. (Leslie), which certainly contains many interesting experiments and much bad reasoning. Upon the whole, however, it appears to me that he will not be an unlikely candidate for your medal of the next year. Pray let me have your opinion of the subject; and, if you disapprove of him, who do you think a more successful promoter of the science you wish to encourage?

I send your medals by Mr. ——. This is the first opportunity I have had, or you would sooner have received them. [These were the first Rumford medals, awarded to Rumford himself.]

SIR JOSEPH BANKS TO COUNT RUMFORD.

Soho Square, June 6, 1804.

As it does not prove convenient to Mr. Livingstone to take with him the Society's transactions or the observations of the Royal Observatory, which I wished to have sent, I am obliged to confine myself to the sending the enclosed books—'Leslie on Heat' for your acceptance, the 'Nautical Almanac' for M. Delambre—and the medals which the Royal Society decreed to you a year and a half ago.

On the subject of the first I much wish for your opinion whether the author may be considered a proper person to receive your medal next year; and, if not, who you think a more deserving candidate?

Be so good as to deliver the 'Nautical Almanac' to M. Delambre with my best regards, and to assure the Institute that I shall never forget the various favours I have in my literary character received from them or those which literary people, my friends, have received from them on my account. I honour and respect them both as a body and as individuals more than ever, and look forward with earnest wishes for the time when I may again communicate with them freely, as I once had the happiness of doing. I have received their medallic diplomas for Mr. Cavendish, Dr. Maskelyne, Dr. Herschel, and myself, and will distribute them without delay. Pray remind them, however, that Mr. James Forbes, F.R.S., is still a prisoner among them; though an old man, possibly he does not wish to return home, as his daughter has married into a French family. Possibly other insurmountable obstacles have prevented his release, as the Institute have so nobly and handsomely proved their wish that the Fellows of the Royal Society should be restored to their pursuits of science.

From the tone of your letter it appears to me that you are likely to take root in the soil in which you now grow. I am sorry that you did not return to England, as you gave me every reason to expect you would, last year. Your house at Brompton is an inadequate pledge of your future residence here, as experience has confirmed me in believing.

In the meantime the Institution has irrevocably fallen into the hands of the enemy, and is now perverted to a hundred uses for which you and I never intended it. I could have successfully resisted their innovations had you been here, but, alone, unsupported, and this year confined to my house for three months by disease (gout), my spirit was too much broken to admit of my engaging singly with the host of H.'s and B.'s[1] who had possession of the fortress. Adieu, then, Institution! I have long ago declared my intention of attending no more.

You desire that Davy may have your papers for insertion in the Journals. Alas! the Journals have ceased for more

[1] Hippesleys and Bernards.

than a year, and the printing office is removed from the house of the Institution. Your papers, however, shall be communicated to him, as they have already been to Sir Charles Blagden.

During this year a series of lectures was begun at the Institution by the Rev. Sydney Smith, which for fashionable attraction surpassed any courses that have ever been delivered there.

Mr. Horner thus wrote to Mr. J. A. Murray:

The Temple, November 15, 1804.

I suppose you know that Smith begins to lecture on Moral Philosophy next Saturday at the Royal Institution? You would be amused to hear the account he gives of his own qualifications for the task and his mode of manufacturing philosophy; he will do the thing very cleverly, I have little doubt, as to general manner, and he is sufficiently aware of all the forbearances to be observed. Profound lectures on metaphysics would be unsuitable to the place; he may do some good if he makes the subject amusing. He will contribute, like his other associates of the Institution, to make the real blue-stockings a little more disagreeable than ever and sensible women a little more sensible. It seems to me, for the interest of general conversation, that these subjects should not be quite so unknown to them as to be thought unintelligible pedantry if mentioned in their company; and the impertinence of those who set up as adepts is the price we must pay for this important acquisition. Your chemists and metaphysicians in petticoats are altogether out of nature—that is, when they make a trade or distinction of such pursuits—but when they take a little general learning as an accomplishment they keep it in very tolerable order. Tell me if I take this rightly. I know it is not well settled, and men of letters usually lean too much on one side. Good afternoon.

Mr. Horner wrote another letter to Mr. Thomas Thompson:

The Temple, November 21, 1804.

Our friend Sydney gave his first lecture on Saturday. I was not there, but all the accounts I have collected from different sorts of people agree in its favour, and that it took extremely well.

During the second course Mr. Horner wrote to Lady Mackintosh at Bombay:

The Temple, April 18, 1805.

We have all this winter had but two topics of conversation—Young Roscius and the lectures of the Right Reverend our Bishop of Mickleham.[1] His Lordship's success has been beyond all possible conjecture—from six to eight hundred hearers; not a seat to be found, even if you go half-an-hour before the time. Nobody else, to be sure, could have executed such an undertaking with the least chance of this sort of success; for who else could make such a mixture of odd paradox, quaint fun, manly sense, liberal opinion, striking language? You must have had more than enough of the other great delight of the public—the Roscius. As it is the propensity of all superior minds to admire, I am sorry that this occasion has added another to my own proofs that I must place myself on a very low form; there never was such a rage except that for Sydney.

In the 'Life of Sydney Smith' Lady Holland mentions that Mr. Bernard obtained these lectures for the Institution. She says:

He obtained considerable increase of reputation by a course of lectures on Moral Philosophy, which Sir Thomas Bernard, who interested himself much about the Royal Institution, proposed to him to give. He continued to lecture for three successive years.

[1] Where Mr. Sharpe, Sydney Smith's friend, lived.

On May 17, 1804, a new proposal was made for the advancement of science at the Royal Institution. A special meeting of the managers and visitors was held, and an address to the proprietors and subscribers was read and approved, and ordered to be circulated, respecting the formation of a mineralogical collection and an assay office on a large scale for the improvement of mineralogy and metallurgy.

The Hon. G. F. Greville, Sir J. St. Aubyn, Sir A. Hume, proposed to raise a fund of 4,000*l.* to arrange a collection in a manner which should exhibit all the interesting series of mineralogical facts; and they proposed to establish an assay office, to be exclusively employed for the advancement of mineralogy and metallurgy. They thought that the whole time of a mineralogist of considerable talent would be employed; and that the continued attention of a chemist of approved abilities would be required.

It was proposed that a mineralogical institution like the library institution should be united to the Royal Institution.

The address relating to the formation of this economic museum ended thus: 'The proprietors and subscribers may be assured that the managers and visitors will never consider their labours as finished, while there remains any effort to be made for the diffusion and useful application of *practical science* in this country. They would indeed have deemed themselves extremely culpable if there had been any delay or neglect on their part in submitting to the consideration of their members, and of the public, a plan which promises essentially to promote the prosperity of the Royal Institution, and at the same time to contribute to the extension of useful science and to the increase of our national resources.'

A plan was drawn up. There were to be hereditary patrons, paying 100*l.* and upwards, and patrons for life, paying 50*l.*, and subscribers of smaller sums might unite when they had subscribed sixty guineas and select one of themselves as patron. The patrons were to elect a chairman, a deputy-chairman, a treasurer and a secretary, committees and sub-committees.

In 1804 Lord Dartmouth gave 200*l.* worth of minerals, and Mr. Hatchett gave the cases for them.

In 1805 Davy gave his own collection of minerals, valued at 100 guineas.

The committee rooms were made into the mineral room, and 250*l.* was spent in fitting it up. Davy went to Wales and Ireland to collect minerals, and the following year he again went to the west and north of Ireland, and took with him William Payne, the boy belonging to the laboratory.

At the end of 1805 the rooms for the mineralogical collection were ready, and the arrangement of the mineralogical and geological specimens was made under the directions of Mr. Davy. The minerals and fossils were removed from the model room, where they had been deposited, and in consequence the models were arranged to more advantage.

On June 9, 1806, a report was made by Mr. Bernard on the total failure of the subscriptions to the mineralogical collection. Thereupon the managers resolved that the three original proposers should receive back their subscriptions, and that thanks should be given to them 'for the benefits which they had conferred upon the Institution by suggesting the idea of a mineralogical collection, and by showing that it will be practicable to establish and to support it out of the funds of the Institution.'

In their answer the proposers said:

We concur in your opinion that the space allotted for minerals and the plan pursued by the managers, according to the funds which the Institution can supply, will be found equal to the illustration of very interesting courses of mineralogy and geology, and it is bare justice to Mr. Davy to state that his activity and intelligence in bringing to notice the important facts of the natural history of Great Britain and Ireland, with the aid of the managers to make his assays keep pace with his discoveries, will ensure much credit to the Royal Institution and great benefit to the public.

. . . .

We are still of opinion that, when the importance of a general collection and of a laboratory of assay in constant activity is felt as it ought to be, the influence of the Royal Institution will not be exerted in vain. The plan, which the managers have limited to the present scale of their building and to the funds of their Institution, has obtained general approbation. Its success will give a bias to public opinion favourable to the progress of mineralogy and chemistry, and enable the managers at a future time to extend their buildings, establishments, and plan to the scale which unsuccessfully we ventured to suggest to be better proportioned to their importance.

The original proposal was too scientific and not sufficiently fashionable to agree with the management of Mr. Bernard at this time.

During this year another proposal was made for the good of science at the Institution. This is to be seen in a letter from Mr. Davy to Mr. Bernard, written on June 2:

Dear Sir,—I have reflected on our conversation at Brighthelmstone with regard to the utility of some new arrangements that may be made in the chemical department of the Royal Institution, and I still entertain the same opinions on the subject.

In all universities and places of public scientific instruction it is, I believe, usual for the professors or teachers to admit into their laboratories a certain number of private or operating pupils, who give their aid in the processes that are carried on, and at the same time gain practical information and are of use to the experimenter. I have several times been applied to by subscribers to the Royal Institution who wished to assist in the experiments carried on in the laboratory; but, as I have had no instructions on this point from the managers, I have been unable to give them permission. I do not think any inconvenience could arise from the admission of private pupils in the chemical department of the Institution. Such a plan would gratify many persons, would tend to facilitate the execution of such operations as are carried on, and would coincide with the ends of the establishment without burthening it with any new expense. If you should think that the idea would not be disagreeable to the managers, perhaps you will have the goodness to mention it on Monday.

I enclose a sketch of some regulations for Mr. Sadler and for myself; perhaps similar ones or better ones might be framed for the other persons in the service of the Institution.

I have been thinking upon the lectures of which you furnished the title, and I shall be very glad to give them at the end of the next season.

I am, dear Sir, with the warmest respect, your obliged and grateful H. Davy.

It was resolved by the managers 'that Mr. Davy have permission to admit six subscribers as private pupils in the laboratory in the manner proposed in his letter.' The regulations drawn up by Mr. Davy were read, as well as a draft of the duties of the Professor of Chemistry and the experimental operator at the Institution.

In 1805 the endeavour of Mr. Bernard to make the Royal Institution fashionable was persevered in with zeal and success. Early in the spring he announced eighteen courses of lectures for the following autumn and spring. The visitors reported that 'the success of the Royal Institution was a matter of public notoriety,' that 'all the debts which were owing from the Institution have been paid, and there is every prospect of future surplus. The investments directed by the bye-laws have been continued; these amount to 1,334*l.* 4*s.* The engagement of lecturers of talent and reputation has given increased interest and effect to the Institution, and with little additional expense. Even if otherwise, no contraction of scale ought to be admitted in this most interesting part of the Institution, which furnishes not only an abundant source of amusement, but also the solid materials of instruction and improvement.'

'Though the mineral collection has not proceeded with the same rapidity of success as the library of reference, yet a considerable advance has been made. The subscriptions and the minerals presented already amount to the value of about 1,500*l.* The managers have laudably given up their board and committee rooms in order to prepare suitable apartments for the collection, and have resolved to hold their committees in the library on the days when it is not open to subscribers in general. Notice has been given that the laboratory of assay is ready for that useful and essential part of the plan the analysis of ores and mineral substances.'

The report said that, 'with a view to the permanent success of the Institution, as the popularity of the lectures was so much increased, the terms of subscription were altered and a supplementary list was made of ladies subscribing three guineas and gentlemen six guineas.' The ordinary subscription being two guineas and four guineas, the ladies and unmarried daughters of proprietors were required to subscribe only one guinea, 'as, by relinquishing the transferable right of one of their tickets, they had contributed to the success of the plans which the managers had formed for the improvement of the Institution.'

The visitors ended thus: 'The great degree of improvement and advancement under the auspices of the present managers is shown by this report relating to the accommodation and convenience of those who attend the Institution, instead of dwelling upon the means by which the members might be increased.'

The number of proprietors at this time was four hundred, and the qualification was raised to one hundred and fifty guineas.

A committee of proprietors, managers, and visitors was appointed to revise the bye-laws.

The Rev. Sydney Smith began his second course of lectures on March 23.

He thus wrote in April to Francis Jefferey, Esq.:

Doughty Street, April 1805.

My lectures are just now at such an absurd pitch of celebrity that I must lose a good deal of reputation before the public settles into a just equilibrium respecting them. I am most heartily ashamed of my own fame, because I am conscious I do not deserve it, and that the moment men of sense are provoked by the clamour to look into my claims it will be at an end.

Mr. Landseer gave three lectures on Engraving. From some personal allusions the managers resolved 'that it is their earnest wish that no allusion of a personal nature be ever offered on any account at the lectures of the Institution.' The next year Mr. Landseer was engaged to give six lectures on Engraving, including the substance of those already given, on the same terms as those of the preceding year. In the announcement of the engagement it was said, 'He will endeavour to add a few lectures of a more general nature on the Philosophy of Art.' The lectures were given early in 1806, and on March 17, after the fourth lecture, the minutes of the managers state that Mr. Landseer was called in and informed that the managers understood that his two last lectures, particulary the last, were exceptionable from the personal allusions they contained, and, he having admitted that they were intended as personal allusions, although introduced with a view to vindicate and support the art, and it appearing that Mr. Landseer had before introduced personal allusions in his lectures, notwithstanding notice last season from the managers, it was resolved 'that Mr. Landseer be informed that it is with great regret that the managers feel themselves obliged to direct that his lectures be discontinued.' The steward was ordered to pay Mr. Landseer 30*l*., the sum he was to receive for his course of lectures.

On March 25 Mr. Bernard reported to the managers 'that Mr. Davy will give three courses of lectures in the ensuing season—the first in November, December, and January, upon that part of Practical Chemistry that relates to the Experimental History of Water, the Atmospheric Heat, and Electricity; the second in February and March next, upon the Chemical History of Water and the Atmosphere; and the third in April and May, upon the Modern History of Science.'

On April 1 the clock in the gallery was ordered.

Mr. Dibden agreed to give ten or twelve lectures on the Use and Progress of English Literature.

At the first meeting in May the following professors were proposed for election at the meeting of managers: Professor of Chemistry, Mr. Davy; Natural Philosophy, Mr. Allen; Poetry, Rev. W. Crowe; Belles Lettres, Rev. John Hewlett; and Moral Philosophy, the Rev. Sydney Smith.

The proprietorship was raised to 150 guineas, and at the end of the year to 200 guineas. The mineralogical room was fitted up for the minerals. The laboratory was opened for analyses for persons paying 10*l*. at most. Ventilators were placed in the roof and under the gallery of the theatre. It was impossible to keep out the wet because of the settlement in the foundations, so the roof was new-leaded; and Mr. Soane, the architect, advised that the roof should be examined twice yearly.

On May 29 Mr. Bernard reported to the managers 'that he had been requested by Sir Francis Baring to inform them that a plan similar to that of the Royal Institution was intended to be adopted in London, with a view to the same laudable and beneficial effects as have been produced with such extraordinary success in Westminster under the auspices of the managers of the Royal Institution; that the gentlemen who had taken the active part in the proposed establishment had no other object in view but that of promoting, concurrently with the Royal Institution, the prevalence of science and literature in the metropolis, and in this they have flattered themselves that they shall receive the approbation and assistance of the managers of the Royal Institution.' It was resolved unanimously 'that Sir Francis Baring be informed that the managers view with great satisfaction the exertions of him and the other gentlemen to extend the beneficial effects of science and literature in the metropolis, and that the managers will be ready to give them any aid and assistance which they can with propriety in the execution of their plan, conceiving as they do that the two institutions will not interfere with each other, but will rather increase the public interest in favour of their objects and promote the success of both by the mutual assistance and beneficial co-operation which they may be enabled to render to each other.'

In October Sir Francis Baring invited Sir Joseph Banks to become a vice-president. This he declined by a letter writen on October 14. He, however, expressed his wish to purchase a share in the Institution. He said:

I confess, however, I do not at present foresee the period at which the utility of your new Institution is likely to commence. The Royal Society was set on foot by a number of persons well versed in those matters which its constitution was intended to promote. The Royal Institution was at first wholly under the direction of persons entirely addicted to science, and has not improved since the management of it has passed into other hands. The Athenæum at Liverpool has been formed, I may say, wholly under the immediate superintendence of Mr. Roscow and Dr. Currie. All this I can understand, but how the very worthy and most respectable men you at present look up to as managers of your new Institution will be able to guide it into the paths of science and literature is not to me quite so evident as I sincerely wish it to be.

In 1806 Sir James Mackintosh, writing from India to his friend Mr. Sharp, also shows how fashion, rather than science, had become the characteristic of the Royal Institution.

Your account of the London Institution has delighted and tantalised me. I wish I were a professor! But the printed paper is too general to admit of any discussion. You do not say how many and who are to be professors. It may surely be a little more solid than the fashionable nerves of Albemarle Street could endure without ceasing to be popular.

In 1806 'the attempt to make the Institution fashionable' by means of the number and quality of the lectures seemed to attain the success that Mr. Bernard desired. There was an increase of nearly 3,000*l.* in proprietors' shares and in subscriptions. The debt of 2,000*l.* formed in 1802 was paid off, and the sum in the funds amounted to nearly 4,000*l.* The library was completed by a separate subscription; this amounted to nearly 7,000*l.*, of which about 5,000*l.* was spent in books.

With the exception of the Professor of Moral Philosophy the same professors were this year re-elected.

In the report of the visitors in 1807 the following statement of the lectures and of the general result of the management in 1805–6 and in 1806–7 is made:

Lecturers	Subjects	Number of Lectures. Season 1805–6	Season 1806–7
Mr. Davy . . .	Geology and Chemistry . .	22	28
Mr. Allen. . .	Natural Philosophy . . .	25	32
Rev. W. Crowe .	Poetry and Dramatic Poetry	21	24
Rev. T. F. Dibden	English Literature	10	12
Rev. J. Hewlett	Belles Lettres	8	8
Dr. Crotch . .	Music	13	25
Rev. E. Foster .	History of Commerce . . .	—	8
Mr. Douglas Guest	State of the Fine Arts in Spain	—	4
Mr. Wood . .	Perspective	—	9
Dr. Shaw . . .	Zoology	12	12
Dr. Smith (afterwards Sir James)	Botany	14	14
Mr. Craig. . .	Drawing in Water Colours .	8	8
Rev. Sydney Smith	Moral Philosophy	14	
Mr. Opie . . .	Painting	6	
Mr. Landseer .	Engraving	4	

'Nothing,' the visitors said, 'seems necessary for substantiating and promoting the interests of the Institution but that the managers should proceed in the track which they have hitherto pursued, and should continue to receive that approbation which has so fully rewarded their former labours.'

On May 26, 1806, Mr. Bernard reported to the managers that Mr. Davy would in November next begin a course of twenty lectures in the higher departments of experimental chemistry, on Vegetable and Animal Analysis and on the Experimental History of Heat, Light, and Electricity; and that in the spring he would begin another course of twenty lectures on the Chemistry of Nature, containing elucidations of the design, order, and harmony of the chemical arrangements in the globe. In the first course he proposed to give two lectures a week, on Wednesdays and Saturdays, and in the second course one lecture a week, on Wednesdays; the hour of the lecture to be two o'clock. The ventilation of the lecture room was considered this day.

Mr. Bernard later reported that Mr. Coleridge would give two courses of eight lectures on the Principles Common to the Fine Arts for 120*l.*; to commence in November, every Thursday at two.

Mr. Lawrence, the surgeon, proposed to give a course of lectures on the Animal Economy. These were not accepted. The Rev. Sydney Smith proposed to give a fifth course of eight lectures in the ensuing spring for a compliment of 90*l.*; 'and, in case it should be in his power, he would give some additional lectures, not exceeding six, for a compliment of 10*l.* a lecture.' These lectures circumstances obliged him to give up. He was paid 120*l.* for his third and fourth courses, which he gave in 1806. His lectures were not printed until after his death.

But it was not by the success of the lectures that this year deserves to be remembered in the history of the Institution. Lectures, indeed, are the support of the Institution, but discovery constitutes its great success; and this year is famous for the first of those great discoveries on which the credit of the Institution depends. The union of chemistry and electricity was established by Davy.

Volta sent the first account of his discovery of the voltaic pile to Sir Joseph Banks. His paper was printed in the 'Philosophical Transactions' for 1800—on the 'Electricity Excited by the mere Contact of Conducting Substances of Different Kinds.' Davy, on October 20, 1800, wrote, 'Galvanism I have found, by numerous experiments, to be a process purely chemical,' and on June 18, 1801, the first paper Davy sent to the Royal Society was on a galvanic combination of a single metallic plate and two fluids. In May 1802 he says, 'A battery of immense size has been made for the Institution, and I am now examining the agencies of it upon certain substances that have not been decomposed.' His lectures on Agriculture, Mineralogy, and Geology so occupied his time that very little remained for original research, and it was not until this year that a close examination of the decomposition of water by electricity led him to investigate the action of the voltaic battery, and to establish the union of electricity and chemistry. For this and his former work the name of Davy ought for ever to be inseparably united with the discovery of chemical electricity. But the honour at that time paid to Davy was not for establishing the production of electricity by chemistry, but for endeavouring to prove that all chemical action was caused by electricity. He received no praise as the founder of chemical electricity, but he was looked on as the discoverer of electro-chemistry—that is, of the theory that the electrical condition or polarity of each element determined its chemical action.

The following year (1807) is still more memorable in the annals of the Institution on account of the originality of the discoveries made in the laboratory. No year in the life of the Institution has equalled this in the magic novelty of the results that were obtained. Davy (æt. 28) proved that the bases of the alkalies were solid metals. He called them potassium and sodium, and he showed that they made potass and soda when united with oxygen.

The year 1831 was a noble year for the Royal Institution. In it Faraday (æt. 40) discovered that the magnet produced electricity and founded magneto-electricity.

Great discoveries in different sciences made at different periods do not admit of any accurate comparison. It may, however, be said that in unimagined novelty the results of Davy far surpassed the results of Faraday; for the discovery of magneto-electricity had been foreshadowed by the discovery of electro-magnetism; but in its telegraphic and other applications the discovery of magneto-electricity will keep the name of Faraday for ever in the remembrance of the world.

How much the prosperity of the Institution depended upon Davy was made very evident by his illness, which occurred soon after his discoveries were made. In the early part of the year the managers had not recognised the fact that original discovery belonged to him, and that their committees were useless for investigation. They did give Davy early in the year a new assistant;[1] but on March 9 they resolved that, in consequence of the completion of the chemical laboratory, which was furnished with the necessary utensils and materials for carrying on operations and experiments, 'the chemical professor, besides his regular annual courses of lectures delivered in the lecture room, shall make, direct, superintend, and explain as far as may be necessary all chemical experiments, or courses of experiments, which the managers from time to time shall direct to be made in the laboratory, and give his assistance in all committees appointed by the managers for the purpose of scientific investigation which may require his aid or stand in need of the use of the laboratory for prosecuting their experiments or researches.'

In May the visitors said 'the Institution continued to afford every prospect of realising in their fullest extent those results which its original promoters had in view.'

On July 13 the lectures of Mr. Davy were announced to the managers. In the autumnal session, which was to begin the first week of December, he intended to give twenty-six lectures on the General Elements of Chemistry, and in the spring sixteen lectures on Chemistry in its Connexion with Physiology and the Phenomena of Animated Nature. The same day Mr. Davy informed the managers that he proposed going into Cornwall for five weeks, with a view to collect

[1] Mr. E. Davy, his cousin.

specimens for the collection of minerals, and that he wished William Payne, the attendant on the laboratory, to accompany him. It was resolved that William Payne's expenses in the journey, and those incurred by Mr. Davy in collecting the specimens, should be defrayed by the managers.

In October Davy made his great discoveries,[1] and the last week of November he was laid low with fever, caught whilst disinfecting Newgate Prison.

On December 7 the following notice was ordered to be sent round to the proprietors and subscribers: 'Mr. Davy having been confined to his bed this last fortnight by a severe illness, the managers are under the painful necessity of giving notice that the lectures will not commence until the first week of January next.'

The lectures began on January 13, but Davy did not lecture until March 12.

This interruption of the lectures stopped the income of the Institution in the autumn. The difficulties regarding the finances became urgent. From the time when Davy's support was temporarily removed until the reign of Faraday was far advanced the Institution remained in a state of great poverty.

In 1808 the visitors made the following report on the state of the Institution:

'Since 1803 the bills of each preceding year have been paid out of the subscriptions received in the beginning of the succeeding year. The amount has varied in different years, and is now about 2,000*l*. This was not attended with inconvenience until this year,

[1] See below, p. 350, *Life of Professor Davy*.

when, by some disappointment as to lectures and by the postponement of the autumnal course in consequence of the lamented illness of their excellent Professor of Chemistry, the subscriptions have been diminished and their payment postponed.

'The expenses have increased. The library required 520*l*. There was some extra expense—about 166*l*.—in the laboratory, so honourable to the Royal Institution and so beneficial to the interests of science in every part of the world. The fitting up and forming the mineralogical collection has cost 404*l*.

'It is proposed that 1,461*l*., to be paid by the representatives of Mr. Edward Gray for renewing his lease of one of the adjoining houses, should be spent, and that the cost of the proprietors' shares should be reduced.

'Mr. Soane, the architect of the corporation, and Mr. Harris, the librarian, have made a valuation of the Institution property.

House and buildings, with the two adjoining houses, subject to the existing under-leases and to the proposed lease	£13,000
Books and manuscripts	7,000
Mineralogical collection	1,000
Laboratory and apparatus	450
Mechanical apparatus and models	1,000
Furniture of the house	900
Consols 3½, 1,375 at 64	880
„ 4½, 2,684 „ 83	2,297

'With such a property, exempt from any mortgage or encumbrance, and with views directed to the great and important advantages which science, literature, and morality are deriving and may derive from this royal and public establishment, the anticipation of a part of the next year's income will not be deemed of much importance.

'When it is considered that in the last five years the library of reference and the mineralogical collection have been formed and newly completed, the laboratory very greatly enlarged and improved, and money invested, we trust there will be no one disposed to think unfavourably of the progress of the Institution.

'An anticipation of a part of the next year's income under circumstances from which a more considerable deficiency might have been expected will not make the friends of science and literature doubt of the Royal Institution being now established on a solid and permanent basis.'

The income was stated to be 1,929*l.*, and the expenditure 1,917*l.*

The draft of this report was read by Mr. Bernard to the managers, and they referred it to a sub-committee, who approved it. The Committee of Visitors was then introduced, consisting of Lord Berkeley, Dr. Glasse, Mr. Hammersley, who considered and approved it.

Mr. Dibden was requested to read his opening lecture on Literature on January 13. He began with a short statement of Davy's great discovery and of his illness. Probably Davy was at this time ill in bed; for the managers did not buy him a sofa, for which they paid three guineas, until January 25.

On February 22 Mr. Davy attended the meeting of managers at their request, and said he would commence his course of lectures on Electro-Chemical Science on Saturday, March 12, at two, and those on Geology on Wednesday evening, March 16, at eight.

At the end of the previous year Mr. Bernard had reported that Mr. Coleridge would give in the ensuing session five courses of five lectures each on the Distinguished English Poets, in illustration of the general principles of poetry arranged under the following heads: 1. Shakespear. 2. Spencer and Allegorical Poetry. 3. Milton. 4. Dryden and Pope, and the fifth course Modern Poetry. These lectures were to begin immediately, one or two weekly, as might be convenient, for a compliment of 140*l*., of which 60*l*. was proposed to be paid in advance.

In February Mr. Bernard paid Mr. Coleridge 40*l*. in advance. The lectures were still delayed.

At the end of April Mr. Bernard reported that Mr. Coleridge had offered gratuitously to give a lecture on Education on Tuesday, May 3, proposing it to be twice the length of his other lectures.[1]

On June 13 the steward, Mr. Savage, laid before the managers the following letter from Mr. Coleridge:

DEAR SIR,—Painful as it is to me, almost to anguish, yet I find my health in such a state as to make it almost death to me to give any further lectures. I beg that you would acquaint the managers that, instead of expecting any re-

[1] This lecture was given. In it Mr. Coleridge made a violent personal attack on Mr. Joseph Lancaster, and a year afterwards, at the annual meeting of proprietors, a resolution was carried unanimously that 'this attack was in direct violation of a known and established rule of the Royal Institution, prohibiting any personal animadversions in the lectures there delivered.'

muneration, I shall as soon as I can repay the sum I have received. I am, indeed, more likely to repay it by my executors than myself. If I could quit my bedroom, I would have hazarded everything rather than not have come, but I have such violent fits of sickness and diarrhœa that it is literally impossible. S. T. COLERIDGE.

'Ordered,—That Mr. Coleridge's lectures be discontinued, and that Mr. Savage make out an account of the number of lectures that Mr. Coleridge has given, in order that a proportional payment may be made.'

On June 20, 2,000*l.* being wanted for the payment of the tradesmen's bills and salaries, the managers and visitors subscribed it as a loan without interest. The tradesmen were paid to December 1806.

The terms of subscription to the Institution were altered thus: Annual, four guineas; and life subscription, forty guineas; the qualification for proprietors was reduced to a hundred guineas.

The position of the Royal Institution is well seen in the following report, which the Committee of Managers made to the Committee of Visitors, on the deficiency of the income of the Institution, &c., on March 20, 1809.

They begin by stating 'that the 700 transferable tickets of the proprietors stopped the annual income from subscribers. In January 1803 the corporation were 3,000*l.* in debt. A subscription was made; transferable rights were reduced one-half, so as to allow of a greater number of annual subscribers.

'The effects of the measures were soon felt. The income was more than doubled and public interest attracted to a very great degree. The debts were discharged and near 3,000*l*. invested.'

'The additions that have been made to the Institution by the library of reference, the mineralogical collection (which, by the assistance and exertions of the Professor of Chemistry, has been made at an expense which bears no comparison to its use and value), the laboratory, the seat of his interesting and extraordinary discoveries, the increased variety of the lectures far exceeding anything in contemplation on the forming of the Institution, have frustrated every attempt to keep the scale of expenditure within the average amount of income.

'The annual expenditure, including 1,055*l*. for professors and lectures, is 3,295*l*. To meet this there is 133*l*. dividends, and life and annual subscriptions of not more than 2,000*l*. It is for the interest of the proprietors that some early and decisive measures should be taken for the preservation of their hereditary property, either by new modelling the constitution, so as to make their life and annual subscriptions more productive, or by reducing the expenditure, or by the proprietors and life members paying some annual sum. The proprietors now enjoy much greater advantages than they originally had from the libraries, collections, lectures, and laboratory, and from that in which all Englishmen, and particularly the proprietors of the Royal Institution, must glory, that in our laboratory those discoveries have been made, and are now making, which excite the surprise and admiration of the scientific in every part of the civilised world.

'For the present support of the Institution, and for the discharge of their bills up to January 1808, some of the managers and visitors have advanced on loan without interest 2,300*l*. The sale of the stock and the fine for the sublease will pay the debts of the corporation. The proprietors must decide what it will be prudent and practical to adopt for the support of the Institution.

'If the support of scientific men is to be obtained, something must be done to give the Institution more the form of a public establishment than of private and hereditary property. The managers have no doubt that the friends of science will come forward when the Institution interests the country at large, and they believe the body of proprietors will make any sacrifice of personal interest and advantage to erect a public, national, and permanent establishment devoted to the cultivation of science and to the promotion of every improvement in agriculture, manufactures, and the useful arts of life that may be conducive to the happiness and prosperity of the British Empire. The important researches which have distinguished the laboratory of the Royal Institution, are not only honourable to the proprietors but to the kingdom at large.

'The managers trust that an active co-operation of the proprietors in increasing the number of life and annual subscribers, and a moderate annual subscription for the transferable ticket of each proprietor, will be adequate to secure the stability and prosperity of the Institution, and to continue and extend its influence by the promotion of science and literature, and by the supply of innocent and useful sources of intellectual pleasure.'

The visitors made their report to the proprietors, April 18, thus:

'The circumstances attending our present situation seem to call for much consideration and reflection, and it would become our duty to state what reasonable expectation could be entertained of more income or less expenditure. But the managers have done this, and therefore we forward their report.

'Upon inspection there seems no deficiency of anything which could contribute to the success or general utility of the Institution, and our financial state alone leads us to concur in the necessity of resorting to new measures for the support of so valuable an establishment.

'The visitors heartily concur with the managers in their recommendations.'

In May a committee of the proprietors, with the managers and visitors, was appointed to consider the general state of the affairs of the Institution. The first step was to request Mr. Davy to prepare a plan for the future management of the Institution, and every member of the committee was asked to lay before the committee in writing his ideas or plan. One proposal was to put an annual tax on the transferable tickets; another to get a new charter; another to get an Act of Parliament; and another to shut the Institution at six o'clock daily. By the end of the year the joint committee had formed a plan which was in the following year proposed to Parliament.

The whole of the stock possessed by the Institution, amounting to 4,058*l.*, was sold; the managers and visitors were paid their loan of 100*l.* each without interest, and the bills of 1807 and 1808 were paid.

A communication was made to the Lords Commissioners of the Admiralty and other public boards, suggesting the employment of the Royal Institution laboratory for analyses and reports.

In November the managers decided to publish a statement regarding the Royal Institution. This was probably written by Davy.

The objects of the Royal Institution in it were said to be 'the advancement and diffusion of useful knowledge and the application of experimental science to the purposes of life.'

Regarding the laboratory it said: 'In the laboratory, which is under the direction of the Professor of Chemistry, and which is open to any scientific persons who may propose important chemical investigations, series of experiments are continually carried on. Minerals and substances likely to be useful in agriculture, arts, and manufactures are analysed and researches tending to the progress of useful discovery prosecuted. Of the results of these many have been already published, particularly researches upon tanning; the principles of electrical decomposition; and the nature of the alkalies, earths, inflammable bodies, and acids. In this laboratory there is constructed, in consequence of the liberal contributions of a few individuals, a voltaic apparatus of great power, which will be exhibited in the lectures, and many new experiments will be performed with it and applications of it made to new scientific researches.'

Regarding the lectures it said: 'There are two terms for lectures, one from December 10 to March 1, and the other from March 10 to July 7.'

On November 13 Mr. Hatchett and Mr. Davy reported that Mr. Dalton proposed to give twenty lectures: 3 Mechanics, 2 Pneumatics, 1 Hydrostatics, 2 Steam Engine, 2 Electricity, 2 Meteorology, 2 Astronomy, 6 on Heat and Elementary Principles, to be delivered immediately after Christmas, in the course of six weeks, for a compliment of eighty guineas. Twenty other lectures were to be given by Mr. Allen and Mr. Pond. An evening course on Electro-Chemical Science, to consist of twelve lectures, was to be given by Mr. Davy, to commence in December. A morning course on General Chemistry and its Applications to Nature and to Art, to commence after Easter, and to continue through the session, was also to be given by him.

At the commencement of the year 1810 the managers refused lectures on Physiology and Comparative Anatomy, 'because they could not convince themselves that scientific lectures can be given on these subjects without offence to a part of their audience.'

A few facts will show what the difficulties of the Royal Institution at this time were. Mr. Allen, the Lecturer on Natural Philosophy, was in February paid a hundred guineas for his lectures in 1807. The fine to the city of London for the lease of the house was due at Michaelmas 1809. The lease lapsed because no payment was made. It was not until April that the Institution could arrange the payment. In the spring Mr. Easingwood, the Steward and Clerk of Accounts, left the Institution without notice. The sum he misappropriated was said to be 179*l*. 10*s*. 10*d*.; it was more than 300*l*., and may have been much more. His successor in the office afterwards robbed the Institution of a much greater amount. Temporary relief from some debts was gained by the payment of a fine of 1,500*l*. from the tenant of the corner house in Albemarle St.

The proprietors met early in the year, and agreed to an immediate application to Parliament for an Act for altering and amending the charter, and for enlarging and more effectually promoting the objects of the Institution.

Great expectations of the permanent prosperity of the Institution were formed, in consequence of the proposed conversion of the Institution by Act of Parliament from a private into a public body. Sir John Sinclair took charge of the Bill and conducted it through the House of Commons. It received the royal assent, April 23. The visitors, in their report, said: 'There is every reason to believe that the establishment on its new foundation will at once contribute to our national prosperity and glory. The conduct of the proprietors upon this occasion has been honourable both to themselves and to their country. A fund has been proposed to be raised on the plan of a loan for three years without interest, and payable by instalments of 10 per cent., for carrying the new scheme into effect.' 12,500*l.* was subscribed, but a small part only was wanted, as very few proprietors accepted the composition which was offered to them. The actuary of the Westminster Life Office estimated the value of each life proprietor's share of 100*l.* at 42*l.*

On March 3 Davy gave a lecture on the 'Plan which it is proposed to adopt for improving the Royal Institution and rendering it permanent.' It was printed by desire of the managers. As a record of the Institution in its earlier and in its existing state, and as a reflection of Davy in his full power, this lecture is of surpassing interest. He said:

'The first plan of the Royal Institution was that of a school for promulgating the knowledge and use of important mechanical inventions, for connecting the views of men of science and artisans, and for the application of the sciences to the arts of life. The great feature of the establishment was to be a collection of models of things used for the common purposes of life, and to teach their use and relations to science by lectures. Hence the instruction of manufacturers and workmen was of equal importance with the promotion of the useful arts.

'Soon after the foundation of the Royal Institution, a request was made to one of the greatest practical mechanical philosophers of the age[1] that he would examine the details of the establishment, and become in some way connected with the body. His refusal was prompt and his expression of disapprobation strong. "Your object," says he, "is one that every practical in-

[1] Probably Mr. Boulton Birmingham.

ventor ought to discountenance. You would destroy the value of the labour of the industrious; by laying open his invention you would take away the great stimulus to exertion. Suppose a man, by a great devotion of time and of labour, by skill and ingenuity, has made an important combination in chemistry or mechanics, your object is to publish the details of his labours, to enable every speculator to profit by his knowledge. This, could it happen, would be ruinous to individuals, and would ultimately interfere with the commercial prosperity of Britain; for your enemies would profit by such disclosure more than your country-men, and it would be absolutely throwing away your superiority. Were I persuaded such a plan of models could be executed, I should be seriously alarmed for the manufacturing interest of the country; but I am convinced, from the nature of this part of the scheme, that it will be ephemeral and that it will die even in its cradle." I am not sure that these were the very words of this able reasoner, but I am sure that they convey his sentiments, which were expressed in my hearing.

'The object which at first was only secondary—that of teaching the principles of the sciences by courses of public lectures—soon became the prime object. The only difficulty resulted from the nature of the audiences. To afford satisfaction to all by one series of subjects was impossible. Numerous courses were consequently established. A great library of reference was added, and a mineral collection has likewise been formed. An object which I hope I shall be pardoned for being partial to is the laboratory, which, though formed upon a small scale and supplied with a small apparatus only, may yet, by its effects, tend to demonstrate the importance and uses of such a foundation in the metropolis.

'It would be indelicate for me to be the historian of the whole of the progress of this part of the establishment, nor should I have entered upon it at all except in consequence of the circumstance that though it is generally known that some new philosophical facts have been ascertained here, yet it is not generally known that the chemical apparatus of the Royal Institution has given aid upon several occasions to the useful arts, and that assistance has been afforded to various great public bodies.

'There is another object on which I can dwell with more pleasure and more propriety; I mean the voltaic apparatus, which has been formed in consequence of a fund raised by subscription. Without a public establishment like the Royal Institution this great light of new science might have been lost to us, and it is not the less honourable to the character of the nation that the efforts of private individuals have effected what in other countries flows only from the Government.

'The new plan of the Royal Institution is intended to exalt and enlarge all those parts of the establishment which are acknowledged to be useful and profitable, so as to create a permanent foundation and means which can never be misapplied for the advancement of every species of useful knowledge.

'Besides the diffusion of knowledge by popular philosophical lectures, and by other more elementary and more scientific lectures, the new plan will also embrace a design for the promotion of knowledge by experiments and original investigations. It is proposed that the members of the body shall meet at least once every week for the purpose of inquiry and discussion. At these meetings any new facts that have arisen in the progress of science will be stated, any important hints for experiments pursued, and in the progress of investigation those subjects will be most particularly attended to which promise to increase the perfection of arts and manufactures.

'That the diffusion and improvement of science may not be limited to those persons only who can personally attend the Institution, it is proposed to publish Journals at least quarterly.

'Having described the philosophical objects, it may be necessary to say something of the manner in which it is conceived the income of the Institution may be made permanent.

'In the original plan, as the prime object was the founding a collection of models and the diffusing the knowledge of useful mechanical inventions, it was but strict justice that these models should be regarded as private property, and belong to the persons by whom they were originally purchased or their heirs, and that this property, being of the nature of common property, might be also transferred by sale.

'But, this idea being found impracticable, and new and more exalted objects having arisen from this foundation, and the Royal Institution having fortunately taken the form of a body for promoting experimental science and for diffusing every species of philosophical knowledge, it is obvious that the principles upon which its funds are to be raised and its members elected will require considerable alteration.

'On the new plan it is proposed upon a compensation, which, after long discussion, has been regarded as the most equitable, to do away entirely the saleable and hereditary rights, so as to leave no vestiges of them in the constitution of the body, and to elect new members, properly recommended, only by ballot.

'The original scheme, by making the proprietary interest perpetual, left no means for the renovation of the funds, except by adding new burdens to the establishment.

'In giving up their private interests for the purpose of founding what may be called a national establishment, the proprietors of the Royal Institution have a right to expect the support and encouragement of their countrymen; and though they will be promoting a general benefit, yet they may perhaps make a particular appeal to some of the most distinguished classes of society—to the great landed proprietors. Whatever specimens they send will be carefully examined and reported upon. The simple truth will be stated by men whose character, as well as motives, will secure them from any suspicion of inaccuracy; and, if a general system of this kind is pursued, much error and disappointment, and even dishonesty, will be prevented.

'On the attention of the statesman and the politician

we have likewise no inconsiderable claim. The Royal Institution is able to offer assistance in investigations of great interest connected with public works and the promotion of arts and manufactures.

'Our doors are to be open to all who wish to profit by knowledge; and I may venture to hope that even the female part of our audiences may not diminish, and that they will honour the plan with an attention which is independent of fashion or the taste of the moment, and connected with the use, the permanence, and the pleasure of intellectual acquisitions. It is not our intention to invite them to assist in the laboratories, but to partake of that healthy and refined amusement which results from a perception of the variety, order, and harmony existing in all the kingdoms of nature, and to encourage the study of those more elegant departments of science which at once tend to exalt the understanding and purify the heart.

'The leisure of the higher female classes is so great, and their influence in society so strong, that it is almost a duty that they should endeavour to awaken and keep alive a love of improvement and instruction.

'Let them make it disgraceful for men to be ignorant, and ignorance will vanish, and that part of their empire founded upon mental improvement will be strengthened and exalted by time, will be untouched by age, will be immortal in its youth.

'Even in the common relations of society how much must be referred to the conduct of the female mind. The mother gives, or ought to give, most of the early impressions to the child, and his future habits may depend in some measure upon her influence. It may in some measure depend upon her whether he become an honour or a disgrace to his country. Her power of enforcing instruction is the most effectual, as flowing from love. We know that without feeling the human being is mere clay, the dust of the earth without the living soul. Whatever is to be permanently infixed on the understanding must be associated with hope, or with joy, or with passion. How much more efficacious must instruction be when communicated by an object beloved and venerated, and in infancy almost adored, and when, instead of being afforded with an effort of pain and of labour, it is carried into the heart by kindness and made delightful by caresses and smiles.

'It has been supposed by some persons who are little acquainted with the nature of the plan and the general objects of philosophical associations, that there is a tendency in them to lessen the importance of our elder establishments for education, and to diminish the love of ancient literature. But nothing is further from the truth. The maxim of improvers is, "Promote whatever can tend to assist the progress of the human mind," and letters will always be the greatest, the most powerful engine to this effect; it is one that all can employ, the strong and the weak, in solitude or in the world. That which is beautiful, that which is pathetic, that which is sublime, can never lose its effects. There is one course of passion and feeling in all times and in all countries; we should never cease to consider with admiration and gratitude those models of excellence which have been happily preserved amongst the wrecks of cultivated nations to be our guides in the Middle Ages, to be our shelter in the storm, and our light in the darkness, the beacons to guide us to pure taste, to correct our wanderings, to bring us to nature and truth. Let us regard them with all respect, but let not our veneration for them be exclusive; let us admire them as we admire the works of art of antiquity. The Apollo Belvidere or the Venus de Medicis were designed by their artists to be objects of adoration; let us wonder at them as statues, as models of perfection, but not worship them as deities, nor even make them our only household gods.

'Greek and Roman literature will always maintain their importance, always exert their influence; but let us not neglect that basis on which the greatness of modern times and of our own country so peculiarly rests —experimental philosophy and the experimental arts. Let their merits be justly estimated and set forth with dignity and truth; let not the countrymen of Bacon, of Newton, and of Boyle neglect those pure springs of knowledge from which those great men drew such copious supplies both for profit and for glory; and let it not be forgotten that science has its moral and intellectual as well as its common uses, that its object is not only to apply the different substances in nature for the advantages, comfort, and benefit of man, but likewise to set forth that wonderful and magnificent history of wisdom and intelligence which is written in legible characters both in the heavens and on the earth.'

On May 1, at the annual meeting of the proprietors, it

was resolved unanimously that the election of managers and visitors should be for one year only. Notice was given of alterations of the bye-laws on June 4, for the election of members in accordance with the new Act of Parliament.

The first monthly meeting of *members* was held on Monday, May 7. A committee of members was appointed to act with a committee of managers and visitors in drawing up bye-laws.

On June 4 the bye-laws were read, and on July 2 they were proposed to the members chapter by chapter and article by article, and their consideration was continued on the 4th and 5th. On the 6th the election of thirty-two members took place; among them was Davy.

On August 6 'Humphry Davy, Esq.,' the first of the newly-elected members, 'having paid his admission fee and given his bond for his annual payments, was admitted a member of the Royal Institution.' Dr. Wollaston was this day proposed as member.

On November 29 a special general meeting of members was held to ballot for three scientific and literary committees. The ballot lasted for ten minutes. For mathematics, mechanics, and mechanical inventions, twenty-five members were elected; the same number for chemistry, geology, and mineralagy; and twenty-five for general science, literature, and arts.

At the December meeting of the members Mr. Auriol signified his desire of resigning the secretaryship.

This year, by order of a committee of the House of Lords, the clerk of the House wrote to the secretary of the Institution, to request him to attend with any gentleman belonging to the Institution who might give advice and assistance to the committee on the subject of warming and ventilating their House. In this roundabout way Davy was asked to give his advice. He made a report and his plan was adopted, without success.

At the monthly meeting of managers in February 1811 the following letter from Sir T. Bernard, who, by the death of his brother, had become a baronet, was read:

It has been for some time my desire and intention to resign my place in the Committee of Managers, but the state of the Institution has made me apprehensive of some inconvenience from withdrawing before the new constitution was formed and the primary difficulties surmounted.

Nothing more, I conceive, is now wanting except a continuance of that union and friendly co-operation by which it has been established; and, as I can no longer continue a regular attendant, I resign my situation as a manager of the Royal Institution. At the same time I beg leave to add that if the annual meeting should hereafter elect me a visitor, I will with great pleasure continue my services in that situation. I beg you will communicate the above to the next monthly meeting, and have the honour to be, with the greatest respect, your obedient and very faithful Servant,

T. Bernard.

The managers resolved 'that they could not avoid on this occasion expressing their deep regret at the prospect of losing the assistance of a gentleman whose zeal, abilities, and indefatigable industry had so eminently contributed to the prosperity of the Institution. They therefore unanimously expressed their wish that Sir Thomas Bernard would consent to defer his resignation till the annual meeting in May.' The next week Sir T. Bernard confirmed his resignation, and Lord Darnley was elected in his place.

At the annual meeting in May Sir Thomas Bernard was not nominated as a visitor, but the following November he was unanimously elected. In 1815 he was again elected a manager, and he was re-elected until his death in the autumn of 1818.

In February the energy of the committees of the Institution gave some signs of activity. The Committee of Chemistry and Geology, &c., chose Humphry Davy chairman, Charles Hatchett chairman, and James Laird, M.D., secretary. The Committee of Mathematics, Mechanics, and Mechanical Inventions elected the Earl of Stanhope chairman, the Hon. R. Clifford chairman, and John Day, Esq., secretary. The Committee of General Science, Literature, and Arts elected Daniel Moore, Esq., F.R.S., L.S, chairman, John Disney chairman, and John Hinckley, Esq., secretary. For eleven months Mr. Hinckley had acted as 'honorary secretary assistant,' and he wished to be elected 'honorary secretary' of the Institution; but in May Mr. Guillemard was elected secretary in the place of Mr. Auriol, who for nine years had apparently taken very slight care of the records of the Institution.

In March it was proposed at the monthly meeting of members that a professorship of astronomy should be created. Reports from the Committee of General Science were read.

This year all the bills due for 1807, 1808, 1809, and 1810 were paid.

Very few managers attended the meetings; so few, that

at the end of the year it was necessary to call a special meeting, stating that it was impossible to announce the lectures for the ensuing year. This brought twelve managers to the first meeting of 1812, and they decided that the lectures were to begin on January 25.

Mr. Lawrence the surgeon, Dr. Birkbeck, Dr. Wollaston, and Mr. Campbell were asked, but declined, to lecture.

At the monthly meeting in April it was moved that a scientific journal should be published. The question of having a Professor of Astronomy and other sciences connected therewith was again discussed. Dr. Jenner was proposed as member by Sir H. Davy and three others. On April 5, at an adjourned general monthly meeting, a report from the Committee of Mathematics and Mechanics was read and referred to the managers as proper to be printed.

On April 20 the first report of the visitors since the passing of the Act of Parliament was made.

They say 'only fifteen proprietors withdrew, and received compensation amounting to 630*l.* 12*s.* 6*d.* The rest remained with the enlarged view of rendering the establishment more eminently what it was designed to be—a great national laboratory and theatre for the improvement and promulgation of science in all its branches.'

'Five per cent. only of the intended loan was required.'

The Committee closed their report by congratulating their brother members on the promotion, progress, and diffusion of science, particularly of chemical discovery, owing to the experiments carried on and the lectures delivered at the Royal Institution. 'And they hope, from the energetic spirit of its members, that it will continue to flourish and tend in its progress to improve arts and manufactures, increase the resources, and exalt the scientific glory of the country.'

On May 6, at the monthly meeting, a professorship of astronomy was established, but no appointment was made. Three fresh committees of twenty-five members each were formed. The resolution for publishing journals was carried, but no journals were published.

On June 8 the election of chairmen and secretaries to the committees was reported to the members.

In 1812 a great change was about to come over the Royal Institution. Sir Humphry Davy, by his splendid discoveries, had made the Institution famous, and, by his attractive lectures, had brought it most material support. How little it could afford to lose his help is seen by the balance to December 31, 1811. This was only 3*l.* 9*s.* 11*d.* Early in 1812 a committee was formed for the publication of a journal, and in April Mr. Wyatt presented a plan for a proposed new theatre. Davy was married on April 11; the day previous he gave his last lecture. The new theatre was no longer needed.

On May 11 Mr. Hatchett reported 'that Sir H. Davy, though he cannot pledge himself to deliver lectures, will be willing to accept the offices of Professor of Chemistry and Director of the Laboratory and Mineralogical Collection without salary.' It was immediately resolved 'that the managers hear with great regret the notification which they have just received that Sir

Humphry Davy cannot pledge himself to continue the lectures which he has been accustomed to deliver with so much honour to the Institution and advantage to the public; but, at the same time, they congratulate themselves on the liberal offer which Sir Humphry Davy has made to superintend the chemical department, and to assist and advise any lecturer the managers may be pleased to appoint.' The managers immediately appointed him Director of the Laboratory and Mineralogical Collection, and expressed their high sense of his past services, gave him their thanks, and ordered a special general meeting to be called to nominate him Professor of Chemistry. He was elected Professor of Chemistry on June 1. On the same day twenty-five members were also elected on each of the committees.

A quarrel in the Institution must here be mentioned, because it shows that the changed circumstances of Davy led to the engagement of Faraday. The apparatus and models of the Institution had been under Davy's care; they were now placed under the care of Mr. Pepys, and he was made Honorary Inspector of the Models and Apparatus, and Mr. Newman, the instrument maker, was put under him. Soon after the managers ordered that William Payne, originally the laboratory boy, should be employed in cleaning and repairing the apparatus in conjunction with Mr. Newman.

In December Dr. Smith was appointed to lecture on Botany; Dr. Roget on Comparative Anatomy; T. Campbell on Poetry; Mr. Brande on Chemical Philosophy;

Rev. J. Powell on Natural Philosophy; Mr. Thompson on Sculpture.

Before the lectures began in 1813 Mr. Edmund Davy, chemical assistant in the laboratory, resigned; and, at the beginning of the year, Payne's salary was increased to 25*s*. weekly. He had had a room in the house for nearly six months. On the increase of his salary his duties were thus laid down by the managers, and five weeks afterwards they became the duties of Mr. Faraday: 'To attend and assist the lecturers and professors in preparing for and during lectures. Where any instruments or apparatus may be required, to attend to their careful removal from the model room and laboratory to the lecture room, and to clean and replace them after being used, reporting to the managers such accidents as shall require repair, a constant diary being kept by him for that purpose. That in one day in each week he be employed in keeping clean the models in the repository, and that all the instruments in the glass cases be cleaned and dusted at least once within a month.'

Towards the end of February Mr. Harris, the Librarian and Superintendent of the House, reported to the managers 'that, hearing a great noise one evening in the lecture room, he went to see the cause of it. He found Mr. Payne and Mr. Newman at high words, and Mr. Newman complained of having been struck by Payne for representing to him his neglect of duty in being absent when he should have attended on Mr. Brande.' The managers immediately resolved that Mr. Payne should be dismissed from the Royal Institution, and that a gratuity of 10*l.* should be paid him in consideration of his long services. He had come as a boy to the Institution before November 1803.

At the following meeting (March 1) Sir Humphry Davy 'had the honour to inform the managers that he had found Michael Faraday,' and the managers engaged him and resolved 'that the clerk furnish him with a copy of the order relating to his duties accordingly.'

In March 1813 the chairman of the Committee of Chemistry having through Sir H. Davy expressed a desire that an open committee of chemistry should be held in the ensuing week, the managers resolved that 'a committee of chemistry, open to all members and gentlemen personally introduced by members, should be held in the theatre of the Institution on Wednesday, March 31, at three o'clock, when the Professor of Chemistry will demonstrate a new series of facts on the fluoric principle' (fluorine).

At the general meeting of members on April 5 Sir Humphry Davy begged leave to resign his situation of Professor of Chemistry. 'He by no means wished to give up his connection with the Royal Institution, as he should ever be happy to communicate his researches in the first instance to the Institution in the manner he did in the presence of the members last Wednesday, and to do all in his power to promote the interest and success of this Institution.' Sir H. Davy having retired, Earl Spencer moved 'that the thanks of this meeting be returned to Sir Humphry Davy for the inestimable services rendered by him to the Royal Institution.' The motion was seconded by the Earl of Darnley and agreed to unanimously. Earl Spencer further moved 'that, in order more strongly to mark the high sense of this meeting of the merits of Sir Humphry Davy, he be elected Honorary Professor of Chemistry.' The Earl of Winchester, the President of the Royal Institution, was requested to sign these resolutions and to convey them to Sir Humphry Davy, and Mr. Brande was elected to the professorship of chemistry.

At the end of June the two rooms that had been occupied by Sir Humphry Davy were ordered to be prepared for Mr. Brande. A few months later he was appointed Superintendent of the House, and was allowed to transfer his chemical class of students of medicine to the laboratory.

On October 4 Sir H. Davy reported to the managers that 'Michael Faraday had expressed a wish to accompany him on his scientific travels, but that he would not engage Mr. Faraday if the Professor of Chemistry considered his services as at all essential to the Institution, or if the managers had the slightest objection to the measure.' Mr. Brande reported that 'arrangements could be made to prevent Mr. Faraday's resignation being felt, and that, as he had shown considerable diligence and attention in cleaning and arranging the mineral collection, he recommended his services to the managers' attention, as this was not his immediate duty.'

The managers permitted Mr. Faraday to resign his situation, and ordered that he should be paid a month's wages on the day of his departure.

The assistant porter was engaged as assistant in the laboratory on the same terms as Michael Faraday.

This year Campbell again lectured on Poetry, and Southey and Moore declined to lecture. Flaxman gave two lectures gratuitously, and was elected a life subscriber. Two o'clock was tried as the lecture hour, but a change was soon made back to three as heretofore.

In 1814, during the absence of Sir H. Davy, the Institution did little for science, but, though poor, it strove to be fashionable. On May 23 it gave 'a cold collation' to the Grand Duchess of Oldenburgh, for which Gunter, of Berkeley Square, was paid by contract twenty guineas. The funds of the Institution were by no means flourishing; the balance in favour of the Institution on the accounts of 1813 was 66*l.*, but many bills were paid out of the 'benefactions to the fund for discharging the debts and for providing for the future support of the Institution.' A list of the benefactors was ordered to be sent round to the members and subscribers on the two last Saturdays in June.

For the promotion of science the three committees (1) on chemistry and geology, (2) on general science and literature, and (3) on mathematics and mechanics were requested by the managers to meet and to elect each two chairmen and a secretary.

In 1815, in February, Mr. Babbage began a course of lectures on Astronomy.

On May 15 Sir Humphry Davy was present at the meeting of managers. That day Mr. Brande stated that he wanted assistance in the laboratory, and that Michael Faraday was 'willing to resume his situation.' The managers resolved that the assistant porter should be discharged, and that the former assistant porter should take his place, and 'that Michael Faraday be engaged as assistant in the laboratory and mineralogical collection and superintendent of the apparatus at a salary of 30*s.* a week, and that he be accommodated with apartments in the house under the superintendence of Mr. Brande.'

The rooms given to him were 25 and 26, the two furthest on the attic floor. The sister of the librarian, Mr. Harris, occupied the smallest of these (26), and there were difficulties about any other arrangement, so that a few weeks afterwards the librarian asked permission to reside out of the house.

In 1816 the managers decided that, in consideration of the additional labour caused to Michael Faraday by the lectures of Mr. Brande in the laboratory, his salary should be raised to 100*l.* per annum. The pecuniary difficulties of the Institution were increasing, and Sir Humphry Davy, Mr. Auriol, and Mr. Solly were appointed as a sub-committee to examine the expenditure. In 1817 the debts increased.

In 1818 the bill for coals in 1816 was paid. Mr. Fuller, who ultimately founded the Fullerian Professorships, allowed one thousand pounds, which he had invested for the benefit of the Institution, to be used for the payment of debts. In the autumn Sir Thomas Bernard died.

In 1819 Mr. Brande applied to the board, on the part of Mr. Faraday, for permission to occupy the two southernmost front rooms on the second floor.

In 1820 an anniversary dinner was held on May 8 at Willis's Rooms. The following year Mr. Faraday was given the use of two more rooms on the second floor, and appointed Superintendent of the House and Laboratory in the absence of Mr. Brande.

In 1822 the treasurer had to advance 1,000*l.* to pay the bills, and in 1823 a loan of 4,000*l.* without interest was raised amongst the members.

In 1824 Faraday first lectured at the Royal Institution, and was elected a Fellow of the Royal Society for his discoveries made in the laboratory.

From 1815 the life of Faraday and the history of the Royal Institution became inseparable, and from 1824 it was kept alive by his unselfish devotion to its welfare.

CHAPTER VI.

LIFE OF DAVY.

1778 to 1829.

THE history of thirteen years of the life of Davy, like that of fifty of the life of Faraday, is closely interwoven with the history of the Royal Institution. Their lives were the life of the place; and hence, to complete the history of the Institution to the time of Faraday, a sketch of Davy and his scientific life must be given here.

Humphry Davy was born on December 17, 1778, at Penzance. He was the son of a wood carver and was apprenticed to a surgeon.

Mr. Davies Gilbert heard that the boy was fond of making chemical experiments. He encouraged him and spoke of him to Dr. Beddoes, Professor of Geology and Chemistry at Oxford, who happened to be at work upon the 'Geology of Cornwall.'

Afterwards Dr. Beddoes established the Pneumatic Institution at Clifton, and he required an assistant to prepare the gases and superintend the Pneumatic Hospital, and Mr. Gilbert proposed Davy. He went on October 2, 1798, 'to superintend experiments on the medical powers of factitious airs or gases.'

Davy thus wrote to Mr. Davies Gilbert:

November 12, 1798.

I have purposely delayed writing until I could communicate to you some intelligence of importance concerning the new Pneumatic Institution. The speedy execution of the plan will, I think, interest you both as a subscriber and a friend to science and mankind. The present subscription is, we suppose, nearly adequate to the purpose of investigating the medicinal powers of factitious airs. It still continues to increase, and we may hope for the ability of pursuing the investigation to its full extent. We are negotiating for a house in Downe Square, the proximity of which to Bristol and its general situation and advantages render it very suitable for the purpose. The funds will, I suppose, enable us to provide for eight or ten patients in the Hospital, and for as many out of it as we can procure. We shall try the gases in every possible way.

. . . .

We are printing in Bristol the first volume of the 'West Country Collection,' which will, I suppose, be out the beginning of January.

. . . .

Believe me, dear Sir, with affection and respect, truly yours,

HUMPHRY DAVY.

The first two hundred pages of this collection, constituting very nearly half the volume, consist of essays of Davy on 'Heat, Light, and the Combinations of Light,' on 'Phos-Oxygen or Oxygen and its Combinations,' and on the 'Theory of Respiration.'

He wrote on February 22, 1799, to Davies Gilbert:

DEAR FRIEND,—(For I love you too well to call you by a more ceremonious name), I have delayed writing to you, expecting that some of our experiments would produce results worthy of communication.

I am now as much convinced of the non-existence of caloric as I am of the existence of light.

Our laboratory in the Pneumatic Institution is nearly finished.

I hope the gaseous oxide of azote will prove to be a specific stimulus for the absorbents.

. . . .

I know of little general scientific news. Berthollet makes sulphuretted hydrogen out to be an acid.

. . . .

I remain, with affection and respect, yours,

HUMPHRY DAVY.

Again on April 10, 1799, to Mr. Gilbert, writing of light and heat, he said:

The supposition of active powers common to all matter from the different modifications of which all the phenomena of its changes result, appears to me more reasonable than the assumption of certain imaginary fluids, alone endowed with active powers, and bearing the same relation to common matter as the vulgar philosophy supposes spirit to bear to matter.

It is only by forming theories, and then comparing them with facts, that we can hope to discover the true system of nature.

I made a discovery yesterday which proves how necessary it is to repeat experiments. The gaseous oxide of azote is perfectly respirable when pure. It is never deleterious but when it contains nitrous gas. I have found a mode of obtaining it pure, and I breathed it to-day in the presence of Dr. Beddoes and some others—sixteen quarts of it for near seven minutes. It appears to support life longer than even oxygen gas, and absolutely intoxicated me. Pure oxygen gas produced no alteration in my pulse nor any other material effect, whereas this gas raised my pulse upwards of twenty strokes, made me dance about the laboratory as a madman, and has kept my spirits in a glow ever since.

. . . .

Yours, with affection and respect,

HUMPHRY DAVY.

Dr. Paris says Coleridge gave him this account of of the caution of Davy at this time:

Dr. Beddoes thought nitrous oxide gas would cure paralysis. A patient was to be treated by Davy. He first took the temperature by means of a small thermometer placed under the tongue. The patient immediately declared that he felt better. The opportunity was too tempting to be lost. Davy cast an intelligent glance at Mr. Coleridge, and desired the patient to renew his visit on the following day, when the same ceremony was again performed, and repeated every succeeding day for a fortnight, the patient gradually improving during that period, when he was dismissed as cured, no other application having been used than that of the thermometer.

Southey thus wrote his opinion and that of Coleridge regarding Davy at this time: 'He is a marvellous young man, whose talents I can only wonder at.'

Later he wrote:

My residence at Westbury was one of the happiest portions of my life. . . . I was in habits of the most frequent and intimate intercourse with Davy, then in the flower and freshness of his youth. We were within an easy walk of each other over some of the most beautiful ground in that beautiful part of England. When I went to the Pneumatic Institution he had to tell me of some new experiment or discovery and of the views which it opened for him, and when he came to Westbury there was a fresh portion of Madoc for his hearing.

On July 3, 1800, Davy wrote from Bristol to Gilbert:

We have been repeating the galvanic experiments with success. Nicholson, by means of a hundred pieces of silver and zinc, has procured a visible spark. Cruickshank has revived oxidated metals in solution by means of the nascent hydrogen produced from the decomposition of water by the shock, and both he and Carlisle have absolutely resolved water into oxygen and hydrogen by means of it, making use of silver and platina wires. An immense field of investigation seems opened by this discovery; may it be pursued so as to acquaint us with some of the laws of life!

You have undoubtedly heard of Herschel's discovery concerning the production of heat by invisible rays emitted from the sun?

Coleridge is gone to reside in Cumberland.

. . . .

Yours, with sincere affection,

HUMPHRY DAVY.

On October 20, 1800, again he wrote to Gilbert:

In pursuing experiments on galvanism during the last two months I have met with unexpected and unhoped-for success. Some of the new facts on this subject promise to afford instruments capable of destroying the mysterious veil which nature has thrown over the operation and properties of ethereal fluids.

Galvanism I have found, by numerous experiments, to be a process purely chemical.

I remain, with sincere respect and affection, yours,

HUMPHRY DAVY.

During this year he published a volume entitled 'Researches, Chemical and Philosophical, chiefly concerning Nitrous Oxide and its Respiration.'

In the spring of 1800 Mr. Underwood, a geologist and artist, had become a proprietor of the Royal Institution. He had several conversations with Count Rumford on the subject of Davy's superior talents and the advantages that would accrue to the Institution from engaging him as a lecturer. 'The Count called on me,' Underwood says, 'on January 5, 1801, having received from the managers of the Institution full powers to negotiate upon this subject. On this occasion, however, I thought it advisable to introduce the Count to Mr. James Thompson, as being the more eligible person to treat in behalf of Davy, not only on account of his greater intimacy with him, but because, not being a proprietor, he was unconnected with the interests of the Institution. Mr. Thompson wrote to Davy. With his characteristic energy Davy answered in person, and had several conferences with Count Rumford. The following letter from Count Rumford to Davy, written from the Royal Institution, is dated February 16, 1801:

DEAR SIR,—In consequence of the conversations I have had with you, respecting your engaging in the service of the Royal Institution of Great Britain, I this day laid the matter before the managers of the Institution at their meeting,[1] and I have the pleasure to acquaint you that the proposal I made to them was approved, and the following resolution unanimously taken by them: 'Resolved,—That Mr. Humphry Davy be engaged in the service of the Royal Institution in the capacity of Assistant Lecturer in Chemistry, Director of the Chemical Laboratory, and As-

[1] Present, Sir Joseph Banks, Earl of Morton, Count Rumford, and Richard Clark, Esq.

sistant Editor of the Journals of the Institution, and that he be allowed to occupy a room in the house and be furnished with coals and candles, and that he be paid a salary of 100*l*. per annum.'

On this occasion I did not neglect to give an account to the managers of the whole of what passed between us respecting the situation it was intended you should fill in the Institution on your engaging in its service, and the prospects that could with propriety be held out to you of future advantages, and the managers agreed with me in thinking that, as you had expressed your willingness to devote yourself entirely and permanently to the Institution, it would be right and proper to hold out to you the prospect of becoming, in the course of two or three years, Professor of Chemistry in the Institution, with a salary of 300*l*. per annum, provided that within that period you shall have given proofs of your fitness to hold that distinguished situation.

Although you must ever consider the duties of the offices you may hold under the Institution as the primary objects of your care and attention, yet the managers are so far from being desirous that you should relinquish the private philosophical investigations in which you have hitherto been engaged, and by which you have so honourably distinguished yourself and attracted their attention, that it will afford them the sincerest pleasure to encourage and assist you in these laudable pursuits, and give you every facility which the philosophical apparatus at the Institution can afford to make new and interesting experiments.

You will naturally consider the Journals of the Institution as the most proper vehicle for communicating to the public from time to time short accounts of the progress you may make in your investigations; this will, however, by no means be considered as precluding you in any degree from presenting to the Royal Society of London, or any other earned body, philosophical papers or memoirs on such scientific subjects as may engage your attention, or from publishing in any other manner the results of your researches.

As you are fully informed with respect to the nature and objects of the Royal Institution and are acquainted with the respectable character of those distinguished persons with whom I have the honour to act in the management of its concerns, you cannot, I think, entertain the smallest doubt of their constant protection and of their readiness on all occasions to do full justice to the zeal and abilities you may display in the situation in which they have placed you.

It is with much esteem and a sincere desire that the talents which at so early a period of life you discovered may be cultivated with care, and always employed with success, that I am, dear Sir, your most obedient Servant,

RUMFORD.

On March 8 Davy wrote to Davies Gilbert:

I cannot think of quitting the Pneumatic Institution without giving you information of it in a letter; indeed, I believe I should have done this some time ago had not the hurry of business and the fever of emotion produced by the prospect of novel changes in futurity destroyed to a certain extent my powers of consistent action.

You, my dear sir, have behaved to me with great kindness, and the little ability I possess you have very much contributed to develope; I should therefore accuse myself of ingratitude were I to neglect to ask your approbation of the measures I have adopted with regard to the change of my situation and the enlargement of my views in life.

In consequence of an invitation from Count Rumford, given to me with some proposals relative to the Royal Institution, I visited London in the middle of February, where, after several conferences with that gentleman, I was invited by the managers of the Royal Institution to become the director of their laboratory and their assistant professor of chemistry. At the same time I was assured that, within the space of two or three seasons, I should be made sole professor of chemistry, still continuing director of the laboratory.

The immediate emolument offered was sufficient for my wants, and the sole and uncontrolled use of the apparatus in the Institution for private experiments was to be granted me.

The behaviour of Count Rumford, Sir Joseph Banks, Mr. Cavendish, and the other principal managers was liberal and polite, and they promised me any apparatus that I might need for new experiments.

The time required to be devoted to the services of the Institution was but short, being limited chiefly to the winter and spring. The emoluments to be attached to the office of sole professor of chemistry are great, and, above all, the situation is permanent and held very honourable.

These motives, joined to the approbation of Dr. Beddoes, who, with great liberality, has absolved me from my engagements at the Pneumatic Institution, and the strong wishes of most of my friends in London and Bristol determined my conduct.

Thus I am quietly to be transferred to London, whilst my sphere of action is considerably enlarged, and as much power as I could reasonably expect, or even wish for at my time of life, secured to me without the obligation of labouring at a profession.

The Royal Institution will, I hope, be of some utility to society. It has undoubtedly the capability of becoming a great instrument of moral and intellectual improvement. Its funds are very great. It has attached to it the feelings of a great number of people of fashion and property, and consequently may be the means of employing to useful purposes money which would otherwise be squandered in luxury and in the production of unnecessary labour.

Count Rumford professes that it will be kept distinct from party politics. I sincerely wish that such may be the case, though I fear it. As for myself, I shall become attached to it, full of hope, with the resolution of employing all my feeble powers towards promoting its true interests.

. . . .

I have been pursuing galvanism with labour and some success; I have been able to produce galvanic power from single plates, by effecting on them different oxidating and deoxidating processes.

After the 11th I shall be in town—my direction, Royal Institution.

I am, my dear Friend, with respect and affection, yours,

HUMPHRY DAVY.

At the meeting of the managers of the Royal Institution on February 16 (present, Sir J. Banks, Earl Morton, Count Rumford, and Mr. R. Clark, Chamberlain of the City of London), it was resolved 'that Mr. Humphry Davy be engaged in the service of the Royal Institution in the capacities of Assistant Lecturer in Chemistry, Director of the Laboratory, and Assistant Editor of the Journals of the Institution; that he be allowed to occupy a room in the house, and be furnished with coals and candles; and that he be paid a salary of one hundred guineas per annum.'

On March 16 Count Rumford, after reporting that a room had beeen prepared and furnished, stated that Mr. Davy had arrived at the Institution on Wednesday, March 11, and taken possession of his situation.

Davy gave three courses of lectures in the spring of 1801.

His first course consisted of five lectures on the 'New Branch of Philosophy'—the galvanic phenomena.

His first lecture was on Tuesday evening, April 25. He began with the history of galvanism, detailed the successive discoveries, and described the different methods of accumulating galvanic influence. Polished plates of different metals and the effect of their lying together in contact with water and air were exhibited. 'Air is absolutely necessary to the oxydating process.' He observed that 'it was difficult to prove that hydrogen was given out in the decomposition of water in this way, and that it seemed rather probable that alkali was formed.' He showed the effects of galvanism on the legs of frogs, and exhibited some interesting experiments on the galvanic effects on the solution of metals in acids. As a recent discovery of his own he showed that with one kind of metal only, more powerful effects may be produced than with two, as heretofore employed; but in this case there must be more than one liquid interposed between the plates. He stated that copper, for example, and discs of cloth or pasteboard, moistened with diluted nitrous acid and solutions of muriat of soda and sulphuret of potash, and arranged in the order named (viz. copper, nitrous acid, muriat of soda, sulphuret of potash, &c.), give much more sensible shocks than the pile as at first constructed. The reporter added: 'Sir Joseph Banks, Count Rumford, and other distinguished philosophers were present. The audience was highly gratified, and testified their satisfaction by general applause. Mr. Davy, who appears to be very young, acquitted himself admirably well; from the sparkling intelligence of his eye, his animated manner, and the *tout ensemble* we have no doubt of his attaining a distinguished eminence.'

The second lecture was given on the 28th, and the others were to be delivered on the Tuesday and Saturday evenings till completed. He gave another short course on Pneumatic Chemistry. 'The lectures were extremely ingenious and excited considerable attention.' The concluding lecture was on June 20, on Respiration, and after the lecture an opportunity was given to such as wished it to breathe some of the nitrous oxide. The reporter said, 'Mr. Grosvenor Bedford, Mr. Stodart, and Mr. Underwood breathed the gas, and the effects it produced, and especially on the last, were truly wonderful. Mr. Underwood experienced so much pleasure from breathing it that he lost all sense of everything else, and the breathing bag could only be taken from him at last by force.' 'The irresistible tendency to muscular action produced by this gas was such as cannot be described. It must be witnessed to be conceived.'

'Professor Pictet, of Geneva, who is now on a visit in this country, Count Rumford, and other philosophers of eminence were present, and seemed not a little gratified with the exhibition of the gas.' [1]

'Another galvanic course was also given by Mr. Davy, which, being delivered in the fore part of the day, was attended not only by men of science, but by numbers of people of rank and fashion, a proof that the Institution bids fair to promote a taste for philosophical pursuits among those whose wealth has but too often

[1] The substance of these lectures was published in the fourth number of the Journals of the Royal Institution, p. 49, edited by Dr. Young. The paper is called *Outlines of a View of Galvanism*. It is dated September 1801.

fostered the idea that such subjects were beneath the notice of independence.'

At a meeting of managers, held on June 1, it was resolved 'that Mr. Humphry Davy, Director of the Chemical Laboratory and Assistant Lecturer in Chemistry, since he has been employed at the Institution, has given satisfactory proofs of his talents as a lecturer, and also it was resolved that he be appointed and in future denominated Lecturer on Chemistry at the Royal Institution, instead of continuing to occupy the place of Assistant Lecturer, which he has hitherto filled.'

On June 18 his first paper was read at the Royal Society. It was an account of some galvanic combinations formed by an arrangement of single metallic plates and fluids analogous to the galvanic apparatus of M. Volta.

On June 29 a permanent committee for the general purposes of chemical investigation and analysis was appointed at the Royal Institution, and the Minutes say that Mr. Davy was instructed to prepare himself to give in the month of December next a course of lectures on the Philosophical and Chemical Principles of the Art of Dyeing, or on the Arts of Staining or Printing with Colours, Woollen, Linen, and Cotton Goods. 'That Mr. Davy have permission to absent himself during the months of July, August, and September for the purpose of making himself more particularly acquainted with the practical part of the business of tanning.'

Davy first went to Bristol, and thence he wrote to his friend Mr. Underwood to join him for a tour in Cornwall.

MY DEAR UNDERWOOD,—That part of Almighty God which resides in the rocks and woods, in the blue and tranquil sea, in the clouds and sunbeams of the sky, is calling upon thee with a loud voice; religiously obey its commands, and come and worship with me on the ancient altars of Cornwall.

I shall leave Bristol on Thursday next, possibly before; so that by this day week I shall probably be at Penzance. Ten days or a fortnight after I shall expect to see you, and to rejoice with you. We will admire together the wonders of God—rocks and the sea, dead hills and living hills covered with verdure. Amen.

Write to me immediately, and say when you will come. Direct, H. Davy, Penzance. Farewell, being of energy. Yours with unfeigned affection,

H. DAVY.

On November 14 he wrote to Davies Gilbert from the Royal Institution:

I didn't arrive in London until the 20th of September. On my arrival I found that Count Rumford had altered his plans of absence, and had left London on that very day for the Continent, purposing to return in about two months. He is now at Paris, and in about a fortnight we expect him here.

. . . .

I yesterday ascertained rather an important fact; namely, that a galvanic battery may be constructed *without any metallic substance.* By means of ten pieces of well-burnt charcoal, nitrous acid, and water, arranged alternately in wine-glasses, I produced all the effects usually obtained from zinc, silver, and water.

The Bakerian lecture[1] by Dr. Young, our Lecturer on Natural Philosophy, is now reading before the Royal

[1] This was the first memoir on the *Theory of Light and Colours,* read Nov. 12, 1801.

Society. He attempts to revive the doctrine of Huygens and Euler, that light depends upon undulations of an ethereal medium. His proofs (*i.e.* his presumptive proofs) are drawn from some strong and curious analogies he has discovered between light and sound.

. . . .

You should fix your permanent residence in London, where alone you can do what you ought—instruct and delight numbers of improved men. I am, my Friend, yours with unfeigned esteem and respect,

HUMPHRY DAVY.

On January 5, 1802, a syllabus of Davy's course of lectures on Chemistry was printed at the press of the Royal Institution. He wrote for it the following advertisement:

It is generally admitted that the best method of teaching the sciences is to begin with simple facts, and gradually to proceed from them to the more complicated phenomena.

In the following pages, which contain the outlines of a course of lectures on Chemistry, an attempt has been made to employ such a method. Hence the abstruse doctrines concerning the imponderable fluids have been separated from the history of simple chemical action, and the applications of the science from the science itself. The classification of substances adopted is founded rather upon facts than analogies, and in consequence certain bodies have been placed among the simple principles which, from their resemblance to other bodies of known composition, have been generally arranged in the class of compounds. This is an imperfection, but on the principles assumed it could not easily be avoided. And it will be fortunate for the author if a discerning public should not discover many more important imperfections.

Part I. 'The Chemistry of Ponderable Substances.'

Part II. 'The Chemistry of Imponderable Substances.'

Div. 1, of Heat or Caloric; Div. 2, of Light; Div. 3, of the Electric Influence; Div. 4, of Galvanism.

Part III. 'The Chemistry of the Arts.' Div. 1, of Agriculture; Div. 2, of Tanning; Div. 3, of Bleaching; Div. 4, of Dyeing; Div. 5, of Metallurgy; Div. 6, of the Manufactory of Glass and Porcelain; Div. 7, of the Preparation of Food and Drink; Div. 8, of the Management of Heat and Light Artificially Produced.

He gave his introductory lecture to the morning course on General Chemistry on Thursday, January 21, and to the evening course on Outlines of Chemical Science and Chemistry of the Arts on February 9. The allusion to the Royal Institution with which he ended his first lecture was full of poetry.

'In reasoning concerning the future hopes of the human species we may look forward with confidence to a state of society in which the different orders and classes of men will contribute more effectually to the support of each other than they have hitherto done. This state, indeed, seems to be approaching fast; for, in consequence of the multiplication of the means of instruction, the man of science and the manufacturer are daily becoming more assimilated to each other.

'The arts and sciences also are in high degree patronised by the rich and privileged orders.

'The unequal division of property and of labour, the differences of rank and condition amongst mankind, are the sources of power in civilised life—its moving causes and even its very soul. In considering and hoping that the human species is capable of becoming more enlightened and more happy we can only expect that the different parts of the great whole of society should be intimately united together by means of knowledge and the useful arts, that they should act as the children of one great parent with one determinate end, so that no power may be rendered useless, no exertions thrown away.

'In this view we do not look to distant ages or amuse ourselves with brilliant though delusive dreams concerning the infinite improvability of man, the annihilation of labour, disease, and even death; but we reason by analogy from simple facts; we consider only a state of human progression arising out of its present condition; we look for a time that we may reasonably expect, FOR A BRIGHT DAY OF WHICH WE ALREADY BEHOLD THE DAWN.'

The following day Sir H. Englefield wrote to Mr. Underwood from Tilney Street, 'Davy, covered with glory, dines with me at five to-day. If you could meet him it would give me great pleasure.'

At this dinner Sir Henry wrote a request to Davy to print his lecture.

A friend of Davy's some years afterwards thus mentioned the success of his lectures to Dr. Paris:

'The sensation created by his lectures at the Institution and the enthusiastic admiration which they obtained is at this period scarcely to be imagined. Men of the first rank and talent, the literary and the scientific, the practical and the theoretical, bluestockings and women of fashion, the old and the young, all crowded, eagerly crowded, the lecture room. His youth, his simplicity, his natural eloquence, his chemical knowledge, his happy illustrations and well-conducted experiments excited universal attention and unbounded applause.

'Compliments, invitations, and presents were showered upon him in abundance from all quarters. His society was courted by all, and all appeared proud of his acquaintance.'

On February 5 he again dined with Sir H. Englefield at his house at Blackheath. Eighteen long years afterwards, looking back through Davy's career, Sir H. Englefield said of this evening, 'It was the last flash of expiring nature.'

On May 31, 1802, at the managers' meeting, it was resolved that Mr. Humphry Davy be for the future styled Professor of Chemistry to the Royal Institution. In July 'he respectfully requested leave of the managers that he may be permitted to spend a few weeks during the summer in the country. It is not amusement alone that he hopes to gain during his short absence, but he believes that he may be able to collect some information that may be useful in the lectures to be given on Agriculture in the spring, and which may be in other ways connected with the views of the Institution. He will take care that his absence shall not interfere with the regular publication of the Journals, and he will never be so far from town but that he can speedily return whenever his presence may be necessary.'

He wrote to Davies Gilbert, October 26:

DEAR FRIEND,—The anxieties and hopes connected with a new occupation have prevented me from paying sufficient attention even to the common duties and affections of life. . . . Your correspondence is to me a real source of pleasure, and, believe me, I would suffer no opportunity to escape of making it more frequent and regular.

My labours in the theatre of the Royal Institution have been more successful than I could have hoped from the nature of them. In lectures the effect produced upon the mind is generally transitory; for the most part they amuse rather than instruct, and stimulate to inquiry rather than give information. My audience has often amounted to four or five hundred and upwards, and amongst them some promise to become permanently attached to chemistry. This science is much the fashion of the day.

I mentioned to you in a former letter the great powers of galvanism in effecting the combustion of metals. I have lately had constructed for the laboratory of the Institution a battery of immense size; it consists of four hundred plates of five inches in diameter and forty of a foot in diameter.

I am now examining the agencies of it upon certain substances that have not as yet been decomposed.

. . . .

Have you seen the theory of my colleague, Dr. Young, on the undulations of an ethereal medium as the cause of light? It is not likely to be a popular hypothesis after what has been said by Newton concerning it. He would be very much flattered if you could offer any observations upon it, whether for or against it.

. . . .

We are publishing at the Royal Institution a 'Journal of Science,' which contains chiefly abridged accounts of what is going on in different parts of Europe, with some original papers; and, in hopes that its diffusion may become more general, we have fixed its price at one shilling.

. . . .

I am beginning to think of my course of lectures for the winter. In addition to the common course of the Institution, I have to deliver a few lectures on Vegetable Substances, and on the Connexion of Chemistry with Vegetable Physiology, before the Board of Agriculture.

. . . .

I am, dear Sir, with affection and respect, yours,

H. DAVY.

In April Davy joined Dr. Young in editing the eighth number of the Journal. Count Rumford had edited the three first and Dr. Young the four following numbers. In the third number Davy had given an account of a new eudiometer, and in the fourth outlines of a view of galvanism. In another number he gave an account of a method of copying paintings upon glass, and of making profiles by the agency of light upon nitrate of silver, invented by T. Wedgwood, Esq. He says, 'Nothing but a method of preventing the unshaded parts of the delineation from being coloured by exposure to the day is wanting to render the process as useful as it is elegant.'

On February 24, 1803, an account of some experiments and observations on the constituent parts of certain astringent vegetables, and on their operation in tanning, was read by Davy at the Royal Society.

He was proposed as a Fellow of the Royal Society on April 20, and elected on November 17.

A letter from Coleridge to Mr. Purkis, dated February 17, 1803, from Nether Stowey, thus speaks of Davy at this time:

I rejoice in Davy's progress. There are three suns recorded in Scripture—Joshua's, that stood still; Hezekiah's, that went backward; and David's, that went forth and hastened on his course like a bridegroom from his chamber. May our friend prove the latter! It is a melancholy thing to see a man, like the sun in the close of the Lapland summer, meridional in his horizon, or like wheat in a rainy season, that shoots up well in the stalk, but does not kern. As I have hoped and do hope more proudly of Davy than of any other man, and as he has been endeared to me more than any other man by the being a thing of hope to me (more, far more, than myself to my own self in my most genial moments), so of course my disappointment would be proportionably severe. It were a falsehood if I said that I think his present situation most calculated of all others to foster either his genius or the clearness and uncorruptness of his opinions and moral feelings. I see two serpents at the cradle of his genius—dissipation with a perpetual increase of acquaintances and the constant presence of inferiors and devotees, with that too great facility of attaining admiration which degrades ambition into vanity; but the Hercules will strangle both the reptile monsters. I have thought it possible to exert talents with perseverance, and to attain true greatness wholly pure even from the impulses of ambition, but on this subject Davy and I always differed. . . My book is not, strictly speaking, metaphysical, but historical. It, perhaps, will merit the title of a history of metaphysics in England, from Lord Bacon to Mr. Hume inclusive. I confine myself to facts in every part of the work, excepting that which treats of Mr. Hume; *him* I have assuredly besprinkled copiously from the fountains of bitterness and contempt. As to this and the other works which you have mentioned, 'have patience, lord, and I will pay thee all.'

Mr. T. Wedgwood goes to Italy in the first days of May. Whether I accompany him is uncertain; he is apprehensive that my health may incapacitate me. If I do not go with him, I shall go off myself in the first week of April if possible.

Davy himself wrote, on May 5, to his friend Mr. Thomas Poole:

Be not alarmed, my dear friend, as to the effect of worldly society on my mind. The age of danger has passed away; there are in the intellectual being of all men permanent elements, certain habits and passions that cannot change. I am a lover of nature with an ungratified imagination; I shall continue to search for untasted charms, for hidden beauties.

My *real*, my *waking* existence is amongst the objects of scientific research; common amusements and enjoyments are necessary to me only as dreams to interrupt the flow of thoughts too nearly analogous to enlighten and to vivify. Coleridge has left London for Keswick. During his stay in town I saw him seldomer than usual; when I did see him it was generally in the midst of large companies, where he is the image of power and activity. His eloquence is unimpaired; perhaps it is softer and stronger. His will is probably less than ever commensurate with his ability. Brilliant images of greatness float upon his mind like the images of the morning clouds upon the waters: their forms are changed by the motions of the waves, they are agitated by every breeze, and modified by every sunbeam. He talked in the course of one hour of beginning three works, and he recited the poem of 'Christabel' unfinished and as I had before heard it. What talent does he not waste in forming visions sublime, but unconnected with the real world! I have looked to his efforts as the efforts of a creating being, but as yet he has not even laid the foundation for the new world of intellectual forms.

When my agricultural lectures are finished I propose to visit Paris, and perhaps Geneva.

On May 10 the first lecture was given before the Board of Agriculture, and five others on succeeding Fridays and Tuesdays. They were corrected and published in 1813.

Later he wrote again to Mr. Poole:

Often, very often, in the midst of the tumults of the multitude in this great city has my spirit turned in quietness and solitude towards you.

I hope soon to see you in Somersetshire, where we may worship nature and the Spirit that dwells in nature in your green fields and under your tranquil sky. My communications with you, and Coleridge, and Southey, and other ornaments of the great existing Being have excited feelings which cheer me in the apathy of London, and which make me love human nature.

In December 1803 Dr. Dalton gave a course of lectures at the Royal Institution. Early in January he wrote to a friend from the Royal Institution:

I was introduced to Mr. Davy, who has rooms adjoining mine; he is a very agreeable and intelligent young man, and we have interesting conversations in the evening; the principal failing in his character as a philosopher is that he does not smoke. Mr. Davy advised me to labour at my first lecture; he told me the people here would be inclined to form their opinion from it. Accordingly I resolved to *write* my first lecture wholly; to *do* nothing, but to tell them what I would do and enlarge upon the importance and utility of science. I studied and wrote for near two days, then calculated to a minute how long it would take me reading, endeavouring to make my discourse about fifty minutes. The evening before the lecture Davy and I went into the theatre; he made me read the whole of it, and he went into the farthest corner. Then he read it, and I was the audience. We criticised each other's method. Next day I read it to an audience of about 150 or 200 people, which was more than were expected. They gave a very general plaudit at the conclusion, and several came up to compliment me upon the excellence of the introduction. Since that I have scarcely written anything; all has been experiment and verbal explanation. In general my experiments have uniformly succeeded, and I have never once faltered in the elucidation of them; in fact, I can now enter the lecture room with as little emotion nearly as I can smoke a pipe with you on Sunday or Wednesday evening.

Before Coleridge left for Malta Davy wrote to him:

Twelve o'clock, Monday (probably March 1804).

MY DEAR COLERIDGE,—My mind is disturbed and my body harassed by many labours, yet I cannot suffer you to depart without endeavouring to express to you some of the unbroken higher feelings of my spirit, which have you at once as their cause and object.

Years have passed away since we first met, and your presence, and recollections with regard to you have afforded me continued sources of enjoyment.

Some of the better feelings of my nature have been elevated by your converse, and thoughts which you have nursed have been to me an eternal source of consolation.

In whatever part of the world you are you will often live with me, not as a fleeting idea, but as a recollection possessed of creative energy, as an imagination winged with fire, inspiring and rejoicing.

You must not live much longer without giving to all men the proof of power which those who know you feel in admiration. Perhaps, at a distance from the applauding and censuring murmurs of the world, you will be best able to execute those great works which are justly expected from you; you are to be the historian of the philosophy of feeling. Do not in any way dissipate your noble nature. Do not give up your birthright. May you soon recover perfect health, the health of strength and happiness! may you soon return to us confirmed in all the powers essential to the exertion of genius! You were born for your country, and your native land must be the scene of your activity. I shall expect the time when your spirit, bursting through the clouds of ill-health, will appear to all men, not as an uncertain and brilliant flame, but as a fair and permanent light, fixed, though constantly in motion, as a sun which gives its fire not only to its attendant planets, but which sends beams from all its parts into all worlds.

May blessings attend you, my dear friend! Do not forget me; we live for different ends and with different habits and pursuits, but our feelings with regard to each other have, I believe, never altered. They must continue; they can have no natural death. I trust they can never be destroyed by fortune, chance, or accident.

H. DAVY.

In October Davy thus wrote to a friend on the death of Gregory Watt, the son of James Watt:

We are deceived, my dear Clayfield, if we suppose that the human being who has formed himself for action, but who has been unable to act, is lost in the mass of being. There is some arrangement of things which we can never comprehend, but in which his faculties will be applied.

The caterpillar, in being converted into an inert scaly mass, does not appear to be fitting itself for an inhabitant of the air, and can have no consciousness of the brilliancy of its future being. We are masters of the earth, but perhaps we are the slaves of some great but unknown beings. The fly that we crush with our finger or feed with our viands, has no knowledge of man and no consciousness of his superiority. We suppose that we are acquainted with matter and with all its elements, and yet we cannot even guess at the cause of electricity or explain the laws of the formation of the stones which fall from meteors.

There may be beings—thinking beings—near us, surrounding us, which we do not perceive, which we can never imagine. We know very little, but, in my opinion, we know enough to hope for the immortality—the *individual immortality—of the better part of man.*

I have been led into all this speculation, which you may well think wild, in reflecting upon the fate of Gregory; my feeling has given erring wings to my mind. He was a noble fellow and would have been a great man.

His letters to me only three or four months ago were full of spirit, and spoke not of any infirmity of body, but of an increasing strength of mind. Why is this in the order of nature, that there is such a difference in the duration and destruction of her works? If the mere stone decays, it is to produce a soil which is capable of nourishing the moss and the lichen; when the moss and the lichen die and decompose, they produce a mould which becomes the bed of life to grass and to a more exalted species of vegetables. Vegetables are the food of animals, the less perfect animals of the more perfect, but in man the faculties and intellect are perfected; he rises, exists for a little while in disease and misery, and then would seem to disappear without an end and without producing any effect.

Another mention of Coleridge occurs in February, when Davy wrote to Mr. Poole:

There has been no news lately from Coleridge; the last accounts state that he was well in the autumn and in Sicily. On that poetic ground we may hope and trust that his genius will call forth some new creations, and that he may bring back to us some garlands of never-dying verse. I have written to urge him strongly to give a course of lectures on Poetry at the Royal Institution, where his feeling would strongly impress and his eloquence greatly delight.

In January 1805 Davy presented his collection of minerals to the Royal Institution. They were valued at one hundred guineas.

On February 4, as Director of the Laboratory, he received an addition of 100*l.* to his salary.

He had two papers read at the Royal Society, one on a 'New Mineral, consisting of Alumine and Water,' and the other on a 'New Mode of Analysing Minerals containing Fixed Alkali by Boracic Acid,' and for these and his other papers he received the Copley medal.

In September he thus wrote to Davies Gilbert:

I came from Ireland by the Western Road about a fortnight ago.

The Irish are a noble race degraded by slavery and bearing the insignia of persecution—extreme savageness or the lowest servility. Yet they are ingenious and active, and seem to me to possess all the elements of power and usefulness; but amongst the lower orders there is a most unfortunate equality, destructive of all great and efficient exertion, and amongst the higher classes the greatest degree of activity is awakened only by the desire of imitating the English, and that not so much in their virtues as in their luxuries and follies.

And to his friend Poole he wrote, October 9:

I have very much to say about Ireland. It is an island that might be made a new and a great country. It now boasts a fertile soil, an ingenious and robust peasantry, and a rich aristocracy, but the bane of the nation is the equality of poverty amongst the lower orders. All are slaves without the probability of becoming free. They are in the state of equality which the sans-culottes wished for in France, and until emulation and riches and the love of clothes and neat houses are introduced amongst them there will be no permanent improvement.

Changes in political institutions can at first do little towards serving them; it must be by altering their habits, by diffusing manufactures, by destroying middle men, by dividing farms, and by promoting industry, by making the pay proportioned to the work. But I ought not to attempt to say anything on the subject when my limits are so narrow.

Up to 1806 the lectures given by Davy had brought to him repute and to the Royal Institution success. To his high reputation as a lecturer he was now about to add that of a great original discoverer. As early as July 3, 1800, he wrote to Davies Gilbert, 'We have been repeating the galvanic experiments with success.' (See p. 316.) These experiments led him to think that all chemical decompositions might be polar. He electrised different compounds at the different poles of the battery, but he made no great discovery for five years. The assertion that acid and alkali were generated by the action of the voltaic pile in the decomposition of water led him to undertake fresh galvanic experiments in 1806. Before long he was rewarded by his great discoveries regarding chemical electricity, the decomposition of the alkalies, and the composition of chlorine.

It appears from the Laboratory Books that in September he first made experiments on phosphorus with the galvanic spark, and in the last week of October he 'tried to decompose phosphorus by the galvanic fluid.' He fused the phosphorus into a tube through which a platinum wire passed. This was the form of the experiment which he made a year afterwards to compel potash to give up its oxygen.

On November 20 his first Bakerian lecture was given at the Royal Society. It had this long title: On the 'Chemical Agencies of Electricity;' on the

'Changes Produced in Water by Electricity;' on the 'Agencies of Electricity;' on the 'Decomposition of various Compound Bodies;' on the 'Transfer of certain Constituent Parts of Bodies by the Action of Electricity;' on the 'Passage of Acids, Alkalies, and other Substances through various Attracting Chemical Menstrua by Means of Electricity;' 'Some General Observations on these Phenomena, and on the Mode of Decomposition and Transition;' on the 'General Principles of the Chemical Changes Produced by Electricity;' on the 'Relations between the Electrical Energies of Bodies and their Chemical Affinities;' on the 'Mode of Action of the Pile of Volta, with Experimental Elucidations;' on 'Some General Illustrations and Applications of the Foregoing Facts and Principles.'

This was the first dawn of light regarding the inseparable union between chemical and electrical motions. The two ends of the pile of metals gave in quantity and quality different chemical results, and the chemical products varied with the variations of the liquid into which the poles were put. The identity of chemical affinity and electricity was imagined, and a new division of elements was made into electro-positive and electro-negative, according as the one or other end of the pile attracted them. The kind of polarity of each matter was thought to determine the electrical and chemical actions shown by it.

Napoleon had founded a prize of 2,400*l.* for a discovery comparable to that of Franklin or Volta, and at the same time he founded with the interest a medal, of 120*l.* value yearly, for the best experiment on the galvanic fluid. This medal for the year 1807 was given to Davy for this paper, which was then printed. Davy wrote to Mr. Poole, 'Some people say I ought not to accept this prize, and there have been foolish paragraphs in the papers to that effect; but if the two countries or governments are at war, the men of science are not. That would indeed be a civil war of the worst description; we should rather, through the instrumentality of men of science, soften the asperities of national hostility.'

On January 22, 1807, Davy was elected secretary of the Royal Society.

Dr. Young wrote to a friend:

I believe your pheasants have assisted in bringing my friend Davy into a hundred a year and the office of secretary of the Royal Society. It had never occurred to him to offer himself till I suggested it to him one day when he dined with me. The next day he heard of poor Gray's death, and, upon applying to the President, he was, after some deliberation, approved, although another person had before been encouraged. If I had not been a member of an *illiberal* profession I should have liked the situation myself, but perhaps the public is right in discouraging a divided attention.

At the end of August Davy wrote to Mr. Poole:

I am obliged to be in the neighbourhood of town during the greater part of the summer for the purpose of correcting the proofs for the 'Philosophical Transactions.'

If Coleridge is still with you, be kind enough to say to him that I wrote nearly a week ago two letters about lectures, and, not knowing where he was, I addressed them to him at different places. I wish very much he would seriously determine on this point. The managers of the Royal Institution are very anxious to engage him, and I think he might be of material service to the public and of benefit to his own mind, to say nothing of the benefit his purse might also receive. In the present condition of society his opinions in matters of taste, literature, and metaphysics must have a healthy influence; and, unless he soon becomes an active member of the living world, he must expect to be hereafter brought to judgment for hiding his light.

Seven months afterwards Davy again wrote to Mr. Poole:

Coleridge, after disappointing his audience twice from illness, is announced to lecture again this week. He has suffered greatly from excessive sensibility, the disease of genius. His mind is a wilderness in which the cedar and the oak, which might aspire to the skies, are stunted in their growth by underwood, thorns, briars, and other parasitical plants. With the most exalted genius, enlarged views, sensitive heart, and enlightened mind he will be the victim of want of order, precision, and regularity. I cannot think of him without experiencing the mingled feelings of admiration, regard, and pity.

Why do you not come to London? Many would be happy to see you, but no one more so than your very sincere Friend, my dear Poole,

H. DAVY.

The Laboratory Books show that the last week in September 1807 he exposed magnesia upon a glass plate at the positive pole with distilled water. Four days afterwards he put oxide of zinc in a coagulated state round the positive pole.

On October 6 he began 'a new series of experiments on polarity.'

From the account he gives of one experiment, it appears that he exposed different substances on a glass plate to the action of the platinum wires from a galvanic battery of 100 plates of 6 inches.

He tried the following substances: oxalic acid, dry; succinic acid; oxalic acid; soap; alcohol; water; carbonate of ammonia; nitrate of potash. He wrote, 'Pure potash, as dry as it can be made, discharges the negative in a remarkable degree and insulates the positive.'

'*Remarkable Phenomena with Potash.* It soon—' Here the laboratory note ends, but his paper in the 'Philosophical Transactions' says—'fused, became a conductor, and gave brilliant light with the appearance of flame at the negative wire. When it was slightly moistened, to make it a better conductor, the potash began to fuse at both its points of electrisation; there was a violent effusion at its upper or positive surface, while at the lower or negative surface there was no liberation of an elastic fluid, but a formation of small granules resembling quicksilver, which occasionally burst with explosion.'

He then tried carbonate of ammonia, sulphuric acid and water, soap, and the flame of a candle.

The following day carbonate of ammonia and oxalic acid were tried, sulphuric acid, water, and alcohol.

From the 7th to the 16th no experiments were entered in the Laboratory Book; but to the substance that produced the gas and globules he gave the name first of alkaligen; for on the 16th he says, 'Gas from alkaligen in alcohol;' also 'gas from ether and gas from oil of turpentine.'

On the 17th he again experimented on this gas from the alkaligen in ether and turpentine, and says, 'The gas which had been collected from the globules under oil of turpentine by the action of water burnt in contact with the air. Does it (the matter of the globules) not form gaseous compounds with ether, alcohol, and the oils?'

Then he notes the action of the alkaligen on mercury. 'Forms with it a solid amalgam, which soon loses its alkaligen in the air.' 'This amalgam amalgamates with platina and iron, but soon flies off on exposure to the air.' 'Query, Does it amalgamate with phosphorus?'

'Probably whenever it meets with hydrogen it dissolves in it.' 'Probably forms an æriform compound with ether.'

On October 19 he made his famous experiment by which he showed beyond question that potash can give up its oxygen. 'When potash was introduced into a tube having a platina wire attached to it, so (fig.), and fused into the tube so as to be a conductor —*i.e.* so as to contain just water enough, though solid—and inserted over mercury, when the platina was made negative, no gas was formed and the mercury became oxydated, and a small quantity of the alkaligen was produced round the

platina wire, as was evident from its quick inflammation by the action of water. When the mercury was made the negative, gas was developed in great quantities from the positive wire, and none from the negative mercury, and this gas proved to be pure oxygen—a capital experiment, proving the decomposition of potash. 'A small quantity of alkaligen was produced round the platina wire.'

'The gas produced from alkaligen confined under mercury by the contact of water seemed to be hydrogen nearly pure. Soda decomposed with different phenomena.'

Davy made no more notes on that day.

On the 20th he worked on the gas obtained from sodagen and potagen, and writes, 'Barytes gave at the oxygen side, when touched with the wire, an appearance like combustion—a bright rose-coloured light. Mem.: To try what effect the hydrogen side will have upon it.'

On the 21st he again worked on the gas, and says the gas from ether, when properly washed, seemed to be pure hydrogen.

He then says, 'Examined the effect of heat this day and last night of the peculiar substance.' Then he notes the results, and then he continues, 'what can be the reason if the metallic globule is composed of A and H (alkaligen and hydrogen)—What is the reason that water and ether and alcohol saturated with potash still act on it so energetically?'

On the 24th he tried the substance with sulphur and phosphorus.

On the 25th, 26th, and 27th he worked on barytes, &c.

On the 27th barytes heated to whiteness did not become a conductor.

On October 30 he was still at work on the gas.

On October 31 he says, 'When the substance amalgamated with mercury, was distilled in a glass retort, and the contents received over mercury, no air was generated; nor over water till the sublimed substance came in contact with the water, when hydrogen was evolved.'

On November 2 he was still working on potagen.

'Probably this substance combines with oxygen in two proportions, the *red colour* owing to this; and it is owing to this that it acts upon plate-glass.'

'The first oxide a peculiar substance capable of being procured with much difficulty, the second potash.'

In the midst of his discovery the condition of the laboratory made him write in the book 'some regulations with regard to the state of the laboratory.'

'1. Everything is to be put in its proper place in the evening, and everything to be arranged for the next day's operations.

'2. The fire to be lighted at eight o'clock, and the apparatus for the experiments to be prepared by nine.'

On November 4 he writes, 'The result of the distillation of as pure a piece (of potagen) as I could obtain seemed to be hydrogene nearly pure.

'The gas given out from an amalgam of it with mercury likewise hydrogene.'

On November 5 many experiments were made.

On November 6 he still worked on the gas. His notes say 'on the combustion of sodagen and potagen with oxygen.'

'Potagen certainly sublimes unaltered at a temperature below red heat. It is twenty times lighter than mercury.'

On November 13 he wrote to his friend Mr. Pepys:

I have decomposed and recomposed the fixed alkalies and discovered their bases to be two new inflammable substitutes very like metals, but one of them lighter than ether and infinitely [more] combustible; so that there are two bodies decomposed and two new elementary bodies found.

The Bakerian lecture was read on November 19, only four days before Davy was obliged to take to his bed by illness. The first sketch of this famous paper was thus made in the Laboratory Book:

'The substance is analogous to some of those imagined to exist by the alchemical visionaries.

'Possessing all the physical properties of metals except high specific gravity, it seems to combine with all of them, and form with them truly metallic amalgams; but in all cases it is capable of being separated from them by its greater facility of oxidation.'

Then he gives the action on water and ice.

The theory of its operation upon water is extremely simple.

3. 'When,' he says, 'the peculiar substance was brought in contact with a thin piece of phosphorus and pressed upon, there is a considerable action.'

4. 'When it was brought in contact with sulphur in fusion in tubes filled with the vapour of naphtha, they combine with varied ignition.'

5. 'The new substance produces some beautiful results with mercury.'

Then he describes the alloys.

'The basis of potash, when thrown into the strong mineral acids, inflames and burns on the surface.'

Then he describes the effects with sulphuric acid, and nitrous acid.

'The action of the basis of potash on fat and volatile oils, and on various bodies, is less violent than on any other class of compound substances containing oxygen, as might have been expected from the small quantity of this principle which they hold in combination.

'The application of naphtha to its preservation I have already mentioned. On the colourless and perfectly transparent naphtha distilled from petroleum or from brown naphtha at a low heat, and defended from air, it has scarcely any action at common temperatures.'

Then he describes the further action on naphtha.

'The fat and volatile oils closely related to naphtha in composition resemble it likewise in their habitudes with the basis of potash. The lightest naphtha that I have been able to procure by double distillation was of spec. gr. 770, water being 1,000, and was almost colourless. In this fluid, confined in close vessels, the globules swam for hours without apparently affecting it, but by degrees a yellow film formed upon them, the naphtha became brown at its point of contact, and the globules sank to the bottom of the vessel. After some days the fluid surrounding the globule appeared black and turbid.

'The fat and volatile oils approach to naphtha in their habitudes with respect to the basis of potash.

'The fat oils follow naphtha in the order of bodies

that slightly act upon it; and the volatile oils, the fat oils; but they all contain sufficient oxygen to render the basis of potash alkaline, if it is exposed to them for a sufficient time and in proper quantities, and that more or less rapidly, according to the circumstances. When naphtha or the oils are exposed to air they soon alkalise the basis. Oxygen is absorbed from the air, and a soap is formed, brown from the decomposition of the compound fluid during the time of the alkalisation. If air be excluded the process is a much longer time in taking place; no gas is emitted in the fixed oils or in naphtha; but in the volatile oils hydrocarbonate is produced in small quantities, and in all these cases charcoal is deposited. In oil of turpentine the process is more rapid than in any other oil I have tried, and this oil contains either water or the elements of water, and perhaps a larger proportion of oxygen to its inflammable matter.

'Nor ought we to be surprised that these substances have never been produced in nature. Their strong attraction for oxygen renders it impossible.'

'The division into two poles:

'The basis of potash, by its strong attraction for oxygen, decomposes all the metallic oxides which I *have* exposed to it by a gentle heat.

'The oxides of lead it instantly acts upon, and the metal is revived and alkali formed. In consequence of this operation it cannot be preserved in tubes of flint glass.

'Are the bases of the fixed alkalies simple bodies? I perhaps shall be asked.

'But are these singular bodies themselves compounds? Have we reached the limits of our analysis—More capable of combining with oxygene than the basis of water?

'The basis of potash serves almost as an accurate indication of the proportion of oxygene in bodies and exactly in proportion—camphor, spermaceti, wax, volatile oils.

'In the course of my inquiries many circumstances arose at first anomalous, but which soon were capable of being explained, and which, when understood, seemed to extend the general facts which had been detailed.'

A long break here occurs in the Laboratory Notes. On November 23, 1807, Davy was taken ill with fever.

On December 7 the Managers' Minutes say, 'Mr. Davy having been confined to his bed for the last fortnight by a severe illness, the managers are under the painful necessity of giving notice that the lectures will not commence until the first week in January next.'

On January 18 the managers of the Royal Institution ordered 500 copies of the following paper to be printed:

NEW DISCOVERY IN CHEMISTRY.

January 18, 1808.

For the satisfaction of those proprietors who were not present at the opening of the Rev. Mr. Dibden's introductory lecture on Wednesday last the managers have obtained and printed the following note of it:

'Before I solicit your attention to the opening of those lectures which I shall have the honour of delivering in the course of the season, permit me to trespass upon it for a few minutes by stating the peculiar circumstances under which this Institution is now again opened, and how it comes to pass that it has fallen to me rather than to a more deserving lecturer to be the first to address you.

'The managers of this Institution have directed me to impart to you that intelligence which no one who is alive to the best feelings of human nature can hear without the mixed emotions of sorrow and delight.

'Mr. Davy, whose frequent and powerful addresses from this place, supported by his ingenious experiments, have been so long and so well known to you, has for the last five weeks been struggling between life and death. The effects of those experiments recently made in illustration of his late splendid discovery, added to consequent bodily weakness, brought on a fever so violent as to threaten the extinction of life. Over him it might emphatically be said, in the language of the immortal Milton, that—

Death his dart shook, but delayed to strike.

If it had pleased Providence to deprive the world of all *further* benefit from his original talents and intense application there has certainly been sufficient *already* effected by him to entitle him to be classed among the brightest scientific luminaries of his country. That this may not appear to be unfounded eulogium I shall proceed, at the particular request of the managers, to give you an outline of the splendid discovery just alluded to, and I do so with the greater pleasure as that outline has been drawn in a very masterly manner by a gentleman of all others perhaps the best qualified to do it effectually (Cavendish ?)

'In the course of the last twenty-five or thirty years the science of chemistry has undergone great changes and has been astonishingly augmented by various important discoveries, amongst which the most remarkable have been the decomposition and recomposition of water and of nitric acid, discovered by Mr. Cavendish, and the consequent knowledge of the nature of metallic calces (now called oxides) with that of acids in general.

'But although the two fixed alkalies called soda and potash were attacked by the most eminent chemists with every known chemical agent and by every method which the improved state of science could suggest, not the smallest effect could be produced on them; so that the nature of these two common substances remained totally unascertained and became a grand desideratum of chemical science. When, however, M. Volta had communicated to the Royal Society his great discovery of the galvanic pile, and when this had been modified into the more convenient form of troughs by Crookshank of Woolwich, the electro-galvanic power was found by various philosophers to produce surprising effects when applied to different substances, and Mr. Davy in particular distinguished himself in these researches and made a number of valuable experiments and observations, some of the more remarkable of which he communicated to the Royal Society in the Bakerian lecture read in November 1806. Mr. Davy conceived, however, from what he had then accomplished, that much more might be done; and with equal skill and perseverance he performed a new series of experiments, in the course of which, by various means, he again tried the effect of the powerful galvanic batteries belonging to the laboratory of the Royal Institution, and particularly devoted his attention to the two fixed alkalies (soda and potash), with the view of effecting their decomposition and of ascertaining the nature of them by means of that powerful agent galvanism.

'This great discovery he at length effected; and, to the high gratification of all men of science, he proved that soda and potash are compound bodies, each consisting of a peculiar metal, which has so great a tendency to combine with oxygen that no agent but galvanism can separate them. The two metals, therefore, of soda and potash have always hitherto been presented to us in this state of combination with oxygen, forming the two alkalies. But some of the primitive earths (as they are called), such as barytes and strontites, have many alkaline properties, which induced Mr. Davy to subject them to similar experiments; and in like manner he discovered that these consisted of metallic bases united to oxygen, forming compound bodies analogous to the two fixed alkalies. These may justly be placed amongst the most brilliant and valuable discoveries which have ever been made in chemistry, for a great chasm in the chemical system has been filled up; a blaze of light has been diffused over that part which before was utterly dark; and new views have been opened so numerous and interesting that the more any man who is versed in chemistry reflects on them, the more he finds to admire and to heighten his expectation of future important results. Mr. Davy's name, in consequence of these discoveries, will be always recorded in the annals of science amongst those of the most illustrious philosophers of his time. His country, with reason, will be proud of him; and it is no small honour to the Royal Institution that these great discoveries have been made within its walls, in that laboratory and by those instruments which, from the zeal of promoting useful knowledge, have with so much propriety been placed at the disposal and for the use of the Professor of Chemistry.

'This recital [said Dr. Dibden] will be sufficient to convince those who hear of the celebrity which the author of such a discovery has a right to attach to himself; and yet no one, I am confident, has less inclination to challenge it. To us and to every enlightened Englishman it will be a matter of just congratulation that the country which has produced the two Bacons and Boyle has in these days shown itself worthy of its former renown by the labours of Cavendish and Davy.

'The illness of the latter, severe as it has been, is now beginning to abate,[1] and we may reasonably hope, from

[1] Davy always thought he caught the fever during an experiment for disinfecting Newgate Prison.

present appearances at least, that the period of convalescence is not very remote.'[1]

The recovery of Davy was slow.

On February 22 he attended at the request of the Committee of Managers, and informed them that he should be able to commence his course of lectures on Electro-Chemical Science on Saturday, March 12, at two o'clock, and those on Geology on Wednesday evening, the sixteenth of that month. In his opening lecture he thus spoke of electro-chemistry and its power of analysis: 'In this it will be seen that Volta has presented to us a key which promises to lay open some of the most mysterious recesses of nature. Till this discovery our means were limited; the field of pneumatic research had been exhausted, and little remained for the experimentalist except minute and laborious processes. There is now before us a boundless prospect of novelty in science, a country unexplored but noble and fertile in aspect, a land of promise in philosophy.'

In the Laboratory Book, probably about this time, he wrote, 'An instrument for procuring those metals that have not yet been reduced—*for decomposing muriatic acid gas*, fluoric, &c., and *boracic acid gas*.'

[1] Some time after his recovery it was said in the Institution that his laboratory experiments caused his illness.

'Says Davy to Baryt, "I've a strong inclination
To try to effect your deoxidation;"
But Baryt replied, "Have a care of your mirth,
Lest I should retaliate and change you to earth."'

On April 19 and 20 Davy was again at work with the battery of 520 pair of plates.

He began thus: 'Indications of the decomposition of muriatic acid. To use every effort to ensure accuracy in the results.'

'A given quantity of muriatic acid gas was acted upon by dry charcoal; there was continued vivid light in the galvanic circuit. The action was continued for ten minutes; when a little water was added no absorption took place, so that all the muriatic acid gas was decomposed. Some other experiments were made with dry muriate of lime and mercury and with a solution of muriate of lime, strontium, and soda.'

On June 30 he had a paper read at the Royal Society on the 'Decomposition of the Earths Strontia, Lime, Magnesia, by Means of Iron at the Negative End of the Battery.' Berzelius having mentioned in a letter that he had succeeded by using mercury as the negative pole, Davy repeated Berzelius's experiment, and decomposed alumina and silica by an amalgam of mercury and potassium at the negative end of the battery.

On July 11 he laid before the managers of the Royal Institution the following paper:

A new path of discovery having been opened in the agencies of the electrical battery of Volta, which promises to lead to the greatest improvements in chemistry and natural philosophy and the useful arts connected with them; and since the increase of the size of the apparatus is absolutely necessary for pursuing it to its full extent, it is proposed to raise a fund by subscription for constructing a powerful battery, worthy of a national establishment and capable of promoting the great objects of science.

Already in other countries public and ample means have been provided for pursuing these investigations. They have had their origin in this country, and it would be dishonourable to a nation so great, so powerful, and so rich if, from the want of pecuniary resources, they should be completed abroad.

An appeal to enlightened individuals on this subject can scarcely be made in vain. It is proposed that the instrument and apparatus be erected in the laboratory of the Royal Institution, where it shall be employed in the advancement of this new department of science.

The Managers' Minutes then say:

The above paper having been laid before the board of managers, they felt it their indispensable duty instantly to communicate the same to every member of the Institution, lest the slightest delay might furnish an opportunity to other countries for accomplishing this great work, which originated in the brilliant discoveries recently made at the Royal Institution.

Lord Dundas, W. Watson, Thomas Bernard, and C. Hatchett, the managers present, agreed to subscribe to this undertaking, and ordered that a book be opened at the steward's office for the purpose of entering the names of all those who may wish to contribute towards this important national object.[1]

The sum wanted was soon raised, and Davy thus described the battery:

'It consists of 200 instruments, connected together in regular order, each composed of ten double plates, arranged in cells of porcelain, and containing in each

[1] The voltaic subscriptions amounted to 520*l.*

plate thirty-two square inches; so that the whole number of double plates is 2,000, and the whole surface 128,000 square inches. This battery was charged with sixty parts water and one part of nitric acid. It gave a spark from charcoal points through four inches of air.'

On July 12 the Laboratory Notes say, 'Tried the experiments upon the decomposition of the earths by iron wire with the happiest results.' These were obtained with the battery of only twenty pair.

On July 18 he wrote, 'In pursuit of the researches on the deoxygenation of diamond and charcoal.

'Is not diamond the 2-oxide of carbon, charcoal the 1-oxide, the gaseous oxide of carbon a triple compound of hydrogen, nitrogen, and charcoal?'

On September 21, 22, 23, 24, 25, 26, 27 experiments were tried on the production of cold by induced electricity. He tried the decomposition of sulphur 'with success.' He tried to decompose mercury in the Torricellian vacuum 'with success apparently.'

'Sulphur, after giving out hydrogen by electricity, had lost its yellow colour and *was become brownish*, but still non-conducting, crystalline, and transparent.'

Numberless experiments were made on the action of potassium on ammonia and on nitrogen.

In November he must have injured his right hand, for his notes are made with his left hand on thè 19th and 20th of this month.

On December 15 he gave another Bakerian lecture on New Analytical Researches on Alkalies, Phosphorus, Sulphur, &c. In this paper he says his chief object was to show that there was oxygen in ammonia, and that potassium was not a compound of the metal and hydrogen. He made further experiments also on the decomposition of boracic, fluoric, and muriatic acids.

On December 27, 1808, Davy wrote to Coleridge:

Alas, poor Beddoes is dead! He died on Christmas Eve. He wrote to me two letters on two successive days—22nd and 23rd. From the first, which was full of affection and new feeling, I anticipated his state. He is gone at the moment when his mind was purified and exalted for noble affections and great works.

My heart is heavy. I would talk to you of your own plans, which I shall endeavour in every way to promote; I would talk to you of my own labours, which have been incessant since I saw you and not without result; but I am interrupted by very melancholy feelings, which, when you see this, I know you will partake of. Ever, my dear Coleridge, very affectionately yours,

H. DAVY.

On December 28 he wrote in the Laboratory Book, 'We have tried a number of experiments within the last few days on the muriatic and fluoric acids, heating them with potassium.'

Early in 1809 Davy sent an appendix to his last Bakerian lecture to the Royal Society. In it he spoke 'of the general results being decisive with regard to a decomposition of nitrogen having been effected.'

In a letter at this time he told his friend Mr. Children 'he hoped to show him nitrogen as a complete wreck, torn to pieces in different ways.'

On January 18 he wrote, 'Capital result from the

action of potassium on ammonia. Nitrogen was lost. If the nitrogen is to be considered as converted into oxygen and hydrogen, it must be regarded as containing much more oxygen than water; and if we do not adopt this supposition, the only alternative is that water is the ponderable matter which, under different modifications of electro-chemical existence, constitutes oxygen, hydrogen, nitrogen, and the nitrous compounds.'

On February 15 he wrote in the Laboratory Book, 'Were a description, indeed, to be given of all the experiments I have made, of all the difficulties I have encountered, of the doubts that have occurred, and the hypotheses formed—' The sentence was not finished, and more time was lost on the investigation.

Throughout the spring and summer more experiments were made on ammonia and nitrogen.

He ignited potassium by the voltaic spark in nitrogen, and found that some hydrogen was evolved and some nitrogen lost; but when the potassium was free from potash this did not occur, and at last he gave up trying to show that nitrogen was a compound of oxygen and a metallic basis.

At the end of August he was working on tellurium and made telluretted hydrogen.

To his mother he wrote in August:

At present, except when I resolve to be idle for health's sake, I devote every moment to labours which I hope will not be wholly ineffectual in benefiting society, and which will not be wholly inglorious for my country hereafter; and the feeling of this is the reward which will continue to keep me employed.

On September 13 he wrote in the Laboratory Book this verbal picture of his laboratory:

Objects much wanted in the laboratory of the Royal Institution: Cleanliness, neatness, and regularity.

The laboratory must be cleaned every morning when operations are going on before ten o'clock.

It is the business of W. Payne [1] to do this, and it is the duty of Mr. E. Davy to see that it is done and to take care of and keep in order the apparatus.

There must be in the laboratory pen, ink, paper, and wafers, and these must not be kept in the slovenly manner in which they usually are kept. I am now writing with a pen and ink such as was never used in any other place.

There are wanting small graduated glass tubes blown here and measured to ten grains of mercury.

There are wanting four new stopcocks fitted to our air-pump.

There are wanting twelve green glass retorts.

There are wanting most of the common metallic and saline solutions, such as acetate of copper, nitrate of silver, nitrate of barytes—most of these made in the laboratory.

All the wine-glasses should be cleaned.

And, as all operation ceases at six o'clock in the evening, there is plenty of time for getting things in order before night; but if they are not got into order the same night, they must be by ten o'clock the next day.

The laboratory is constantly in a state of dirt and confusion.

There must be a roller with a coarse towel for washing the hands and a basin of water and soap, and every week at least a whole morning must be devoted to the inspection and ordering of the voltaic battery.

For Thursday—*i.e.* to-morrow—the experiments in the

[1] The predecessor of Mr. Faraday.

morning are on the excitation of radiant heat and electricity in different gases. For the experiments on Friday, which will be on tellurium, there are wanting very pure hydrogen; two bottles of *new*, very pure oxymuriatic gas; two new stopcocks cemented into retorts, with stoppers, either green or white; some tubes of this bore  or near it, closed at one end and six inches long; a spirit lamp made from a phial of large bore and the tube larger than that at present used.

On September 14 he tried various experiments on the excitation of electricity. The Laboratory Book says, 'Present in these and the former experiments, Mr. Cavendish, Dr. Herschel, Mr. Herschel, Sir Charles Blagden (not in the second set on electricity); Dr. Wollaston, Mr. Warburton.'

The repulsion of the machine was compared to the repulsion in a partial vacuum, in hydrogen, in carbonic acid, and in rarefied carbonic acid. The former experiments the same day were on the rise of a thermometer heated by a coil of platinum wire in different gases.

On September 21 the Note-Book says:

An Experiment to Decompose Muriatic Acid Gas.—A balloon having three openings, to one of which a stopcock was cemented, and in the other two were corks containing wires, so adapted to each other that a contact might be made. Pieces of well-burnt charcoal were fastened to the ends of the wires. The apparatus, being air-tight, was exhausted and filled with hydrogen; another exhaustion being made, the balloon was filled with oxymuriatic gas from a gas-holder, with which it was connected by means of a stopcock. The two wires being joined to the voltaic apparatus and a contact of the charcoal made, the ignition was brilliant without any apparent combustion; white fumes were presently produced, which in a short time disappeared again, and were afterwards, during the remaining time the experiment was in hand, only formed when two new points of charcoal came in contact, or when the flame played on the copper wire which fastened the charcoal. The light emitted was a brilliant yellowish colour, frequently assuming a fine lake. After an hour's time the gas appeared unaltered, of its original colour. The higher parts of the pieces of charcoal were covered with a fine greenish-yellow powder, otherwise unaltered.

Tin-leaf thrown in through one of the openings began immediately to form with the oxymuriatic acid gas the fuming liquor of Libavius. When shook it inflamed.

On September 23, 1809, in a letter to Mr. Children, he mentions this experiment, and says 'it is as difficult to decompose as nitrogen, except when all its elements can be made to enter into new combinations.'

On October 3, among 'the hints for experiments' in the Note-Book is this, to detonate together hydrogen and oxymuriatic acid.

Another Bakerian lecture was given, and then he continued his researches on ammonia.

On November 24 'experiments to be in progress' are thus entered in the Laboratory Book:

1. To decompose sulphuretted hydrogen by electricity in an apparatus by which the results can be accurately known.

2. To pass potassium through ignited powdered quartz.

3. To decompose muriatic acid gas by potassium, so as to ascertain the quantity of hydrogen formed.

4. To weigh ammonia, hydrogen, and nitrogen,

sulphuretted hydrogen and gaseous fluoric acid, nitrous oxide, and oxymuriatic acid gas.

5. To make a series of experiments upon the ores and products of cast iron.

6. To ascertain with greater precision than has been yet obtained the nature of the acid matter formed in pure water, oxygenated or not.

7. To decompose fluoric acid gas, and to ascertain the source of the hydrogen which it gives by the operation of potassium.

8. To make various experiments on the amalgamation of ammonia, using different amalgams of mercury and different modes of excluding water.

9. To endeavour to bring the ὑδὼρ theory to a test of producing oxygen from water without hydrogen.

10. To decompose muriate of soda and litharge and other bodies that contain no water by electricity, and to see what happens.

In the early part of 1810 the experiments were chiefly on the action of potassium on sulphur and phosphorus.

From analogy oxygen had been considered as the acidifying principle of the muriatic acid, or spirit of salt. It was thought to combine with more oxygen, and then was called oxygenated muriatic acid, although its powers as an acid were weakened and it became more volatile and bleached.

Davy sent two papers to the Royal Society, on this subject. The first was on July 12, 'Researches on Oxymuriatic Acid and the Elements of Muriatic Acid; with Experiments on Sulphur and Phosphorus,' and the second, on November 15, was the 'Bakerian Lecture on Some of the Combinations of Oxymuriatic Gas and

Oxygen, and on the Chemical Relations of these Principles to Inflammable Bodies.'

In the first paper he says, 'Scheele considered oxymuriatic acid as more simple than muriatic acid, and that it became muriatic acid by union with phlogiston. Berthollet said it contained oxygen. The vivid combustion of many bodies in this gas has favoured the presumption that it contained oxygen very loosely combined, and ready to exert its utmost power of affinity; but it is mere presumption, since heat and light result also from the intense agency of any other combination without the presence of oxygen.'

On July 3 he wrote, 'Equal parts of oxymuriatic acid and hydrogene, both dried, were detonated. There was a diminution equal to about $\frac{1}{12}$, and muriatic gas was formed; and this was over mercury, and some of the oxymuriatic acid burnt the mercury, and there was an excess of $\frac{1}{4}$ hydrogene. Equal parts of oxymuriatic acid and sulphuretted hydrogene, diminution about $\frac{1}{12}$. Muriatic gas formed; sulphuretted hydrogene apparently in excess.'

A most important experiment had been made on September 21, 1809, on the resistance of oxymuriatic acid to galvanic decomposition; and as long previously as April 19, 1808, he had decomposed muriatic acid with a battery of 520 pair of plates.[1]

[1] The discovery of the simplicity of chlorine was claimed by the French chemists. Davy afterwards said of Gay-Lussac's paper in the *Annales de Chimie* for July 1814, 'The historical notes attached to it are of a nature not to be passed over without animadversion. M. Gay-Lussac states that he and M. Thénard were the first to advance the hypothesis that chlorine was a simple body, and he quotes M. Ampère as having

The experiments which were detailed in the Bakerian lecture read during the absence of Davy on November 15, were made in July and August.

On August 30, after entering things wanted, he wrote in the Laboratory Book:

'No experiments are to be made or carried on in the laboratory without the consent and approbation of the Professor of Chemistry. The attempt at original experiment, unless preceded by knowledge, merely interferes with the progress of discovery. There are a sufficient number of new and interesting objects which a modest student would wish to pursue, and in which the path is marked and distinct.'

On September 8 he was again experimenting on the decomposition of nitrogen. He wrote, 'And if it be said that no air and no water were present (in the potassium, boracic acid, and ammonia), the experiment is decisive as to the destruction of nitrogen and its containing the same kind of elementary matter as water.'

To the like experiment, September 13, he wrote, 'This experiment seems almost decisive on the decomposition of nitrogen.'

Soon after he wrote, 'Query, Does not the general tenor of the last experiments lead to the suspicion of the decomposition of nitrogen?'

entertained that opinion before me. On the subject of the originality of the idea of chlorine being a simple body I have always vindicated the claims of Scheele, but I must assume for myself the labour of having demonstrated its properties and combinations and of having explained the chemical phenomena it produces, and I am in possession of a letter from M. Ampère that shows he has no claims of this kind to make.'

On September 16 he made this note: 'Objects to be attempted during the next week: To-morrow, oxy-muriatic acid pure, to try absorption by two grains of different metals—tin, arsenic, antimony, bismuth, copper, platina, lead, zinc.'

On October 4, when he was about to start for Dublin, he wrote in the Laboratory Book, 'The principal thing, the laboratory in complete order.' He was absent from October 4 to the middle of December. No experiments were entered until October 27; then there are some on oxymuriatic acid by E. Davy.

On November 15 the action of oxymuriatic gas on dried nitrous gas was repeated.

The next experiment was on November 24. 'Two grains of silver were entirely converted into horn-silver; the absorption of chlorine gas was $\frac{9}{10}$ of a cubic inch.' This was the first use of the word CHLORINE in the Note-Book; it occurs daily afterwards. Oxymuriatic gas continued the chief subject of the experiments in the laboratory up to the end of February in the following year.

This year Davy was invited to deliver a course of lectures on Electro-Chemical Science, and another course of six lectures on the Application of Chemistry to Agriculture, in the new laboratory of the Dublin Society. Having obtained permission as secretary to be absent from the meetings of the Royal Society, he commenced his course on November 8 and finished it on the 29th, and the Society requested his acceptance of 500 guineas.

In 1811 he again delivered two courses, one on the

Elements of Chemical Philosophy and the other on Geology. For these he received 750*l.*, and Trinity College made him a Doctor of Laws. Such consideration for lectures on this side of the Atlantic sounds fabulous.

He wrote to his mother:

Balina, Ireland, October 24, 1811.

The laboratory in Dublin, which has been enlarged, so as to hold 550 people, will not hold half the persons who desire to hear my lectures. The 550 tickets issued for the course by the Dublin Society at two guineas each were all disposed of the first week, and I am told now that from ten to twenty guineas are offered for a ticket.

This is merely for your eye; it may please you to know that your son is not unpopular or useless. Every person here, from the highest to the lowest, shows me every attention and kindness.

I shall come to see you as soon as I can. I hear with infinite delight of your health, and I hope Heaven will continue to preserve and bless a mother who deserves so well of her children.

I am, your very affectionate Son,

H. DAVY.

During 1811 he made the acquaintance of Mrs. Appreece, the daughter and heiress of Charles Carr, of Kelso, and about the end of the year probably he wrote to his mother:

MY DEAR MOTHER,—You possibly may have heard reports of my intended marriage. Till within the last few days it was mere report. It is, I trust, now a settled arrangement. I am the happiest of men in the hope of a union with a woman equally distinguished for virtues, talent, and accomplishments.

. . . .

You, I am sure, will sympathise in my happiness. I believe I should never have married but for this charming woman, whose views and whose tastes coincide with my own, and who is eminently qualified to promote my best efforts and objects in life.

I am, your affectionate Son,

H. DAVY.

He wrote to his brother, at that time a medical student at Edinburgh:

MY DEAR JOHN,—Many thanks for your last letter. I have been very miserable. The lady whom I love best of any human being has been very ill. She is now well and I am happy. Mrs. Appreece has consented to marry me, and when the event takes place I shall not envy kings, princes, or potentates.

I am, my dear Brother, ever most affectionately yours,

H. DAVY.

The Laboratory Note-Book at this time contains very little work.

On February 21, 1811, he had a paper read to the Royal Society on a 'Combination of Oxymuriatic Gas and Oxygen Gas, called Euchlorine.'

In July the action of chlorine on carbonic oxide, exposed for hours to bright sunshine, was examined. He wrote, 'The new gas seems to consist of equal volumes of chlorine and carbonic oxide condensed to one volume.'

On August 7 Davy wrote in the Laboratory Book, 'To get nitrous oxide, nitrous gas, and very pure chlorine for experiments. To try to decompose nitrogen or to combine it with *chlorine*.'

On the 10th the exposure to the light had been continued two days without result.

In the middle of August he experimented on the action of potassium on silicated fluoric gas.

From September 2 to December 20 there are no entries in the Laboratory Book. That day—the first after his return from Ireland—there are experiments on the electrolization of water.

Early in the following year Sir Joseph Banks wrote to Sir George Staunton (in China):

. . . .

We are going on here as usual, but I think the taste for science is on the increase. The Royal Society has been well supplied with papers, and continues to be so. Davy, our secretary, is said to be on the point of marrying a rich and handsome widow, who has fallen in love with science and marries him in order to obtain a footing in the academic groves; her name is Apreece, the daughter of Mr. Carr, who made a fortune in India, and the niece of Dr. Carr, of Northampton. If this takes place, it will give to science a kind of new éclat; we want nothing so much as the countenance of the ladies to increase our popularity.

Very little laboratory work was done in 1812. It appears from Davy's notes that a few experiments on euchlorine were made in January. In February he was again working on sulphur and phosphorus and chlorine. In March he was experimenting on borum with oxygen, and with chlorine.

In August an experiment was made to ascertain whether there is, according to the received belief, a neutral part in the voltaic circle.

The battery consisted of forty double plates, thus arranged: Each trough, excepting the end ones, was separately connected with a glassful of mercury by polished copper wire, and each pair of glasses was connected by very fine polished iron wire.

The effects took place at the moment of contact at all the wires, so that there could have been no *neutral point.*

For the last time, after innumerable failures, he returned to the decomposition of nitrogen.

On August 13 'experiment very cautiously made of the action of potassium on nitrogene. Light green when mercury is employed, red when potassium.'

On October 23 the Laboratory Book says:

'A series of experiments to attempt to decompose hydrofluoric acid, and to ascertain the constitution of the *fluoric combinations.*

'1. To obtain pure hydrofluoric acid.

'2. To obtain silicofluoric acid gas, and to decompose it by potassium and by potash, and to ascertain the quantity of fluate of lime they will give.

'3. To make pure prussic acid.

'4. To act upon pure prussic acid by chlorine.'

On November 5 a new detonating compound was formed; this was the chloride of nitrogen.

This year Davy gave his last course of lectures on Chemical Philosophy at the Royal Institution.

An account of four of these lectures 'was taken off from notes by Mr. Faraday.' The subjects were Radiant Matter, Chlorine, Simple Inflammables, and Metals. After the report of each lecture he gave the experiments as a sequel, illustrated with drawings; the whole made a small quarto of 386 pages, with an index of twenty-five pages. The volume was bound by Mr. Faraday, and was sent to Davy as an evidence of Faraday's 'knowledge, diligence, and order,' when he asked for an engagement at the Royal Institution.

Davy gave the lecture on Radiant Matter on February 29. He said, 'With respect to radiant or ethereal substances all our knowledge of it is obtained from the effect it produces on us and terrestrial bodies when in motion.

'In our consideration of this subject it will be essentially necessary that we distinguish between knowledge and speculation. These terms in their meaning are palpably different, but yet have been intermixed and *combined* together in a very singular manner. The French chemists in particular speak of the materiality of heat, and of the nature of the compounds it forms, as confidently and as fluently as if they had undeniably proved it to be a body. They have blended their knowledge with speculation, and formed a theory that is very possibly untrue. The most eminent phenomena of radiation are to be observed in light.'

And then he passed on to the laws of light and dwelt on Herschel's discovery that the heating power of red rays was to the green as fifty-five to sixteen, and that he had himself found the thermometer rose still higher beyond the red, and that heating rays are less refrangible than light rays; then he showed a wire heated by the voltaic battery in air and in vacuo, and said that he had proved 'that the radiating power is three times as strong in an exhausted receiver as in the open air,' and, 'fully proves that radiation is not caused by undulations in the atmosphere. It is strongest when no atmosphere is present.' He ends his account of the effects of radiant heat thus: 'Were it not for this terrestrial radiation of earthly bodies, the heat would accumulate from the rays of the sun until at last the whole world would be uninhabitable.

'But, besides the effects produced by the two species of radiant matter—radiant light and radiant heat—there are other effects—chemical effects—that take place caused by the action of some radiant matter that comes to us from the sun, perhaps a single substance that, independent of light and heat, causes effects by its own power.' And then he showed an experiment of chlorine and hydrogen exposed to light.

He says, 'There is a very singular analogy that exists between the rays at the violet end of the spectrum, hydrogen gas, and the negative pole of the voltaic battery; and opposed to it stands the analogy of the rays at the red end of the spectrum to positive electricity; they produce opposite effects to the first-mentioned arrangement, but act similar to each other.

'If that sublime idea of the ancients that there is only one species of matter in the universe, and that its different properties depend on the difference of size, shape and other qualities should be confirmed, it would simplify the science in a most eminent degree, and at the same time it would raise it to the acme of perfection.'

Opposing the view that oxygen gas contained light combined with it, and gave light out in oxidation, he contrasted slowly oxidised iron with an iron turning burnt in oxygen.

'When the laws which govern in chemical science are fully known, there is no doubt it will become a much more simple science. It cannot fail to be so, since then it will be complete. Already it is one of the most useful of the whole circle to man, and when in its utmost state of improvement it will be one of the most sublime. It will, I have no doubt, connect mechanical and chemical sciences together; it will concentrate them into one and in that one comprehend the whole universe.

'The first step to truth is the confession of ignorance. No man could have made the immortal discoveries of Newton unless he had first thrown up the ridiculous doctrines of Des Cartes. To attend to our errors and own them, to sacrifice all selfishness to the science, not to support errors for the sake of vanity, ought to be the leading precepts of a philosopher. He should turn his endeavour to the advancement of science and not to the increase of his reputation. Let him fix steps for others to rise on, and he does more real good to science than if he had spent years in controversy on an equivocal point. Let him turn his thoughts to general views and try to contain the whole science in his grasp; he will then be calculated to arrange it, improve it, and reform it and place it in that order which tends so materially to its advancement.'

His lecture on Chlorine was given on Saturday, March

14; the previous week he had given a lecture on Oxygen, which was not reported by Faraday.

'I will demonstrate what I affirm in a positive and satisfactory manner.

'Accustomed for years to consider the chemical principles of the French School of Physical Sciences as correct, I had adopted them and put faith in them until they became prejudices, and I even felt unwilling to give them up when my judgment was fully convinced by experiment that they were erroneous. I know that this is the case in some degree with almost every person; he is unwilling to believe that he is wrong, and therefore feels averse to adopt what is right when it opposes his principles.

'Pelletier died from inhaling this gas (chlorine). It supports combustion of a taper [experiment]; it does not contain oxygen.' He showed by experiment that pure dry chlorine and hydrogen, when exploded, caused no moisture; no water was formed. This was the synthetical proof. Decomposition of muriatic acid gas by potassium was shown as the analytical proof. Compounds with phosphorus, ammonia, and sulphur all free from oxygen. 'Oxygen does combine with chlorine. I have ventured to name the compound euchlorine; it is of a very bright yellow green colour. Names should represent things, not opinions, for in the last case they often tend to misrepresent and mislead.

'As chlorine contained no oxygen, it became an inquiry well worth investigation to ascertain the part which chlorine acted in bleaching. It decomposes water and forms hydrochloric acid.'

'Had Mr. Berthollet obtained oxygen from chlorine there would have been no error in his theory, but by not attending to the minute circumstances of his experiment, by not ascertaining that the water present acted no part and was not decomposed, he fell into an error, and of course all the conclusions he drew were false and erroneous. Nothing should be allowed but what can be proved by experiment, and nothing should be taken for granted upon analogy or supposition.'

Faraday concludes this lecture thus: 'Mr. Davy now proceeded to comment and make observations on the former theory of chlorine gas. Here I was unable to follow him. The plan which I pursue in taking of notes is convenient and sufficient with respect to the theoretical and also the practical part of the lecture, but for the embellishments and ornaments of it it will not answer. Mr. Davy's language at those times is so superior (and indeed throughout the whole course of the lecture) that then I am infinitely below him and am incapable of following him even in an humble style. Therefore I shall not attempt it; it will be sufficient to give a kind of contents of it.

'He said that hypotheses should not be considered as facts and built upon accordingly. Nevertheless, if cautiously pursued, they might lead to mature fruit. That nothing should be taken for granted unless proved. By considering oxygen as contained in chlorine the whole chemical world had been wrapped in error respecting that body for more than one-third of a century.

'He noticed that all the truly great scientific men

were possessed of great humility and diffidence of their own opinions and powers. He spoke of Scheele, the discoverer of chlorine ; observed that he possessed a truly philosophical spirit, gave up his opinions when he supposed them to be erroneous, and without hesitation or reluctance adopted those of others which he considered more correct; admired his spirit and recommended it to all philosophers; compared it to corn, which looked but simple and insignificant in blossom and asked for little praise, yet was the support of man.'

In this lecture Faraday gives the details of twenty experiments.

On April 8 Professor Davy lectured on Simple Inflammable Bodies. 'Their number, excepting the metals, is six, which unite with oxygen and chlorine, the subjects of the two last lectures.' He showed a jet of oxygen burning in hydrogen, and said, 'In the burning of tallow, wax, oil, and wood it is the hydrogen of their bodies that causes the flame; though in most cases it is also combined with carbon, yet it is the hydrogen that produces the flame. . . .

'I have here a bladder filled with nitrous oxide gas; I will breathe it once or twice, but not so far as to incapacitate me from continuing the lecture. It produces a very pleasing sensation (far superior to the most exquisite liquors, such as champagne), and I have no doubt that if I were to continue it a few minutes longer I should make a very interesting exhibition to the company; but I would rather be excused. . . .

'If we suppose that the diamond is pure carbon,

and is therefore the same as charcoal, we have a very strong presumptive reason to suppose that all matter is alike in all substances. If substances so opposite and so different as charcoal and diamond are in reality the same kind of matter, then the difference in other bodies is no proof that they also are not of the same kind of matter; and this would lead us to suppose that there is but one matter in nature, and that the difference in different bodies is owing to variety in the distance of the particles, to shape, and to size. . . .

'In conclusion several of these six simple combustibles I suspect to be compounds, and perhaps their nature may shortly be discovered. . . .

'What gives a strong colour to the idea of the compound nature of nitrogen is the quantity of it that can be obtained from animal bodies, whereas they imbibe none, they combine with none.

'Sulphur and phosphorus both appear to be compound bodies when they are subjected to the power of a voltaic battery. A great quantity of hydrogen gas is evolved, so that it appears hydrogen is one of their constituent parts. . . .

'Whether these bodies are compound or not, they are objects of new research; they present new fields for the great, the industrious, the scientific, and the penetrating mind. Our horizon extends the higher we rise. The result of future inquiries will probably lay a foundation on which future ages and future generations may erect an edifice that will reach from earth to heaven.'

In this lecture Faraday noted twenty-two experiments.

The next day, April 9, Davy was knighted by the Prince Regent.

On April 10 Sir Humphry Davy gave his last lecture at the Royal Institution; it was on the Metals.

'All the volatile metals burn with flame, and all those that are not volatile with sparks. . . .

'These, with the metals of the alkalies and the alkaline earths which I have had the good fortune to discover, make up the number to about forty.'

He shewed the mode of obtaining alkaline metals by voltaic decomposition; and earths by potassium.

The mode of obtaining the alkaline metals by chemical action alone was shown, but the experiment was not made. A quantity of potassium from common potash by iron was on the table.

'The combustion of metals is according to their electricity, those containing the most electricity burning with the most energy. All those metals that are positive to others are also more inflammable than those others, and burn more readily. . . .

'That the metals of the earths and alkalies cannot exist at the surface of our globe we are well assured, but they may exist in the interior, and if so they will offer a very complete and a very probable solution of the phenomena of earthquakes and volcanoes; and perhaps, considered thus, they may lay the foundation of a new and perfect system of geology.

'We have here a small volcano formed of clay, &c., in the shape of a mountain, and having two or three pieces of the alkaline metals introduced here and there. Now by adding a little water to this volcano I shall be able to inflame it and cause it to burn briskly. . . .

'Meteors consist of alkaline metals and iron; the iron burns last if it be burnt at all.

'What I conceive is, that there are certain bodies that revolve round our earth—a kind of satellites—and are the same with respect to our globe that comets are to the sun. Their orbits are ellipses, whose longer diameters, like those of the comets, far exceed their shorter ones. They must move with very great velocity to counteract the attraction of the earth. . . .

Regarding transmutation of metals he said 'the beginning was deceit, the progress falsehood, and the end beggary, said Lemery.'

'It was supposed till lately that the fixed alkalies were simple bodies, but I have had the good fortune to prove them compounds; and that pure potash should contain a metal, oxygen, and water is not more probable than that the metals are compounds, yet it not only is probable but it is possible, and in reality is so. . . .

'From the mercurial amalgam and from the quantity of hydrogen given out by metals when exposed to the action of a vigorous voltaic battery, either this hydrogen is combined with the metal or it is one of its constituent parts. . . .

'If, then, we suppose that hydrogen constitutes a part of all metals, they will be compounds of it and a base. The hydrogen will give them their genuine characters and make them metals, and their base will bestow on them their own peculiar properties.

'I should wish particularly on this point to be understood rightly. I am not an advocate for alchemy and its attendant frauds; that will appear from the tenor of my discourse; but I conceive it to be a noble and glorious object to follow up the paths trod by those chemists who wish for the improvement of science to ascertain the compound nature of metals. It is a subject well worthy of pursuit, and whenever the discovery is made it will confer immortal honour on the discoverer, the age, and the country that it is made in.'

Faraday then says, 'Having thus given the general character of the metals, Sir H. Davy proceeded to make a few observations on the connection of science with the other parts of polished and social life. Here it would be improper for me to follow him. I should merely injure and destroy the beautiful, the sublime observations that fell from his lips. He spoke in the most energetic and luminous manner of the advancement of the arts and sciences, of the connection that had always existed between them and other parts of a nation's economy. He noticed the peculiar congeries of great men in all departments of life that generally appeared together, noticed Anaximander, Anaximenes, Socrates, Newton, Bacon, Elizabeth, &c., but, by an unaccountable omission, forgot himself, though I will venture to say no one else present did.

'During the whole of these observations his delivery

was easy, his diction elegant, his tone good, and his sentiments sublime.'

Faraday ends his volume with the notes of eighteen experiments that were made in this lecture.

The same day Davy wrote to his brother. It was the eve of his wedding.

Friday, April 10, 1812.

My dear Brother,—You will have excused me for not writing to you on subjects of science. I have been absorbed by arrangements on which the happiness of my future life depends. Before you receive this these arrangements will, I trust, be settled, and in a few weeks I shall be able to return to my habits of study and scientific research. I am going to be married to-morrow, and I have a fair prospect of happiness with the most amiable and intellectual woman I have ever known.

The Prince Regent, unsolicited by me or by any of my intimate friends, was pleased to confer the honour of knighthood on me at the last levée. This distinction has not often been bestowed on scientific men, but I am proud of it, as the greatest of human geniuses bore it; and it is at least a proof that the world has not overlooked my humble efforts in the cause of science.

. . . . . .

I am, my dear Brother, most affectionately yours,

H. Davy.

On June 12 he published his 'Elements of Chemical Philosophy.' It is dedicated to Lady Davy, 'as a pledge that he shall continue to pursue science with unabated ardour.'

Dr. Thomas Young, in the 'Quarterly Review' for September 1812, enables us to see what was thought of Sir H. Davy and of his book at this time.

'In attempting a review of this work we cannot avoid professing that we are far from entertaining the impression of sitting down as competent judges to decide upon the merits or demerits of the author; on this point the public voice, not only within our own islands, but wherever science is cultivated, has already pronounced too definite a sentence to be weakened or confirmed by anything that we can suggest of exception or approbation. Our humble labours on such an occasion must be much more analytical and historical than critical; at the same time we are too well acquainted with the author's candour to suppress any remark which may occur to us as tending to correction or improvement. It has most assuredly fallen to the lot of no one individual to contribute to the progress of chemical knowledge by discoveries so numerous and important as those which have been made by Sir Humphry Davy; and, with regard to mere experimental investigation, we do not hesitate to rank his researches as more splendidly successful than any which have ever before illustrated the physical sciences in any of their departments. We are aware that the "Optics" of Newton will immediately occur to our readers as an exception; but, without attempting to convince those who may differ from us on this point, we are disposed to abide by the opinion that for a series of well-devised experiments and brilliant discoveries the contents of Davy's "Bakerian Lectures" are as much superior to those of Newton's "Optics" as the "Principia" are to those or to any other human work for the accurate and refined application of a sublime and simple theory to the most intricate and apparently anomalous results derived from previous observation.

. . . . . .

'Until the year 1806 Sir Humphry Davy had been remarkable for the industrious and ingenious application of those means of experiment only which had been long known to chemists. He had acquired at a very early period of his life a well-established celebrity among men of science throughout Europe by the originality and accuracy of his researches, and at the same time the fluent and impressive delivery of his lectures had obtained him the most flattering marks of approbation from the public of the metropolis. But it was in the summer of that year that, in repeating some electro-chemical experiments of very doubtful authority (the production of acid and alkali by the decomposition of water), he was led into a new train of reasoning and investigation, which enabled him to demonstrate the important laws of the connection between the electrical affections of bodies and their chemical powers. This was his first great discovery. . . . Our author's next great step was the decomposition of the alkalies, which he effected the succeeding year; and this, though less interesting and important with regard to the fundamental theory of the science, was more brilliant and imposing from its capability of being exhibited in a visible, tangible form. The third striking feature which distinguishes the system advanced in the present work is the assertion of the existence of at least two empyreal principles—oxygen and the elastic fluid called the oxymuriatic acid gas (chlorine). . . .

'A fourth peculiarity, which, however, is less exclusively and originally a doctrine of Sir Humphry Davy, is the theory of the simplicity of the proportions in which all bodies combine—a theory the explicit illustration and general and minute application of which the science is principally indebted to our countryman Mr. Dalton.'

How far later discoveries have advanced our knowledge can be seen in the strange words, as they now sound, which Dr. Young uses when he mentions the first researches of Davy.

'Certain bodies which attract each other chemically, and combine when their particles have freedom of motion, when brought into contact still preserving their aggregation, exhibit what may be called electrical polarities, and by certain combinations these polarities may be highly exalted; and in this case they become subservient to chemical decompositions, and, by means of chemical arrangements, the constituent parts of bodies are separated in uniform order and in definite proportions.'

. . . . . .

The review then gives the account of the discovery of potassium, sodium, barium, strontium, magnesium, aluminum, glycinium, zirconium, silicium, and itrium and boron.

On the subject of oxymuriatic acid gas Dr. Young says 'we cannot help thinking his tone somewhat more decisive than the present state of the investigation altogether authorises,' and he strongly objects to Davy's terminology; which never was adopted by chemists.

As no table of the proportional weights of chemical substances entering into combination is to be found in Sir H. Davy's work, Dr. Young says he took the liberty of inserting one formed from Davy's numbers and from the experiments of Berzelius and Richter.

He thus ended his review, 'The character of Sir Humphry Davy's researches has always been that of the most interesting originality, and we have certainly no reason to complain that he has in his experiments very commonly forsaken the beaten path.

. . . . . .

'With all its excellences this work must be allowed to bear no inconsiderable marks of haste, and we would easily have conjectured, even if the author had not expressly told us so in his dedication, that the period employed on it "has been the happiest of his life." In that and in every other happiness which may have befallen him we shall ever most sincerely rejoice; nor shall we think the public will have any reason to reproach him with having done too little for science, even if he should fail at any future time in his avowed resolution of pursuing it "with unabated ardour;" that he has not yet so failed is become from a late accident a matter of public notoriety, and if we may expect perseverance to be at all commensurate to success, we have no reason to be apprehensive of his passing any part of his life in inactivity.

'The style and manner of this work are nearly the same with those of the author's lectures delivered in the theatre of the Royal Institution. They have been much admired by some of the most competent judges of good language and good taste, and it has been remarked that Davy was born a poet, and has only become a chemist by accident. Certainly the situation in which he was placed induced him to cultivate an ornamented and popular style of expression and embellishment, and what was encouraged by temporary motives has become natural to him from habit. Hence have arisen a multitude of sentimental reflections and appeals to the feelings, which many will think beauties and some only prettinesses; nor is it necessary for us to decide in which of the two classes of readers we wish ourselves to be arranged, conceiving that in matters so indifferent to the immediate object of the work a great latitude may be allowed to the diversity of taste and opinion.'

On June 18 Davy sent a paper to the Royal Society on 'Some Combinations of Phosphorus and Sulphur,' and in July two other papers—'Further Observations on Chloride of Nitrogen; and on Fluorine and Hydrofluoric Acid.'

Late in August he wrote to a friend, 'I have just published a volume of the 'Elements of Chemistry,' and I hope to publish another in the course of the spring. Having given up lecturing, I shall be able to devote my whole time to the pursuit of discovery.'

On October 14, from Edinburgh, he wrote to Mr. Children:

'I have received a very interesting letter from Ampère. He says that a combination of chlorine and azote has been discovered at Paris, which is a fluid and explodes by the heat of the hand, the discovery of which cost an eye and a finger to the author. He gives no details as to the mode of combining them. I have tried in my little apparatus with ammonia cooled very low and chlorine, but without success.'

On October 24 he writes, 'On Wednesday we are to have a meeting at the Institution, to try to make this compound of azote and chlorine.'

On November 5 a letter was read at the Royal Society from Davy to Sir Joseph Banks on this compound, which had been formed by exposing chlorine to a solution of nitrate of ammonia. During his investigation the substance exploded in a tube, and he received a severe wound in the eye.

On November 16 he wrote to his brother, 'It is not safe to experiment upon a globule larger than a pin's head. I have been severely wounded by a piece scarcely bigger.'

In January 1813 he had another severe attack of inflammation in the wounded eye, and it was not perfectly well till April.

On April 4 he wrote to his brother, 'I am now quite recovered, and Jane is very well, and we have both enjoyed the last month in London. I have been hard at work (on fluorine). We have now a triad of supporters of combustion.

'I have just finished printing my 'Agricultural Lectures.'

Soon after he again wrote to his brother:

I communicated to you in a former letter my plans as far as they were matured. I have neither given up the Institution nor am I going to France, and, wherever I am, I shall continue to labour in the cause of science with a zeal not diminished by increase of happiness and (with respect to the world) increased independence.

I have just finished the first part of my 'Chemistry' to my own satisfaction, and I am going to publish my 'Agricultural Lectures,' for which I am to get 1,000 guineas for the copy-right and fifty guineas for each edition, which seems a fair price. As I shall see you so soon I shall not write about any matters of science.

I was appointed professor (honorary) to the Institution at the last meeting (April 5). I do not pledge myself to give lectures. Brande gives twelve.

If I lecture it will be on some new series of discoveries, should it be my fortune to make them, and I give up the routine of lecturing merely that I may have more time to pursue original inquiries and forward more the great objects of science. This has been for some time my intention, and it has been hastened by my marriage.

I shall have great pleasure in making you acquainted with Lady D. She is a noble creature (if I may be permitted so to speak of a wife) and every day adds to my contentment by the powers of her understanding and her amiable and delightful tones of feeling. God bless you!

Believe me to be your affectionate brother,

H. DAVY.

In the minutes of the monthly meetings of members of the Royal Institution, April 5, 1813, it is stated that Sir H. Davy rose and begged leave to resign his situation of Professor of Chemistry; 'but he by no means wished to give up his connection with the Royal Institution, as he should ever be happy to communicate his researches in the first instance to the Institution in the way he did in the presence of the members last Wednesday (on hydrofluoric acid), and to do all in his power to promote the interest and success of this Institution.'

Earl Spencer moved 'that the thanks of this meeting be returned to Sir H. Davy for the inestimable services rendered by him to the Royal Institution, and that, in order more strongly to mark the high sense entertained by this meeting of the merits of Sir H. Davy, he be elected Honorary Professor of Chemistry.'

Mr. Brande was then nominated Professor of Chemistry, with a salary of 200*l.* per annum.

In October Sir H. Davy went abroad with Mr. Faraday.

In May 1815 he came back, and Faraday was re-engaged as the assistant in the laboratory of the Royal Institution. Whilst abroad he had sent as many as seven papers to the Royal Society—on 'Fluoric Acid Compounds and Hydrogen Acids.' Two papers on 'Iodine,' on 'Combustion of the Diamond,' on 'Ancient Colours,' on a 'Solid Compound of Iodine and Oxygen,' on 'Hyperoxy-Muriates.'

When he returned he probably intended to make greater discoveries in chemistry during the following ten years than he had made during the fifteen years that he had been at the Institution. He was in the prime of life. He had won the highest rank as an original inquirer. He had a love of research which, in spite of his marriage, his wealth, and ultimately his ill health, never ceased until his early death. He had Faraday as his assistant, and he soon found a subject more fruitful than the composition of nitrogen, which had so long baffled his genius.

Many of the details of his work in the laboratory

until his last experiment on the diffusion of gases, in February 1826, are to be found in the 'Life of Faraday.' It will be sufficient to give here a statement of the original researches which he communicated to the Royal Society.

In November 1815 and January 1816 his papers on Fire-damp were read. He then worked upon flame, and in January 1817 his researches on flame and his splendid invention of the Davy Lamp were laid before the Royal Society. At this time the popular reputation of Davy reached its climax, and, looking back, we can now see that his life should have ended here; he was then only 38 years old. He was presented with a service of plate as a token of his invaluable invention by the coal owners of the Tyne and Wear. He bequeathed this to the Royal Society for the foundation of a medal, to be given yearly to the chemist who made the greatest discovery. This prize should be looked on as a lasting memorial of the countless lives which Davy and other chemists, by the application of their scientific researches, have preserved.

Year after year, from 1817 to 1826, Davy communicated new investigations to the Royal Society. He worked on chlorine, on phosphorus, on mists. He went abroad again, and he tried chemically to unfold the Herculanean papyri. He returned in 1820, and was elected President of the Royal Society after the death of Sir Joseph Banks. Then he worked on magnetic phenomena produced by electricity, on electric phenomena in vacuo, on water in the cavities of crystals, on new phenomena of electro-magnetism. He became jealous of the discoveries of Faraday, and he sent a paper to the Royal Society on the 'Application of Liquids Formed by the Condensation of Gases as Mechanical Agents.'

In 1823 he began to work on the defence of the copper sheathing of ships, and in 1824 he had two papers published on this subject. He went in a Government steamboat to Norway, Sweden, and Denmark for the purpose of trying the influence of motion on his protectors. He had already suffered for a year at this time from ill health. In 1825 his paper on the 'Preservation of Metals by Electrochemistry' was published. In practice his plan failed, and he was too ill to bear lightly the disappointment of his expectations. In 1826 he had a paper read on the 'Relations of Electrical and Chemical Changes.' It contained but little new matter. On November 30 he was elected President of the Royal Society for the last time. He was dangerously ill on the day of election.

In the middle of December 1826 he was struck with paralysis of the right side.

With the restlessness of disease on January 22, about a month after his attack, he set out for Italy. He had the worst possible journey across Mont Cenis, and, after being three weeks at Ravenna, in the middle of March he wrote to Mr. Poole:

I am, thank God, better, but still very weak and wholly unfit for any kind of business and study. I have, however, considerably recovered the use of all the limbs that were affected, and, as my amendment has been slow and gradual, I hope in time it may be complete. But I am leading the life of an anchorite, obliged to abstain from flesh, wine, business, study, experiments, and all things that I love;

but this discipline is salutary, and, for the sake of being able to do something more for science, and I hope for humanity, I submit to it, believing that the Great Source of intellectual being so wills it for good.

One of the last thoughts in his note-book, written at Ravenna, shows his mind:

'Our *real knowledge* is but to be sure that we know nothing, and I can but doubt if this be a curse or blessing. Those who hope, trust, and believe are surely happier far than those who doubt; and the submissive child, who of his father's goodness is secure, is far more blessed than the froward one, who sets himself against his powerful will, which, after all his struggles and vain efforts, he must at last obey, rebelling against the love which would have made him happy. Is not this the history of man?—of that bright and beauteous garden where in innocence and ignorance he lived and loved till the false taste of knowledge made him wretched and he knew that he must die. And is not this the glory and the consummation of the Christian faith, which gives him back his innocence, his hopes, his confidence in God, which through his life still gilds the future with a golden blessing of an expected immortality? Man fell in Adam; knowledge was his bane; man rose in Christ, recovering his ignorance or substituting hope for what was doubt.'

Four or five days before he left Ravenna he wrote, April 6, 'Did not shoot, but returned thanks to the Great Cause of all being for all His mercies to me, an undeserving and often ungrateful creature, but now most grateful. May I become better and more grateful and more humble-minded every day!'

'Valde miserabilis' is not an unfrequent expression at this time, commonly accompanied with mention of diminished power of limbs and general feebleness, with pain and numbness. Sometimes he was in despair of recovery and resigned to his fate, at other times indulging in hope, thankful for feeling better, and expressing thanks (and he does it very often) by the use of letters; as G. G. D. (Thanks and glory to God); O. O. O.; or more fully thus, G. O. O. O. D.

On July 1 he wrote to his friend Mr. Davies Gilbert, who was on the council of the Royal Society. He says that the expectations of his complete and rapid recovery have not been realised.

Under these circumstances I feel it would be highly imprudent, and perhaps fatal, for me to return and to attempt to perform the official duties of President of the Royal Society; and as I had no other feeling for that high and honourable situation except the hope of being useful to the society, so I would not keep it a moment without the security of being able to devote myself to the labour and attention it demands. I beg, therefore, you will be so good as to communicate my resignation to the council and to the Society at their first meeting in November, stating the circumstances of my severe and long-continued illness as the cause. At the same time I beg you will express to them how grateful I feel for the high honour they have done me in placing me in the chair for so many successive years. Assure them that I shall always take the same interest in the progress of the grand objects of the Society, and throughout the whole of my life endeavour to contribute to their advancement and to the prosperity of the body.

He continued his notes thus:

'*September* 2.—I took my exercise well with less fatigue, and certainly feel better. Offered up my thanksgiving to the O. O. O. with tears of gratitude and feelings of intense adoration.

'*September* 27, ST. GOAR.—A very beautiful and glorious evening. I thought I was going to be quite well, as the weakness of the left wrist, which put an end to my shooting at Spiers, is quite gone; but I found my stiff leg as bad as ever. Yet I can hardly be lower or live lower. Dubito fortissime restaurationem meam.

'As I have so often alluded to the possibility of my dying suddenly, I think it right to mention that I am too intense a believer in the Supreme Intelligence, and have too strong a faith in the optimism of the system of the universe, ever to accelerate my dissolution. The laurel-water and laudanum and opium that are in my dressing-case are medicines. I have been and am taking a care of my health which I fear it is not worth, but which, hoping it may please Providence to preserve me for wise purposes, I think my duty. G. O. O. O.'

He arrived in London on October 6. Not finding his health improve, on March 29, 1828, he left England again. Before he went he sent a paper on Volcanoes to the Royal Society.

In his 'Consolations in Travel' he says, 'I was desirous of again passing some time in Southern Austria and Italy, in the hope of re-establishing a broken constitution, and though this hope was a feeble one, yet at least I expected to spend a few of the last days of life more tranquilly and more agreeably than in the metropolis of my own country. Nature never deceives us. The rocks, the mountains, the streams, always speak the same language. A shower of snow may hide the verdant woods in spring, a thunder-storm may render the blue, limpid streams foul and turbulent; but these effects are rare and transient; in a few hours, or at least days, all the sources of beauty are renovated; and Nature affords no continued trains of misfortunes and miseries, such as depend upon the constitution of humanity, no hopes for ever blighted in the bud, no beings full of life, beauty, and promise taken from us in the prime of youth. Her fruits are all balmy, bright, and sweet; she affords none of those blighted ones so common in the life of man and so like the fabled apples of the Dead Sea, fresh and beautiful to the sight, but when tasted full of bitterness and ashes.'

On May 22 he writes, 'To my old haunt, Wurzen, which is subline in the majesty of Alpine grandeur. The snowy peaks of the Noric Alps rising above thunder-clouds, whilst spring in all its bloom and beauty blooms below, its buds and blossoms adorning the face of nature under a frowning canopy of dark clouds, like some Judith beauty of Italy—a Transteverene brow and eye and a mouth of Venus and the Graces.'

On June 3 he wrote to his brother, Dr. Davy:

Aussee, in Styria.

Notwithstanding the long, severe, and depressing malady under which I still labour I am not entirely without hope of ultimate recovery, and the few pleasures which retain in this my state of earthly purgatory have principally reference to the enjoyments and prospects of my friends;

and I indulge in the idea that you are well and happy and enjoying a life which I can say I only support, supposing that it pleases Omniscience to preserve me for some ends which I cannot understand, but which I trust belong to the great plan of goodness and mercy belonging to the Divine mind.

It suits me better to write away my days in this solitary state of existence in the contemplation of nature than to attempt to enter into London society, where recollections call up the idea of what I was, and the want of bodily power teaches me what a shadow I am. I make notes in natural history, fish, and prepare for another edition of my 'Salmonia;' ride amongst the lakes and mountains; and attach the loose fringe of hope as much as possible to my tattered garments. I am now going to Ischel, where there are warm salt baths, to try if they will renovate the muscular power of my leg and arm.

I wish to go to Trieste in October, to make the experiments I have long projected on the torpedo. God bless you, my dear John!

Your affectionate Friend and Brother,

H. DAVY.

On June 24 he says:

I have used the baths. I have nearly recovered the flexibility of the affected limbs, but not their former strength, and this I can hardly hope to do as long as I am obliged to live so low and to use so much medicine; but I shall go on. Speranza!

In November he sent his last paper to the Royal Society. It was on the Torpedo.

On December 21 he wrote to his brother:

Rome.

Perhaps in the spring you could see me in Illyria. I would then show you my kind little nurse, to whom I owe most of the little happiness I have enjoyed since my illness.

He had stopped his treatment for four months and had lived rather more freely, but in 'every respect I have continued extremely temperate.'

On January 30, 1829, he was still at Rome. He said, 'The palpitation of the heart has increased almost alarmingly, and I do not think I have gained any strength in the weak limbs.'

On February 1 he wrote in his journal, 'Finished the dialogues fifth and sixth' (these ended the 'Consolations in Travel'). 'Si moro, spero che ho fatto il mio dovere, e che la mia vita non e stata vana ed inutile.'

On February 6 he wrote to his friend Poole from Rome:

Would I were better, I would then write to you an agreeable letter from this curious city; but I am here wearing away the winter, a ruin amongst ruins.

I write and philosophise a good deal, and have nearly finished a work with a higher aim than the little 'Salmonia,' which I shall dedicate to you. It contains the essence of my philosophical opinions and some of my poetical reveries. I sometimes think of the lines of Waller:

> The soul's dark cottage, battered and decayed,
> Lets in new light through chinks that time has made.

I have, notwithstanding my infirmities, attended to scientific objects whenever it was in my power, and I have sent to the Royal Society a paper, which they will publish, on the 'Peculiar Electricity of the Torpedo,' which I think bears remotely on the functions of life. I attend a good deal to natural history.

I fight against sickness and fate, believing I have still duties to perform, and that even my illness is connected in some way with my being made useful to my fellow-creatures. I have this conviction full on my mind, that intellectual beings spring from the same breath of Infinite Intelligence, and return to it again, but by different courses, like rivers born amidst the clouds of heaven and lost in the deep and eternal ocean; some in youth rapid and short-lived torrents, some in manhood powerful and copious rivers, and some in age by a winding and slow course, half lost in their career and making their exit by many sandy and shallow mouths. [And then he asks him if he will come and travel with him.] But I write as if I were a strong man, when I am like a pendulum, as it were, swinging between death and life. God bless you, my dear Poole!

Your grateful and affectionate Friend,

H. DAVY.

A fortnight afterwards he had another severe attack of paralysis of the right side.

On February 23, three days after the attack, he dictated a letter to his brother.

MY DEAR JOHN,—Notwithstanding all my care and discipline and ascetic living I am dying from a severe attack of palsy, which has seized the whole of the body with the exception of the intellectual organ. I am under the usual severe discipline of bleeding and blistering, but the weakness increases, and a few hours or days will finish my mortal existence. I shall leave my bones in the Eternal City. I bless God that I have been able to finish all my philosophical labours. . . .

God bless you, my dear brother! may you be happy and prosperous!

Your affectionate Friend and Brother,

H. DAVY.

The 25th he dictated another letter, chiefly on the torpedo; it ends:

Pray do not neglect this subject, which I leave to you as another legacy. God bless you, my dear brother!

Your affectionate Friend,

H. DAVY.

He tried to write a postcript, and he did write 'My dear John;' then he dictated, 'I am dying; come as quickly as you can. You will not see me alive, I am afraid. God bless you!'

On March 16 Dr. Davy reached him. 'Never shall I forget,' he says, 'the manner in which he received me, the joy which lighted up his pale and emaciated countenance, his cheerful words and extreme kindness, and his endeavours to soothe a grief which I had not the power of controlling on finding him so ill, or rather at hearing him speak as if he were a dying man, who had only a few hours to live, and who wished to use every moment of such precious time. With a most cheerful voice, a smile on his countenance, and most warm pressure of the hand, he bade me not be grieved, but consider the event as a philosopher. He expressed his pleasure at seeing me so soon and in having me with him in his last hours, and firmly rejected all expectation and hope of recovery. He had lost all the irritable feeling to which he was very liable, and which generally accompanies paralytic complaints. His own conviction that he was a dying man almost persuaded me that the brilliancy of his mind was a lightening before death.'

The next day he was not only amused but interested deeply with the dissection of a torpedo made by Dr. Davy in an adjoining room.

On the night of March 31, having gradually got

worse, he told Dr. Davy he was sure he should die. 'He took leave of me most tenderly, kissed my cheek, and bade God bless me. I believed that now indeed I was about to lose him and that I should never again hear his voice of kindness. During the night when I went to him he still breathed. The following morning, when I drew back his curtains, he expressed great astonishment at being alive. He said that he had gone through the whole process of dying, and that when he awoke he had difficulty in convincing himself by experiments that he was in his earthly existence. He added that his being alive was quite miraculous, and that he now began to think his recovery not impossible, and that it might be intended by Divine Providence that his life should be prolonged for purposes of usefulness.

'From this day he pretty rapidly improved; as he mended the sentiment of gratitude to Divine Providence was overflowing. On April 20 he wrote his last note at the end of a letter of Dr. Davy's.

'MY DEAR SISTER,—I am very ill, but, thanks to my dearest John, still alive. God bless you all!—H. DAVY.' 'He would have said more, but his feeble hand failed him.'

On April 30 he was able to leave Rome for Switzerland. He stayed a week at Genoa and on May 28 he reached Geneva, and there first heard of the death of Dr. Young, 'which affected him in a manner almost unaccountable.' He dined early and was read to afterwards; at half-past nine he wished to be left alone, 'and I took leave of him,' says Dr. Davy, 'for the night. At half-past two his servant called me. He was insensible, and in a few minutes he expired.'

For the last half-century general opinion has been so charmed by the simple greatness of Faraday, that even the genius of Davy with his love of original research has been partially eclipsed. But, as time lessens the effect of the contrast, the reputation of Davy will recover its former brightness, and the picture drawn of him by Mr. Poole will not be looked on as due to the partiality of his oldest and most attached friend.

'Although the most friendly intercourse existed between us for thirty years, I fear I have little else to communicate than to bear testimony to his general intellectual elevation and to the warmth, sincerity, and simplicity of his heart. I was first introduced to him at the Medical Pneumatic Institution at Clifton in, I think, 1799, where I inhaled his nitrous oxide with the usual extraordinary and transitory sensations; but the interesting conversation, manners, and appearance of the youthful operator were not transitory—nay, riveted my attention—and we soon became friends.

'From that time to his death no interruption of the most cordial goodwill and affection occurred between us. Neither the importance of his discoveries nor the attentions of the exalted in rank or science, whether as individuals or bodies, nor the honour conferred on him by his sovereign, made the least alteration in his personal demeanour or in the tone of his correspondence. No man was ever less spoiled by the world. The truth is, though he conformed to the world and paid due deference to those men and things which are deferred to by the world, his delight was in his intellectual being. He felt that he had the power of investigating the laws of nature beyond that entrusted to the generality of men, and the success with which he acted on this impulse increased his confidence. During his last visit to me in November 1827, when in a very weak state of health, he more than once said, "I do not wish to live as far as I am personally concerned; but I have views which I could develope, if it please God to save my life, which would be useful to science and to mankind." Indeed, to be useful to science and to mankind was that in which he gloried, to use a favourite word of his. He was enthusiastically attached to science and to men of science, and his heart yearned to be useful to mankind, and particularly to the humblest of mankind. How often have I heard him express the satisfaction which the discovery of the safety lamp gave him. "I value it," he said, "more than anything I ever did."

'However his circumstances and situation in society altered, his labours and zeal in the pursuit of science were throughout his life undiminished.

'What from my earliest knowledge of my admirable friend I considered his most striking characteristic was the quickness and truth of his apprehension. It was a power of reasoning so rapid when applied to any subject, that he could hardly himself be conscious of the process, and it must, I think, have been felt by him as it appeared to me pure intuition. I used to say to him, "You understand me before I half understand myself."

'If his mind had been given in that direction he would probably have ranked high among our poets. I recollect hearing perhaps the greatest living poetic genius (Coleridge) say, "Had not Davy been the first chemist, he probably would have been the first poet of his age."

'No man was less a sectarian, if I may use the expression, in religion, in politics, or in science. He regarded with benevolence the sincere convictions of any class on the subject of religion, however they might vary from his own. In politics he was the ardent friend of rational liberty; he gloried in the institutions of his country and was anxious to see them maintained in their purity by timely and temperate reform. Men of science, wherever situated, he considered fellow-subjects of one great republic spread over the world. As to his amusements he would say, "It is not the sport only, though there is a great pleasure in successful dexterity, but it is the ardour of the pursuit, the pure air, the contemplation of the fine country, the exercise, all which invigorate the body and excite the mind to its best efforts."

'When he made his last visit to me in 1827, on his arrival he said, "Here I am, the ruin of what I was." But nevertheless the same activity and ardour of mind continued, though directed to different objects.

'He was not only one of the greatest but one of the most benevolent and amiable of men.'

APPENDIX I.

CONTAINING ORIGINAL DOCUMENTS IN THE LIBRARY OF THE ROYAL INSTITUTION REGARDING THE SERVICE OF COUNT RUMFORD IN THE AMERICAN WAR.

As early as 1782 Sir Guy Carleton had requested permission to return home 'in consequence of his repugnance to a situation merely defensive.' The King's ministers had just determined that active operations should be carried on under his command in the West Indies against the French, and the King had appointed him to the chief command of the army destined to act there on the day he asked for his dismissal. Late in the autumn the Right Hon. T. Townsend, then Secretary of State, directed that 1,500 British troops should be sent to reinforce the islands, but Sir Guy Carleton considered this would be attended with such serious consequences that he determined 'to deviate from a measure so explicitly directed to be carried into execution.' The Secretary suggested that a number of provincials and foreign troops should be sent, and he authorised that every provincial corps embarking for the West Indies should immediately be put upon the British establishment.

On March 14, 1783, Colonel Thompson sent a memorial for himself, brother officers, and men to Sir Guy Carleton. He said

'That the officers were chiefly young men of the first families and connections, and that except the adjutant they were all Americans, and had suffered very considerably by the Rebellion, that in the event of peace and the independency of the provinces all their hopes of returning to their former situations will be at an end, and they will be reduced to the greatest distress. That they are ready to go anywhere. That the regiment is completely appointed to the full establishment of six troops of sixty men each, together with four field-pieces, with their harness, &c., complete for a troop of flying artillery.'

The memorial then begs for employment in the West Indies, or in any other part of his Majesty's dominions, and states, that in case more troops should be wanted Colonel Thompson undertakes to raise a very fine battalion of light infantry from amongst the men then serving in his Majesty's provincial forces.

On the 21st of March Sir Guy Carleton authorised and empowered Colonel Thompson to raise four companies of light infantry, consisting of one captain, one lieutenant, one ensign, three sergeants, three corporals, two drummers, and fifty-two privates each, to be attached to the King's American Dragoons, the whole to be put on the British establishment upon their embarking for the West Indies.

He said, 'All officers, civil and military, particularly the officers commanding provincal corps, and all others his Majesty's liege subjects are hereby required to be aiding and assisting to you and all concerned in the execution of the above services, for which this shall be to you and to them a sufficient warrant and authority.'

The following paper is in Rumford's writing :

Proposed Establishment of a Corps of Light Troops to be raised for his Majesty's Service, to be commanded by Lieutenant-Colonel Thompson, Commandant of the King's American Dragoons.

	Commission Officers						Staff Officers					Non-Commissioned Officers and Privates							Total Officers and Men
	Majors	Captains	Capt.-Lieutenant	Lieutenants	Cornets	Ensigns	Chaplain	Adjutant	Qr.-Masters	Surgeon	Mate	Sergeants	Corporals	Trumpeters	Drummers	Fifers	Privates	Total	
Dismounted Cavalry: King's American Dragoons, 6 troops of 60 men each . . .	2	3	1	5	6		1	1	6	1	1	18	18	6			318	360	388
Light Infantry: 4 companies of 60 men each		4		4		4						12	12		4	4	208	240	252
Artillery: 1 company of 60 men each . .												4	4		2		50	60	60
Total . .	2	7	1	9	6	4	1	1	6	1	1	34	34	6	6	4	576	660	700

'Distribution of the six quarter-masters, two to remain with the six troops of dragoons, one to act as adjutant and one as quarter-master to the four companies of light infantry, two to serve with the company of artillery.

'The four pieces of cannon to be on the flank of the battalion, two on the right and two on the left, and the company of artillery to be formed in two divisions. Each division to be under the command of a quarter-master.

'The privates of the company of artillery to be *blacks*. To have no other arms but swords, and to be accoutred for drawing the guns. The non-commissioned officers to be *whites*, and to be armed with muskets and bayonets. The whole to have infantry pay. Permission to be granted to take one private from each troop of dragoons for a drummer to receive pay as a private. As the trumpeters of the King's American Dragoons are *blacks*, permission to be granted for the drummers and the fifers to be *blacks* also.

'The officers of the four companies of light infantry to be Americans, and to be all taken from the Provincial Line, and the men to be volunteers from the different provincial regiments.'

Peace with France put an end to all these plans, and also to another proposal to raise two regiments of infantry complete to the present establishment of the British regiments of foot; viz. ten companies, 595 officers and men. On April 4 Colonel Thompson wrote to Sir Guy Carleton to return his unfeigned thanks for all the distinguished marks of his Excellency's goodness to him, particularly for the last most flattering proof of his Excellency's approbation in appointing him to the command of light troops, which were to have served in the West Indies had not peace taken place. He begs that the King's American Dragoons may go to some part of Nova Scotia, there to do duty or to be discharged if any wish it, and that he may go to England, there to solicit, in behalf of himself and the corps, that they may be employed in the East Indies or in some other part of his Majesty's dominions where their services may be wanted.

Extract of a letter from an officer of rank in the Provincial Line to Lieutenant-Colonel Thompson, dated April 2, 1783:

'If our petition for half-pay, which I understand is strongly recommended by Sir Guy Carleton, should be disregarded, or, what would be still more grievous to us, if the applications of the refugees in London should be brought into Parliament, and ours and all our faithful services should be neglected! But I will not suppose a case so painful to my feelings, and which I trust is so very unlikely to happen. Sir Guy Carleton has repeatedly said that he has not a doubt but we shall be taken care of; indeed, it would be the height of cruelty as well as injustice in Great Britain to forsake us in this hour of our distress. We have shed our blood in her cause. She surely does not mean to make us the sacrifice of peace. She will not leave us to perish for want, now that she has no longer any occasion for our services; nor will she insult our misfortunes by referring us to the mercy of our enemies. Be assured we must expect no mercy from them.

'I flatter myself before you reach England our petition will have been taken into consideration and our request granted. If this should not be the case, we must depend upon you to solicit for us. You know the ways of office, and can get access to ministers, while others less acquainted with public business and less known, though equally zealous in our cause, would have it much less in their power to assist us. You know our services and our sufferings, and can give every information that can be wanted relative to our present situation.'

As soon as Colonel Thompson arrived in England he sent the following letter to Lord North:

'Pall Mall Court, June 8, 1783.

'MY LORD,—Having assisted in drawing up the representation and petition of the commanding officers of his Majesty's provincial regiments in North America, and having been desired by them to solicit for them in this country, that the prayer of their petition be granted, I take the liberty of troubling your Lordship upon that subject.

'The situation of the provincial officers, particularly such of them as are natives or were formerly inhabitants of the American colonies, is truly distressing. Having sacrificed their property and all their expectations from their rank and connections in civil society, and being now cut off from all hope of returning to their former homes by the articles of the peace, they have no hope left but in the justice and the humanity of the British nation.

'I will not trouble your Lordship with an account either

of their services or their sufferings; their merit, as well as their misfortunes, are known to the whole world, and I believe their claim upon the humanity and upon the justice of this country will not be disputed.

'They have stated their situation in a strong but at the same time in a most respectful manner in their representation, which I am informed has been transmitted to his Majesty's Secretary of State by Sir Guy Carleton, and strongly recommended. As they are extremely anxious to know their fate, I am to request of your Lordship that I may be informed whether any and what resolutions have been taken relative to their petition, and whether their claims of permanent rank in America and half-pay upon the reduction of their regiments will meet with the countenance and support of his Majesty's ministers.

'I know your Lordship will excuse the liberty I take in troubling you upon this occasion, particularly as you will see by the enclosed extract of a letter I have just received from New York how anxious the provincial officers are, and how much they expect that I should exert myself in their behalf.

'If your Lordship should wish for any further information respecting the provincial troops, I will do myself the honour of attending you at any time you may appoint.

'Enclosed I have the honour to transmit to your Lordship two memorials, one from the Muster-Master General of his Majesty's Provincial Forces in North America, the other from his deputy. I know them both to be very deserving of the favour and protection of Government. The former, Colonel Winslow, signed the general representation in behalf of the Provincial Line, and of course was included in Sir Guy Carleton's recommendation. As his is a military appointment by commission from the Commander-in-Chief in America, as well as that of the Inspector General of the Provincial Forces, I should suppose they would both be inclnded with their deputies, should half-pay be given to the provincial officers in general.

'I have the honour to be, with the greatest respect, my Lord, your Lordship's most obedient and most humble servant,

'B. THOMPSON.'

In three days Lord North wrote to Sir Guy Carleton to approve of his recommendation (made nine months previously) of permanent rank and half-pay for the officers of the King's American Dragoons, and in a week he wrote another despatch, to say that his Majesty was extremely disposed to show every possible attention to the remaining provincial corps, although they may not have literally complied with the engagements which entitled them to rank and half-pay, and he made known his Majesty's gracious intention that all the provincial regiments should be disbanded at Halifax. On the 27th of June Parliament voted half-pay to the officers of the different corps which in the course of the year had been raised in America. Colonel Thompson then wrote to Sir Guy Carleton:

'Pall Mall Court, July 6, 1783.

'SIR,—I beg leave to congratulate with your Excellency upon an event which I am confident will afford you great satisfaction—the resolution of Parliament to give half-pay to the provincial officers. We all feel ourselves under infinite obligations to your Excellency upon this occasion. As you have had the goodness to interest yourself so much in our behalf, I think it my duty to acquaint your Excellency with all the steps I have taken in this country relative to the provincial business since my arrival from New York.

'Soon after my arrival in London, finding the session of Parliament drawing near to a conclusion, and that no resolution had been taken by his Majesty's ministers relative to the memorial of the provincial officers recommended by your Excellency, I took the liberty of writing a letter to Lord North upon the subject (copy of which is enclosed) and made personal applications to General Conway, Lord Sheffield, and other gentlemen of the House of Commons, who assisted in bringing the business forward.

'I then, at Lord North's desire, set about to prepare estimates of the expense of half-pay for the provincial officers with other information relative to that matter, copies of which I put into the hands of General Conway and Lord Sheffield, who both interested themselves very warmly in our behalf.

'Enclosed I have the honour to transmit to your Excellency for your information copies of all the papers I took the liberty of laying before Lord North. I earnestly hope they will meet with your approbation, but if I have made any mistakes, your Excellency, being fully acquainted with what I have done, will have it in your power to rectify them.

'The paper No. 1 contains copies of all the letters between the Secretary of State and the Commander-in-Chief in North America relative the provincial corps; to which are added a few observations and a copy of the memorial of commanding officers of provincial regiments. No. 2 is a list of the provincial corps in North America, which was made out from your Excellency's return of the army under your command, dated New York, April 11, 1783. The establishment of the officers of the different corps were taken principally from the printed list of the provincial army published at New York this year. Your Excellency will observe that in this list, as well as in the list No. 3, there is a colonel and a lieutenant-colonel put down to the King's American Dragoons. This was done with the knowledge and consent of Lord North and General Conway, and upon this ground: Being disappointed of getting my regiment put upon the British establishment, I took the liberty of soliciting the rank of Colonel of the King's American Dragoons, and that Major Murray might be promoted to the rank of lieutenant-colonel of the same; which request I flattered myself would not be thought unreasonable, as it was originally intended that there should be a colonel and a lieutenant-colonel to the regiment, and as your Excellency had given me reason to hope that you would have honoured me with the provincial rank of colonel had I embarked for the West Indies with the corps to the command of which you had appointed me.

'I took the liberty of writing to your Excellency upon the subject by the last packet, since which his Majesty has been graciously pleased to approve of the King's American Dragoons having the full establishment of field officers, as was originally intended, and that I should be promoted to the rank of colonel. I cannot help flattering myself that this arrangement will be agreeable to your Excellency, and that I shall be returned in your list of the provincial officers for half-pay as colonel.

'The rank to me is of infinite importance, as I am going abroad in a short time with a view to foreign service; but the half-pay is also an object, as I have little else left to depend on except my industry.

'The paper No. 3 will explain itself. I wished much that the House of Commons would have voted the full or complete establishment of the different corps, but Lord North seemed very desirous of bringing the sum wanted for the provincial staff pay as low as possible, that it might pass the easier. With that view the calculation of the savings of part of the chaplain's half-pay, the adjutants, quarter-masters, &c., were made. But all these regulations will depend entirely upon your Excellency. Whatever you think right I am confident will be done without any kind of objection or difficulty.

'As it was impossible to lay correct estimates before the House at the time, none of the corps have been voted specifically, but their claim to half-pay in general is substantiated by the vote of a certain sum *on account of half-pay*, and so the matter must rest till your Excellency can furnish his Majesty's ministers with such returns of the different provincial regiments and corps as may be proper to lay before Parliament.

'I hope your Excellency will approve of my having made no separate claim or interest between the three provincial corps that are established with permanent rank (of which the King's American Dragoons is one) and the rest. I thought it would have a better appearance if we were all unanimous, and would be more pleasing to the rest of the corps that we should take our chance in common with them and stand or fall together. At the end of the paper No. 3 your Excellency will observe that Major Rooke is returned for half-pay as Deputy Inspector General of Provincial Forces. This was done at the desire of Colonel Innes, who arrived in London after all the papers were prepared. I know nothing of Major Rookes' pretensions, and therefore cannot answer for the propriety of his being included for half-pay, but, as it is a matter that must finally be determined by your Excellency, I am sure nothing but what is perfectly right will be done respecting it.

'In the vote of the House of Commons no mention is made of half-pay for the Muster-Master General or his deputies; but it is by no means intended to exclude them, and, if your Excellency returns their names, the vote for their half-pay will pass of course. I have spoken to Lord North upon the subject, and he thinks it perfectly right that they should be included, as also Mr. Bridgham, Colonel Innes' deputy.

'With regard to the *seconded* provincial officers who are mentioned in the memorandums contained in the papers No. 4 both General Conway and Lord Sheffield strongly advised against bringing their claims before Parliament at the same time with the application of the officers of the provincial corps, as the largeness of the sum wanted for the whole might prevent our success, whereas, if what we then asked should be granted, it would strengthen the claim of the *seconded* officers, and their application would afterwards be brought before Parliament with greater propriety and with a much better prospect of success. I conceal no part of the transaction from your Excellency, and I hope what I have done will meet with your approbation. I am certain that the motives which induced me to take the steps I have followed in the prosecution of this business are such as cannot fail to be approved by your Excellency. I have been indefatigable in my endeavours to carry what I thought your wishes respecting the provincials into execution, and if what I have done meets with your approbation and with the approbation of my deserving countrymen, in whose behalf you have so generously and so nobly interested yourself, I shall amply be repaid for all the trouble and anxiety I have had in the course of my solicitations.

'I have the honour to be, with the greatest respect, and with unfeigned gratitude for all your goodness to me, Sir, your Excellency's most obedient and most faithful Servant,

'B. Thompson.

'His Excellency Sir Guy Carleton, K.B.'

On the 8th of August, 1783, Lord North wrote to Sir Guy Carleton:

'Lieutenant-Colonel Thompson having been particularly distinguished by you in the appointment to the command of the corps of provincial troops intended to be sent upon service in the West Indies (which corps, had it embarked, would, agreeably to the King's commands signified by the late Secretary of State in his letter of the 3rd of January last, have been placed upon the British establishment), and as it appears by your letter of the 15th of June that his conduct has met with your full approbation, and that you consider him to be an officer possessing an uncommon share of merit in his profession, the King for these reasons has consented to his being appointed by commission from you Colonel of the King's American Dragoons upon the American provincial establishment.'

Sir Guy Carleton wrote to Colonel Thompson:

'New York, October 10, 1783.

'SIR,—I have received your letter of July 6, with the several enclosures therein mentioned, and you may be assured that the resolution of Parliament to give the British-American officers half-pay (with which also I find they will all have permanent rank in America) affords me a very sincere satisfaction. Your zeal and assiduity on this occasion appear to have been such as your friends might have expected, and I am sensible of your attention to me in writing so fully on the subject.

'The American officers have, in my opinion, so fair a claim to half-pay that I hope the grant will finally be made for the full establishment of their several regiments without the least exception.'

APPENDIX II.

CONTAINING A LETTER FROM DR. YOUNG TO COUNT RUMFORD, WHEN THE OFFER OF THE PROFESSORSHIP AT THE ROYAL INSTITUTION WAS MADE TO HIM; AND TWO LETTERS TO SIR JOSEPH BANKS ON THE INVENTION OF A MICROMETER TO BE USED FOR MEASURING WOOL. THE ORIGINALS OF THESE LETTERS ARE AMONGST THE PAPERS OF SIR JOSEPH BANKS.

DR. YOUNG TO COUNT RUMFORD.

Welbeck Street, Thursday, July 9, 1801.

SIR,—I have received your obliging letter, and beg leave to return you and the managers thanks for the honour you do me.

I am willing to undertake the various charges which you have the goodness to detail, and I flatter myself that you will have no reason to complain of any want of zeal on my part in the service of the Royal Institution.

But I confess I think it would be in some measure degrading both to me and to the Institution that the salary, which appears to me to have been no more than moderate before, should now be reduced one-fourth,[1] at the same time that the labour and responsibility of the employment are rather increased than lessened. For, whatever might have been expected of the late professor respecting the Journals and the superintendence of the house, I do not apprehend that any specific stipulation was made on the subject; and, as I am determined to devote a greater share of attention to the Institution than he ever appears to have done, I do not see that my education and opportunities

[1] Count Rumford must have proposed a salary of 225*l*. (p. 238).

of literary acquirement have been such as to render me less worthy than he was of a salary which, when compared with the emoluments of other situations of a similar nature, is by no means exorbitant.

It would not be my wish, and the duties of the professorship would certainly render it impossible for me, to attempt any extent of medical practice; but I should be sorry to bind myself to reject the little that might accidentally fall in my way. I do not mention this as a matter of any consequence, but to avoid having it understood, from the conversation I had with you, that I should be obliged to refuse my advice to a friend who might consult me.

As to the Journals, I should not much object to engage that a sheet or more should be ready for publication every week; but I conceive that it would give them additional importance if it were left to the direction of the professor, with the approbation of the committee, with proper notice, to publish a number at the end of a fortnight, instead of a week, whenever there might appear to be a real deficiency of matter to fill it. And I think I should want little or no assistance, either in translating or in transcribing, except what Mr. Davy might have the goodness to give me.

I hope that, when you have reconsidered what I have stated, you will not much differ from me in opinion, and that you will favour me with a further communication of your sentiments on the subject.

I am, Sir, your obliged and obedient humble Servant,

THOMAS YOUNG.

Count Rumford, Royal Institution.

DR. THOMAS YOUNG TO SIR JOSEPH BANKS.

Worthing, September 10, 1810.

DEAR SIR,—Observing from the papers that you have been interesting yourself respecting the arrangement of a micrometer for the purpose of measuring the diameter of the fibres of different kinds of wool, I beg leave to trouble you with the description of a very simple instrument which I invented some time ago for a similar purpose, and which I propose to call an agricultural micrometer. I should imagine it to be sufficiently accurate for all practical purposes, and the great facility and cheapness of its construction may perhaps render it useful to a class of persons who would object to the expense of providing themselves with a more complicated apparatus. If it appear to you in the same point of view, you will be pleased to make any use that you may think proper of this communication. When we look at a distant candle through a lock of wool it appears surrounded by rings of colours, and these rings are invariably so much the larger as the wool is the finer. The cause of these appearances I have endeavoured to explain in my lectures and elsewhere; but for the present purpose the principal object is to ascertain their comparative magnitude. In order to perform this I take a card blackened on one side, describe on it two concentric circles, the outer exactly one inch in diameter, the inner $\frac{11}{20}$, make at the centre a hole about $\frac{1}{20}$ of an inch in diameter, and pierce the card at the circumference of the inner circle, in 10 or 12 points at equal distances, with a small pin, and at that of the larger in 7 or 8 points, at unequal distances, with a large one. I then take a small rod of wood about a yard long and divide it into half-inches, numbering them from one end, at which I fix two or three pins side by side and wind round it a piece of wire—for instance a common knitting needle—in such a form as to hold the card upright between its ends and to slide on the rod. This is the whole apparatus. It is to be used by candle-light in this manner: Attach to the fixed pins a small lock of the wool to be examined, containing 20 or 30 single fibres, and look through them and through the central hole at a candle not very remote from the card, the blackened side of the card being turned towards the eye. The hole will appear to be surrounded by a bright surface, reddish at the margin, by a dark circle or ring, and again by a brighter ring, bluish-green within and red without. If the colours are not seen distinctly, we may conclude that the wool is mixed and not perfectly fit for examination; but in this case we may generally form an estimate of its quality by means of the bright surface only, moving the card along the rod until the holes of the inner circle appear exactly at the extreme margin of that surface, where it is of a reddish hue, the place of the card as indicated by the scale showing the number which characterises the wool. It will also be most convenient to begin by producing this coincidence of the inner circle in other cases where the outer ring of colours is more distinctly seen, and then to adjust the card more accurately; so that the holes in the circumference of the outer circle may appear to coincide with the middle of the coloured ring at the common limit of the red and greenish portions. If the holes be seen in the red ring, the card must be brought nearer to the edge; if in the blue, it must be moved farther off, and the number of the scale must be observed as before. It will require very attentive observation, and perhaps some practice, to obtain always precisely the same number for the same substance, but by taking the mean of several trials we may be perfectly certain of coming within a unit of the true place of the slider, and perhaps even of avoiding any error at all.

I have not yet had an opportunity of examining any

great variety of substances, but I send you the result of such observations as I have made, which will be sufficient to enable you to judge of the accuracy of the instrument.

Fibres of coarse wool from green baize, 52. Southdown, 35. Anglo-merino from a flock of Mr. Henty Tarring, 27. A lock taken from a Paular ewe by Mr. Sheppard, 25 (varying from 24 to 30). Another specimen from the same flock brought by another gentleman as a test of the instrument, 25. Cotton, mixed but about, 19. Vigonia from the Rev. P. Wood, very distinct $14\frac{1}{2}$. Beaver from a hat, 11. Blood diluted with saliva and rubbed on glass, beautifully distinct 5. Milk diluted with water, very indistinct 3. I have sometimes thought of employing the instrument as a nosological test of the state of the blood, of pus, and of other animal fluids.

It is of little consequence to the farmer to know the actual dimensions indicated by these numbers, nor can I at present ascertain them with perfect accuracy. They express, however, very nearly the diameters of the fibres in the 45,000th of an inch. Thus Mr. Henty's wool, standing at No. 27, must measure about $\frac{27}{45000}$ or $\frac{1}{1667}$ of an inch in diameter, and the globules of the blood reduced to spheres about $\frac{1}{9000}$. Probably these results are a little too small, and especially the latter, but by a comparison of a few measurements, made by means of other micrometers with these numbers, it would be easy to form a correct table of their true value, and it may safely be asserted that this instrument will enable us in some cases to be secure of avoiding any error amounting to the hundred-thousandth of an inch, and almost in all of being far within one ten-thousandth of the truth, without the use of any microscope, simple or compound.

In order to render the instrument still more portable we may employ a piece of tape as a measure, fixing to one end of it a double piece of card with an aperture, and with some pins projecting from its edge for holding the wool either between its folds or on the pins, and to the other end a small weight, serving to draw the tape tight through a hole in the blackened card. I enclose you the whole apparatus arranged in this manner, together with a few fibres of the Vigonia wool, which exhibit the colours in great perfection, constantly giving 14½ as the characteristic number. The directions for the use of the instrument might be engraved and printed on the card if it were thought desirable.

I also take the liberty of forwarding to you a letter which I have just received from a French gentleman, who claims the protection of the Royal Society. You will best judge whether the case requires or admits any exertion of your well-known liberality and kindness.

Believe me, dear Sir, with the highest respect and esteem, your faithful and obedient Servant.

DR. THOMAS YOUNG TO SIR JOSEPH BANKS.

Worthing, October 6, 1810.

MY DEAR SIR,—I shall be most happy in assisting you to form a judgment from your own observation of the utility of my little instrument; but I cannot forbear to trouble you with a few specimens of wool, which I imagine will exhibit the appearances so obviously as at least to convince you of the perfect practicability of the method. You will observe, by merely looking through them at a candle, that there is a manifest difference in the size of the rings, and if the colours are not sufficiently conspicuous when the card is used, the central hole may be made a little larger with a bodkin; and a common pair of spectacles, such as you would use in mending a pen, will be amply sufficient for remedying the flatness of the eye.

I do not apprehend that the different magnitude of the different fibres of the same fleeces is any *objection* to the use of the instrument; on the contrary, it possesses the singular advantage of detecting at once the inequality where it exists, and of giving the mean dimensions of the whole at the same time where the difference is not too great. I have mixed together, for example, two small specimens, which measured separately 21 and 31. The mixture, though evidently irregular, gave the dimensions of about 24, varying from 23 to 27, according to the part of the lock which was to be examined, and this is surely a much greater inequality than can ever exist in any *contiguous* part of the same fleece. But, however this may be, the fact is that the circumstance does not actually destroy the validity of the indications of my micrometer, as I shall further exemplify to you by an account of my examinations of some specimens of the finest wool, with which I have been favoured by Mr. H. Sheppard, an ingenious manufacturer at Frome, Somersetshire. You are, perhaps, better acquainted than I am with the history of Mr. Western's flock, which stands in so elevated a situation between the Saxon and the Spanish productions.

Specimens of Wool from Mr. Sheppard, as measured by the Agricultural Thermometer.

Grey beaver wool . . .	No. 11½ to 12
Angola	about 14
Prime Vigonia	14½
Foreign coney	15
American rabbits	15
Yellow rabbits	15
Scotch hares	15
Siberian hares	15, 16
British coney	16
Finest seal	about 18
Alpaca (a single long hair)	18½–20
Goats	19

Saxon	20
Peruvian black	21, 22
Mr. Western's Southdown, 'reckoned the finest in the kingdom'	$23\frac{1}{2}$
Lioneza	24–29
Peruvian light brown	29
Peruvian dark brown	31
Dust of the puff-ball (*Lycoperdon borista*) rubbed on glass, very distinct, giving about $\frac{1}{12000}$ inch diameter	$3\frac{1}{2}$

APPENDIX III.

TABLE OF THE INCOME AND EXPENDITURE OF THE ROYAL INSTITUTION TO 1814, *OMITTING SHILLINGS AND PENCE.*

INCOME.						EXPENDITURE.							
Year	Proprietors	Life Subscribers	Annual Subscribers	Miscellaneous Ground Rents, Dividends, &c.	Grand Total	Year	House	Lectures	Library	Printing	Workshop	Surplus, Funds, Exchequer Bills, Given to the Library, &c.	Grand Total
	£	£	£	£	£		£	£	£	£	£	£	£
1799	5,827	514	37	—	6,379	1799	5,147	—	15	184	—	—	5,777
1800	8,047	2,280	719	—	11,047	1800	4,193	802	174	216	1	4,471	10,115
1801	2,323	363	456	331	3,474	1801	4,868	812	269	376	708	—	7,078
1802	1,417	503	1,003	75	2,999	1802	5,113	844	255	344	502	—	7,059
1803	1,134	245	1,624	512	3,516	1803	1,667	1,014	250	478	326	157	3,894
1804	808	437	2,271	248	3,765	1804	1,777	872	210	181	118	420	3,579
1805	1,837	387	3,845	434	6,504	1805	1,999	1,096	287	193	320	813	4,710
1806	1,134	126	2,691	190	4,141	1806	1,739	1,493	464	384	47 [2]	1,805	5,935
1807	—	—	1,426	133	1,560	1807	1,816	1,451	440	258	—	—	3,967
1808	—	126	1,615	138	1,880	1808	1,834	1,128	422	99	—	—	3,484
1809 [1]	—	279	1,778	289	2,347	1809	1,905	1,326	420	375	—	Debts,	2,068
1810	—	812	1,723	2,334	4,869	1810	562	499	220	375	—	2,524	4,180
1811	—	1,731	1,869	719	4,319	1811	1,796	886	322	157	—	1,784	4,945
1812	—	913	2,172	244	3,329	1812	1,080	533	190	172	—	1,165	3,140
1813	—	584	1,978	542	3,104	1813	872	783	222	150	—	1,175	3,202
1814	—	710	1,763	1,937	4,410	1814	1,322	727	352	180	—	1,870	4,451

[1] Expenditure to June 12.

[2] Abolished in August.

INDEX.

LONDON : PRINTED BY
SPOTTISWOODE AND CO., NEW-STREET SQUARE
AND PARLIAMENT STREET

GENERAL LIST OF WORKS

PUBLISHED BY

MESSRS. LONGMANS, GREEN, AND CO.

PATERNOSTER ROW, LONDON.

History, Politics, Historical Memoirs, &c.

The HISTORY of ENGLAND from the Fall of Wolsey to the Defeat of the Spanish Armada. By JAMES ANTHONY FROUDE, M.A. late Fellow of Exeter College, Oxford.

LIBRARY EDITION, 12 VOLS. 8vo. price £8 18*s*.
CABINET EDITION, in 12 vols. crown 8vo. price 72*s*.

The HISTORY of ENGLAND from the Accession of James II. By Lord MACAULAY.

STUDENT'S EDITION, 2 vols. crown 8vo. 12*s*.
PEOPLE'S EDITION, 4 vols. crown 8vo. 16*s*.
CABINET EDITION, 8 vols. post 8vo. 48*s*.
LIBRARY EDITION, 5 vols. 8vo. £4.

LORD MACAULAY'S WORKS. Complete and Uniform Library Edition. Edited by his Sister, Lady TREVELYAN. 8 vols. 8vo. with Portrait, price £5 5*s*. cloth, or £8 8*s*. bound in tree-calf by Rivière.

VARIETIES of VICE-REGAL LIFE. By Sir WILLIAM DENISON, K.C.B. late Governor-General of the Australian Colonies, and Governor of Madras. With Two Maps. 2 vols. 8vo. 28*s*.

On PARLIAMENTARY GOVERNMENT in ENGLAND: Its Origin, Development, and Practical Operation. By ALPHEUS TODD, Librarian of the Legislative Assembly of Canada. 2 vols. 8vo. price £1 17*s*.

A HISTORICAL ACCOUNT of the NEUTRALITY of GREAT BRITAIN DURING the AMERICAN CIVIL WAR. By MOUNTAGUE BERNARD, M.A. Chichele Professor of International Law and Diplomacy in the University of Oxford. Royal 8vo. 16*s*.

The CONSTITUTIONAL HISTORY of ENGLAND, since the Accession of George III. 1760—1860. By Sir THOMAS ERSKINE MAY, C.B. Second Edition. Cabinet Edition, thoroughly revised. 3 vols. crown 8vo. price 18*s*.

The HISTORY of ENGLAND, from the Earliest Times to the Year 1865. By C. D. YONGE, Regius Professor of Modern History in Queen's College, Belfast. New Edition. Crown 8vo. price 7*s*. 6*d*.

HISTORY of the ROMANS under the EMPIRE. By the Very Rev. C. MERIVALE, D.C.L. Dean of Ely. 8 vols. post 8vo. 48*s.*

The FALL of the ROMAN REPUBLIC; a Short History of the Last Century of the Commonwealth. By the same Author. 12mo. 7*s.* 6*d.*

A STUDENT'S MANUAL of the HISTORY of INDIA, from the Earliest Period to the Present. By Colonel MEADOWS TAYLOR, M.R.A.S. M.R.I.A. Crown 8vo. with Maps, 7*s.* 6*d.*

The HISTORY of INDIA, from the Earliest Period to the close of Lord Dalhousie's Administration. By JOHN CLARK MARSHMAN. 3 vols. crown 8vo. 22*s.* 6*d.*

INDIAN POLITY: a View of the System of Administration in India. By Lieutenant-Colonel GEORGE CHESNEY, Fellow of the University of Calcutta. New Edition, revised; with Map. 8vo. price 21*s.*

HOME POLITICS; being a consideration of the Causes of the Growth of Trade in relation to Labour, Pauperism, and Emigration. By DANIEL GRANT. 8vo. 7*s.*

REALITIES of IRISH LIFE. By W. STEUART TRENCH, Land Agent in Ireland to the Marquess of Lansdowne, the Marquess of Bath, and Lord Digby. Fifth Edition. Crown 8vo. price 6*s.*

The STUDENT'S MANUAL of the HISTORY of IRELAND. By MARY F. CUSACK, Author of 'The Illustrated History of Ireland, from the Earliest Period to the Year of Catholic Emancipation.' Crown 8vo. price 6*s.*

CRITICAL and HISTORICAL ESSAYS contributed to the *Edinburgh Review*. By the Right Hon. LORD MACAULAY.

CABINET EDITION, 4 vols. post 8vo. 24*s.* | LIBRARY EDITION, 3 vols. 8vo. 36*s.*
PEOPLE'S EDITION, 2 vols. crown 8vo. 8*s.* | STUDENT'S EDITION, 1 vol. cr. 8vo. 6*s.*

SAINT-SIMON and SAINT-SIMONISM; a chapter in the History of Socialism in France. By ARTHUR J. BOOTH, M.A. Crown 8vo. price 7*s.* 6*d.*

HISTORY of EUROPEAN MORALS, from Augustus to Charlemagne. By W. E. H. LECKY, M.A. Second Edition. 2 vols. 8vo. price 28*s.*

HISTORY of the RISE and INFLUENCE of the SPIRIT of RATIONALISM in EUROPE. By W. E. H. LECKY, M.A. Cabinet Edition, being the Fourth. 2 vols. crown 8vo. price 16*s.*

GOD in HISTORY; or, the Progress of Man's Faith in the Moral Order of the World. By Baron BUNSEN. Translated by SUSANNA WINKWORTH; with a Preface by Dean STANLEY. 3 vols. 8vo. price 42*s.*

The HISTORY of PHILOSOPHY, from Thales to Comte. By GEORGE HENRY LEWES. Fourth Edition. 2 vols. 8vo. 32*s.*

An HISTORICAL VIEW of LITERATURE and ART in GREAT BRITAIN from the Accession of the House of Hanover to the Reign of Queen Victoria. By J. MURRAY GRAHAM, M.A. 8vo. price 14*s.*

The MYTHOLOGY of the ARYAN NATIONS. By GEORGE W. COX, M.A. late Scholar of Trinity College, Oxford, Joint-Editor, with the late Professor Brande, of the Fourth Edition of 'The Dictionary of Science, Literature, and Art,' Author of 'Tales of Ancient Greece,' &c. 2 vols. 8vo. 28*s.*

HISTORY of CIVILISATION in England and France, Spain and Scotland. By HENRY THOMAS BUCKLE. New Edition of the entire Work with a complete INDEX. 3 vols. crown 8vo. 24*s.*

HISTORY of the CHRISTIAN CHURCH, from the Ascension of Christ to the Conversion of Constantine. By E. BURTON, D.D. late Prof. of Divinity in the Univ. of Oxford. New Edition. Fcp. 3*s.* 6*d.*

SKETCH of the HISTORY of the CHURCH of ENGLAND to the Revolution of 1688. By the Right Rev. T. V. SHORT, D.D. Lord Bishop of St. Asaph. Eighth Edition. Crown 8vo. 7*s.* 6*d.*

HISTORY of the EARLY CHURCH, from the First Preaching of the Gospel to the Council of Nicæa, A.D. 325. By ELIZABETH M. SEWELL, Author of 'Amy Herbert.' New Edition, with Questions. Fcp. 4*s.* 6*d.*

The ENGLISH REFORMATION. By F. C. MASSINGBERD, M.A. Chancellor of Lincoln and Rector of South Ormsby. Fourth Edition, revised. Fcp. 8vo. 7*s.* 6*d.*

MAUNDER'S HISTORICAL TREASURY; comprising a General Introductory Outline of Universal History, and a series of Separate Histories. Latest Edition, revised and brought down to the Present Time by the Rev. GEORGE WILLIAM COX, M.A. Fcp. 6*s.* cloth, or 9*s.* 6*d.* calf.

HISTORICAL and CHRONOLOGICAL ENCYCLOPÆDIA; comprising Chronological Notices of all the Great Events of Universal History: Treaties, Alliances, Wars, Battles, &c.; Incidents in the Lives of Eminent Men and their Works, Scientific and Geographical Discoveries, Mechanical Inventions, and Social, Domestic, and Economical Improvements. By B. B. WOODWARD, B.A. and W. L. R. CATES. 1 vol. 8vo. [*In the press.*

Biographical Works.

A MEMOIR of DANIEL MACLISE, R.A. By W. JUSTIN O'DRISCOLL, M.R.I.A. Barrister-at-Law. With Portrait and Woodcuts. Post 8vo. price 7*s.* 6*d.*

MEMOIRS of the MARQUIS of POMBAL; with Extracts from his Writings and from Despatches in the State Papers Office. By the CONDE DA CARNOTA. New Edition. 8vo. price 7*s.*

REMINISCENCES of FIFTY YEARS. By MARK BOYD. Post 8vo. price 10*s.* 6*d.*

The LIFE of ISAMBARD KINGDOM BRUNEL, Civil Engineer. By ISAMBARD BRUNEL, B.C.L. of Lincoln's Inn; Chancellor of the Diocese of Ely. With Portrait, Plates, and Woodcuts. 8vo. 21*s.*

The LIFE and LETTERS of FARADAY. By Dr. BENCE JONES, Secretary of the Royal Institution. Second Edition, thoroughly revised. 2 vols. 8vo. with Portrait, and Eight Engravings on Wood, price 28*s.*

FARADAY as a DISCOVERER. By JOHN TYNDALL, LL.D. F.R.S. Professor of Natural Philosophy in the Royal Institution. New and Cheaper Edition, with Two Portraits. Fcp. 8vo. 3*s.* 6*d.*

The LIFE and LETTERS of the Rev. SYDNEY SMITH. Edited by his Daughter, Lady HOLLAND, and Mrs. AUSTIN. New Edition, complete in One Volume. Crown 8vo. price 6*s.*

SOME MEMORIALS of R. D. HAMPDEN, Bishop of Hereford. Edited by his Daughter, HENRIETTA HAMPDEN. With Portrait. 8vo. price 12*s.*

The LIFE and TRAVELS of GEORGE WHITEFIELD, M.A. By JAMES PATERSON GLEDSTONE. 8vo. price 14*s.*

LIVES of the LORD CHANCELLORS and KEEPERS of the GREAT SEAL of IRELAND. from the Earliest Times to the Reign of Queen Victoria. By J. R. O'FLANAGAN, M.R.I.A. Barrister-at-Law. 2 vols. 8vo. 36*s.*

DICTIONARY of GENERAL BIOGRAPHY; containing Concise Memoirs and Notices of the most Eminent Persons of all Countries, from the Earliest Ages to the Present Time. Edited by W. L. R. CATES. 8vo. 21*s.*

LIVES of the QUEENS of ENGLAND. By AGNES STRICKLAND. Library Edition, newly revised; with Portraits of every Queen, Autographs, and Vignettes. 8 vols. post 8vo. 7*s.* 6*d.* each.

LIFE of the DUKE of WELLINGTON. By the Rev. G. R. GLEIG, M.A. Popular Edition, carefully revised; with copious Additions. Crown 8vo. with Portrait, 5*s.*

HISTORY of MY RELIGIOUS OPINIONS. By J. H. NEWMAN, D.D. Being the Substance of Apologia pro Vitâ Suâ. Post 8vo. 6*s.*

The PONTIFICATE of PIUS the NINTH; being the Third Edition of 'Rome and its Ruler,' continued to the latest moment and greatly enlarged. By J. F. MAGUIRE, M.P. Post 8vo. with Portrait, 12*s.* 6*d.*

FATHER MATHEW: a Biography. By JOHN FRANCIS MAGUIRE, M.P. for Cork. Popular Edition, with Portrait. Crown 8vo. 3*s.* 6*d.*

FELIX MENDELSSOHN'S LETTERS from *Italy and Switzerland*, and *Letters from* 1833 *to* 1847, translated by Lady WALLACE. New Edition, with Portrait. 2 vols. crown 8vo. 5*s.* each.

MEMOIRS of SIR HENRY HAVELOCK, K.C.B. By JOHN CLARK MARSHMAN. Cabinet Edition, with Portrait. Crown 8vo. price 3*s.* 6*d.*

VICISSITUDES of FAMILIES. By Sir J. BERNARD BURKE, C.B. Ulster King of Arms. New Edition, remodelled and enlarged. 2 vols. crown 8vo. 21*s.*

ESSAYS in ECCLESIASTICAL BIOGRAPHY. By the Right Hon. Sir J. STEPHEN, LL.D. Cabinet Edition, being the Fifth. Crown 8vo. 7*s.* 6*d.*

MAUNDER'S BIOGRAPHICAL TREASURY. Thirteenth Edition, reconstructed, thoroughly revised, and in great part rewritten; with about 1,000 additional Memoirs and Notices, by W. L. R. CATES. Fcp. 6*s.*

LETTERS and LIFE of FRANCIS BACON, including all his Occasional Works. Collected and edited, with a Commentary, by J. SPEDDING, Trin. Coll. Cantab. VOLS. I. and II. 8vo. 24*s.* VOLS. III. and IV. 24*s.* VOL. V. price 12*s.*

Criticism, Philosophy, Polity, &c.

The INSTITUTES of JUSTINIAN; with English Introduction, Translation, and Notes. By T. C. SANDARS, M.A. Barrister, late Fellow of Oriel Coll. Oxon. New Edition. 8vo. 15*s.*

The ELEMENTS of POLITICAL ECONOMY. By HENRY DUNNING MACLEOD, M.A. Barrister-at-Law. 8vo. 16*s.*

A Dictionary of Political Economy; Biographical, Bibliographical, Historical, and Practical. By the same Author. VOL. I. royal 8vo. 30*s.*

The ELECTION of REPRESENTATIVES, Parliamentary and Municipal; a Treatise. By THOMAS HARE, Barrister-at-Law. Third Edition, with Additions. Crown 8vo. 6*s.*

SPEECHES of the RIGHT HON. LORD MACAULAY, corrected by Himself. People's Edition, crown 8vo. 3*s.* 6*d.*

Lord Macaulay's Speeches on Parliamentary Reform in 1831 and 1832. 16mo. 1*s.*

INAUGURAL ADDRESS delivered to the University of St. Andrews. By JOHN STUART MILL. 8vo. 5*s.* People's Edition, crown 8vo. 1*s.*

A DICTIONARY of the ENGLISH LANGUAGE. By R. G. LATHAM, M.A. M.D. F.R.S. Founded on the Dictionary of Dr. SAMUEL JOHNSON, as edited by the Rev. H. J. TODD, with numerous Emendations and Additions. In Four Volumes, 4to. price £7.

THESAURUS of ENGLISH WORDS and PHRASES, classified and arranged so as to facilitate the Expression of Ideas, and assist in Literary Composition. By P. M. ROGET, M.D. New Edition. Crown 8vo. 10*s.* 6*d.*

LECTURES on the SCIENCE of LANGUAGE. By F. MAX MÜLLER, M.A. &c. Foreign Member of the French Institute. Sixth Edition. 2 vols. crown 8vo. price 16*s.*

CHAPTERS on LANGUAGE. By FREDERIC W. FARRAR, F.R.S. Head Master of Marlborough College. Crown 8vo. 8*s.* 6*d.*

The DEBATER; a Series of Complete Debates, Outlines of Debates, and Questions for Discussion. By F. ROWTON. Fcp. 6*s.*

MANUAL of ENGLISH LITERATURE, Historical and Critical. By THOMAS ARNOLD, M.A. Second Edition. Crown 8vo. price 7*s.* 6*d.*

SOUTHEY'S DOCTOR, complete in One Volume. Edited by the Rev. J. W. WARTER, B.D. Square crown 8vo. 12*s.* 6*d.*

HISTORICAL and CRITICAL COMMENTARY on the OLD TESTAMENT; with a New Translation. By M. M. KALISCH, Ph.D. VOL. I. *Genesis*, 8vo. 18*s.* or adapted for the General Reader, 12*s.* VOL. II. *Exodus*, 15*s.* or adapted for the General Reader, 12*s.* VOL. III. *Leviticus*, PART I. 15*s.* or adapted for the General Reader, 8*s.*

A HEBREW GRAMMAR, with EXERCISES. By M. M. KALISCH, Ph.D. PART I. *Outlines with Exercises*, 8vo. 12*s.* 6*d.* KEY, 5*s.* PART II. *Exceptional Forms and Constructions*, 12*s.* 6*d.*

A LATIN-ENGLISH DICTIONARY. By JOHN T. WHITE, D.D. Oxon. and J. E. RIDDLE, M.A. Oxon. Third Edition, revised. 2 vols. 4to. pp. 2,128, price 42*s.* cloth.

White's College Latin-English Dictionary (Intermediate Size), abridged for the use of University Students from the Parent Work (as above). Medium 8vo. pp. 1,048, price 18*s.* cloth.

White's Junior Student's Complete Latin-English and English-Latin Dictionary. New Edition. Square 12mo. pp. 1,058, price 12*s.*

Separately { The ENGLISH-LATIN DICTIONARY, price 5*s.* 6*d.*
The LATIN-ENGLISH DICTIONARY, price 7*s.* 6*d.*

An ENGLISH-GREEK LEXICON, containing all the Greek Words used by Writers of good authority. By C. D. YONGE, B.A. New Edition. 4to. 21*s.*

Mr. YONGE'S NEW LEXICON, English and Greek, abridged from his larger work (as above). Revised Edition. Square 12mo. 8*s.* 6*d.*

A GREEK-ENGLISH LEXICON. Compiled by H. G. LIDDELL, D.D. Dean of Christ Church, and R. SCOTT, D.D. Dean of Rochester. Sixth Edition. Crown 4to. price 36*s.*

A Lexicon, Greek and English, abridged from LIDDELL and SCOTT'S *Greek-English Lexicon.* Twelfth Edition. Square 12mo. 7*s.* 6*d.*

A SANSKRIT-ENGLISH DICTIONARY, the Sanskrit words printed both in the original Devanagari and in Roman Letters. Compiled by T. BENFEY, Prof. in the Univ. of Göttingen. 8vo. 52*s.* 6*d.*

WALKER'S PRONOUNCING DICTIONARY of the ENGLISH LANGUAGE. Thoroughly revised Editions, by B. H. SMART. 8vo. 12*s.* 16mo. 6*s.*

A PRACTICAL DICTIONARY of the FRENCH and ENGLISH LANGUAGES. By L. CONTANSEAU. Fourteenth Edition. Post 8vo. 10*s.* 6*d.*

Contanseau's Pocket Dictionary, French and English, abridged from the above by the Author. New Edition, revised. Square 18mo. 3*s.* 6*d.*

NEW PRACTICAL DICTIONARY of the GERMAN LANGUAGE; German-English and English-German. By the Rev. W. L. BLACKLEY, M.A. and Dr. CARL MARTIN FRIEDLÄNDER. Post 8vo. 7*s.* 6*d.*

The MASTERY of LANGUAGES; or, the Art of Speaking Foreign Tongues Idiomatically. By THOMAS PRENDERGAST, late of the Civil Service at Madras. Second Edition. 8vo. 6*s.*

Miscellaneous Works and *Popular Metaphysics.*

The ESSAYS and CONTRIBUTIONS of A. K. H. B., Author of 'The Recreations of a Country Parson.' Uniform Editions:—

Recreations of a Country Parson. By A. K. H. B. FIRST and SECOND SERIES, crown 8vo. 3*s.* 6*d.* each.

The COMMON-PLACE PHILOSOPHER in TOWN and COUNTRY. By A. K. H. B. Crown 8vo. price 3*s.* 6*d.*

Leisure Hours in Town; Essays Consolatory, Æsthetical, Moral, Social, and Domestic. By A. K. H. B. Crown 8vo. 3*s.* 6*d.*

The Autumn Holidays of a Country Parson; Essays contributed to *Fraser's Magazine* and to *Good Words.* By A. K. H. B. Crown 8vo. 3*s.* 6*d.*

The Graver Thoughts of a Country Parson. By A. K. H. B. FIRST and SECOND SERIES, crown 8vo. 3*s.* 6*d.* each.

Critical Essays of a Country Parson, selected from Essays contributed to *Fraser's Magazine.* By A. K. H. B. Crown 8vo. 3*s.* 6*d.*

Sunday Afternoons at the Parish Church of a Scottish University City. By A. K. H. B. Crown 8vo. 3*s.* 6*d.*

LESSONS of MIDDLE AGE; with some Account of various Cities and Men. By A. K. H. B. Crown 8vo. 3*s*. 6*d*.

Counsel and Comfort spoken from a City Pulpit. By A. K. H. B. Crown 8vo. price 3*s*. 6*d*.

Changed Aspects of Unchanged Truths; Memorials of St. Andrews Sundays. By A. K. H.B. Crown 8vo. 3*s*. 6*d*.

Present-day Thoughts; Memorials of St. Andrews Sundays. By A. K. H. B. Crown 8vo. 3*s*. 6*d*.

SHORT STUDIES on GREAT SUBJECTS. By JAMES ANTHONY FROUDE, M.A. late Fellow of Exeter Coll. Oxford. Third Edition. 8vo. 12*s*. SECOND SERIES. 8vo. price 12*s*.

LORD MACAULAY'S MISCELLANEOUS WRITINGS:—

LIBRARY EDITION. 2 vols. 8vo. Portrait, 21*s*.
PEOPLE'S EDITION. 1 vol. crown 8vo. 4*s*. 6*d*.

LORD MACAULAY'S MISCELLANEOUS WRITINGS and SPEECHES. STUDENT'S EDITION, in crown 8vo. price 6*s*.

The REV. SYDNEY SMITH'S MISCELLANEOUS WORKS; including his Contributions to the *Edinburgh Review*. Crown 8vo. 6*s*.

The Wit and Wisdom of the Rev. Sydney Smith; a Selection of the most memorable Passages in his Writings and Conversation. 16mo. 3*s*. 6*d*.

The ECLIPSE of FAITH; or, a Visit to a Religious Sceptic. By HENRY ROGERS. Twelfth Edition. Fcp. 5*s*.

Defence of the Eclipse of Faith, by its Author; a rejoinder to Dr. Newman's *Reply*. Third Edition. Fcp. 3*s*. 6*d*.

Selections from the Correspondence of R. E. H. Greyson. By the same Author. Third Edition. Crown 8vo. 7*s*. 6*d*.

FAMILIES of SPEECH, Four Lectures delivered at the Royal Institution of Great Britain. By the Rev. F. W. FARRAR, M.A. F.R.S. Head Master of Marlborough College. Post 8vo. with Two Maps, 5*s*. 6*d*.

CHIPS from a GERMAN WORKSHOP; being Essays on the Science of Religion, and on Mythology, Traditions, and Customs. By F. MAX MÜLLER, M.A. &c. Foreign Member of the French Institute. 3 vols. 8vo. £2.

UEBERWEG'S SYSTEM of LOGIC and HISTORY of LOGICAL DOCTRINES. Translated, with Notes and Appendices, by T. M. LINDSAY, M.A. F.R.S.E. Examiner in Philosophy to the University of Edinburgh. 8vo. price 16*s*.

ANALYSIS of the PHENOMENA of the HUMAN MIND. By JAMES MILL. A New Edition, with Notes, Illustrative and Critical, by ALEXANDER BAIN, ANDREW FINDLATER, and GEORGE GROTE. Edited, with additional Notes, by JOHN STUART MILL. 2 vols. 8vo. price 28*s*.

An INTRODUCTION to MENTAL PHILOSOPHY, on the Inductive Method. By J. D. MORELL, M.A. LL.D. 8vo. 12*s*.

ELEMENTS of PSYCHOLOGY, containing the Analysis of the Intellectual Powers. By the same Author. Post 8vo. 7*s*. 6*d*.

The SECRET of HEGEL: being the Hegelian System in Origin, Principle, Form, and Matter. By J. H. STIRLING. 2 vols. 8vo. 28*s*.

SIR WILLIAM HAMILTON; being the Philosophy of Perception: an Analysis. By J. H. STIRLING. 8vo. 5*s*.

The SENSES and the INTELLECT. By ALEXANDER BAIN, M.D. Professor of Logic in the University of Aberdeen. Third Edition. 8vo. 15*s*.

MENTAL and MORAL SCIENCE: a Compendium of Psychology and Ethics. By the same Author. Second Edition. Crown 8vo. 10*s*. 6*d*.

LOGIC, DEDUCTIVE and INDUCTIVE. By the same Author. In TWO PARTS, crown 8vo. 10*s*. 6*d*. Each Part may be had separately:—
PART I. *Deduction*, 4*s*. PART II. *Induction*, 6*s*. 6*d*.

TIME and SPACE; a Metaphysical Essay. By SHADWORTH H. HODGSON. (This work covers the whole ground of Speculative Philosophy.) 8vo. price 16*s*.

The Theory of Practice; an Ethical Inquiry. By the same Author. (This work, in conjunction with the foregoing, completes a system of Philosophy.) 2 vols. 8vo. price 24*s*.

The PHILOSOPHY of NECESSITY; or, Natural Law as applicable to Mental, Moral, and Social Science. By CHARLES BRAY. Second Edition. 8vo. 9*s*.

The Education of the Feelings and Affections. By the same Author. Third Edition. 8vo. 3*s*. 6*d*.

On Force, its Mental and Moral Correlates. By the same Author. 8vo. 5*s*.

A TREATISE on HUMAN NATURE; being an Attempt to Introduce the Experimental Method of Reasoning into Moral Subjects. By DAVID HUME. Edited, with Notes, &c. by T. H. GREEN, Fellow, and T. H. GROSE, late Scholar, of Balliol College, Oxford. [*In the press.*

ESSAYS MORAL, POLITICAL, and LITERARY. By DAVID HUME. By the same Editors. [*In the press.*

Astronomy, Meteorology, Popular Geography, &c.

OUTLINES of ASTRONOMY. By Sir J. F. W. HERSCHEL, Bart. Eleventh Edition, with Plates and Woodcuts. Square crown 8vo. 12*s*.

The SUN; RULER, LIGHT, FIRE, and LIFE of the PLANETARY SYSTEM. By RICHARD A. PROCTOR, B.A. F.R.A.S. With 10 Plates (7 coloured) and 107 Figures on Wood. Crown 8vo. 14*s*.

OTHER WORLDS THAN OURS; the Plurality of Worlds Studied under the Light of Recent Scientific Researches. By the same Author. Second Edition, with 14 Illustrations. Crown 8vo. 10*s*. 6*d*.

SATURN and its SYSTEM. By the same Author. 8vo. with 14 Plates, 14*s*.

SCHALLEN'S SPECTRUM ANALYSIS, in its application to Terrestrial Substances and the Physical Constitution of the Heavenly Bodies. Translated by JANE and C. LASSELL; edited by W. HUGGINS, LL.D. F.R.S. Crown 8vo. with Illustrations. [*Nearly ready.*

CELESTIAL OBJECTS for COMMON TELESCOPES. By the Rev. T. W. WEBB, M.A. F.R.A.S. Second Edition, revised, with a large Map of the Moon, and several Woodcuts. 16mo. 7*s.* 6*d.*

NAVIGATION and NAUTICAL ASTRONOMY (Practical, Theoretical, Scientific) for the use of Students and Practical Men. By J. MERRIFIELD, F.R.A.S and H. EVERS. 8vo. 14*s.*

DOVE'S LAW of STORMS, considered in connexion with the Ordinary Movements of the Atmosphere. Translated by R. H. SCOTT, M.A. T.C.D. 8vo. 10*s.* 6*d.*

The CANADIAN DOMINION. By CHARLES MARSHALL. With 6 Illustrations on Wood. 8vo. price 12*s.* 6*d.*

A GENERAL DICTIONARY of GEOGRAPHY, Descriptive, Physical, Statistical, and Historical: forming a complete Gazetteer of the World. By A. KEITH JOHNSTON, LL.D. F.R.G.S. Revised Edition. 8vo. 31*s.* 6*d.*

A MANUAL of GEOGRAPHY, Physical, Industrial, and Political. By W. HUGHES, F.R.G.S. With 6 Maps. Fcp. 7*s.* 6*d.*

MAUNDER'S TREASURY of GEOGRAPHY, Physical, Historical, Descriptive, and Political. Edited by W. HUGHES, F.R.G.S. Revised Edition, with 7 Maps and 16 Plates. Fcp. 6*s.* cloth, or 9*s.* 6*d.* bound in calf.

The PUBLIC SCHOOLS ATLAS of MODERN GEOGRAPHY. In 31 Maps, exhibiting clearly the more important Physical Features of the Countries delineated, and Noting all the Chief Places of Historical, Commercial, or Social Interest. Edited, with an Introduction, by the Rev. G. BUTLER, M.A. Imp. 4to price 3*s.* 6*d.* sewed, or 5*s.* cloth. [*Nearly ready.*

Natural History and *Popular Science.*

ELEMENTARY TREATISE on PHYSICS, Experimental and Applied. Translated and edited from GANOT'S *Eléments de Physique* (with the Author's sanction) by E. ATKINSON, Ph.D. F.C.S. New Edition, revised and enlarged; with a Coloured Plate and 620 Woodcuts. Post 8vo. 15*s.*

The ELEMENTS of PHYSICS or NATURAL PHILOSOPHY. By NEIL ARNOTT, M.D. F.R.S. Physician Extraordinary to the Queen. Sixth Edition, rewritten and completed. Two Parts. 8vo. 21*s.*

SOUND: a Course of Eight Lectures delivered at the Royal Institution of Great Britain. By JOHN TYNDALL, LL.D. F.R.S. New Edition, crown 8vo. with Portrait of *M. Chladni* and 169 Woodcuts, price 9*s.*

HEAT a MODE of MOTION. By Professor JOHN TYNDALL, LL.D. F.R.S. Fourth Edition. Crown 8vo. with Woodcuts, 10*s.* 6*d.*

RESEARCHES on DIAMAGNETISM and MAGNE-CRYSTALLIC ACTION; including the Question of Diamagnetic Polarity. By the same Author. With 6 Plates and many Woodcuts. 8vo. price 14*s.*

PROFESSOR TYNDALL'S ESSAYS on the USE and LIMIT of the IMAGINATION in SCIENCE. Being the Second Edition, with Additions, of his Discourse on the Scientific Use of the Imagination. 8vo. 3*s.*

NOTES of a COURSE of SEVEN LECTURES on ELECTRICAL PHENOMENA and THEORIES, delivered at the Royal Institution, A.D. 1870. By Professor TYNDALL. Crown 8vo. 1*s.* sewed, or 1*s.* 6*d.* cloth.

NOTES of a COURSE of NINE LECTURES on LIGHT delivered at the Royal Institution, A.D. 1869. By the same Author. Crown 8vo. price 1*s.* sewed, or 1*s.* 6*d.* cloth.

FRAGMENTS of SCIENCE for UNSCIENTIFIC PEOPLE; a Series of detached Essays, Lectures, and Reviews. By JOHN TYNDALL, LL.D. F.R.S. Second Edition. 8vo. price 14*s.*

LIGHT SCIENCE for LEISURE HOURS; a Series of Familiar Essays on Scientific Subjects, Natural Phenomena, &c. By R. A. PROCTOR, B.A. F.R.A.S. Crown 8vo. price 7*s.* 6*d.*

LIGHT: Its Influence on Life and Health. By FORBES WINSLOW, M.D. D.C.L. Oxon. (Hon.). Fcp. 8vo. 6*s.*

A TREATISE on ELECTRICITY, in Theory and Practice. By A. DE LA RIVE, Prof. in the Academy of Geneva. Translated by C. V. WALKER, F.R.S. 3 vols. 8vo. with Woodcuts, £3 13*s.*

The BEGINNING: its When and its How. By MUNGO PONTON, F.R.S.E. Post 8vo. with very numerous Illustrations, price 18*s.*

The CORRELATION of PHYSICAL FORCES. By W. R. GROVE, Q.C. V.P.R.S. Fifth Edition, revised, and followed by a Discourse on Continuity. 8vo. 10*s.* 6*d.* The *Discourse on Continuity*, separately, 2*s.* 6*d.*

MANUAL of GEOLOGY. By S. HAUGHTON, M.D. F.R.S. Revised Edition, with 66 Woodcuts. Fcp. 7*s.* 6*d.*

VAN DER HOEVEN'S HANDBOOK of ZOOLOGY. Translated from the Second Dutch Edition by the Rev. W. CLARK, M.D. F.R.S. 2 vols. 8vo. with 24 Plates of Figures, 60*s.*

Professor OWEN'S LECTURES on the COMPARATIVE ANATOMY and Physiology of the Invertebrate Animals. Second Edition, with 235 Woodcuts. 8vo. 21*s.*

The COMPARATIVE ANATOMY and PHYSIOLOGY of the VERTE-brate Animals. By RICHARD OWEN, F.R.S. D.C.L. With 1,472 Woodcuts. 3 vols. 8vo. £3 13*s.* 6*d.*

The ORIGIN of CIVILISATION and the PRIMITIVE CONDITION of MAN; Mental and Social Condition of Savages. By Sir JOHN LUBBOCK, Bart. M.P. F.R.S. Second Edition, with 25 Woodcuts. 8vo. price 16*s.*

The PRIMITIVE INHABITANTS of SCANDINAVIA: containing a Description of the Implements, Dwellings, Tombs, and Mode of Living of the Savages in the North of Europe during the Stone Age. By SVEN NILSSON. With 16 Plates of Figures and 3 Woodcuts. 8vo. 18*s.*

BIBLE ANIMALS; being a Description of every Living Creature mentioned in the Scriptures, from the Ape to the Coral. By the Rev. J. G. WOOD, M.A. F.L.S. With about 100 Vignettes on Wood. 8vo. 21*s.*

HOMES WITHOUT HANDS: a Description of the Habitations of Animals, classed according to their Principle of Construction. By Rev. J. G. WOOD, M.A. F.L.S. With about 140 Vignettes on Wood, 8vo. 21*s.*

INSECTS AT HOME. By the Rev. J. G. WOOD, M.A. F.L.S. With a Frontispiece in Colours, 21 full-page Illustrations, and about 700 smaller Illustrations from original designs engraved on Wood by G. Pearson. 8vo. price 21*s.*

STRANGE DWELLINGS; being a description of the Habitations of Animals, abridged from 'Homes without Hands.' By J. G. WOOD, M.A. F.L.S. With a New Frontispiece and about 60 other Woodcut Illustrations. Crown 8vo. price 7*s.* 6*d.*

A FAMILIAR HISTORY of BIRDS. By E. STANLEY, D.D. F.R.S. late Lord Bishop of Norwich. Seventh Edition, with Woodcuts. Fcp. 3*s.* 6*d.*

The HARMONIES of NATURE and UNITY of CREATION. By Dr. GEORGE HARTWIG. 8vo. with numerous Illustrations, 18*s.*

The SEA and its LIVING WONDERS. By the same Author. Third (English) Edition. 8vo. with many Illustrations, 21*s.*

The TROPICAL WORLD. By Dr. GEO. HARTWIG. With 8 Chromoxylographs and 172 Woodcuts. 8vo. 21*s.*

The SUBTERRANEAN WORLD. By Dr. GEORGE HARTWIG. With 3 Maps and about 80 Woodcuts, including 8 full size of page. 8vo. price 21*s.*

The POLAR WORLD, a Popular Description of Man and Nature in the Arctic and Antarctic Regions of the Globe. By Dr. GEORGE HARTWIG. With 8 Chromoxylographs, 3 Maps, and 85 Woodcuts. 8vo. 21*s.*

KIRBY and SPENCE'S INTRODUCTION to ENTOMOLOGY, or Elements of the Natural History of Insects. 7th Edition. Crown 8vo. 5*s.*

MAUNDER'S TREASURY of NATURAL HISTORY, or Popular Dictionary of Zoology. Revised and corrected by T. S. COBBOLD, M.D. Fcp. with 900 Woodcuts, 6*s.* cloth, or 9*s.* 6*d.* bound in calf.

The TREASURY of BOTANY, or Popular Dictionary of the Vegetable Kingdom; including a Glossary of Botanical Terms. Edited by J. LINDLEY, F.R.S. and T. MOORE, F.L.S. assisted by eminent Contributors. With 274 Woodcuts and 20 Steel Plates. Two Parts, fcp. 12*s.* cloth, or 19*s.* calf.

The ELEMENTS of BOTANY for FAMILIES and SCHOOLS. Tenth Edition, revised by THOMAS MOORE, F.L.S. Fcp. with 154 Woodcuts, 2*s.* 6*d.*

The ROSE AMATEUR'S GUIDE. By THOMAS RIVERS. Ninth Edition. Fcp. 4*s.*

LOUDON'S ENCYCLOPÆDIA of PLANTS; comprising the Specific Character, Description, Culture, History, &c. of all the Plants found in Great Britain. With upwards of 12,000 Woodcuts. 8vo. 42*s.*

MAUNDER'S SCIENTIFIC and LITERARY TREASURY. New Edition, thoroughly revised and in great part re-written, with above 1,000 new Articles, by J. Y. JOHNSON, Corr. M.Z.S. Fcp. 6*s.* cloth, or 9*s.* 6*d.* calf.

A DICTIONARY of SCIENCE, LITERATURE, and ART. Fourth Edition, re-edited by W. T. BRANDE (the original Author), and GEORGE W. COX, M.A. assisted by contributors of eminent Scientific and Literary Acquirements. 3 vols. medium 8vo. price 63*s.* cloth.

Chemistry, Medicine, Surgery, and the *Allied Sciences.*

A DICTIONARY of CHEMISTRY and the Allied Branches of other Sciences. By HENRY WATTS, F.R.S. assisted by eminent Contributors Complete in 5 vols. medium 8vo. £7 3*s.*

ELEMENTS of CHEMISTRY, Theoretical and Practical. By W. ALLEN MILLER, M.D. late Prof. of Chemistry, King's Coll. London. Fourth Edition. 3 vols. 8vo. £3. PART I. CHEMICAL PHYSICS, 15*s.* PART II. INORGANIC CHEMISTRY, 21*s.* PART III. ORGANIC CHEMISTRY, 24*s.*

A MANUAL of CHEMISTRY, Descriptive and Theoretical. By WILLIAM ODLING, M.B. F.R.S. PART I. 8vo. 9*s.* PART II. *just ready.*

OUTLINES of CHEMISTRY; or, Brief Notes of Chemical Facts. By WILLIAM ODLING, M.B. F.R.S. Crown 8vo. 7*s.* 6*d.*

A Course of Practical Chemistry, for the use of Medical Students. By the same Author. New Edition, with 70 Woodcuts. Crown 8vo. 7*s.* 6*d.*

Lectures on Animal Chemistry, delivered at the Royal College of Physicians in 1865. By the same Author. Crown 8vo. 4*s.* 6*d.*

Lectures on the Chemical Changes of Carbon. Delivered at the Royal Institution of Great Britain. By the same Author. Crown 8vo. price 4*s.* 6*d.*

SELECT METHODS in CHEMICAL ANALYSIS, chiefly INORGANIC. By WILLIAM CROOKES, F.R.S. With 22 Woodcuts. Crown 8vo. price 12*s.* 6*d.*

A TREATISE on MEDICAL ELECTRICITY, THEORETICAL and PRACTICAL; and its Use in the Treatment of Paralysis, Neuralgia, and other Diseases. By JULIUS ALTHAUS, M.D. &c. Second Edition, revised and partly re-written. Post 8vo. with Plate and 2 Woodcuts, price 15*s.*

The DIAGNOSIS, PATHOLOGY, and TREATMENT of DISEASES of Women; including the Diagnosis of Pregnancy. By GRAILY HEWITT, M.D. Second Edition, enlarged; with 116 Woodcut Illustrations. 8vo. 24*s.*

On SOME DISORDERS of the NERVOUS SYSTEM in CHILDHOOD; being the Lumleian Lectures delivered before the Royal College of Physicians in March 1871. By CHARLES WEST, M.D. Crown 8vo. price 5*s.*

LECTURES on the DISEASES of INFANCY and CHILDHOOD. By CHARLES WEST, M.D. &c. Fifth Edition, revised and enlarged. 8vo. 16*s.*

A SYSTEM of SURGERY, Theoretical and Practical. In Treatises by Various Authors. Edited by T. HOLMES, M.A. &c. Surgeon and Lecturer on Surgery at St. George's Hospital, and Surgeon-in-Chief to the Metropolitan Police. Second Edition, thoroughly revised, with numerous Illustrations. 5 vols. 8vo. £5 5*s.*

The SURGICAL TREATMENT of CHILDREN'S DISEASES. By T. HOLMES, M.A. &c. late Surgeon to the Hospital for Sick Children. Second Edition, with 9 Plates and 112 Woodcuts. 8vo. 21*s.*

LECTURES on the PRINCIPLES and PRACTICE of PHYSIC. By Sir THOMAS WATSON, Bart. M.D. Fifth Edition, thoroughly revised. 2 vols. 8vo. price 36*s.*

LECTURES on SURGICAL PATHOLOGY. By Sir JAMES PAGET, Bart. F.R.S. Third Edition, revised and re-edited by the Author and Professor W. TURNER, M.B. 8vo. with 131 Woodcuts, 21*s.*

COOPER'S DICTIONARY of PRACTICAL SURGERY and Encyclopædia of Surgical Science. New Edition, brought down to the present time. By S. A. LANE, Surgeon to St. Mary's Hospital, assisted by various Eminent Surgeons. VOL. II. 8vo. completing the work. [*In the press.*

On CHRONIC BRONCHITIS, especially as connected with GOUT, EMPHYSEMA, and DISEASES of the HEART. By E. HEADLAM GREENHOW, M.D. F.R.C.P. &c. 8vo. 7*s.* 6*d.*

The CLIMATE of the SOUTH of FRANCE as SUITED to INVALIDS; with Notices of Mediterranean and other Winter Stations. By C. T. WILLIAMS, M.A. M.D. Oxon. Assistant-Physician to the Hospital for Consumption at Brompton. Second Edition. Crown 8vo. 6*s.*

REPORTS on the PROGRESS of PRACTICAL and SCIENTIFIC MEDICINE in Different Parts of the World. Edited by HORACE DOBELL, M.D. assisted by numerous and distinguished Coadjutors. Vols. I. and II. 8vo. 18*s.* each.

PULMONARY CONSUMPTION; its Nature, Varieties, and Treatment: with an Analysis of One Thousand Cases to exemplify its Duration. By C. J. B. WILLIAMS, M.D. F.R.S. and C. T. WILLIAMS, M.A. M.D. Oxon. Post 8vo. price 10*s.* 6*d.*

CLINICAL LECTURES on DISEASES of the LIVER, JAUNDICE, and ABDOMINAL DROPSY. By CHARLES MURCHISON, M.D. Post 8vo. with 25 Woodcuts, 10*s.* 6*d.*

ANATOMY, DESCRIPTIVE and SURGICAL. By HENRY GRAY, F.R.S. With about 400 Woodcuts from Dissections. Fifth Edition, by T. HOLMES, M.A. Cantab. with a new Introduction by the Editor. Royal 8vo. 28*s.*

CLINICAL NOTES on DISEASES of the LARYNX, investigated and treated with the assistance of the Laryngoscope. By W. MARCET, M.D. F.R.S. Crown 8vo. with 5 Lithographs, 6*s.*

OUTLINES of PHYSIOLOGY, Human and Comparative. By JOHN MARSHALL, F.R.C.S. Surgeon to the University College Hospital. 2 vols. crown 8vo. with 122 Woodcuts, 32*s.*

PHYSIOLOGICAL ANATOMY and PHYSIOLOGY of MAN. By the late R. B. TODD, M.D. F.R.S. and W. BOWMAN, F.R.S. of King's College. With numerous Illustrations. VOL. II. 8vo. 25*s.*

VOL. I. New Edition by Dr. LIONEL S. BEALE, F.R.S. in course of publication, with many Illustrations. PARTS I. and II. price 7*s.* 6*d.* each.

COPLAND'S DICTIONARY of PRACTICAL MEDICINE, abridged from the larger work and throughout brought down to the present State of Medical Science. 8vo. 36*s.*

REIMANN'S HANDBOOK of ANILINE and its DERIVATIVES; a Treatise on the Manufacture of Aniline and Aniline Colours. Edited by WILLIAM CROOKES, F.R.S. With 5 Woodcuts. 8vo. 10*s.* 6*d.*

On the MANUFACTURE of BEET-ROOT SUGAR in ENGLAND and IRELAND. By WILLIAM CROOKES, F.R.S. Crown 8vo. with 11 Woodcuts, 8*s.* 6*d.*

A MANUAL of MATERIA MEDICA and THERAPEUTICS, abridged from Dr. PEREIRA'S *Elements* by F. J. FARRE, M.D. assisted by R. BENTLEY, M.R.C.S. and by R. WARINGTON, F.R.S. 8vo. with 90 Woodcuts, 21*s.*

THOMSON'S CONSPECTUS of the BRITISH PHARMACOPŒIA. 25th Edition, corrected by E. LLOYD BIRKETT, M.D. 18mo. price 6*s.*

The Fine Arts, and *Illustrated Editions.*

IN FAIRYLAND; Pictures from the Elf-World. By RICHARD DOYLE. With a Poem by W. ALLINGHAM. With Sixteen Plates, containing Thirty-six Designs printed in Colours. Folio, 31*s.* 6*d.*

LIFE of JOHN GIBSON, R.A. SCULPTOR. Edited by Lady EASTLAKE. 8vo. 10*s.* 6*d.*

MATERIALS for a HISTORY of OIL PAINTING. By Sir CHARLES LOCKE EASTLAKE, sometime President of the Royal Academy. 2 vols. 8vo. price 30*s.*

HALF-HOUR LECTURES on the HISTORY and PRACTICE of the Fine and Ornamental Arts. By WILLIAM B. SCOTT. New Edition, revised by the Author; with 50 Woodcuts. Crown 8vo. 8*s.* 6*d.*

ALBERT DURER, HIS LIFE and WORKS; including Autobiographical Papers and Complete Catalogues. By WILLIAM B. SCOTT. With Six Etchings by the Author, and other Illustrations. 8vo. 16*s.*

SIX LECTURES on HARMONY, delivered at the Royal Institution of Great Britain in the Year 1867. By G. A. MACFARREN. With numerous engraved Musical Examples and Specimens. 8vo. 10*s.* 6*d.*

The CHORALE BOOK for ENGLAND: the Hymns translated by Miss C. WINKWORTH; the Tunes arranged by Prof. W. S. BENNETT and OTTO GOLDSCHMIDT. Fcp. 4to. 12*s.* 6*d.*

The NEW TESTAMENT, illustrated with Wood Engravings after the Early Masters, chiefly of the Italian School. Crown 4to. 63*s.* cloth, gilt top; or £5 5*s.* elegantly bound in morocco.

LYRA GERMANICA; the Christian Year. Translated by CATHERINE WINKWORTH; with 125 Illustrations on Wood drawn by J. LEIGHTON, F.S.A. 4to. 21*s.*

LYRA GERMANICA; the Christian Life. Translated by CATHERINE WINKWORTH; with about 200 Woodcut Illustrations by J. LEIGHTON, F.S.A. and other Artists. 4to. 21*s.*

The LIFE of MAN SYMBOLISED by the MONTHS of the YEAR. Text selected by R. PIGOT; Illustrations on Wood from Original Designs by J. LEIGHTON, F.S.A. 4to. 42*s.*

CATS' and FARLIE'S MORAL EMBLEMS; with Aphorisms, Adages, and Proverbs of all Nations. 121 Illustrations on Wood by J. LEIGHTON, F.S.A. Text selected by R. PIGOT. Imperial 8vo. 31*s.* 6*d.*

SACRED and LEGENDARY ART. By Mrs. JAMESON.

Legends of the Saints and Martyrs. Fifth Edition, with 19 Etchings and 187 Woodcuts. 2 vols. square crown 8vo. 31*s*. 6*d*.

Legends of the Monastic Orders. Third Edition, with 11 Etchings and 88 Woodcuts. 1 vol. square crown 8vo. 21*s*.

Legends of the Madonna. Third Edition, with 27 Etchings and 165 Woodcuts. 1 vol. square crown 8vo. 21*s*.

The History of Our Lord, with that of his Types and Precursors. Completed by Lady EASTLAKE. Revised Edition, with 31 Etchings and 281 Woodcuts. 2 vols. square crown 8vo. 42*s*.

The Useful Arts, Manufactures, &c.

HISTORY of the GOTHIC REVIVAL; an Attempt to shew how far the taste for Mediæval Architecture was retained in England during the last two centuries, and has been re-developed in the present. By CHARLES L. EASTLAKE, Architect. With many Illustrations. Imp. 8vo. price 31*s*. 6*d*.

GWILT'S ENCYCLOPÆDIA of ARCHITECTURE, with above 1,600 Engravings on Wood. Fifth Edition, revised and enlarged by WYATT PAPWORTH. 8vo. 52*s*. 6*d*.

A MANUAL of ARCHITECTURE: being a Concise History and Explanation of the principal Styles of European Architecture, Ancient, Mediæval, and Renaissance; with a Glossary of Technical Terms. By THOMAS MITCHELL. Crown 8vo. with 150 Woodcuts, 10*s*. 6*d*.

ITALIAN SCULPTORS; being a History of Sculpture in Northern, Southern, and Eastern Italy. By C. C. PERKINS. With 30 Etchings and 13 Wood Engravings. Imperial 8vo. 42*s*.

TUSCAN SCULPTORS, their Lives, Works, and Times. With 45 Etchings and 28 Woodcuts from Original Drawings and Photographs. By the same Author. 2 vols. imperial 8vo. 63*s*.

HINTS on HOUSEHOLD TASTE in FURNITURE, UPHOLSTERY, and other Details. By CHARLES L. EASTLAKE, Architect. Second Edition, with about 90 Illustrations. Square crown 8vo. 18*s*.

The ENGINEER'S HANDBOOK; explaining the Principles which should guide the Young Engineer in the Construction of Machinery. By C. S. LOWNDES. Post 8vo. 5*s*.

PRINCIPLES of MECHANISM, designed for the Use of Students in the Universities, and for Engineering Students generally. By R. WILLIS, M.A. F.R.S. &c. Jacksonian Professor in the University of Cambridge. Second Edition, enlarged; with 374 Woodcuts. 8vo. 18*s*.

LATHES and TURNING, Simple, Mechanical, and ORNAMENTAL. By W. HENRY NORTHCOTT. With about 240 Illustrations on Steel and Wood. 8vo. 18*s*.

URE'S DICTIONARY of ARTS, MANUFACTURES, and MINES. Sixth Edition, chiefly rewritten and greatly enlarged by ROBERT HUNT, F.R.S. assisted by numerous Contributors eminent in Science and the Arts, and familiar with Manufactures. With above 2,000 Woodcuts. 3 vols. medium 8vo. price £4 14*s*. 6*d*.

HANDBOOK of PRACTICAL TELEGRAPHY. By R. S. Culley, Memb. Inst. C.E. Engineer-in-Chief of Telegraphs to the Post Office. Fifth Edition, with 118 Woodcuts and 9 Plates. 8vo. price 14*s.*

ENCYCLOPÆDIA of CIVIL ENGINEERING, Historical, Theoretical, and Practical. By E. Cresy, C.E. With above 3,000 Woodcuts. 8vo. 42*s.*

TREATISE on MILLS and MILLWORK. By Sir W. Fairbairn, Bart. F.R.S. New Edition, with 18 Plates and 322 Woodcuts. 2 vols. 8vo. 32*s.*

USEFUL INFORMATION for ENGINEERS. By the same Author. First, Second, and Third Series, with many Plates and Woodcuts, 3 vols. crown 8vo. 10*s.* 6*d.* each.

The APPLICATION of CAST and WROUGHT IRON to Building Purposes. By Sir W. Fairbairn, Bart. F.R.S. Fourth Edition, enlarged; with 6 Plates and 118 Woodcuts. 8vo. price 16*s.*

IRON SHIP BUILDING, its History and Progress, as comprised in a Series of Experimental Researches. By the same Author. With 4 Plates and 130 Woodcuts. 8vo. 18*s.*

A TREATISE on the STEAM ENGINE, in its various Applications to Mines, Mills, Steam Navigation, Railways and Agriculture. By J. Bourne, C.E. Eighth Edition; with Portrait, 37 Plates, and 546 Woodcuts. 4to. 42*s.*

CATECHISM of the STEAM ENGINE, in its various Applications to Mines, Mills, Steam Navigation, Railways, and Agriculture. By the same Author. With 89 Woodcuts. Fcp. 6*s.*

HANDBOOK of the STEAM ENGINE. By the same Author, forming a Key to the Catechism of the Steam Engine, with 67 Woodcuts. Fcp. 9*s.*

BOURNE'S RECENT IMPROVEMENTS in the STEAM ENGINE in its various applications to Mines, Mills, Steam Navigation, Railways, and Agriculture. Being a Supplement to the Author's 'Catechism of the Steam Engine.' By John Bourne, C.E. New Edition, including many New Examples; with 124 Woodcuts. Fcp. 8vo. 6*s.*

A TREATISE on the SCREW PROPELLER, SCREW VESSELS, and Screw Engines, as adapted for purposes of Peace and War; with Notices of other Methods of Propulsion, Tables of the Dimensions and Performance of Screw Steamers, and detailed Specifications of Ships and Engines. By J. Bourne, C.E. New Edition, with 54 Plates and 287 Woodcuts. 4to. 63*s.*

EXAMPLES of MODERN STEAM, AIR, and GAS ENGINES of the most Approved Types, as employed for Pumping, for Driving Machinery, for Locomotion, and for Agriculture, minutely and practically described. By John Bourne, C.E. In course of publication in 24 Parts, price 2*s.* 6*d.* each, forming One volume 4to. with about 50 Plates and 400 Woodcuts.

A HISTORY of the MACHINE-WROUGHT HOSIERY and LACE Manufactures. By William Felkin, F.L.S. F.S.S. Royal 8vo. 21*s.*

PRACTICAL TREATISE on METALLURGY, adapted from the last German Edition of Professor Kerl's *Metallurgy* by W. Crookes, F.R.S. &c. and E. Röhrig, Ph.D. M.E. With 625 Woodcuts. 3 vols. 8vo. price £4 19*s.*

MITCHELL'S MANUAL of PRACTICAL ASSAYING. Third Edition, for the most part re-written, with all the recent Discoveries incorporated, by W. Crookes, F.R.S. With 188 Woodcuts. 8vo. 28*s.*

The ART of PERFUMERY; the History and Theory of Odours, and the Methods of Extracting the Aromas of Plants. By Dr. PIESSE, F.C.S. Third Edition, with 53 Woodcuts. Crown 8vo. 10*s.* 6*d.*

Chemical, Natural, and Physical Magic, for Juveniles during the Holidays. By the same Author. Third Edition, with 38 Woodcuts. Fcp. 6*s.*

LOUDON'S ENCYCLOPÆDIA of AGRICULTURE: comprising the Laying-out, Improvement, and Management of Landed Property, and the Cultivation and Economy of the Productions of Agriculture. With 1,100 Woodcuts. 8vo. 21*s.*

Loudon's Encyclopædia of Gardening: comprising the Theory and Practice of Horticulture, Floriculture, Arboriculture, and Landscape Gardening. With 1,000 Woodcuts. 8vo. 21*s.*

BAYLDON'S ART of VALUING RENTS and TILLAGES, and Claims of Tenants upon Quitting Farms, both at Michaelmas and Lady-Day. Eighth Edition, revised by J. C. MORTON. 8vo. 10*s.* 6*d.*

Religious and *Moral Works.*

OLD TESTAMENT SYNONYMS, their BEARING on CHRISTIAN FAITH and PRACTICE. By the Rev. R. B. GIRDLESTONE, M.A. 8vo. [*Nearly ready.*

An INTRODUCTION to the THEOLOGY of the CHURCH of ENGLAND, in an Exposition of the Thirty-nine Articles. By the Rev. T. P. BOULTBEE, M.A. Fcp. 8vo. price 6*s.*

FUNDAMENTALS; or, Bases of Belief concerning MAN and GOD: a Handbook of Mental, Moral, and Religious Philosophy. By the Rev. T. GRIFFITH, M.A. 8vo. price 10*s.* 6*d.*

PRAYERS SELECTED from the COLLECTION of the late BARON BUNSEN, and Translated by CATHERINE WINKWORTH. PART I. For the Family. PART II. Prayers and Meditations for Private Use. Fcp. 8vo. price 3*s.* 6*d.*

The STUDENT'S COMPENDIUM of the BOOK of COMMON PRAYER; being Notes Historical and Explanatory of the Liturgy of the Church of England. By the Rev. H. ALLDEN NASH. Fcp. 8vo. price 2*s.* 6*d.*

The BIBLE and POPULAR THEOLOGY; a Re-statement of Truths and Principles, with special reference to recent works of Dr. Liddon, Lord Hatherley, and the Right Hon. W. E. Gladstone. By G. VANCE SMITH, B.A. Ph.D. 8vo. price 7*s.* 6*d.*

The TRUTH of the BIBLE: Evidence from the Mosaic and other Records of Creation; the Origin and Antiquity of Man; the Science of Scripture; and from the Archæology of Different Nations of the Earth. By the Rev. B. W. SAVILE, M.A. Crown 8vo. price 7*s.* 6*d.*

CHURCHES and their CREEDS. By the Rev. Sir PHILIP PERRING, Bart. late Scholar of Trin. Coll. Cambridge, and University Medallist. Crown 8vo. price 10*s.* 6*d.*

CONSIDERATIONS on the REVISION of the ENGLISH NEW TESTAMENT. By C. J. ELLICOTT, D.D. Lord Bishop of Gloucester and Bristol. Post 8vo. price 5*s.* 6*d.*

An EXPOSITION of the 39 ARTICLES, Historical and Doctrinal. By E. HAROLD BROWNE, D.D. Lord Bishop of Ely. Ninth Edit. 8vo. 16*s.*

The LIFE and EPISTLES of ST. PAUL. By the Rev. W. J. CONYBEARE, M.A., and the Very Rev. J. S. HOWSON, D.D. Dean of Chester :—

LIBRARY EDITION, with all the Original Illustrations, Maps, Landscapes on Steel, Woodcuts, &c. 2 vols. 4to. 48*s.*

INTERMEDIATE EDITION, with a Selection of Maps, Plates, and Woodcuts. 2 vols. square crown 8vo. 31*s.* 6*d.*

STUDENT'S EDITION, revised and condensed, with 46 Illustrations and Maps. 1 vol. crown 8vo. price 9*s.*

The VOYAGE and SHIPWRECK of ST. PAUL; with Dissertations on the Life and Writings of St. Luke and the Ships and Navigation of the Ancients. By JAMES SMITH, F.R.S. Third Edition. Crown 8vo. 10*s.* 6*d.*

A CRITICAL and GRAMMATICAL COMMENTARY on ST. PAUL'S Epistles. By C. J. ELLICOTT, D.D. Lord Bishop of Gloucester & Bristol. 8vo.

Galatians, Fourth Edition, 8*s.* 6*d.*

Ephesians, Fourth Edition, 8*s.* 6*d.*

Pastoral Epistles, Fourth Edition, 10*s.* 6*d.*

Philippians, Colossians, and Philemon, Third Edition, 10*s.* 6*d.*

Thessalonians, Third Edition, 7*s.* 6*d.*

HISTORICAL LECTURES on the LIFE of OUR LORD JESUS CHRIST: being the Hulsean Lectures for 1859. By C. J. ELLICOTT, D.D. Lord Bishop of Gloucester and Bristol. Fifth Edition. 8vo. price 12*s.*

EVIDENCE of the TRUTH of the CHRISTIAN RELIGION derived from the Literal Fulfilment of Prophecy. By ALEXANDER KEITH, D.D. 37th Edition, with numerous Plates, in square 8vo. 12*s.* 6*d.*; also the 39th Edition, in post 8vo. with 5 Plates, 6*s.*

History and Destiny of the World and Church, according to Scripture. By the same Author. Square 8vo. with 40 Illustrations, 10*s.*

An INTRODUCTION to the STUDY of the NEW TESTAMENT, Critical, Exegetical, and Theological. By the Rev. S. DAVIDSON, D.D. LL.D. 2 vols. 8vo. 30*s.*

HARTWELL HORNE'S INTRODUCTION to the CRITICAL STUDY and Knowledge of the Holy Scriptures, as last revised; with 4 Maps and 22 Woodcuts and Facsimiles. 4 vols. 8vo. 42*s.*

Horne's Compendious Introduction to the Study of the Bible. Re-edited by the Rev. JOHN AYRE, M.A. With Maps, &c. Post 8vo. 6*s.*

EWALD'S HISTORY of ISRAEL to the DEATH of MOSES. Translated from the German. Edited, with a Preface and an Appendix, by RUSSELL MARTINEAU, M.A. Second Edition. 2 vols. 8vo. 24*s.*

The HISTORY and LITERATURE of the ISRAELITES, according to the Old Testament and the Apocrypha. By C. DE ROTHSCHILD and A. DE ROTHSCHILD. Second Edition, revised. 2 vols. post 8vo. with Two Maps, price 12*s.* 6*d.*

The SEE of ROME in the MIDDLE AGES. By the Rev. OSWALD J. REICHEL, B.C.L. and M.A. 8vo. price 18*s.*

The TREASURY of BIBLE KNOWLEDGE; being a Dictionary of the Books, Persons, Places, Events, and other matters of which mention is made in Holy Scripture. By Rev. J. AYRE, M.A. With Maps, 16 Plates, and numerous Woodcuts. Fcp. 8vo. price 6*s.* cloth, or 9*s.* 6*d.* neatly bound in calf.

The GREEK TESTAMENT; with Notes, Grammatical and Exegetical. By the Rev. W. WEBSTER, M.A. and the Rev. W. F. WILKINSON, M.A. 2 vols. 8vo. £2 4*s*.

EVERY-DAY SCRIPTURE DIFFICULTIES explained and illustrated. By J. E. PRESCOTT, M.A. VOL. I. *Matthew* and *Mark*; VOL. II. *Luke* and *John*. 2 vols. 8vo. 9*s*. each.

The PENTATEUCH and BOOK of JOSHUA CRITICALLY EXAMINED. By the Right Rev. J. W. COLENSO, D.D. Lord Bishop of Natal. People's Edition, in 1 vol. crown 8vo. 6*s*.

SIX SERMONS on the FOUR CARDINAL VIRTUES in relation to the Public and Private Life of Catholics. By the Rev. ORBY SHIPLEY, M.A. Crown 8vo. with Frontispiece, price 7*s*. 6*d*.

The FORMATION of CHRISTENDOM. By T. W. ALLIES. PARTS I. and II. 8vo. price 12*s*. each Part.

ENGLAND and CHRISTENDOM. By ARCHBISHOP MANNING, D.D. Post 8vo. price 10*s*. 6*d*.

CHRISTENDOM'S DIVISIONS, PART I., a Philosophical Sketch of the Divisions of the Christian Family in East and West. By EDMUND S. FFOULKES. Post 8vo. price 7*s*. 6*d*.

Christendom's Divisions, PART II. Greeks and Latins, being a History of their Dissensions and Overtures for Peace down to the Reformation. By the same Author. Post 8vo. 15*s*.

A VIEW of the SCRIPTURE REVELATIONS CONCERNING a FUTURE STATE. By RICHARD WHATELY, D.D. late Archbishop of Dublin. Ninth Edition. Fcp. 8vo. 5*s*.

THOUGHTS for the AGE. By ELIZABETH M. SEWELL, Author of 'Amy Herbert' &c. New Edition, revised. Fcp. 8vo. price 5*s*.

Passing Thoughts on Religion. By the same Author. Fcp. 8vo. 5*s*.

Self-Examination before Confirmation. By the same Author. 32mo. price 1*s*. 6*d*.

Readings for a Month Preparatory to Confirmation, from Writers of the Early and English Church. By the same Author. Fcp. 4*s*.

Readings for Every Day in Lent, compiled from the Writings of Bishop JEREMY TAYLOR. By the same Author. Fcp. 5*s*.

Preparation for the Holy Communion; the Devotions chiefly from the works of JEREMY TAYLOR. By the same Author. 32mo. 3*s*.

THOUGHTS for the HOLY WEEK for Young Persons. By the Author of 'Amy Herbert.' New Edition. Fcp. 8vo. 2*s*.

PRINCIPLES of EDUCATION Drawn from Nature and Revelation, and applied to Female Education in the Upper Classes. By the Author of 'Amy Herbert.' 2 vols. fcp. 12*s*. 6*d*.

SINGERS and SONGS of the CHURCH: being Biographical Sketches of the Hymn-Writers in all the principal Collections; with Notes on their Psalms and Hymns. By JOSIAH MILLER, M.A. Post 8vo. price 10*s*. 6*d*.

LYRA GERMANICA, translated from the German by Miss C. WINKWORTH. FIRST SERIES, Hymns for the Sundays and Chief Festivals. SECOND SERIES, the Christian Life. Fcp. 3*s*. 6*d*. each SERIES.

'SPIRITUAL SONGS' for the SUNDAYS and HOLIDAYS throughout the Year. By J. S. B. MONSELL, LL.D. Vicar of Egham and Rural Dean. Fourth Edition, Sixth Thousand. Fcp. 4*s.* 6*d.*

The BEATITUDES: Abasement before God; Sorrow for Sin; Meekness of Spirit; Desire for Holiness; Gentleness; Purity of Heart; the Peacemakers; Sufferings for Christ. By the same. Third Edition. Fcp. 3*s.* 6*d.*

His PRESENCE—not his MEMORY, 1855. By the same Author, in Memory of his SON. Sixth Edition. 16mo. 1*s.*

LYRA EUCHARISTICA; Hymns and Verses on the Holy Communion, Ancient and Modern: with other Poems. Edited by the Rev. ORBY SHIPLEY, M.A. Second Edition. Fcp. 5*s.*

Lyra Messianica; Hymns and Verses on the Life of Christ, Ancient and Modern; with other Poems. By the same Editor. Second Edition, altered and enlarged. Fcp. 5*s.*

Lyra Mystica; Hymns and Verses on Sacred Subjects, Ancient and Modern. By the same Editor. Fcp. 5*s.*

ENDEAVOURS after the CHRISTIAN LIFE: Discourses. By JAMES MARTINEAU. Fourth Edition, carefully revised. Post 8vo. 7*s.* 6*d.*

INVOCATION of SAINTS and ANGELS, for the use of Members of the English Church. Edited by the Rev. ORBY SHIPLEY. 24mo. 3*s.* 6*d.*

WHATELY'S INTRODUCTORY LESSONS on the CHRISTIAN Evidences. 18mo. 6*d.*

FOUR DISCOURSES of CHRYSOSTOM, chiefly on the Parable of the Rich Man and Lazarus. Translated by F. ALLEN, B.A. Crown 8vo. 3*s.* 6*d.*

BISHOP JEREMY TAYLOR'S ENTIRE WORKS. With Life by BISHOP HEBER. Revised and corrected by the Rev. C. P. EDEN, 10 vols. price £5 5*s.*

Travels, Voyages, &c.

HOW to SEE NORWAY. By Captain J. R. CAMPBELL. With Map and 5 Woodcuts. Fcp. 8vo. price 5*s.*

PAU and the PYRENEES. By Count HENRY RUSSELL, Member of the Alpine Club, &c. With 2 Maps. Fcp. 8vo. price 5*s.*

SCENES in the SUNNY SOUTH; including the Atlas Mountains and the Oases of the Sahara in Algeria. By Lieut.-Col. the Hon. C. S. VEREKER, M.A. Commandant of the Limerick Artillery Militia. 2 vols. post 8vo. price 21*s.*

The PLAYGROUND of EUROPE. By LESLIE STEPHEN, late President of the Alpine Club. With 4 Illustrations engraved on Wood by E. Whymper. Crown 8vo. price 10*s.* 6*d.*

CADORE; or, TITIAN'S COUNTRY. By JOSIAH GILBERT, one of the Authors of 'The Dolomite Mountains.' With Map, Facsimile, and 40 Illustrations. Imperial 8vo. 31*s.* 6*d.*

HOURS of EXERCISE in the ALPS. By JOHN TYNDALL, LL.D. F.R.S. Second Edition, with 7 Woodcuts by E. WHYMPER. Crown 8vo. price 12*s.* 6*d.*

TRAVELS in the CENTRAL CAUCASUS and BASHAN. Including Visits to Ararat and Tabreez and Ascents of Kazbek and Elbruz. By D. W. FRESHFIELD. Square crown 8vo. with Maps, &c. 18*s.*

PICTURES in TYROL and Elsewhere. From a Family Sketch-Book. By the Authoress of 'A Voyage en Zigzag,' &c. Second Edition. Small 4to. with numerous Illustrations, 21*s.*

HOW WE SPENT the SUMMER; or, a Voyage en Zigzag in Switzerland and Tyrol with some Members of the ALPINE CLUB. From the Sketch-Book of one of the Party. In oblong 4to. with 300 Illustrations, 15*s.*

BEATEN TRACKS; or, Pen and Pencil Sketches in Italy. By the Authoress of 'A Voyage en Zigzag.' With 42 Plates, containing about 200 Sketches from Drawings made on the Spot. 8vo. 16*s.*

MAP of the CHAIN of MONT BLANC, from an actual Survey in 1863—1864. By A. ADAMS-REILLY, F.R.G.S. M.A.C. Published under the Authority of the Alpine Club. In Chromolithography on extra stout drawing-paper 28in. × 17in. price 10*s.* or mounted on canvas in a folding case, 12*s.* 6*d.*

WESTWARD by RAIL; the New Route to the East. By W. F. RAE. With Map shewing the Lines of Rail between the Atlantic and the Pacific and Sections of the Railway. Second Edition, enlarged. Post 8vo. 10*s.* 6*d.*

HISTORY of DISCOVERY in our AUSTRALASIAN COLONIES, Australia, Tasmania, and New Zealand, from the Earliest Date to the Present Day. By WILLIAM HOWITT. 2 vols. 8vo. with 3 Maps, 20*s.*

The CAPITAL of the TYCOON; a Narrative of a Three Years' Residence in Japan. By Sir RUTHERFORD ALCOCK, K.C.B. 2 vols. 8vo. with numerous Illustrations, 42*s.*

ZIGZAGGING AMONGST DOLOMITES. By the Author of 'How we Spent the Summer, or a Voyage en Zigzag in Switzerland and Tyrol.' With upwards of 300 Illustrations by the Author. Oblong 4to. price 15*s.*

The DOLOMITE MOUNTAINS; Excursions through Tyrol, Carinthia, Carniola, and Friuli, 1861-1863. By J. GILBERT and G. C. CHURCHILL, F.R.G.S. With numerous Illustrations. Square crown 8vo. 21*s.*

GUIDE to the PYRENEES, for the use of Mountaineers. By CHARLES PACKE. 2nd Edition, with Map and Illustrations. Cr. 8vo. 7*s.* 6*d.*

The ALPINE GUIDE. By JOHN BALL, M.R.I.A. late President of the Alpine Club. Thoroughly Revised Editions, in Three Volumes, post 8vo. with Maps and other Illustrations:—

GUIDE to the WESTERN ALPS, including Mont Blanc, Monte Rosa, Zermatt, &c. Price 6*s.* 6*d.*

GUIDE to the CENTRAL ALPS, including all the Oberland District. Price 7*s.* 6*d.*

GUIDE to the EASTERN ALPS, price 10*s.* 6*d.*

Introduction on Alpine Travelling in General, and on the Geology of the Alps, price 1*s.* Each of the Three Volumes or Parts of the *Alpine Guide* may be had with this INTRODUCTION prefixed, price 1*s.* extra.

The NORTHERN HEIGHTS of LONDON; or, Historical Associations of Hampstead, Highgate, Muswell Hill, Hornsey, and Islington. By WILLIAM HOWITT. With about 40 Woodcuts. Square crown 8vo. 21*s.*

VISITS to REMARKABLE PLACES: Old Halls, Battle-Fields, and Stones Illustrative of Striking Passages in English History and Poetry. By WILLIAM HOWITT. 2 vols. square crown 8vo. with Woodcuts, 25*s.*

The **RURAL LIFE of ENGLAND.** By the same Author. With Woodcuts by Bewick and Williams. Medium 8vo. 12*s.* 6*d.*

PILGRIMAGES in the PYRENEES and LANDES. By DENYS SHYNE LAWLOR. Crown 8vo. with Frontispiece and Vignette, price 15*s.*

Works of Fiction.

NOVELS and TALES. By the Right Hon. B. DISRAELI, M.P. Cabinet Edition, complete in Ten Volumes, crown 8vo. price 6*s.* each, as follows:—

LOTHAIR, 6*s.*
CONINGSBY, 6*s.*
SYBIL, 6*s.*
TANCRED, 6*s.*
VENETIA, 6*s.*
HENRIETTA TEMPLE, 6*s.*
CONTARINI FLEMING, &c. 6*s.*
ALROY, IXION, &c. 6*s.*
The YOUNG DUKE, &c. 6*s.*
VIVIAN GREY, 6*s.*

The **MODERN NOVELIST'S LIBRARY.** Each Work, in crown 8vo. complete in a Single Volume:—

MELVILLE'S GLADIATORS, 2*s.* boards; 2*s.* 6*d.* cloth.
——— GOOD FOR NOTHING, 2*s.* boards; 2*s.* 6*d.* cloth.
——— HOLMBY HOUSE, 2*s.* boards; 2*s.* 6*d.* cloth.
——— INTERPRETER, 2*s.* boards; 2*s.* 6*d.* cloth.
——— KATE COVENTRY, 2*s.* boards; 2*s.* 6*d.* cloth.
——— QUEEN'S MARIES, 2*s.* boards; 2*s.* 6*d.* cloth.
TROLLOPE'S WARDEN, 1*s.* 6*d.* boards; 2*s.* cloth.
——— BARCHESTER TOWERS, 2*s.* boards; 2*s.* 6*d.* cloth.
BRAMLEY-MOORE'S SIX SISTERS *of the* VALLEYS, 2*s.* boards; 2*s.* 6*d.* cloth.

IERNE; a Tale. By W. STEUART TRENCH, Author of 'Realities of Irish Life.' Second Edition. 2 vols. post 8vo. price 21*s.*

The **HOME at HEATHERBRAE**; a Tale. By the Author of 'Everley.' Fcp. 8vo. price 5*s.*

CABINET EDITION of STORIES and TALES by MISS SEWELL:—

AMY HERBERT, 2*s.* 6*d.*
GERTRUDE, 2*s.* 6*d.*
The EARL'S DAUGHTER, 2*s.* 6*d.*
EXPERIENCE *of* LIFE, 2*s.* 6*d.*
CLEVE HALL, 3*s.* 6*d.*
IVORS, 3*s.* 6*d.*
KATHARINE ASHTON, 3*s.* 6*d.*
MARGARET PERCIVAL, 5*s.*
LANETON PARSONAGE, 4*s.* 6*d.*
URSULA, 4*s.* 6*d.*

STORIES and TALES. By E. M. SEWELL. Comprising:—Amy Herbert; Gertrude; The Earl's Daughter; The Experience of Life; Cleve Hall; Ivors; Katharine Ashton; Margaret Percival; Laneton Parsonage; *and* Ursula. The Ten Works, complete in Eight Volumes, crown 8vo. bound in leather, and contained in a Box, price 42*s.*

A Glimpse of the World. By the Author of 'Amy Herbert.' Fcp. 7*s.* 6*d.*

The Journal of a Home Life. By the same Author. Post 8vo. 9*s.* 6*d.*

After Life; a Sequel to 'The Journal of a Home Life.' Price 10*s.* 6*d.*

UNCLE PETER'S FAIRY TALE for the NINETEENTH CENTURY. Edited by E. M. SEWELL, Author of 'Amy Herbert,' &c. Fcp. 8vo. 7*s.* 6*d.*

THE GIANT; A Witch's Story for English Boys. By the same Author and Editor. Fcp. 8vo. price 5*s.*

WONDERFUL STORIES from NORWAY, SWEDEN, and ICELAND. Adapted and arranged by JULIA GODDARD. With an Introductory Essay by the Rev. G. W. Cox, M.A. and Six Woodcuts. Square post 8vo. 6*s.*

A VISIT to MY DISCONTENTED COUSIN. Reprinted, with some Additions, from *Fraser's Magazine.* Crown 8vo. price 7*s.* 6*d.*

BECKER'S GALLUS; or, Roman Scenes of the Time of Augustus: with Notes and Excursuses. New Edition. Post 8vo. 7*s.* 6*d.*

BECKER'S CHARICLES; a Tale illustrative of Private Life among the Ancient Greeks: with Notes and Excursuses. New Edition. Post 8vo. 7*s.* 6*d.*

CABINET EDITION of NOVELS and TALES by G. J. WHYTE MELVILLE:—

- *The* GLADIATORS, 5*s.*
- DIGBY GRAND, 5*s.*
- KATE COVENTRY, 5*s.*
- GENERAL BOUNCE, 5*s.*
- HOLMBY HOUSE, 5*s.*
- GOOD *for* NOTHING, 6*s.*
- *The* QUEEN'S MARIES, 6*s.*
- *The* INTERPRETER, 5*s.*

TALES of ANCIENT GREECE. By GEORGE W. COX, M.A. late Scholar of Trin. Coll. Oxon. Crown 8vo. price 6*s.* 6*d.*

A MANUAL of MYTHOLOGY, in the form of Question and Answer. By the same Author. Fcp. 3*s.*

OUR CHILDREN'S STORY, by one of their Gossips. By the Author of 'Voyage en Zigzag,' 'Pictures in Tyrol,' &c. Small 4to. with Sixty Illustrations by the Author, price 10*s.* 6*d.*

Poetry and *The Drama.*

THOMAS MOORE'S POETICAL WORKS, the only Editions containing the Author's last Copyright Additions:—

- CABINET EDITION, 10 vols. fcp. 8vo. price 35*s.*
- SHAMROCK EDITION, crown 8vo. price 3*s.* 6*d.*
- RUBY EDITION, crown 8vo. with Portrait, price 6*s.*
- LIBRARY EDITION, medium 8vo. Portrait and Vignette, 14*s.*
- PEOPLE'S EDITION, square crown 8vo. with Portrait, &c. 10*s.* 6*d.*

MOORE'S IRISH MELODIES, Maclise's Edition, with 161 Steel Plates from Original Drawings. Super-royal 8vo. 31*s.* 6*d.*

Miniature Edition of Moore's Irish Melodies with Maclise's Designs (as above) reduced in Lithography. Imp. 16mo. 10*s.* 6*d.*

MOORE'S LALLA ROOKH. Tenniel's Edition, with 68 Wood Engravings from original Drawings and other Illustrations. Fcp. 4to. 21*s.*

SOUTHEY'S POETICAL WORKS, with the Author's last Corrections and copyright Additions. Library Edition, in 1 vol. medium 8vo. with Portrait and Vignette, 14*s.*

LAYS of ANCIENT ROME; with *Ivry* and the *Armada.* By the Right Hon. LORD MACAULAY. 16mo. 4*s.* 6*d.*

Lord Macaulay's Lays of Ancient Rome. With 90 Illustrations on Wood, from the Antique, from Drawings by G. SCHARF. Fcp. 4to. 21*s.*

Miniature Edition of Lord Macaulay's Lays of Ancient Rome, with the Illustrations (as above) reduced in Lithography. Imp. 16mo. 10*s.* 6*d.*

GOLDSMITH'S POETICAL WORKS, with Wood Engravings from Designs by Members of the ETCHING CLUB. Imperial 16mo. 7*s.* 6*d.*

JOHN JERNINGHAM'S JOURNAL. Fcp. 8vo. price 3*s.* 6*d.*

POEMS OF BYGONE YEARS. Edited by the Author of 'Amy Herbert,' &c. Fcp. 8vo. price 5*s.*

POEMS. By JEAN INGELOW. Fifteenth Edition. Fcp. 8vo. 5*s.*

EUCHARIS; a Poem. By F. REGINALD STATHAM (Francis Reynolds), Author of 'Alice Rushton, and other Poems' and 'Glaphyra, and other Poems.' Fcp. 8vo. price 3*s.* 6*d.*

POEMS by Jean Ingelow. With nearly 100 Illustrations by Eminent Artists, engraved on Wood by the Brothers DALZIEL. Fcp. 4to. 21*s.*

The MAD WAR PLANET, and other POEMS. By WILLIAM HOWITT, Author of 'Visits to Remarkable Places,' &c. Fcp. 8vo. price 5*s.*

MOPSA the FAIRY. By JEAN INGELOW. Pp. 256, with Eight Illustrations engraved on Wood. Fcp. 8vo. 6*s.*

A STORY of DOOM, and other Poems. By JEAN INGELOW. Third Edition. Fcp. 5*s.*

WORKS by EDWARD YARDLEY:—

FANTASTIC STORIES. Fcp. 3*s.* 6*d.*
MELUSINE *and* OTHER POEMS. Fcp. 5*s.*
HORACE'S ODES, *translated into* English Verse. Crown 8vo. 6*s.*
SUPPLEMENTARY STORIES *and* POEMS. Fcp. 3*s.* 6*d.*

BOWDLER'S FAMILY SHAKSPEARE, cheaper Genuine Editions. Medium 8vo. large type, with 36 WOODCUTS, price 14*s.* Cabinet Edition, with the same ILLUSTRATIONS, 6 vols. fcp. 3*s.* 6*d.* each.

HORATII OPERA, Pocket Edition, with carefully corrected Text, Marginal References, and Introduction. Edited by the Rev. J. E. YONGE, M.A. Square 18mo. 4*s.* 6*d.*

HORATII OPERA. Library Edition, with Marginal References and English Notes. Edited by the Rev. J. E. YONGE. 8vo. 21*s.*

The ÆNEID of VIRGIL Translated into English Verse. By JOHN CONINGTON, M.A. New Edition. Crown 8vo. 9*s.*

ARUNDINES CAMI, sive Musarum Cantabrigiensium Lusus canori. Collegit atque edidit H. DRURY, M.A. Editio Sexta, curavit H. J. HODGSON, M.A. Crown 8vo. 7*s.* 6*d.*

HUNTING SONGS and MISCELLANEOUS VERSES. By R. E. EGERTON WARBURTON. Second Edition. Fcp. 8vo. 5*s.*

Rural Sports, &c.

ENCYCLOPÆDIA of RURAL SPORTS; a complete Account, Historical, Practical, and Descriptive, of Hunting, Shooting, Fishing, Racing, and all other Rural and Athletic Sports and Pastimes. By D. P. BLAINE. With above 600 Woodcuts (20 from Designs by JOHN LEECH). 8vo. 21*s.*

The DEAD SHOT, or Sportsman's Complete Guide; a Treatise on the Use of the Gun, Dog-breaking, Pigeon-shooting, &c. By MARKSMAN. Revised Edition. Fcp. 8vo. with Plates, 5*s*.

The FLY-FISHER'S ENTOMOLOGY. By ALFRED RONALDS. With coloured Representations of the Natural and Artificial Insect. Sixth Edition; with 20 coloured Plates. 8vo. 14*s*.

A BOOK on ANGLING; a complete Treatise on the Art of Angling in every branch. By FRANCIS FRANCIS. Second Edition, with Portrait and 15 other Plates, plain and coloured. Post 8vo. 15*s*.

The BOOK of the ROACH. By GREVILLE FENNELL, of 'The Field.' Fcp. 8vo. price 2*s*. 6*d*.

WILCOCKS'S SEA-FISHERMAN; comprising the Chief Methods of Hook and Line Fishing in the British and other Seas, a Glance at Nets, and Remarks on Boats and Boating. Second Edition, enlarged; with 80 Woodcuts. Post 8vo. 12*s*. 6*d*.

HORSES and STABLES. By Colonel F. FITZWYGRAM, XV. the King's Hussars. With Twenty-four Plates of Illustrations, containing very numerous Figures engraved on Wood. 8vo. 15*s*.

The HORSE'S FOOT, and HOW to KEEP IT SOUND. By W. MILES, Esq. Ninth Edition, with Illustrations. Imperial 8vo. 12*s*. 6*d*.

A PLAIN TREATISE on HORSE-SHOEING. By the same Author. Sixth Edition. Post 8vo. with Illustrations, 2*s*. 6*d*.

STABLES and STABLE-FITTINGS. By the same. Imp. 8vo. with 13 Plates, 15*s*.

REMARKS on HORSES' TEETH, addressed to Purchasers. By the same. Post 8vo. 1*s*. 6*d*.

ROBBINS'S CAVALRY CATECHISM, or Instructions on Cavalry Exercise and Field Movements, Brigade Movements, Out-post Duty, Cavalry supporting Artillery, Artillery attached to Cavalry. 12mo. 5*s*.

BLAINE'S VETERINARY ART; a Treatise on the Anatomy, Physiology, and Curative Treatment of the Diseases of the Horse, Neat Cattle and Sheep. Seventh Edition, revised and enlarged by C. STEEL, M.R.C.V.S.L. 8vo. with Plates and Woodcuts, 18*s*.

The HORSE: with a Treatise on Draught. By WILLIAM YOUATT. New Edition, revised and enlarged. 8vo. with numerous Woodcuts, 12*s*. 6*d*.

The DOG. By the same Author. 8vo. with numerous Woodcuts, 6*s*.

The DOG in HEALTH and DISEASE. By STONEHENGE. With 70 Wood Engravings. Square crown 8vo. 10*s*. 6*d*.

The GREYHOUND. By STONEHENGE. Revised Edition, with 24 Portraits of Greyhounds. Square crown 8vo. 10*s*. 6*d*.

The OX; his Diseases and their Treatment: with an Essay on Parturition in the Cow. By J. R. DOBSON. Crown 8vo. with Illustrations, 7*s*. 6*d*.

Works of *Utility* and *General Information.*

The THEORY and PRACTICE of BANKING. By H. D. MACLEOD, M.A. Barrister-at-Law. Second Edition, entirely remodelled. 2 vols. 8vo. 30*s*.

A DICTIONARY, Practical, Theoretical, and Historical, of Commerce and Commercial Navigation. By J. R. M'CULLOCH. New and thoroughly revised Edition. 8vo. price 63*s.* cloth, or 70*s.* half-bd. in russia.

The LAW of NATIONS Considered as Independent Political Communities. By Sir TRAVERS TWISS, D.C.L. 2 vols. 8vo. 30*s.*; or separately, PART I. *Peace,* 12*s.* PART II. *War,* 18*s.*

The CABINET LAWYER; a Popular Digest of the Laws of England, Civil, Criminal, and Constitutional: intended for Practical Use and General Information. Twenty-third Edition. Fcp. 8vo. price 7*s.* 6*d.*

PEWTNER'S COMPREHENSIVE SPECIFIER; A Guide to the Practical Specification of every kind of Building-Artificers' Work; with Forms of Building Conditions and Agreements, an Appendix, Foot-Notes, and a copious Index. Edited by W. YOUNG, Architect. Crown 8vo. price 6*s.*

The LAW RELATING to BENEFIT BUILDING SOCIETIES; with Practical Observations on the Act and all the Cases decided thereon; also a Form of Rules and Forms of Mortgages. By W. TIDD PRATT, Barrister. Second Edition. Fcp. 3*s.* 6*d.*

COLLIERIES and COLLIERS: a Handbook of the Law and Leading Cases relating thereto. By J. C. FOWLER, of the Inner Temple, Barrister. Second Edition. Fcp. 8vo. 7*s.* 6*d.*

The MATERNAL MANAGEMENT of CHILDREN in HEALTH and Disease. By THOMAS BULL, M.D. Fcp. 5*s.*

HINTS to MOTHERS on the MANAGEMENT of their HEALTH during the Period of Pregnancy and in the Lying-in Room. By the late THOMAS BULL, M.D. Fcp. 5*s.*

HOW to NURSE SICK CHILDREN; containing Directions which may be found of service to all who have charge of the Young. By CHARLES WEST, M.D. Second Edition. Fcp. 8vo. 1*s.* 6*d.*

NOTES on LYING-IN INSTITUTIONS; with a Proposal for Organising an Institution for Training Midwives and Midwifery Nurses. By FLORENCE NIGHTINGALE. With several Illustrations. 8vo. price 7*s.* 6*d.*

NOTES on HOSPITALS. By FLORENCE NIGHTINGALE. Third Edition, enlarged; with 13 Plans. Post 4to. 18*s.*

CHESS OPENINGS. By F. W. LONGMAN, Balliol College, Oxford. Fcp. 8vo. 2*s.* 6*d.*

A PRACTICAL TREATISE on BREWING; with Formulæ for Public Brewers, and Instructions for Private Families. By W. BLACK. 8vo. 10*s.* 6*d.*

MODERN COOKERY for PRIVATE FAMILIES, reduced to a System of Easy Practice in a Series of carefully-tested Receipts. By ELIZA ACTON. Newly revised and enlarged Edition; with 8 Plates of Figures and 150 Woodcuts. Fcp. 6*s.*

WILLICH'S POPULAR TABLES, for ascertaining, according to the Carlisle Table of Mortality, the value of Lifehold, Leasehold, and Church Property, Renewal Fines, Reversions, &c. Seventh Edition, edited by MONTAGUE MARRIOTT, Barrister-at-Law. Post 8vo. price 10*s.*

MAUNDER'S TREASURY of KNOWLEDGE and LIBRARY of Reference: comprising an English Dictionary and Grammar, Universal Gazetteer, Classical Dictionary, Chronology, Law Dictionary, a Synopsis of the Peerage, useful Tables, &c. Revised Edition. Fcp. 8vo. price 6*s.*

INDEX.

Spottiswoode & Co., Printers, New-street Square, London.

23440042R00271

Printed in Great Britain
by Amazon